The
WELL-SPOKEN
Thesaurus

The Most Powerful
Ways to Say
Everyday Words and Phrases

·····································

TOM HEEHLER

sourcebooks

Published by Sourcebooks, Inc.
P.O. Box 4410, Naperville, Illinois 60567-4410
(630) 961-3900
Fax: (630) 961-2168
www.sourcebooks.com

Library of Congress Cataloging-in-Publication Data

Heehler, Tom.
    The well-spoken thesaurus : the most powerful ways to say everyday words and phrases / Tom Heehler.
        p. cm.
    1. English language—Synonyms and antonyms. 2. English language—Terms and phrases. I. Title.
    PE1591.H397 2011
    413'.12—dc22

                            2010047798

            Printed and bound in the United States of America.
                DRC   30 29 28 27

Dedicated to my mom.

Contents

....

Acknowledgments

Literary Agent: Jessica Faust

Acquisitions Editor: Peter Lynch

Publisher: Dominique Raccah

Editor: Kelly Bale

Production Editors: Michelle Lecuyer
                                                             Anne Hartman

Cover Designer: Will Riley

Production Designers: Ashley Haag
                                                             Holly Bahn
                                                           Danielle Trejo
                                                             Tina Silva

English Teachers: Mrs. Tune, Second Grade, Una Elementary;
                                   Mrs. Lawrence, Fourth Grade, Una Elementary;
                                 Professor Lisa Hinrichsen, Harvard Extension

Important People: Ruth Ellen Keiper,
                                                         Matt Killikelly,
                                                        Jeannie Ehrhardt

On Becoming Articulate

....

Why Should You Care?

Words are like little gods. The pronoun "him" instead of "her," if used often enough, can dissuade a girl from science or math. The words you use determine the density of gray matter in your brain. They affect your political leanings, influence how you see reality, determine your level of confidence and thus, define what it means to be you. That's what words do.

As important as your words are in shaping your behavior, they are even more important in the way they shape the behavior of others. Your manner of speaking is, if nothing else, the central factor upon which people form assumptions about you. Whatever is your ultimate goal in life, chances are good you're going to have to communicate your way to it. And if greatness is your goal, well-spoken words are essential. Think about it. From Homer to Hemingway, Lincoln, Churchill, King, Obama—their *words* are why you know them.

The well-spoken few are viewed by others in a different way. They are thought of as more knowledgeable, more informed, and therefore expected to do more things. This law of great expectations is a powerful motivator. We all have an inherent need to meet expectations, whether they be high or low, and when expectations rise, we're inclined to rise with them. Our improvement then becomes a self-fulfilling prophecy: as others expect us to be better, we become so, and as we become so, they expect it further still.

How to Speak Like an Academic without Sounding Like One

The most accomplished speakers use words in ways that compliment their thoughts and ideas, not overshadow them. They are able to adopt a scholarly air of authority, but without all those pretentious scholarly words. Take Barack Obama for instance, a man for whom the well-spoken word is a major source of power. President Obama understands, obeys, and exploits the most important command-ment of communication: that it's not so much the words we use, as it is the way we use them. You hear it all the time: "Barack Obama is so articulate, so eloquent, so intelligent." But has he ever used a word any child couldn't comprehend?

It's not easy becoming articulate. For most of us, the process is a never-ending exercise in trial and error. We fumble our way along with the occasional foreign word here or big word there, all the while praying we're pronouncing and using these words correctly. And when we do dare to use these words, we risk casting ourselves as pretentious, awkwardly formal, academic, or nerdy. Have you ever used a lofty word and felt embarrassed at having done so? We've all been there. We hear others use these words with ease, but when we try them for size, they don't always fit. That's because we confuse formality with what we believe to be articulate speech. We deploy such language in an attempt to present ourselves as professional when, ironically, usually the opposite effect is achieved.

The same can be said for those who attempt to impress with big professorial words. While such language may seem "indubitably" clear and appropriate to them, it strikes the rest of us as more than a bit eccentric. The trick here is to achieve the authoritative and persuasive effects of formality and intellectualism without sounding too, well, formal or intellectual. What you are aiming for is an effect: you want to be regarded as the smartest authority in the room but without the least trace of awkwardness or pretension. And to that end, I present to you this book. Whether it be for writing or speaking, I think you will find it quite helpful.

A Few Words about Me

I began writing what would become this book when I decided, in the spring of 2006, to go back to school and complete my education. It was there in Cambridge that I would come to realize just how inarticulate I really was. And because I could find no easy way to lift my speech and prose quickly, I resolved to invent a way. It began simply enough; whenever I would happen upon an eloquent word or phrase, I would write it down and pair it with what *I* would have said otherwise. (All those common word entries you see in this thesaurus? That's me talking.) I did this for years, collecting words like butterflies, until it became increasingly apparent that my collection could be of use to others. So you could say that my authority on this subject stems not only from a determination to do something about my own predicament, but to do something about yours. My only hope is that this remarkable collection of words does as much for you in that regard as it has for me.

Rhetorical Form
and Design

It's not enough to replace ordinary words with the extraordinary words contained within this book. You need to know *why* these words are extraordinary, and the best way to do this is to examine the language of history's greatest writers and speakers, verbal alchemists like Margaret Atwood, Ernest Hemingway, T. S. Eliot, and Barack Obama. It is by their example that we come to know how words are powerful not in and of themselves, but in and of each other, in the way they combine to form that which they could never be otherwise.

Take for example the word, *leave*. In most contexts, such as, *when she leaves tonight*, this particular word is nothing if not ordinary and hardly the sort one would expect to find in a vocabulary builder or style guide. But take a moment to imagine how such a word might be used to improve the following sentence: *It makes me want more.*

Did you come up with, *It leaves me wanting more?* The difference is rather striking; is it not? This kind of linguistic chemistry happens not by flash of insight, but by rhetorical formula, and as you progress through this chapter, these formulas will become your own. Use them, learn from them, and apply what you learn to your everyday business correspondence, your résumés, your college papers, your novels, your news accounts, and, yes, even your casual conversation.

Lesson 1: T. S. Eliot

The Poetry of Ordinary Things

Most of us don't consider ourselves poetic, but we are. Filmmakers are keenly aware of our fascination with poetry. Why do you think so many leading men drive poetic cars like Karmann Ghias, and live in poetic places like marinas or in converted abandoned warehouses? Poetry isn't just words on a page that rhyme, it's the feeling you get from words, and the feeling you get from the actual things those words represent. Poetry is the smell of a freshly pressed white cotton shirt. Poetry is the color of lightning.

Certain everyday words are poetic too. See if you can spot one here in this line from T. S. Eliot's "The Love Song of J. Alfred Prufrock":

> **In the room the women come and go**
> **Talking of Michelangelo.**

While "Michelangelo" is poetic, it's hardly an everyday word. "Of" is the poetic word here. Talking *about* Michelangelo just doesn't do it for me; talking *of him* does. Try replacing your "abouts" with "ofs," as in this example:

> **Before:** There is talk about a takeover, but the would-be CEO knows nothing about the publishing business.
>
> **After:** There is talk *of* a takeover, but the would-be CEO knows nothing *of* the publishing business.

So you see, even a no-nonsense business memo can be improved upon with a bit of poetry.

Here are ten other poetic replacements and omissions:

1. Drop "of."
    – She thinks *of* herself as an expert.
    – She thinks herself an expert.

2. Drop "is."
    – Do you think it *is* impertinent?
    – Do you think it impertinent?

3. Drop the second "is."
    – "Every look is a cordial smile, every gesture a familiar caress."—T. B. McCauley, *Machiavelli*

4. Replace "very" with "-est of."
    – It is a *very rare* event.
    – It is the *rarest of* events.

5. Replace "are" with a comma.
    – These *are* the men who stood their ground.
    – These, the men who stood their ground.

6. Replace "-able" with "a matter of."
    – It's *disputable*.
    – It's *a matter of dispute*.

7. Drop "that are."
    – I have a taste for all things *that are* classical.
    – I have a taste for all things classical.

8. Replace "that he was" with "him."
    – I thought *that he was* wise.
    – I thought *him* wise.

9. Replace "-ful" with "a source of."
    – Her continued absence is *regretful* for us all.
    – Her continued absence is *a source of regret* for us all.

10. Replace "with" with "of."
    – "They were sitting in the blind that Wanderobo hunters had built *with* twigs and branches…"
    – "They were sitting in the blind that Wanderobo hunters had built *of* twigs and branches…"—E. Hemingway

Lesson 2: Margaret Atwood

···

The Conversion of the Figurative

If someone were to empathize with you and say, "I know where you're coming from," they would be using a figure of speech, and so their expression would be considered *figurative*, as opposed to *literal*. If they knew where you were coming from literally, they would know where you had been an hour earlier, and that would be a little creepy.

This is the sort of thing that gives AI programers serious indigestion. Computers have a tough time drawing distinctions between the figurative and the literal. Tell a computer that you're freezing, and it's likely to call for an ambulance. Tell me that, and I'll get you a sweater. That's because I'm a person, and like all people, I inherently know what you mean. In fact, I'm so accustomed to knowing what should be figurative and what should be literal that if you were to change it up on me, I would consider that to be a breath of fresh air—and I mean that figuratively. Witness this breath of fresh air as Margaret Atwood takes what we normally accept as figurative and interprets it in a literal way a few pages into *The Handmaid's Tale*:

> *We would exchange remedies and try to outdo each other in the recital of our physical miseries; gently we would complain, our voices soft and minor key and mournful as pigeons in the eaves troughs. I know what you mean, we'd say. Or, a quaint expression you sometimes hear, still, from older people:* <u>*I know where you're coming from, as if the voice itself were a traveler from a distant place. Which it would be, which it is.*</u>

When people read that, they don't think to themselves, Margaret Atwood sure is good at converting the figurative to the literal. Instead they think, Wow, what a writer!

The trick here is to come up with a figure of speech that relates to your subject, then try to provoke your creative instincts into going literal. For instance, let's assume that you had written the following expression in rough-draft form:

I remember once how I let myself fall in love; now I'm more careful with my emotions.

Are you yawning yet? I am. So let's get to work:

> **Step 1:** Find a figure of speech that relates to falling in love. Can you think of one? How about "head over heels in love," "tough love," "puppy love," or even the most obvious of all, "falling in love"?
>
> **Step 2:** Interpret your figure of speech in a literal way. Can you? "I remember once how I let myself fall in love; _____."

There are dozens of possibilities. Here's mine:

I remember once how I let myself fall in love; now I always work with a net.

What makes this sentence interesting is the way the second half implies a literal translation of the first—that the fall was literal.

Now see if you can convert the figurative to the literal by filling in this blank with a single word.

Your clue: It's a quote by Albert Einstein.

"_____is not responsible for people falling in love."

Lesson 3: Ernest Hemingway

....

Verb Displacement

Minimalism, the art of simplifying literature to its most basic form, is actually quite complicated. You can't just dumb down everything you write to a third-grade reading level and be done with it. If that's all it took, then everybody would be able to write like Hemingway, which is not the case.

What makes Hemingway remarkable is his ability to make simplicity sophisticated, to give ordinary language a timeless and poetic feel. Consider this example from the novel *For Whom the Bell Tolls*. Pay particular attention to the last sentence of this passage, which has been altered so as to be without the Hemingway aesthetic.

> *"Kashkin," Robert Jordan said. "That would be Kashkin."*
>
> *"Yes," said Pablo. "It was a very rare name. Something like that. What has become of him?"*
>
> *"He died in April."*

It's hard to imagine how one might improve upon the wording here. But in the last sentence, watch as the verb "died" is displaced by "is," and the remainder of the sentence modified to accommodate the change:

Before verb displacement: He died in April.

After verb displacement: He *is dead since* April.

While the meaning of the expression hasn't changed, the feel is more poetic, yes? Impressively, Hemingway does this with an unaffected manner. That is, we don't get the feeling that the characters are poets reciting poetry or actors succumbing to melodrama. Instead, because the language is so simple, we accept Hemingway's poetic enhancements as perfectly natural, perhaps the broken English of everyday Spaniards. In so doing, Hemingway endows his ordinary prose—and the ordinary people who speak it—with a kind of primitive nobility that lesser writers might not think or know how to bestow.

Here's another example from Hemingway's *Green Hills of Africa*. Among the verbs in the alternate or "un-displaced" version below, only one is particularly well suited for displacement. Find it and do what Hemingway does: displace that verb with "is" or its past tense, "was."

Un-displaced version: We were sitting in the blind that Wanderobo hunters had built of twigs and branches at the edge of the salt-lick when we heard the truck coming. At first it was far away and no one could tell what the noise was. Then it stopped and we hoped it had been nothing or perhaps only the wind.

Hemingway's version: At first it was far away and no one could tell what the noise was. Then it *was stopped* and we hoped it had been nothing or perhaps only the wind.

If you were able to find the verb and make the change, or even if you could not but you now see why the latter example is a stylistic improvement on the former, then you're catching on.

This is fairly nuanced stuff, so let's try one more for good measure. Here's a passage from Hemingway's *Garden of Eden*. Find the only verb suitable for displacement and replace it with "is" or "was," then see if you can modify the sentence to accommodate the change.

Un-displaced version: They were hungry for breakfast which they ate at the café, ordering brioche and café au lait and eggs, and the type of preserve that they chose and the manner in which the eggs were to be cooked excited them.

Hemingway's version: They were hungry for breakfast which they ate at the café, ordering brioche and café au lait and eggs, and the type of preserve that they chose and the manner in which the eggs were to be cooked *was an excitement.*

Lesson 4: Cormac McCarthy

···

Creating Abstractions

Recall this scene from the movie *Gladiator*: the emperor Commodus stands enthralled before a scale model of the city of Rome. As he lowers his humongous head over tiny intricate buildings for a close-in look, his shadow is fallen over the Coliseum.

Now take a moment to reflect upon that. The emperor's head and shadow are actual concrete things. But they are meant instead as abstractions (things that exist only in the mind). In this case, the emperor's looming head and shadow are meant to evoke the abstraction of the fear and imperial force under which all of Rome was subjected. When a writer—or director—does this, when she compels her readers to think of concrete things in abstract ways, she becomes less a writer of one-dimensional stories and more a writer of literature.

Let's see if you can write some literature. Begin by reading this excerpt from Cormac McCarthy's *No Country for Old Men*. As McCarthy's character Llewellyn Moss scans "the desert below him with a pair of 12-power German binoculars," what he does not know is that somewhere out there is a deadly thing. (I would tell you what that deadly thing is if it wouldn't spoil the story.)

> *The sun was up less than an hour and the shadow of the ridge and the yucca plants and the rocks fell far out across the floodplain below him. (_____.)*

At this point, try to visualize not the shadows of the plants or rocks, but Moss's shadow. Now say something about that shadow, but do it in a way that turns the shadow to abstraction, to a harbinger of impending doom perhaps, but without using any explicit words like "impending doom."

Hopefully you came up with something like this:

> **The sun was up less than an hour and the shadow of the ridge and the yucca plants and the rocks fell far out across the floodplain below him. <u>Somewhere out there was the shadow of Moss himself.</u>**

Foreboding, right? McCarthy doesn't mean Moss's actual shadow, but something more akin to his own ghost, his own fate.

Shadows are easy to imagine as abstractions because of their ethereal ways. But anything can be turned to abstraction—even a murderer's eyes:

> **"They say the eyes are the windows to the soul. I don't know what them eyes was the windows to and I guess I'd as soon not know. But there is another view of the world out there and other eyes to see it and that's where this is goin'. It has done brought me to a place in my life I would not of thought I'd of come to."** No Country for Old Men

Can you transform a psychopathic killer's coin into an abstraction? Here's your clue: *Call it in the air.*

Lesson 5: John Steinbeck

....

Intuitive Description

If I were to ask you to describe the flowers on your window sill, chances are good that your physical description would be precisely that: physical. Color, shape, and smell. But watch how John Steinbeck describes the flowers in *East of Eden*:

> *Then there were harebells, tiny lanterns, cream white and almost sinful looking,* <u>*and these were so rare and magical that a child, finding one, felt singled out and special all day long.*</u>

Brilliant, right? That's because emotional feelings trump physical feelings every time. You say the sky is blue? That's nice. Now relate that to something human, as I do here:

> *The sky was the kind of blue if blue could burn, blue on fire, lit by the sun blazing high above the hills in winter on a morning when there are no clouds.* <u>*A sky like that makes it easier for a soldier to die. It's the last thing he sees, and there is comfort in knowing some things will live forever.*</u>

In this excerpt from Steinbeck's *In Dubious Battle*, how might you relate a simple scar to a human emotion or motivation?

Ordinary description: His thick hair was combed straight down over a white scar half an inch wide that lay horizontally over his right ear.

> **Steinbeck's intuitive description:** His thick hair was combed straight down *from each side at the top in a vain attempt to cover* a white scar half an inch wide that lay horizontally over the right ear.

That may not be a brilliant example of intuitive description, but the expression carries with it more impact than it would otherwise. That's because human feelings and motivations make us care about what's being described. While it's nice to know that leaves are green and flowers are pretty and hair is combed a certain way, unless you can relate those facts to a human emotion or motivation, readers will not so easily connect with your words on a personal, human, intuitive level.

Here's one more from the novel *Cannery Row*. Note how Steinbeck likes to begin his paragraph with physical description, and conclude with intuitive description:

> *Mary Talbot, Mrs. Tom Talbot, that is, was lovely. She had red hair with green lights in it. Her skin was golden with a green under cast and her eyes were green with little golden spots. Her face was triangular, with wide cheekbones, wide-set eyes, and her chin was pointed. She had long dancer's legs and dancer's feet and she seemed never to touch the ground when she walked.* <u>When she was excited, and she was excited a good deal of the time, her face flushed with gold. Her great-great-great-great-great grandmother had been burned as a witch.</u>

A lesser writer might have simply concluded, "Mary looked like a witch." But Steinbeck finds a way to make that point intuitively, connecting Mary's physical features to something personal to Mary.

Lesson 6: Norman Mailer

....

Poetic Articles

The words "the" and "a" are surely the least regarded words in the English language. But sometimes when you omit these words from where they ordinarily belong, or include them where they do not, they become quite interesting. Do what you can to enhance this passage from *The Armies of the Night* by either adding or omitting an "a."

> **Alternate version:** Still, Mailer had a complex mind of sorts. Like a later generation that was to burn holes in their brain on Speed, he had given his own head the texture of fine Swiss cheese.
>
> **Mailer's version:** Still, Mailer had a complex mind of sorts. Like a later generation that was to burn holes in their brain on Speed, he had given his own head the texture of *a* fine Swiss cheese.

Still not convinced that article can be poetic? Try this one from Mailer's *The Castle in the Forest:*

> **Alternate version:** I know that I will sail into a sea of turbulence, for I must uproot many conventional beliefs.

> **Mailer's version:** I know that I will sail into a sea of turbulence, for I must uproot many *a* conventional belief.

Here's one I'm particularly fond of. See if you can either add or omit an "a" in this passage from *The Fight*:

> **Alternate version:** In contrast, a five-punch combination in which every shot lands is certain to stampede any opponent into unconsciousness. No matter how light the blows, a jackpot has been struck. The sudden over-loading of the victim's message center is bound to produce that inrush of confusion known as a coma.
>
> **Mailer's version:** In contrast, a five-punch combination in which every shot lands is certain to stampede any opponent into unconsciousness. No matter how light the blows, a jackpot has been struck. The sudden over-loading of the victim's message center is bound to produce that inrush of confusion known as *coma*.

And now for your final test. Add or omit an "a" or a "the" to ensure there are no clichés in this passage from Mailer's *The Armies of the Night*. For this you'll want to rely on a pronoun to accommodate the change:

> **Alternate version:** But for the record, it had best be stated that his imme-diate reaction was one of woe—he did not wish to speak to the man on the other end.
>
> **Mailer's version:** But for *our* record, it had best be stated that his immedi-ate reaction was one of woe—he did not wish to speak to the man on the other end.

Lesson 7: Edith Wharton

··

Objectification

Simple and clear expression is generally considered to be the hallmark of proper rhetorical form, but complicated and opaque can be so much more interesting. Take this expression for instance:

He considered her to be out of his league.

That's about as simple and as clear as one can be. But watch here as Edith Wharton uses objectification (the regarding of people as objects) to imply as much in this excerpt from *The House of Mirth*:

Everything about her was at once vigorous and exquisite, at once strong and fine. He had a confused sense that she must have cost a great deal to make, that a great many dull and ugly people must, in some mysterious way, have been sacrificed to produce her.

The first expression is direct and unambiguous. The second is nothing of the kind. But the second is vastly more interesting, yes? That's the power of objectification, a technique used to imply what people think. When one person objectifies another, it implies the level of regard between them, and because all of human interaction is a function of regard, objectification informs just about everything that goes on between two people. In this case, Lily Bart is regarded by Lawrence Selden as an *object* of excessive beauty and social standing. But Wharton never says that. Instead, she leads readers to *infer* it from the way Mr. Selden is objectifying Miss Bart. You infer his regard in the same way that you are required to infer the feelings of everyone in life. Nobody spoon-feeds you through your daily existence, so why should it be any different in fiction? That's one reason why writers like Wharton can engage us on such a powerful level. They pull us into the story by requiring of us what real life requires of us: thought.

Let's try another. The following is a clear and simple sentiment that prevails throughout the *The House of Mirth*:

> **Lily Bart was everything to Lawrence Selden.**

So how might you use objectification to imply as much? Here's how Wharton does it—by depicting Lily Bart as an object, in this case a heavenly body, about which her would-be suitor Mr. Selden revolves:

> **As a spectator he had always enjoyed Lily Bart, and his course lay so far out of her orbit that it amused him to be drawn for a moment into the sudden intimacy which her proposal implied.**

Objectification doesn't get any better than that.

Lesson 8: E. B. White

....

Rhetorical Tension

Play in your head the first four notes to Beethoven's Fifth Symphony. Got that? Now play them again, only this time without the final fourth note—just the first *three*.

You don't like the way that sounds, do you? That's because the first three notes create within your mind a kind of tension that needs to be released. In the same way, if you play that fourth note of would-be release without the preceding three notes of tension, the effect is equally unsatisfying. Only when all four notes are played in series—when *released tension* is created—do you feel satisfied. But here's what's really interesting: just as released tension creates a feeling of satisfaction in song, it also creates a feeling of satisfaction in prose.

Here are two versions of the same excerpt from E. B. White's *Charlotte's Web*. The first has been stripped of tension and is therefore without release:

> *He handed her a newborn pig, a white one. The morning sun shone through its ears, turning them pink.*

Reading that is a little like listening to Beethoven's fourth note of release without the first three notes of tension. It's unsatisfying because it's monotone. Now compare that to the passage as White actually wrote it. Listen for the first few notes of tension and the subsequent notes of release:

> *Fern came slowly down the stairs. Her eyes were red from crying. As she approached her chair, the carton wobbled, and there was a scratching noise. Fern looked at her father. Then she lifted the lid*

of the carton. There, inside, looking up at her, was the newborn
pig. It was a white one. The morning sun shone through its ears,
turning them pink.

What White is doing here is creating tension with a kind of rhetorical foreplay—the wobbling carton, the scratching noise from within. He then releases that tension with "*There, inside, looking up at her, was the newborn pig.*" It's instant gratification.

You may be tempted to regard rhetorical tension as a type of suspense, but there are important distinctions. While suspense is tension that goes unresolved for long periods of time, rhetorical tension is resolved quickly, usually within the same paragraph or page. It's less about uncertainty of outcome and more about provoking questions, inviting wonder or speculation, prolonging the inevitable for a few moments longer, or begging resolution. Fern already knows what's in the box, and so do we, but White manufactures the tension and release nonetheless.

Is this opening to White's *The Trumpet of the Swan* an example of suspense or of rhetorical tension?

Walking back to camp through the swamp, Sam wondered whether
to tell his father what he had seen.

We're not concerned about Sam making it out of the swamp, so this is not suspense, but White does have us wondering about Sam's encounter. As the page unfolds, he keeps us uninformed for another two paragraphs before unveiling a pair of nearly extinct birds almost twice Sam's size. If White had been forthcoming about those exotic creatures from the start, the passage would not have required any wonder on our part, nor would it have provided any satisfaction from the resolution of that wonder.

Now you know why kids—and adults—love the prose of E. B. White. It sounds like music.

Lesson 9: J.M. Coetzee

Rhetorical Agency

If you were to perform an action of some kind, let's say for example that you were to *understand the irony of a situation*, then it would be you doing the understanding, and therefore you, as the *agent* of that action, would be said to have *agency*.

Unlike you, however, inanimate objects and abstractions do not have agency, because they don't do things—at least not of their own accord. But that doesn't mean we can't speak of them as though they do, as though they have *rhetorical agency*.

Read this altered excerpt from J.M. Coetzee's *Disgrace*. Note that "he" retains the agency in the highlighted clause.

> *He continues to teach because it provides him with a livelihood;*
> ~~*also because it teaches him humility, brings it home to him who he*~~
> *is in the world.* <u>*He understands the irony;*</u> *that the one who comes*
> *to teach learns the keenest of lessons, while those who come to*
> *learn learn nothing.*

Now see if you can manipulate the clause to allow "irony" to perform the action instead of "he":

> *He continues to teach because it provides him with a livelihood;*
> *also because it teaches him humility, brings it home to him who he*
> *is in the world.* <u>*The irony does not escape him;*</u> *that the one who*
> *comes to teach learns the keenest of lessons, while those who come*
> *to learn learn nothing.*

In the first example, "he" is performing the action "to understand." In the second example, "irony" is performing the action "to escape"—or rather not to escape. By transferring the agency from a person (he) to an abstraction (irony) the prose becomes more interesting and engaged.

Rhetorical agency can also help to correct awkward wording. In this altered excerpt from *Disgrace*, see if you can detect a problem:

> *In the kitchen of the flat in Green Point there are a kettle, plastic cups, a jar of instant coffee, a bowl with sachets of sugar. In the refrigerator there is a supply of bottled water. In the bathroom there is soap and a pile of towels, in the cupboard clean bed linen.*

It should be obvious that too many sentences—all of them in fact—begin with the same two words. This problem can be solved by simply extending agency to the refrigerator:

> *In the kitchen of the flat in Green Point there are a kettle, plastic cups, a jar of instant coffee, a bowl with sachets of sugar. <u>The refrigerator holds</u> a supply of bottled water. In the bathroom there is soap and a pile of towels, in the cupboard clean bed linen.*

Lesson 10: John Steinbeck

....

Creative Number

The lyrics to the song "Human" by The Killers are a curious thing. For instance, what do you make of this:

Are we human, or are we dancer?

Notwithstanding the confusion in meaning, you'd think The Killers would have enough grammatical sense to change the word *dancer* to its plural form, *dancers*. I mean, really, why would anyone speak like that? Who do The Killers think they are?

But when you think about it, if we can be *human*, and not necessarily *humans*, then why can't we be *dancer*, and not necessarily *dancers*? The point is, plurality is relative. You can change it to give your prose a special feel. In this passage from John Steinbeck's *East of Eden*, see if you can find a plural noun that would sound a little special if it were singular.

Alternate version: I remember where the toads lived and what time the birds awaken in the summer, and what trees and seasons smelled like—how people looked and walked and smelled even.

Steinbeck's version: I remember where *a toad may live* and what time the birds awaken in the summer, and what trees and seasons smelled like—how people looked and walked and smelled even.

"Where a toad may live" is more interesting than "where the toads lived" because it is specific to a single toad. Specifics tend to carry more interest than generalities. For this reason, Steinbeck is quick to default to the singular tense when occasion permits. Here is another instance of that default to the singular in *East of Eden*. Find the plural nouns and singularize them:

Alternate version: The Salinas was only a part-time river. The summer sun drove it underground. It was not a fine river at all, but it was the only one we had and so we boasted about it—how dangerous it was in wet winters and how dry it was in dry summers.

Steinbeck's version: The Salinas was only a part-time river. The summer sun drove it underground. It was not a fine river at all, but it was the only one we had and so we boasted about it—how dangerous it was *in a wet winter* and how dry it was *in a dry summer*.

Here's one more from the same novel, but this time render two singular nouns plural:

Alternate version: February in Salinas is likely to be damp and cold and full of misery. The heaviest rain falls then, and if the river is going to rise, it rises then. February of 1915 was a year heavy with water.

Steinbeck's version: February in Salinas is likely to be damp and cold and full of *miseries*. The heaviest *rains* fall then, and if the river is going to rise, it rises then. February of 1915 was a year heavy with water.

Lesson 11: Barbara Kingsolver

The Objective Correlative

Read this excerpt from Barbara Kingsolver's *The Lacuna* and see if you can identify the specific words and combinations of words that lend a certain feel to the
prose. Try to define what that feel is and why you are feeling it.

> *In the beginning were the howlers. They always commenced their
> bellowing in the first hour of dawn, just as the hem of the sky
> began to whiten. It would start with just one: his forced, rhythmic
> groaning, like a saw blade. That aroused others near him, nudging
> them to bawl along with his monstrous tune. Soon the maroon-
> throated howls would echo back from other trees, farther down the
> beach, until the whole jungle filled with roaring trees. As it was in
> the beginning, so it is every morning of the world.*

First, the phrases "In the beginning" and "As it was in the beginning, so it is
every morning of the world" recall the Bible and give the passage a sacred feel.
But in Kingsolver's beginning there is no light, only bellowing, groaning, bawling,
and monstrous maroon-throated howls and roars. The effect is at once sacred *and*
sacrilege, good *and* evil. It's an incongruent collage that's hard to describe but easy
to feel. Can you?

That feel you get from the words you read is a consequence of the *objective correlative*. *Correlative* refers to the correlation between specific words and the feelings they inspire when we read or hear them. The correlation is *objective* because
the feelings created by certain words are felt by everyone in the same way: objec-
tively. When you understand this, you can draw upon the objective correlative to

unlock the human psyche, to provoke whatever feelings you wish, and to provoke them in *everyone*. It's how movie directors compel everyone to cry on cue. It's how comedians provoke everyone to laugh. Certain words and combinations of words will do certain things, and do them to everybody in the same way. It's as if a single rhetorical key can open a billion psychological locks.

The first version of this next selection from *The Lacuna* has been altered so as to be without regard to the objective correlative. The second is very much informed by it, as a boy and his single mother find themselves in a strange land with creatures who dwell outside, and one creature in particular who dwells within—their would-be stepfather and husband, Enrique.

Alternate version: Enrique was their keeper, observing their fear while eating breakfast. "That howling is the aullaros," he would say. "They howl at one-another to settle out their territories, before they begin a day of hunting."

Kingsolver's version: Enrique was their *captor, surveying* their *terror* with a *cool eye* while eating *his* breakfast. "That howling is the aullaros," he would say, *as he pulled the white napkin out of its silver ring into his silver-ringed fingers*, placing it on his lap and *slicing into* his breakfast with a fork and knife. "They howl at one-another to settle out their territories, before they begin a day of *hunting for food*."

Note the careful words and phrases Kingsolver uses to transform an otherwise well-mannered gentleman at breakfast, into something quite dangerous, disturbed, calculated, cold, creepy, and violent even. Note also that Kingsolver doesn't rely upon any of those obvious adjectives. Instead she allows her readers to feel the meaning of those adjectives by way of the objective correlative. From the nouns she uses to the verbs, to the pronouns, to the way Enrique watches them, moves, even the way he eats, everything about this passage is designed to evoke a certain feel. Anything Kingsolver can do to achieve that feeling she does by virtue of the careful words at her command.

Lesson 12: Joshua Ferris

Falling into Lingo

If you've ever used a walkie-talkie, you know how hard it is to resist falling into walkie-talkie lingo. Based solely on the fact that these communication devices require one to press and hold down a knob while talking, things otherwise *heard* are suddenly and inexplicably *copied*: "Copy that victor tango three niner out." At least that's what I do.

This bit of human nature, this urge to affect a special language for every special circumstance, is a little unnecessary, and so it lends itself to satire. That's why falling into lingo is a particularly effective way of poking fun. See if you can poke some fun by falling into lingo in this passage from Joshua Ferris's *Then We Came to the End*. Here's some help: use clichéd corporate lingo in place of the word "quickly" and cheesy advertising lingo in place of the phrase "order the product."

Alternate version: Ordinarily jobs came in and we completed them quickly. Sometimes fuck-ups did occur. Printing errors, transposed numbers. Our business was advertising and details were important. If the third number after the second hyphen in a client's toll-free number was a six instead of an eight, and if it went to print like that, and showed up in *Time* magazine, no one reading the ad could order the product.

Ferris's version: Ordinarily jobs came in and we completed them *in a timely and professional manner*. Sometimes fuck-ups did occur. Printing errors, transposed numbers. Our business was advertising and details were important. If the third number after the second hyphen in a client's toll-free number was a six instead of an eight, and if it went to print like that, and showed up in *Time* magazine, no one reading the ad could *call now and order today*.

Can you see how falling into lingo gives the prose a satirical bent?

Sometimes it's necessary to set your lingo in quotation marks, to ensure that your fall into lingo is not lost on anyone, as in the following passage from this book's introduction:

To some extent, formality creeps into just about every profession. People deploy such language in an attempt to present themselves as professional when, ironically, usually the opposite effect is achieved. The same can be said for those who attempt to impress with big professorial words. While such language may seem "indubitably" clear and appropriate to them, it strikes the rest of us as more than a bit eccentric.

Lesson 13: Ken Kesey

....

Couching Metaphors

Read this portrayal of a house on a river from Ken Kesey's *Sometimes a Great Notion*. Can you name the animal to which the language alludes?

> *No bridges span its first ten miles. And yet, across, on that southern shore, an ancient two-story wood-frame house rests on a structure of tangled steel, of wood and earth and sacks of sand.*

If the allusion to a bird in a nest escaped you, Kesey's simile makes it all too clear:

> *No bridges span its first ten miles. And yet, across, on that southern shore, an ancient two-story wood-frame house rests on a structure of tangled steel, of wood and earth and sacks of sand,* <u>like a two-story bird with split-shake feathers, sitting fierce in its tangled nest.</u>

The point is, good writers do more than simply conjure up clever comparisons for the things they describe; they couch those comparisons in language that relates to them or is suggestive of them.

Let's try one ourselves. Assume the subject about which we are writing is an asylum, and we are in search of a title.

Step 1: Create a comparison.
Animals and the places they live make outstanding comparisons. Let's go with a cuckoo's nest.

Step 2: Couch your comparison in related language.

We may create our own related language or we may borrow it. Poems,
Bibles, and children's rhymes all lend themselves well to this exercise.
In this case we'll pick from rhyme:

One flew east, one flew west,

One flew over the cuckoo's nest.

Lesson 14: Martin Luther King, Jr.

....

Shape-Shifting

Let's assume that your company has been taken over by new management, and you have been tasked with creating a new slogan to whip whatever employees are left into shape. After some consideration, your new slogan goes like this:

> **Don't cause a problem; find a solution.**

That may be a little nondescript, but fear not. Watch what happens when a piece of the structure—or shape—of the first clause is *shifted* to the second:

Before shift: Don't cause a problem; find a solution.

After shift: Don't cause a problem; *cause* a solution.
Now *that's* much improved.

Shape-shifting gives your words an aphoristic feel, which is to say that it makes what you say seem wise and clever—because it is. So it's no coincidence that shape-shifting is used by people who want to persuade and inspire. Consider this excerpt from the Reverend Martin Luther King's "A knock at midnight" speech, as he examines the problem of racism in America.

> **The problem isn't so much that we don't know enough, but it's as if we aren't good enough. The trouble isn't so much**

> *that our scientific genius lags behind, but that our moral genius*
> *lags behind.*

Here, King uses two shape-shifts back to back, which creates an automatic rhythm to his prose. The first shift is good, but the second shift is remarkable because it creates a set of words not ordinarily seen or heard. Just as we are unaccustomed to "causing solutions," we are equally unaccustomed to having a "moral genius," let alone allowing it to lag behind.

Here's one from this very book. See if you can shape-shift part of the structure of the first clause to the second, and thereby create a more interesting effect:

Before shift:
…words are powerful not in and of themselves, but in the way they combine to form that which they could never be otherwise.

After shift:
…words are powerful not in and of themselves, but *in and of* each other, in the way they combine to form that which they could never be otherwise.

Lesson 15: Henry James

....

Creative Prepositions

Prepositions—words that convey relationship like "on," "in," "above," and "through"—are rarely given any thought at all. But because they are so few in number, and because they must be used in nearly every sentence, prepositions have a way of seeding clichés.

It therefore becomes necessary to replace the prepositions we're accustomed to with ones we are not. Read this excerpt from *The Turn of the Screw* as the narrator waits to hear what he presumes to be a true account of unspeakable horror. Mind you, the passage has been altered so as to be without a creative preposition. So begin by locating the ordinary preposition, and its cliché:

> **This I took for a sign that he had himself something to produce and**
> **that we should only have to wait. We waited in fact till two nights**
> **later; but that same evening, before we scattered, he brought out**
> **what was on his mind.**

Hopefully you have identified the cliché "what was on his mind." So do what James does, and replace the preposition "on," with one from the list on page 41:

> **We waited in fact till two nights later; but that same evening,**
> **before we scattered, he brought out what was in his mind.**

This seemingly minor change in preposition does three things. It destroys the cliché, it adds a haunted feel to the prose, and it serves as an opposing foil to the word "out."

Here's another excerpt from *The Turn of the Screw*, altered so as to be without creative preposition.

He never took his eyes off me.

Now replace "off" with a less-usual preposition:

He never took his eyes from me.

Again, the cliché is destroyed.

Not every preposition is meant to be replaced by another. Sometimes prepositions should be replaced by adjectives, as James does here in *The Turn of the Screw*:

Before preposition replacement: She has been dead for twenty years.

After preposition replacement: She has been dead *these* twenty years.

And now for your final test. In this next excerpt from *A Moveable Feast*, Ernest Hemingway—an admirer of James and in some respects an emulator—takes equal care in his choice of preposition.

Before creative preposition: Then there was the bad weather. It would come in one day when the fall was over. We would have to shut the windows at night against the rain and the cold wind would strip the leaves from the trees in the Place Contrescarpe.

After creative preposition: We would have to shut the windows *in the* night against the rain and the cold wind would strip the leaves from the trees in the Place Contrescarpe.

It would seem that what good writers do "at night," brilliant writers do "in the night."

And you thought Ernest Hemingway and Henry James were diametrically opposed. Shame on you.

Here's a fairly extensive list of prepositions taken from Wikipedia. Use this list to find substitutions that destroy clichés and improve your speech and prose.

- aboard
- about
- above
- across
- after
- against
- along
- alongside
- amid
- amidst
- among
- amongst
- around
- as
- aside
- astride
- at
- athwart
- atop
- barring
- before
- behind
- below
- beneath
- beside
- besides
- between
- beyond
- but
- by
- circa
- concerning

- despite
- down
- during
- except
- excluding
- failing
- following
- for
- from
- given
- in
- including
- inside
- into
- like
- minus
- near
- next
- notwithstanding
- of
- off
- on
- onto
- opposite
- out
- outside
- over
- pace
- past
- per
- plus
- qua

- regarding
- round
- save
- since
- than
- through
- throughout
- till
- times
- to
- toward
- towards
- under
- underneath
- unlike
- until
- up
- upon
- versus
- via
- with
- within
- without

Lesson 16: Barack Obama

....

Eloquence and Power

When you write and speak using eloquent language, two curious things happen. One: your audience cannot help but to associate that eloquent language with power. And two: they will then associate that power with you. It's as if by the mere *use* of eloquent language, writers and speakers are able to acquire and project power. Think about it: The leader of the free world, arguably the most powerful person on this planet, is also among the most eloquent public speakers of the twenty-first century. Coincidence?

While there are good reasons why some words and phrases are more powerful than others—many of which are the subjects of lessons in this book—some words are powerful just because they are. Read this altered excerpt from Barack Obama's "A More Perfect Union" speech and try to come up with a more powerful replacement for the word in bold. Feel free to look up the word in this very thesaurus.

Altered: Farmers and scholars; statesmen and patriots who had traveled across an ocean to escape tyranny and persecution finally ratified the Declaration of Independence at a Philadelphia convention that lasted through the spring of 1787.

Original: Farmers and scholars; statesmen and patriots who had traveled across an ocean to escape tyranny and persecution finally *made real* their declaration of independence at a Philadelphia convention that lasted through the spring of 1787.

I can't tell you exactly why in this particular context "made real" is more eloquent than "ratified." It just is. That's why for every ordinary word you look up in this book there are usually several options from which to choose. Everything depends on context and your ability to choose wisely. So let's test that ability by replacing the highlighted words in this passage from *Dreams from My Father*. Again, refer to *The Well-Spoken Thesaurus* if need be, but try to do this one yourself.

Altered: I enjoyed those moments—but only briefly. If the talk began to wander, or become too familiar, I would quickly find a reason to excuse myself. I had grown too comfortable in my privacy, the safest place I knew.

Original: I enjoyed *such* moments—but only *in brief*. If the talk began to wander, or *cross the border* into familiarity, I would *soon* find (_) reason to excuse myself. I had grown too comfortable in my *solitude*, the safest place I knew.

Lesson 17: Cintra Wilson

....

Wordplay

When you think of words and phrases, it helps to think of them not so much as what they are—little groupings of letters on a page—but more as what they could be: three-dimensional objects, like pieces of a 3-D puzzle. Think of each word or phrase as a unique shape so that, as you rotate it, the face of the object—or the meaning—changes. Turn a word or phrase one way, and it conveys a certain meaning. Turn it upside down or on to its side, and it means something else entirely. When you think like this, it becomes easier to play with words in a creative way.

Let's say you're writing about a resurgence of '80s fashions, and so you plan to make some cultural references to movies like *Flashdance* or *Back to the Future*. Looking at *Back to the Future* straight on, it's a movie and nothing more. But if you were to pick it up and rotate it ever so slightly in your mind, it would appear physically altered, perhaps without any capitalization, and therefore less movie-like and more phrase-like. You could then seamlessly weave "back to the future" into a sentence, as Cintra Wilson does in this excerpt from the 2009 *New York Times* article "Where the Bad '80s Has a Niche":

> *Fashion is currently obsessed with a redux of the New Wave '80s, which, for the most part, has also been sanitized for your re-consumption. The sleazy, over-stimulated parts were left on the old side of the fin de siècle, and only the off-shoulder Tiffany tops and "Flashdance" leggings were welcomed back to the future.*

If this kind of clever wordplay seems especially familiar, it's because you encountered the very same thing on the preceding page, where Barack Obama describes America's Founding Fathers, not as ratifying The Declaration of Independence, but as "making real their declaration of independence."

Again, the easiest way to write like this is to think of words and phrases as three-dimensional objects. So let's think in 3-D, shall we? In this excerpt from a 2008 Salon.com article, Cintra Wilson makes the point that the Oscars have become tired, old, and uncool. But before we go any further, consider that word-pair: the Oscars. It's just begging to be played with, don't you think? Pick it up and turn it about in your mind. It shouldn't take you long to come up with "Oscar," which is precisely what Wilson does here:

> *Oscar is elderly, and in dire need of hipness-replacement surgery.*
> *In his dotage he is tiresome, dull and earnest, and employs a lot*
> *of doddering repetition about how movies "touch the soul" and*
> *"inspire others to dream."*

What's more, Wilson takes the term "hip-replacement surgery," interprets "hip" to mean cool, then modifies it to read "hipness-replacement surgery."

And that's how you play with words.

The Well-Spoken Vocabulary

....

How Our Words Can Change the Way We Think

Have you ever learned a new word, and then after having done so, a few days later, happened upon that very word again, and then again a couple of weeks later? You realize that in all your past readings, never once did you really notice that word until you had taken the time to learn its meaning. The truth is, you had probably encountered the word a hundred times, but because you never understood it, for all intents and purposes, it wasn't there. That's because your mind has a way of papering over what it does not understand with what little it does. In each occurrence, your brain fills in the empty spaces as best it knows how, based on the incomplete aspects of your incomplete vocabulary. Here's why that's a very bad thing.

When presented with pictures of the following animals—a robin, a bear, and an eagle—and called upon to group two of the animals together, most young children will pair the robin with the eagle.[1] Children do this because they recognize the concept of birdness by virtue of the word "bird" in their limited vocabularies. But older kids will more often give a different answer.

Take a moment to group two of the animals yourself. Done? Hopefully you've paired the eagle with the bear, because, as do older kids, you possess the word

---

1   Based on experiments conducted by Dr. Stephen J. Ceci at Cornell University.

"predator" in your vocabulary. Only because you know the word "predator" do you have a rhetorical awareness that allows you to see predation. You and the older kids can see what the younger children can't, not because the younger children lack intellect, but because they lack a developed vocabulary. They simply have not yet been introduced to that particular concept or word.

This experiment suggests that the introduction of a single word into your vocabulary can transform the way you perceive reality. The implications are immediate. If words allow you to see that which you cannot otherwise see, then imagine what you are missing in your life today. It raises the question: how blind are you really?

As a case in point, let's turn our attention to a word you may or may not know—*de-familiarization*. Using this word as our "predator" example, I'm going to show you how an understanding of something as arcane as an obscure literary term can change the way you see reality. To do this, we must first agree on the word's meaning.

> De-familiarization is anything a writer does that is unusual or out of the ordinary. Writers and speakers de-familiarize what they say because they want your attention, and they want to more effectively make their points. One easy way to de-familiarize a point is to use a strategically placed expletive. Think about it: If someone who never swears were to drop the F-bomb in public, you'd listen, and you'd remember what they said. Why? Because that sort of language would be completely out of the ordinary for such a person, and hardly in keeping with decorum. Such outbursts can be pretty head-turning—and eyebrow-raising—so they must occur as if by mistake.

So now that you have an understanding of the word *de-familiarization*, suppose you were to overhear the vice president of the United States characterize the recent passage of health care legislation as "a big fucking deal." Would you be so quick to assume his remark an unintended faux pas? Or, would you suspect that the vice president *wanted* his remark to be picked up by the mic he knew was there, that he *wanted*—and succeeded in getting—all major news outlets to spend the next seventy-two hours talking about what a "big fucking deal" is the Obama-led health care bill?

The point is, maybe it was a gaff, and maybe it wasn't, but without a rhetorical awareness of the word *de-familiarization*, you would have assumed only one of those two possibilities. You would have paired the robin with the eagle.

Expletives can also be used when their corresponding euphemisms fail to convey the gravity of a specific point, as we can see in this excerpt from Barack Obama's *Dreams from My Father*:

> **When the weather was good, my roommate and I might sit out on the fire escape to smoke cigarettes and study the dusk washing blue over the city, or watch white people from the better neighborhoods nearby walk their dogs down our block to let the animals shit on our curbs—"Scoop the poop, you bastards!" my roommate would shout with impressive rage, and we'd laugh at the faces of both master and beast, grim and unapologetic as they hunkered down to do the deed.**

Again, without an understanding of the word *de-familiarization*, you could easily come away from this passage wondering why a respected public figure like Barack Obama wouldn't just use a less offensive word like "crap" in place of "shit." You might therefore conclude unwittingly that President Obama was just being vulgar or trying too hard to be cool, and so you would have missed his attempt to de-familiarize his point, to describe the indignities imposed by one group of people upon another, using harsh language for effect. You would not have seen de-familiarization occurring before your very eyes, because it was not a part of your vocabulary. Unless you happen to be that rare breed given to discovering new phenomena, you need the word to see the thing. That's how the act of learning new words can transform the way you see reality. That's how acquiring a proper vocabulary forces your mind to stop seeing only those things that conform to what you think you already know.

The Seven Rhetorical Sins

....

Here are seven of the most common rhetorical offenses. Your efforts in reducing the frequency with which they occur are greatly appreciated.

1. Melodrama: Jacqueline Susann, *Valley of the Dolls*

> *The temperature hit ninety degrees the day she arrived. New York was steaming, an angry concrete animal caught unawares in an unseasonable hot spell.*

This recalls that famous *Seinfeld* scene: "The sea was angry that day, my friends—like an old man trying to send back soup in a deli."

2. Needlessness: Lee Child, *The Enemy*

> *I was alone in a borrowed office. There was a clock on the wall. It had no second hand. Just an hour hand, and a minute hand. It was electric. It didn't tick. It was <u>completely</u> silent, like the room. I was watching the minute hand intently. It wasn't moving.*

As Simon and Garfunkel used to say, it's "The Sound of Silence," not "The Sound of Complete Silence"—and for good reason.

3. Cliché: Steven King, *Insomnia*

> *By then the ticking had grown very loud, and when Ralph lay in bed beside her on those* <u>hot summer nights</u> *when even a single sheet seemed to weigh ten pounds and he believed every dog in Derry was* <u>barking at the moon</u>, *he listened to it, to the deathwatch ticking inside Carolyn, and it seemed to him that* <u>his heart would break</u> *with sorrow and terror.*

While there is little harm in using an occasional cliché, they should never inform your prose or your speech. The only good cliché is the one you coin yourself.

4. Pretension: Elias Canetti, *Crowds and Power*

> *There is nothing that* <u>man</u> *fears more than the touch of the unknown.* <u>He</u> *wants to see what is reaching towards* <u>him</u>, *and to be able to recognize or at least classify it.* <u>Man</u> *always tends to avoid physical contact with anything strange.*

Why would you want to rhetorically dismiss half the people on the planet every time you communicate some grand universal notion? What's wrong with "humankind" or even the occasional "she" or "her"? Speak to everyone. It's the twenty-first century.

5. Craftiness: Glenn Beck, *Common Sense*

> *I think I know who you are. After September 11, 2001, you thought our country had changed for the better. But the months that followed proved otherwise. We began to divide ourselves and the partisan bickering that had been absent from blood donor lines and church services started all over again.*

From this, the opening paragraph to *Common Sense*, if you didn't know any better you would think that Glenn Beck was sorry to see our country divided. But don't be fooled. Propagandists crave division, and come well versed in language designed to sow it. They exploit our fear of terrorists, our suspicion of science, our resentment of the "edumacated," and our bias against other cultures, religions, races, and nationalities. They manipulate our opinions by hyping obscure fringe groups which then serve as unwitting foils to the propagandists' more "moderate" views. And with that oft-repeated whisper "those people think they're better than you," propagandists exploit our lack of self-esteem, and dismiss as corrupt, arrogant, or misinformed anyone with whom they disagree.

Whether you lean right or left, never let "common sense" deprive you of reason.

6. Perkiness: Janet Evanovich, *How I Write*

> *Three people are actually responsible for writing this book. Alex, my webmaster daughter, is the third author. When asked if she preferred the money or the glory, there wasn't a contest, so for design purposes Alex's name isn't on the cover. Bad enough we had to fit Evanovich on once, much less twice!*

This is insufferable. I'd rather read Glenn Beck.

7. Wordiness: Henry James, *The Turn of the Screw*

> *The case, I may mention, was that of an apparition in just such an old house as had gathered us for the occasion—an appearance, of a dreadful kind, to a little boy sleeping in the room with his mother and waking her up in the terror of it; <u>waking her not to dissipate his dread and soothe him to sleep again, but to encounter also, herself, before she had succeeded in doing so, the same sight that had shaken him.</u>*

Sometimes even the greatest of writers need to be reminded to take in the slack.

How This
Book Works

....

To get a sense for what this thesaurus can do, consider its preamble as it was originally written in rough draft form:

> *These words are like spices. Be careful selecting the right ratios and flavors. Too much sugar will make your writing seem flowery and pretentious. Too much garlic, and your writing will taste academic and stiff. Not enough salt, and you'll be labeled bland.*

Suppose you had written the above passage as part of a rough draft, and now the time had come to polish it up a bit with *The Well-Spoken Thesaurus*. For starters, you might try looking up "be careful," where you would find the alternative "take care to." You could then look up "right" and replace it with "proper," and then look up "too much" to find "an embarrassment of." Not exactly a synonym of "too much," but it works, doesn't it? That's because it's rhetorically related to what you are trying to say. You see, because your ultimate objective is not simply to find a synonymous word, but a more powerful word, this book has been designed to provide you with precisely that—what I like to call *powernyms*.

And so, with the powernym for "make your" being "leave your," the final product speaks for itself:

> *These words are like spices.* <u>Take care to</u> *select the* <u>proper</u> *ratios and flavors.* <u>An embarrassment of</u> *sugar will* <u>leave your</u> *prose flowery and pretentious. Too much garlic, and your writing will taste academic and stiff. Too little salt, and you'll be* <u>dismissed</u> *as* <u>pedestrian.</u> *And always* <u>be mindful of</u> *your audience. Try not to serve vichyssoise to a coal miner, and do not give Cheerios to the queen of England. Neither will be amused.*

No conventional thesaurus can do that. No vocabulary builder. No style guide.

As effective as this book can be as a writer's reference, my hope is that you take the time to use it as a learning aid for speaking. After all, if you're going to be well-spoken, you can't be continually looking up words every time you have something to say. You're going to need to memorize a few things. Start with the boxes. They contain some of the most impressive examples of eloquence this book has to offer. Then move to the common word entries, under which you will often find not one but several eloquent alternatives. Of these alternatives, only the first—arguably the most eloquent—is meant to be memorized and used regularly in your everyday speech. It must not be thought, however, that my choices are informed by anything other than personal taste. So feel free to take exception, and memorize the one alternative that most appeals to you. In any case, the quickest and most effective way to do this is to write each of your favored alternatives on flash cards paired against their corresponding common word entries and review them daily. Only then will these words begin to inform the way you speak. Also, as a general rule, limit the use of foreign and academic words to those occasions when your subject is foreign or, when your audience is peopled with academics. I include both categories as words that are good to know but not necessarily to use at every occasion.

Finally, should you ever happen upon any eloquent words or phrases that I have neglected, email them to me along with your name and address. If I use them in a future edition, I'll be delighted to mention your contribution in that edition's acknowledgments.

Preamble

....

These words are like spices. Take care to select the proper ratios and flavors. An embarrassment of sugar will leave your prose flowery and pretentious. Too much garlic, and your writing will taste academic and stiff. Too little salt, and you'll be dismissed as pedestrian. And always be mindful of your audience. Try not to serve vichyssoise to a coal miner, and do not give Cheerios to the queen of England. Neither will be amused.

The Well-Spoken Thesaurus

Aa

A BIT
-rather
-somewhat
-in part
-to some degree
-to some extent

"*Perhaps to some extent, but I think her judicial decisions are based less on politics than on natural justice.*"

A BIT OF
-a remnant of

"*To the peasants of old times, the world outside their own direct experience was a region of vagueness and mystery: to their untravelled thought a state of wandering was a conception as dim as the winter life of the swallows that came back with the spring; and even a settler, if he came from distant parts, hardly ever ceased to be viewed with a remnant of distrust...*" Mary Anne Evans, *Silas Marner*

A CERTAIN AMOUNT OF
-a measure of

A CERTAIN SOMETHING
-je ne sais quoi {French, *zhuh nuh say KWAH*}

A CERTAIN WAY
-a given manner

A DIFFERENT STORY
-another matter entirely

A DONE DEAL
-an accomplished fact
-a fait accompli {French, *fate uh-com-PLEE*}

"*I'm sorry, but the court has spoken; it's a fait accompli.*"

A FEW YEARS AGO
-some years ago

"*Some years ago there was in the city of York a society of magicians. They met upon the third Wednesday of every month and read each other long, dull papers upon the history of English magic.*" Susanna Clarke, *Jonathan Strange and Mr. Norrell*

A KIND OF ____
-a ____ of sorts

A LITTLE BIT
-somewhat
-in part

-to some degree
-to some extent

"Perhaps to some extent, but I think her judicial decisions are based less on politics than on natural justice."

A LITTLE BIT OF (I DETECT A LITTLE BIT OF)
-a degree of
-a remnant of

"To the peasants of old times, the world outside their own direct experience was a region of vagueness and mystery: to their untravelled thought a state of wandering was a conception as dim as the winter life of the swallows that came back with the spring; and even a settler, if he came from distant parts, hardly ever ceased to be viewed with a remnant of distrust..." Mary Anne Evans, *Silas Marner*

A LITTLE BIT OF A
-something of a

"We used to be more productive in verse. Maybe that was a young man's thing, because every novelist, especially in the early phases of his work, is something of a poet." Derek Walcott, speaking of West Indian writers

A LOT
-a great deal

"You'll come to learn a great deal if you study the Insignificant in depth." Odysseus Elytis

A LOT HAPPENED DURING
-much did happen during

A LOT LIKE
-it recalls a certain
-it's much like
-it is reminiscent of
-it is akin to
-it is much the same as
-it's ____ian
-it bears a resemblance to

A LOT OF
-a wealth of
-a host of
-extensive
-a goodly number of [playful]
-a fair amount of
-fuming not a little
-hordes of
-legions of
-profuse
-a great many
-a litany of
-considerable

A MAN
-the man

"For all men live by truth and stand in need of expression. In love, in art, in avarice, in politics, in labor, in games, we study to utter our painful secret. The man is only half himself, the other half is his expression." Ralph Waldo Emerson, "The Poet"

A MILE AWAY
-a mile distant

"Because the intersection was on this tiny rise, you could see our buildings, a mile distant, at the southern edge of the farm." Jane Smiley, *A Thousand Acres*

A REGULAR (HE'S A REGULAR AT THIS PUB)
-one of the usual suspects

"The usual suspects begin to mosey on in at around five o' five."
-a client
-a habitué {French, *huh-BICH-oo-ay*, one who frequents an establishment habitually}

"Of all the customers, he was the bartender's most loyal habitué."

A SPECIFIC WAY
-a given manner

A TIME WHEN (IT WAS A TIME WHEN)
-years that saw

"These were years that saw the rise of Mussolini and the Fascist Party."

A WHILE (FOR A WHILE)
-for some time now
-for a considerable space in time

ABANDON (TO ABANDON)
-abandon the sanctuary of

"This king, to say no more of him, and this queen, and their infant children (who once would have been the pride and hope of a great and generous people) were then forced to abandon the sanctuary of the most splendid palace in the world, which they left swimming in blood..." Edmund Burke, *Reflections on the Revolution in France*

-consign
-relinquish
-forsake
-forswear
-cede
-lay aside

"Lay aside your personal feelings, and view this as a professional matter."

ABANDONED (IS ABANDONED)
-derelict

ABILITIES
-prowess
-facility in
-instincts

"His instincts as a lawyer are what got him where he is today."

____ ABILITY
-command of
-authority in the handling of
-a capacity for

"You certainly have a capacity for mathematics and engineering."
-the faculty for
-capacity to

"The chief weapon of the sea pirates, however, was their capacity to astonish. Nobody else could believe, until it was much too late, how heartless and greedy they were." Kurt Vonnegut, *Breakfast of Champions*

ABLE TO (ARE YOU ABLE TO)
-can you manage to

ABOUT
-of

"I know nothing of the house I was born in. The look of the town is all I remember. And yet I can hear the sound of the door as we closed it behind us for good." Andrew O'Hagan, *Our Fathers*

There is talk about a merger.

There is talk of a merger.

ABOUT (APPROXIMATELY)
-on the order of
-some ten million
-there or thereabouts
-to the tune of
-circa {Latin, SIR-cuh, lit. around}

"The Mencius was written circa 4th century BCE."

ABOUT TO HAPPEN
-poised to
-in the offing
-impending
-approaching
-looming
-imminent

ABSENT
-unaccounted for
-elsewhere
-in absentia {Latin, *in ab-SENT-shee-ya*}

"He was wrongfully tried and convicted in absentia."

ABSOLUTE
-unmitigated

"Christianity has operated with an un-mitigated arrogance and cruelty—necessarily, since a religion ordinarily imposes on those who have discovered the true faith the spiritual duty of liberating the infidels." James Baldwin
-sheer
-uncompromising
-stark
-unqualified

ABSOLUTE POWER
-imperium {Latin, *im-PEER-ee-um*}

"She rules with imperium."

ABSOLUTELY
-without question
-without exception
-without doubt
-by any measure
-undoubtedly
-unmistakably
-in no measured terms
-soundly
-categorically
-decidedly
-invariably
-indeed
-in every respect
-out and out
-to be sure
-patently
-without reservation
-in no uncertain terms
-is nothing other than
-utterly [often derogatory]

> This is absolutely the best beer on the menu.
>
> This is without question the best beer on the menu.

ABSOLUTELY NOT
-by no means

"The issue is by no means resolved."
-emphatically not

ABUNDANTLY
-profusely

"Maria Concepción walked carefully, keeping to the middle of the white dusty road, where the maguey thorns and the treacherous curved spines of organ cactus had not gathered so profusely." Katherine Anne Porter, *The Collected Stories of Katherine Anne Porter.*

ABUSED
-maltreated

"The book was thick and black and covered with dust. Its boards were bowed and creaking; it had been maltreated in its own time." A. S. Byatt, *Possession*

ACADEMIC FIELD
-academic discipline

ACCEPT
-embrace

"Science embraces the facts and debates opinion; religion embraces opinion and debates the facts."

ACCEPT THAT (I RELUCTANTLY ACCEPT THAT)
-I am resigned to
-I will allow that
-I have come to terms with

ACCEPT THE COST
-bear the cost

ACCEPT THE RESPONSIBILITY
-bear the responsibility

ACCEPTABLE (GOOD ENOUGH BUT NOT GREAT)
-palatable
-admissible

ACCEPTED AND ESTABLISHED
-canonical

"It has been three centuries since Dr. (Samuel) Johnson was born, on Sept. 7, 1709. He died on Dec. 13, 1784, still struggling for the mixed blessing of more life. His Falstaffian vitalism is always my first thought when I reread, teach again or continue brooding upon the canonical critic of Western literature." Harold Bloom, New York Times, Nov. 5, 2009

ACCEPTED IDEA [BUT IRONI-CALLY A PLATITUDE]
-idée recue [pejorative]
{French, *ee-day ru-SUE*}

"When a company tells its workers to think outside the box, that is the kind of idée recue that can suck the life out of everyone there."

ACCESS TO
-recourse to
-avail yourself of
-immediacy to

"Immediacy to everything the new hospital had to offer was his first concern."

ACCESSIBLE (ARE ACCESSIBLE)
-lie within the reach of

"Very simple ideas lie within the reach only of complex minds." Remy De Gourmont

ACCESSORIES
-embellishments
-accoutrements
-trappings

ACCIDENT
-mishap

ACCOMPANIED BY
-attended by
-punctuated by

"Football combines the two worst features of American life. It is violence punctuated by committee meetings." George Will

ACCOMPANYING
-attendant
-concomitant [academic]

ACCORDING TO
-by various accounts
-as viewed by
-in what some say is
-it was by all accounts

> According to everyone there, it was an awkward exchange.
>
> It was by all accounts an awkward exchange.

ACCOUNT FOR (DID YOU ACCOUNT FOR)
-render an account of

ACCUMULATION OF
-an assemblage of
-a repository of
-a trove of

ACCURATELY
-faithfully

ACCURATENESS
-the inerrancy of [academic]

ACCUSATION
-incrimination
-indictment
-denunciation

ACCUSE
-point an accusatory finger

ACCUSED OF
-come under fire for

"She has come under fire for her imperious management style."

ACHIEVE
-fulfill
-realize
-make strides toward

-carry off
-produce

ACHIEVE GREAT THINGS
-achieve great ends

"Every man of action has a strong dose of egoism, pride, hardness and cunning. But all those things will be regarded as high qualities if he can make them the means to achieve great ends." Giorgos Seferis

ACHIEVEMENT
-a triumph
-a significant point of arrival
-a tour de force {French, *tour du* FORCE}

"Victor Hugo's Les Miserables is considered a literary tour de force."

ACKNOWLEDGING (OUT OF REGARD FOR)
-in a nod to

"In a nod to the gloomy economy, Ford Motor Company will forgo up to twelve monthly payments for car buyers who lose their jobs."

ACROSS FROM (SAT ACROSS FROM)
-sat opposite

ACT AS
-function as
-serve as

ACT OF
-in a gesture of

ACT OF GOD
-a force majeure {French, *force mu-* ZHURE, lit. supreme force}

"Because there is a force majeure clause in the contract, we are not obliged to pay for damage caused by the earthquake."
-vis major {Latin, *vis* MAY-jer, lit. higher force}

ACT OF VIOLENT REVENGE
-a blood reckoning

ACTION (A SPECIFIC ACTION)
-measure
-deed
-gesture
-exploit
-venture
-undertaking
-pursuit

ACTION (IN A GENERAL SENSE)
-agency

"And like a big teacup at the county fair, they would sit and spin in their little round boat, and want for rain and want for land, until they had only to want for the agency of God."
-instrumentality [academic]

ACTIONABLE INTELLIGENCE [MILITARY JINGOISM]
-timely information

ACTIONS
-deeds
-doings

"They are dead, all of them. I am caught and tangled around by their doings. It is as if their lives left a weaving of invisible threads in the air of this house, of this town, of this county. And I stumbled and fell into them." Shirley Ann Grau, *The Keepers of the House*
-good offices

"It was only her good offices that saved his job."

ACTIVITIES
-affairs
-proceedings
-goings on
-endeavors
-pursuits

ACTUAL (IN PRACTICE, BUT NOT OFFICIALLY)
-de facto {Latin, *de FAC-toe*, lit. in fact}

"Though he is only a radio commentator, many consider Rush Limbaugh to be the de facto leader of the Republican Party."

ACTUAL (REAL)
-tangible
-substantive

"I want you to make substantive improvements."

ACTUAL BUSINESS
-a going concern

ACTUALLY (AS A WAY TO BEGIN A STATEMENT)
-as it happens
-the fact of the matter is
-truth be told
-I would have you know
-it is in point of fact

ACTUALLY (REALLY)
-in truth
-in any real sense

"But even though the number of those who really think seriously before they begin to write is small, extremely few of them think about the subject itself: the remainder think only about the books that have been written on the subject, and what has been said by others. In order to think at all, such writers need the more direct and powerful stimulus of having other people's thoughts before them. These become their immediate theme; and the result is that they are always under their influence, and so never, in any real sense of the word, are original." Arthur Schopenhauer, *The Art of Literature*

ADAPTABLE
-compliant
-malleable
-pliant

ADD BEAUTY TO
-grace with
-adorn with
-array with

ADD TO
-inject a dose of
-augment
-supplement
-infuse
-leaven with
-endow with
-install
-instill with

ADD TO PROBLEMS
-exacerbate the problems
-only compound the problems

ADD TO THAT THE
-couple that with

ADDED BONUS (AS AN ADDED BONUS)
-for good measure

ADDING FILLER
-larding

"You are larding the narrative with needless adjectives."

ADDITION
-addendum
-supplement

ADDITIONAL (BUT SUBORDINATE)
-ancillary
-collateral

ADJUST
-tailor
-calibrate

ADJUSTED HIMSELF TO
-attuned himself to

ADMINISTERING (CONSERVING)
-husbanding

"The Master once observed that to rule well one of the larger States meant strict attention to its affairs and conscientiousness on the part of the ruler; careful husbanding of its resources, with at the same time a tender care for the interests of all classes; and the employing of the masses in the public service at suitable seasons." Confucius, The Analects

ADMINISTRATIVE OFFICES
-the secretariat [formal]

ADMIRABLE
-laudable
-deserving
-commendable
-praiseworthy

ADMIRE
-there's something to be said for
-the quality I most esteem

ADMIRED BY
-the darling of
-found favor among

"She found favor among the country's leading conservatives."

ADMIT THAT
-make no secret of
-will allow that
-will grant you
-recognize
-come to terms with
-by your own account

I admit that I have a past.

I make no secret of my past.

ADMITTEDLY
-albeit
-it has to be said that
-truth be told

ADVANCE GRADUALLY
-encroach

ADVANCEMENT
-progression
-furtherance

ADVERSELY AFFECTED BY
-suffers from
-subject to

"Civilization exists by geological consent, subject to change without notice." Will Durant

ADVERTISED
-trumpeted

ADVICE
-counsel

ADVISE
-counsel
-impress upon
-caution

ADVISES ME TO
-recommends me to

ADVISOR
-consigliere {Italian, cun-sig-lee-AIR-ay}

ADVISORS
-brain trust
-intellectual blood bank

ADVOCATE (AN ADVOCATE)
-proponent
-apostle
-firebrand

ADVOCATE (TO ADVOCATE)
-espouse
-proselytize
-countenance

AFFAIR
-intrigue

"Everything was in confusion in the Oblonskys' house. The wife had discovered that the husband was carrying on an intrigue with a French girl, who had been a governess in their family, and she had

announced to her husband that she could not go on living in the same house with him." Leo Tolstoy, *Anna Karenina*
-entanglement
-liaison {French, *lee-AY-zohn*}

AFFECT
-inform
-color

"*Sensations, feelings, volitions, ideas— such are the changes into which my existence is divided and which color it in turns.*" Henri Bergson, *Creative Evolution*

AFFECTED BY
-subject to
-suffer from

AFFECTED HER WITH
-produced upon her

"*She had never been pretty; her whole life, which had been but a succession of pious works, had produced upon her a kind of transparent whiteness, and in growing old she had acquired what may be called the beauty of goodness.*" Victor Hugo, *Les Miserables*

AFRAID (I'M AFRAID)
-I fear that he will
-I go in fear of my life

AFTER
-in the wake of
-after having
-afterward
-after which
-in the aftermath
-coming on the heels of
-thereafter
-from _____ onwards
-post _____

"*Fashions occurring after the reign of King Edward are said to be post-Edwardian.*"

It comes right after a full moon.

It comes in the wake of a full moon.

AFTER A WHILE
-in time
-over the course of a few short weeks

AFTER BEING
-after having been

AFTER I'M GONE, ALL HELL WILL BREAK LOOSE
-Après moi le deluge {French, *ah-pray mwah lay day-LOOZSH*, lit. after me, the deluge}

"*He betrayed not a little arrogance with his reply: 'Après moi le deluge.'*"

AFTER THE EVENT
-post hoc

AFTER THE WAR
-postbellum {Latin, *post-BEL-um*, lit. after the war}

"*When the killing was ended, the postbellum government enacted measures to lessen the likelihood of another war.*"

AFTER THE YEAR _____
-in the years following _____

AFTER THINKING ABOUT IT
-on reflection

AGAIN
-once again
-here again
-yet again
-_____ redux {Latin, *re-DUX*, lit. brought back again}

"*Upon its release in 2001, Francis Ford Coppola's 1979 film* Apocalypse Now *was aptly re-titled* Apocalypse Now Redux."

AGAIN AND AGAIN
-several times over

AGAINST (ARE AGAINST)
-have come out against

AGAINST THE RULES
-at odds with
-at variance with
-flies in the face of
-heresy

AGAINST THE WISHES OF
-over strong objections
-in defiance of

AGE (THE SAME AGE)
-of similar date

> The age of this pottery is the same.
>
> This pottery is of similar date.

AGGRAVATE
-inflame

AGGRESSIVE
-sharp elbowed
-going for the jugular

AGGRESSIVELY HOSTILE
-truculent
-vitriolic
-belligerent

AGONIZING ISSUES
-wrenching issues
-the thorniest of issues

AGONIZINGLY
-murderously

"The day was murderously hot and there was no wind and the dust hung above the army like a yellow veil." Michael Shaara, *The Killer Angels*

AGREE TO DISAGREE
-modus vivendi {Latin, *MODE-us vi-VEN-dee*}

"Israel and Palestine have been unable to reach a modus vivendi regarding disputed territories."

AGREE TO IN A CONDESCENDING WAY
-deign to

"He didn't even deign to reply to her inquiry."

AGREEABLE
-amenable

"The union is amenable to the latest corporate offer."
-complaisant (very agreeable)
-obliging (very agreeable)

AGREED ON
-was agreed upon
-was settled between us

AGREEING
-in accord with
-in agreement
-well disposed to
-concordant {*cun-COR-dunt*} [academic]

AGREEMENT
-accommodation
-consensus
-concurrence [academic]
-accord
-covenant [poetic]
-perfect coincidence between

"Those who discourse…of the nature of truth…affirm a perfect coincidence between truth and goodness." Robert South, *Sermons Preached Upon Several Occasions*

AGREES WITH (GOES WITH)
-is in keeping with
-comports with
-is consistent with the views of
-echoes

-reflects
-accords with

"It is not because the truth is too difficult to see that we make mistakes…we make mistakes because the easiest and most comfortable course for us is to seek insight where it accords with our emotions—especially selfish ones." Alexander Solzhenitsyn

AHEAD OF
-in advance of

AID
-facilitate

"My attorney had taken his shirt off and was pouring beer on his chest, to facilitate the tanning process. 'What the hell are you yelling about?' he muttered, staring up at the sun with his eyes closed and covered with wraparound Spanish sunglasses. 'Never mind,' I said. 'It's your turn to drive.'" Hunter S. Thompson, *Fear and Loathing in Las Vegas*

AIMLESS REMARK (OFF TOPIC)
-a desultory remark

AIR
-atmosphere

"Pierre plunged into the subway. A feverish, a brutal crowd. On his feet near the door, closely pressed in a bank of human bodies and sharing the heavy atmosphere passing in and out of their mouths, he stared without seeing them at the black and rumbling vaults over which flickered the shining eyes of the train." Romain Rolland, *Pierre and Luce*

AIRY
-ethereal

ALL
-among those who
-each with its own
-the whole of

ALL AROUND THE ROOM
-all about the room

ALL FOR NOTHING
-all for naught

ALL HELL BREAKS LOOSE
-war of all against all

ALL I HAVE IS A
-I have only a

ALL KINDS OF
- _____ of every sort
-all manner of

"He is a man of action, but at the same time a scholar who finds time for everything and likes to discuss all manner of subjects under heaven and on earth." Pär Lagerkvist, *The Dwarf*

ALL KNOWING
-omniscient

ALL MY LIFE
-all the days of my life

"…I have the feeling that whatever happened would have happened whether I had been on hand or not, whether I had spoken or been still, whether I had known the Carmodys all the days of my life or had met them for the first time one sunlit afternoon in the middle of last week." Edwin O'Connor, *The Edge of Sadness*

ALL NIGHT
-the whole night through

"A councilor ought not to sleep the whole night through, a man to whom the populace is entrusted, and who has many responsibilities." Homer, *The Iliad*

ALL OF
-the whole of

"The life of a nomad is surprising. You cover nine hundred miles in two weeks: the whole of Anatolia in a cloud of dust." Nicolas Bouvier, *The Way of the World*

ALL OF ITS
-the full measure of its

ALL OF THE SUDDEN I SAW
-all at once I saw

ALL OF THEM
-altogether
-without exception
-in toto {Latin, *in TOE-TOE*}

ALL OUT ENDORSEMENT
-a full-throated endorsement

ALL OVER
-widespread
-pervasive
-systemic
-prevailing

ALL OVER THE PLACE
-indiscriminately

ALL OVER THE WORLD
-the world over

ALL THAT IS ASKED OF HIM IS THAT HE
-no more is asked of him than to

"For readers reared on traveler's tales, the words 'desert isle' may conjure up a place of soft sands and shady trees where brooks run to quench a castaway's thirst and ripe fruit falls into his hand, where no more is asked of him than to drowse the days away till a ship calls to fetch him home."
J. M. Coetzee, *Foe*

ALL THE WAY
-to its full extent

ALL THEY WANT
-with impunity

They violate company policy all they want.

They violate company policy with impunity.

ALL TOGETHER
-all told
-en masse
-in toto {Latin, *in TOE-TOE*}

ALL WE CAN SAY IS
-all that can be said is
-all that is known is that

ALL YOU HAVE TO DO IS
-you have only to
-we should only have to

ALL YOU WANT
-to your heart's content

ALLIANCE
-anschluss (an unseemly political alliance) {German, *ON-shlus*}

ALLOCATE
-apportion
-appropriate
-earmark

ALLOW
-enable
-play host to
-perpetuate

ALLOWABLE
-permissible

ALLOWED
-permissible
-admissible
-perfectly at liberty to
-in order for

"Rolland asked if it was in order for him to study these jottings. He gave his credentials; he was part-time research assistant to

Professor Blackladder, who had been editing Ash's Complete Works since 1951."
A. S. Byatt, *Possession*

ALLY (SUPPORTER)
-a ready patron

"Jack found a ready patron in Lisa, the new head of Product Development."

ALLY WITH
-make common cause with

ALMOST
-nearly
-all but the most
-near to
-nearly so
-most anything
-almost to the point of
-every chance but one

ALMOST DEAD
-moribund

ALMOST DONE
-almost in hand

ALONG WITH
-in tandem with
-alongside those of
-in the midst of

ALREADY BEEN DECIDED
-an accomplished fact
-a foregone conclusion
-a fait accompli {French, *fate a-com-PLEE*}

"Do not write to my sister yet. When all is a 'fait accompli' then we will tell her, because then it will be useless for her to do other than to accept." D. H. Lawrence, *Selected Letters*

It's already been decided.
It's a fait accompli.

ALREADY EXIST
-preexist

"Man is explicable by nothing less than all his history. Without hurry, without rest, the human spirit goes forth from the beginning to embody every faculty, every thought, every emotion, which belongs to it, in appropriate events. But the thought is always prior to the fact; all the facts of history preexist in the mind as laws." Ralph Waldo Emerson, "Essay on History"

ALREADY GOING ON
-already afoot

ALSO
-what's more,
-to say nothing of
-it may be added that
-also to be found
-among other things
-here again
-in turn
-likewise
-moreover
-not the least of which
-and on top of that
-notwithstanding the fact that
-otherwise known as
-parenthetically
-so too did
-if not
-even beyond that
-as a further matter
-as did
-____ no less

"This work is in excellent condition—and signed no less."

ALTERED
-doctored [derogatory]

ALTHOUGH
-albeit

"The trip abroad was enjoyable, albeit brief."

-but then again

-even if
-if

"*The speech was well written, if uncertainly delivered.*"

ALWAYS
-invariably
-never hesitates to
-on every occasion
-eternally [poetic]
-evermore [poetic]
-ever [poetic]

ALWAYS BE CAREFUL TO
-be ever mindful of

ALWAYS RIGHT
-unerring

AM (I AM)
-I remain

AMATEUR
-dilettante {French, *DIL-uh-tahnt*}
  [pejorative]

AMAZING
-remarkable
-astonishing
-staggering

AMOUNT OF
-measure of
-degree of
-a quotient of
-reckoning of
-a quantity of
-application of

"*From the freezer she pulled out a bottle and poured herself a serious application of vodka.*" Tim Winton, *Dirt Music*

AMUSING DIVERSION
-divertissement {French,
  div-ER-tis-ment}

AMUSING IN AN ODD WAY
-droll

AN ENJOYMENT
-a relish

"*The constant attention of Mr. and Mrs. Henry Dashwood to his wishes, which proceeded not merely from interest, but from goodness of heart, gave him every degree of solid comfort which his age could receive; and the cheerfulness of the children added a relish to his existence.*" Jane Austen, *Sense and Sensibility*

AN EXAMPLE OF
-an instance of

ANALYZE
-parse
-assay [academic]
-attempt some analysis of

ANARCHIST PHILOSOPHY
-Hobbesian {HOB-zee-in}

ANCESTORS
-forebears
-antecedents [academic]

ANCIENT
-archaic
-paleo
-primordial
-primeval
-antediluvian
-antiquarian

ANCIENT TIMES
-antiquity

AND
-as well as
-this, together with
-both in
-moreover
-and alike
-and what's more
-with

"*We would tell our children: If you travel as far as you can that way, as far as you can that way, you will come to places that lie more distant from our sun than we do.*"

You will find thick water, not light and quick moving as it is with us. The water is slow **with** *cold, and on its surface it wrinkles as it moves, or even, sometimes, makes plates or flakes that are solid. This is ice."* Doris Lessing, *The Making of the Representative for Planet 8*

AND ALSO
-and on top of that

AND BY THAT I MEAN
-which is to say

"They were gentlemen-magicians, which is to say they had never harmed any one by magic—nor done any one the slightest good." Susanna Clarke, *Jonathan Strange and Mr. Norrell*

AND I DON'T THINK
-nor do I think

AND OTHERS
-et al

AND SO IT IS
-and there it rests

AND SO ON
-and so forth

AND SURE ENOUGH
-and indeed

"'Ready to sleep,' she says; and indeed, en route, she falls asleep briefly, her head slumped against the window." J.M. Coetzee, *The Lives of Animals*

AND THEREFORE
-and as such
-and as befits that background

ANGELIC
-seraphic {SARE-uh-fic}
-cherubic {chuh-RUBE-ic}
-ethereal

ANGER (TO ANGER)
-infuriate
-incense

ANGER (HAVE ANGER)
-malevolence
-animosity
-animus
-ire

ANGRY
-heated
-acrimonious
-indignant
-incensed
-seething

ANIMAL LIFE
-fauna

ANIMAL SCULPTURES
-totemic sculptures
-topiary sculptures (bushes shaped like animals) {TOPE-ee-air-ee}

> You should have seen the bushes shaped like animals at Disney.
>
> You should have seen Disney's topiary sculptures.

ANIMALS
-creepers
-beasts

"In the first days of December the birds, after frequent biting frosts, flew into villages and towns, and even wild beasts came out of dense forests and drew near the houses of people." Henryk Sienkiewicz, *On the Field of Glory*

ANNOUNCING
-proclaiming
-calling attention to

ANNOY
-irk
-exasperate
-tire
-rankle
-displease

ANNOYED
-displeased
-piqued
-vexed

ANNOYING
-tiresome
-vexing
-displeasing
-incessant
-irksome
-nettlesome
-infernal
-bothersome

ANNOYING PERSON
-gadfly

ANOTHER
-a further class of
-yet another

ANSWER (AN ANSWER)
-rejoinder
-retort

ANSWER EVASIVELY
-parry
-equivocate

ANSWER HIS QUESTION
-address his concern

> Which of you can answer her question?
>
> Which of you can address her concern?

ANXIOUS TO
-keen on
-keen to know

ANXIOUS TO FIGHT
-spoiling for action.

"One man, however, was in fighting mood, awake and on edge, spoiling for action." Anonymous, *Beowulf* {BAY-uh-wolf}

ANY GOOD
-the slightest good

"They were gentlemen-magicians, which is to say they had never harmed any one by magic—nor done any one the slightest good." Susanna Clarke, *Jonathan Strange and Mr. Norrell*

ANYHOW
-be that as it may
-nonetheless
-nevertheless
-notwithstanding
-in any case
-in any event

"In any event, no harm was done."

ANYTHING THEY
-that which they

ANYTIME THEY WANT
-at will
-with impunity

ANYWAY
-at any rate
-in any event
-nevertheless
-in any case
-be that as it may
-nonetheless
-notwithstanding

ANYWHERE
-arbitrarily

ANXIETY
-disquiet
-angst

APART FROM EACH OTHER
-asunder [poetic]

APATHY
-torpor {TOR-pur}

APOLOGY
-mea culpa {Latin, ME-uh KULP-uh}

APPARENT
-much in evidence
-semblant
-putative

APPARENTLY
-ostensibly
-by all accounts
-by all appearances
-presumably
-purportedly
-seemingly
-is said to be the
-it would seem
-on the face of it
-at first blush
-we are told

"…there lies a small market town or rural port, which by some is called Greensburgh, but which is more generally and properly known by the name of Tarry Town. This name was given, we are told, in former days, by the good housewives of the adjacent country, from the inveterate propensity of their husbands to linger about the village tavern on market days." Washington Irving, *The Legend of Sleepy Hollow*

APPEAL TO A HIGHER AUTHORITY
-invoke

"At the beginning of an epic poem, the protagonist often invokes a muse for protection."

APPEAR
-present oneself
-shows itself in
-surface
-make an appearance
-emerge

APPEARANCE (LOOK)
-facade
-outward show
-visage
-a pretense
-mien {*meen*}

-patina
-semblance
-veneer

APPEARANCE OF (OCCURRENCE)
-emergence of
-presence of
-ascendancy of

APPEARED IN
-graced our

APPEARING
-without casting oneself as

APPEARS TO BE
-strikes one as
-has every appearance of
-has all the earmarks of
-assumes the guise of

APPEASE
-placate
-mollify

APPLY PRESSURE
-bring to bear
-exert

APPLY TO (THEY APPLY TO)
-extend to

APPRECIATE
-savor

"Almost every day for five years I had left for somewhere and arrived somewhere; in the morning I had gone up station steps and down again, in the afternoon down station steps and up again, signaled for a taxi, felt in my pockets for money to pay for my ticket, bought evening papers at kiosks, and savored in the corner of my mind the studied casualness of these mechanical actions." Heinrich Böll, *The Clown*

APPRECIATING LOCAL CULTURE
-collecting local color

APPROACH (A WAY)
-treatment

APPROACH (TO APPROACH)
-draw near
-come upon

APPROACH AGGRESSIVELY
-accost

APPROACHING
-oncoming
-winter drawing on

APPROPRIATE FOR
-in keeping with
-most suited for
-lends itself to
-apropos
-befitting
-only fitting
-commensurate
-apt
-in accordance with
-felicitous
-in order for
-aptly chosen

> This painting is appropriate for the room's décor.
>
> This painting is in keeping with the room's décor.

APPROPRIATENESS OF
-the propriety of

APPROVAL
-assent
-adoption
-approbation [academic]
-imprimatur {Latin, *im -pri-MAH-tour*}

"We could not proceed without the court's imprimatur."

APPROVE
-sanction
-condone

APPROVED
-vested

"She has a vested right to half of the estate."
-not without sanction

"Her right to the estate is not without sanction."

APPROVED OF
-well received
-hailed
-welcomed
-applauded
-rapturously received
-was supportive of

> His presentation was approved of.
>
> His presentation was well-received.

APPROXIMATELY
-some ten million
-on the order of
-there or thereabouts
-by and large
-to the tune of

ARE
-are to be found
-are in fact
-are judged
-are among the most
-happen to be
-_____ they are not
-they remain

ARE ACCESSIBLE
-lie within the reach of

ARE ALL OVER THE PLACE
-abound
-are ubiquitous

ARE BECAUSE
-are rooted mainly in the

ARE CAUSED BY
-stem from

ARE DIFFERENT
-make quite a contrast

ARE EXAMPLES OF
-stand as examples of

ARE EXPENSIVE
-command high prices

ARE FARTHER FROM
-lie more distant from

"We would tell our children: If you travel as far as you can [this] way, as far as you can that way, you will come to places that lie more distant from our sun than we do. You will find thick water, not light and quick moving as it is with us. The water is slow with cold, and on its surface it wrinkles as it moves, or even, sometimes, makes plates or flakes that are solid. This is ice." Doris Lessing, *The Making of the Representative for Planet 8*

ARE HIDDEN
-are indistinguishable from

ARE IN
-are to be found in
-lie in

"Although he devotes hours of each day to his new discipline, he finds its first premise, as enunciated in the Communications 101 handbook, preposterous: 'Human society has created language in order that we may communicate our thoughts, feelings and intentions to each other.' His own opinion, which he does not air, is that the origins of speech lie in song, and the origins of song in the need to fill out with sound the overlarge and rather empty human soul." J. M. Coetzee, *Disgrace*

ARE LUCKY
-lucky are they who

ARE MANY
-abound

ARE NOT
-_____ they are not
-it is clearly not the case that

> They are not free.
>
> Free they are not.

ARE NOT AS IMPORTANT AS
-take a back seat to

"Reflections on politics, though, take a back seat to the practicalities of surviving on the road and, in the style of Herodotus, collecting dubious bits of lore." Richard B. Woodward, *New York Times*, Nov. 1, 2009

ARE NOT SUCCESSFUL
-never know success

"For the traveler we see leaning on his neighbor is an honest and well-meaning man and full of melancholy, like those Chekhov characters so laden with virtues that they never know success in life." Orhan Pamuk, *Snow*

ARE NOT WELL KNOWN
-are too little known

ARE ONLY
-remain, at best, no more than

ARE PROOF OF
-attest to
-stand as proof of

ARE REMEMBERED AS
-stand in memory as

ARE SIMILAR
-bear a resemblance to
-have close affinities to
-are close in style to
-might be mistaken for

ARE STILL
-remain

ARE SUPPOSED TO
-are to

ARE THE SAME
-are one

ARE THE SYMPTOMS OF
-reflect

ARE UNABLE TO
-are in no position to

ARE VALID
-bear scrutiny
-bear inspection

"*As political analysis, there's something to be said for Krugman's Manichean view of the world. But Krugman is also an economist—a very good one—and the economics of what is proposed bear inspection.*" John Cassidy, *The New Yorker*, Nov. 4, 2009

ARE YOU ABLE TO
-can you manage to

ARE YOU AFRAID FOR THEM?
-Do you fear for them?

AREA
-sphere
-dominion
-domain
-sphere of influence
-theater of war
-expanse
-swath
-locale
-realm

"*In the brand-new, state-of-the-art condominium, mother and daughter will each have her own realm, Erika here, Mother there, both realms neatly divided.*" Elfriede Jelinek, *The Piano Teacher*

AREA OF EXPERTISE
-my bailiwick
-the province of

"*Success is the province of those who work hardest.*"

AREN'T MANY ____
-are few ____ to be found

ARGUE THAT
-hold that
-contend that
-maintain that

ARGUING
-at loggerheads
-wrangling
-trading public insults

ARGUMENT
-quarrel
-impasse
-great divide
-source of antagonism between

ARGUMENTATIVE
-polemical
-contentious

ARISTOCRAT
-a patrician

AROSE FROM
-found expression in

AROUND
-about
-round about

> She drags the broom around the rooms.
>
> She drags the broom about the rooms.

ARRANGE
-configure
-orchestrate
-array

ARRANGE INTO A SYSTEM (ESTABLISH)
-codify

"Abner Doubleday was the first to codify the rules of what would become modern baseball."

ARRANGED
-deployed

ARRANGEMENT
-configuration
-a certain geometry of purpose
-a disposition of

ARRIVAL
-advent of

ARROGANCE
-hauteur {French, *oh-TER*, *oh* as in snow}

ARROGANT
-haughty
-imperious

ART OF CONTROVERSY
-polemics

ART OF DEBATE
-forensics

ARTICLE
-a piece on

ARTIFICIAL
-ersatz {*AIR-zahts*}
-faux

"New London, in southeastern Connecticut about midway between New York and Boston, seems on paper a lot like Mystic, its neighbor to the east—all sea views, seafood, and seafaring history. But unlike that quaint (or perhaps faux quaint) town, New London is becoming as recognized for its independent art scene as for its handsome harbor." Laura Siciliano-Rosen, *New York Times*, Nov. 1, 2009

ARTIFICIAL BEHAVIOR
-affectation
-pretense
-in a highly mannered fashion

ARTIFICIAL DEVICE
-contrivance
-deus ex machina {Latin, *DAY-us ex MAH-kuh-nuh*, lit. God from the machine}

ARTIST
-executant [academic]

ARTISTIC
-aesthetic
-symmetric
-geometric

"The outfit was acceptable by any theological and geometrical standards, however abstruse, and suggested a rich inner life." John Kennedy Toole, *A Confederacy of Dunces*

ARTIST'S LIFEWORK ON DISPLAY
-a retrospective

ARTWORK
-a work
-a piece

AS
-as _____ as it is _____
-as is

"She was fair as is the rose in May." Geoffrey Chaucer

AS ____ ONCE SAID
-to borrow the words of ____
-it is, in the lexicon of ____, a very...
-to approximate ____'s remark

"It was only that, having written down the first few fine paragraphs, I could not produce any others—or, to approximate Gertrude Stein's remark about a lesser writer of The Lost Generation—I had the syrup but it wouldn't pour." William Styron, *Sophie's Choice*

AS A FAVOR
-do it ex gratia {Latin, *ex GRAY-she-uh*}

AS A FORMALITY
-pro forma {Latin, *pro FOR-muh*, lit. for form}

AS A MATTER OF FACT
-as it happens
-the fact of the matter is
-truth be told
-as a matter of course

"Nevertheless on most topics the atmosphere was liberal. For instance, Darwinism was accepted as a matter of course." Bertrand Russell, *On God and Religion*

AS A RESULT
-consequently
-hence
-thus
-as a consequence
-in consequence

> Her dismissal came as the result of her own poor decisions.
>
> Her dismissal came as a consequence of her own making.

AS A WAY OF
-as a means of

AS AN ADDED BONUS
-for good measure

AS AN EXPRESSION OF
-in token of their mutual affection

AS EXPECTED
-true to form

AS FAR AS
-to the extent that
-insofar as
-inasmuch as
-considering that

-insomuch as
-to such an extent that

AS FAR AS I'M CONCERNED
-and I, for my part,
-it is, in my estimation

AS FAR AS WE KNOW
-as far as we can see
-on the face of it
-so far as it appeared
-to all appearances
-or so it goes

AS FOR
-with respect to
-as to
-apropos of
-with regard to

AS GOOD
-comparable
-anything that bears comparison

"Now I cannot recall, any fight you entered, Unferth, that bears comparison." Anonymous, *Beowulf* {BAY-uh-wolf}

AS GREAT AS
-as great as any that can be named
-the equal of _____

AS HE SEES IT
-to his mind
-by his reckoning
-in his judgement

"To a man of his age, 52, divorced, he has, to his mind, solved the problem of sex rather well. On Thursday afternoons he drives to Greenpoint. Punctually at 2 p.m., he presses the buzzer at the entrance to Windsor Mansions, speaks his name, and enters." J.M. Coetzee, *Disgrace*

AS IF
-as though

"Leaning far out the window, the girl called to the station manager as though he were a

great distance away." Yasunari Kawabata, *Snow Country*

AS IF HE OWNED HER
-in a proprietary sort of way

> He looked her over, as if he owned her.
>
> He looked her over, in a proprietary sort of way.

AS IF IT WERE REAL [PERTAINING TO FILM]
-cinéma vérité {French, *SIN-e-ma vair-e-TAY*}

AS IS USUALLY THE CASE
-as is usual

AS LONG AS IT IS
-insofar as it is
-provided it is

AS MANY AS YOU WANT
-any number of

AS MUCH AS
-no less than
-as fully as

AS MUCH AS I
-much as I

AS MUCH AS WE TRY
-try as we might

AS OPPOSED TO
-in contrast to

AS PROMISED
-true to his word

AS REQUIRED
-as the occasion may require

AS SO OFTEN
-as is usual in

AS STATED BY
-if I may paraphrase

AS TIME WENT BY
-in the course of time

AS USUAL
-in typical fashion

AS YOUNG AS
-no older than

ASH COLORED
-ashen

ASHAMED
-quite cast down

ASIDE FROM
-otherwise
-in other respects
-apart from that
-among other

ASK
-raise the question
-pose the question
-pursue that line of inquiry
-inquire
-trouble
-invite
-put to
-inquire after
-make inquiries
-call upon
-put the question to
-put it to

ASK FOR HELP
-appeal
-solicit
-enlist the help of
-petition him in favor of
-make inquiries
-occasion
-invite
-call upon you for

ASK HER THIS QUESTION
-put this question to her
-ask this of her

ASKED FOR
-expressed the need for

ASKED TO (WAS ASKED TO)
-called upon to

ASKING FOR TROUBLE
-courting disaster

ASLEEP
-dormant

ASPECT
-component
-facet
-dimension
-dynamic
-feature

"The irony does not escape him: that the one who comes to teach learns the keenest of lessons, while those who come to learn learn nothing. It is a feature of his profession on which he does not remark to Soraya." J. M. Coetzee, *Disgrace*

ASS KISSER
-lackey
-obsequious person
-sycophant

ASSEMBLED
-marshaled

ASSESSMENT
-an accounting of

ASSIGNED TO DO
-charged with

ASSIGNMENT
-stint

ASSIMILATION
-acculturation

ASSIST
-accommodate
-cater to their needs
-minister to

ASSISTANT
-adjunct
-underling [derogatory]
-subordinate
-understudy
-attaché {French, *a-tash-AYE*}

ASSISTANT CHEF
-sous chef {French, *SUE shef*}

ASSISTANTS
-retinue
-entourage
-coterie {*KOE-ter-ee*}
-cortège {French, *cor-TEZH*}

ASSISTED
-tended upon
-ministered to

ASSOCIATE (AN ASSOCIATE)
-collaborator
-confederate

ASSOCIATE WITH
-lend one's name to

ASSOCIATED WITH
-affiliated with
-linked to
-home to
-once synonymous with
-centered around
-attributed to
-incidental to
-allied to
-bound up with

ASSUME
-posit
-postulate
-take as an indication that

ASSUMED POWER
-possessed himself of

ASSUMES THAT THERE IS
-presupposes a

ASSUMPTION
-presumption
-premise
-postulate [academic]

ASSURE
-dispel any doubts

AT ALL
-by any means
-in the least
-remotely
-in the slightest degree
-whatsoever
-in any sense
-not even for a moment

AT AROUND
-circa {Latin, *SIR-cuh*, lit. around}

"The Mencius was written circa 4th century BCE."

AT HOME
-in one's element

AT LEAST
-accept the consolation that
-at the very least

AT LENGTH
-in extenso {Latin, *in ek-STENT-so*} [academic]

AT NOON HE
-noon found him

"Noon found him momentarily alone, while the family prepared lunch in the kitchen." Paul Harding, *Tinkers*

AT RISK
-at hazard
-in peril of

"And I think a man would have to put his soul at hazard. And I won't do that. I think now that maybe I never would." Cormac McCarthy, *No Country for Old Men*

AT THAT MOMENT
-on that instant

"Either we live by accident and die by accident, or we live by plan and die by plan. And on that instant Brother Juniper made the resolve to inquire into the secret lives of those five persons, that moment falling through the air, and to surprise the reason of their taking off." Thornton Wilder, *The Bridge of San Luis Rey*

AT THAT POINT
-with that

AT THE AGE OF _____
-in her _____ year

AT THE BEGINNING
-at the outset
-from the outset

AT THE END OF THE DAY
-in the final analysis
-ultimately

"Ultimately, literature is nothing but carpentry. With both you are working with reality, a material just as hard as wood." Gabriel Garcia Marquez

AT THE HOUSE OF
-chez {French, *shay*}

"In France, instead of eating at Spencer's, you eat at Chez Spencer."

AT THE POINT OF DEATH
-in extremis {Latin, *in eck-STREAM-is*}

AT THE SAME TIME
-meanwhile
-in the meantime
-is at once his _____, and his _____
-it is at once, _____, _____

AT THIS JUNCTURE [CORPORATE CLICHÉ]
-at this time

AT THIS MOMENT IN TIME
-at this moment

AT THIS PACE
-apace

AT WHAT HE SAID
-at his words

> He was dismayed at what the president said.
>
> He was dismayed at the president's words.

AT WHICH TIME
-whereupon

AT WILL
-with impunity
-at one's will and pleasure
-at one's discretion
-as far as one desires
-of one's own accord

ATE BREAKFAST
-took his breakfast

"At 8 a.m., he took his breakfast of toast and eggs." Victor Hugo, *Les Miserables*

ATHEISM
-skepticism
-existentialism (secular existentialism)

"Existentialism explained in under 140 characters: Gd does not exist, so U are free to make yr own inwardly passionate, individual choices; some are wrthy of this responsibility, most are not, wich is why life is absrd."

ATMOSPHERE
-color
-an air of
-a note of
-with distinct ___ undertones
-flavor
-aura
-milieu
-genius loci {JEEN-yus LOW-sigh} [academic]

ATTACH
-append

ATTACHED
-adjoining

ATTACHED TO
-moored to

ATTACK (TO ATTACK)
-have at
-lay siege to
-lay into
-take a swipe at
-set upon
-savage
-besiege
-assail

"The terror and hurt in my story happened because when I was young I thought others were the authors of my fortune and misfortune; I did not know that a person could hold up a wall made of imaginary bricks and mortar against the horrors and cruel, dark tricks of time that assail us, and be the author therefore of themselves." Sebastian Barry, *The Secret Scripture*

ATTACK (AN ATTACK)
-incursion
-foray
-onslaught
-barrage
-salvo of
-the latest salvo in the battle against
-sortie

ATTACK VERBALLY
-inveigh against
-cast aspersions upon

> It's considered poor form to verbally attack the dead.
>
> It's considered poor form to cast aspersions upon the dead.

ATTACKED BY
-came under fire
-subject to
-set upon
-beset by

ATTACKER OF CHERISHED BELIEFS
-an iconoclast

ATTEMPT
-a bid to
-endeavor to
-have a go at
-venture
-a push for

ATTEMPTS AT
-forays into

ATTENTIVE
-discerning

ATTENTIVE TO THE VIEWS OF
-solicitous of the views of

ATTITUDE
-manner
-predisposition
-disposition

ATTRACT
-appeal to
-draw
-collect
-invite

ATTRACT ATTENTION TO
-draw their gazes
-accentuate
-engage
-invite attention

"After pointing heavenward for half a century, the steeple appeared to have swerved suddenly from its purpose, and to invite now the attention of the wayfarer to the bar beneath." E. A. G. Glasgow, *The Miller of Old Church*

ATTRACTED ATTENTION
-had been the object of much attention
-drew close scrutiny from

ATTRACTED TO
-drawn to

"Although I was first drawn to math and science by the certainty they promised, today I find the unanswered questions and the unexpected connections at least as attractive." Professor Lisa Randall, *Warped Passages*

ATTRACTION TO
-fondness for
-allure of
-the appeal lay in
-affinity for
-gravitation towards

ATTRACTIVE
-engaging
"She is quite engaging."
-inviting

ATTRIBUTE
-ascribe
-invest it with qualities of
-assign

AUTHORITY
-standing

AUTHORIZE
-license
-vest with

AVAILABLE TO USE
-discretionary
-at one's disposal

We have a limited amount of money available to use.

We have a limited amount of money at our disposal.

AVERAGE LOOKING
-nondescript

AVIATRIX
-pilot

AVOID
-circumvent
-avert
-steer clear
-give a wide berth
-pointedly avoid
-finesse
-forbear
-shun

AVOID THE QUESTION
-hedge around the question
-defer

"In his response to our pointed questions, he deferred to his counterparts within the agency."

AVOIDANCE
-forbearance

AVOIDED
-averted

"The crisis was averted when the European Union voted on a bailout package for Greece."

AWARD
-accolade

AWARDING
-granting

AWARE OF
-acquainted with
-conscious of
-mindful of
-privy to the secret
-in tune with
-attuned to
-heedful of

AWAY (KEEP IT AWAY)
-at bay

AWAY FROM
-secluded from
-apart from

"She stood apart from the crowd, letting it drift by her to the platform or the street, and wearing an air of irresolution which might, as he surmised, be the mask of a very definite purpose." Edith Wharton, *The House of Mirth*

AWFUL (IMMORAL)
-reprehensible
-reproachful
-deplorable
-wretched
-grievous
-depraved
-perverse
-wayward
-worthy of censure
-un-redeeming

AWFUL QUALITY
-of little merit
-leave much to be desired

AWKWARD
-ill at ease
-discomfited

Bb

B MOVIES
-psychotronic films
-psychotronica [noun]

BACK AND FORTH
-vacillating
-oscillating
-passing from ___ to ___
-flitting between
-moving to and fro
-with some interplay

BACK AWAY FROM WHAT WAS SAID
-backpedal
-roll that one back

BACK OF THE BOAT
-the stern
-go aft (towards the back)

BACK THEM UP
-lend support

> She refused to back up either party.
>
> She refused to lend support to either party.

BACK THEN
-at the time

BACK UP (MOVE BACK)
-draw back

BACK-UP PLAN
-contingency

BACKED UP
-drew back

BACKFIRED (THE PLAN BACKFIRED)
-hoisted with one's own petard

BACKGROUND (IN THE BACKGROUND)
-backdrop

"The president gave his speech with Mt. Rushmore as his backdrop."

BACKLIGHTING
-contre-jour {French, *kawn-tre ZHOOR*}

"The contre-jour photographic technique will create a silhouette every time."

BAD
-perverse
-wayward

-wretched
-un-redeeming
-depraved

BAD ACTS
-indiscretions
-transgressions
-misdeeds
-improprieties
-wrongs
-vices

BAD AT
-inept
-not well suited

"It's not a game in which I'm particularly well suited."

BAD AT MATH
-innumerate [academic]

BAD BEHAVIOR
-villainy [often playful]

"Come to spread your villainy, have you?"

BAD DEEDS
-corruptions
-pollutions

BAD EFFECTS
-adverse effects

BAD FOR
-ill suited for
-do not lend themselves easily to
-detrimental to
-poisonous to

"Mother Nature determines what is poisonous to the soul and body, and sometimes it is easy to avoid that which is baneful and unclean: e.g., we naturally have no desire to eat fetid corpses and drink motor oil."
Cintra Wilson, A Massive Swelling

BAD GIRL
-femme fatale {French, FEM *feh-TAL*}

BAD GUY
-the heavy

BAD IDEA
-ill-advised
-inadvisable
-a non-starter (no chance of success)

BAD IMAGE
-troubled image

BAD LUCK
-misfortune

BAD-MOUTH
-speak harshly of
-throw aspersions on
-deride
-refer to derisively
-disparage
-denigrate
-express contempt for
-traduce [academic]
-belittle
-libel

"You cannot libel the dead, I think, you can only console them." Anne Enright, *The Gathering*

BAD POET
-poetaster [academic] {*POH-et-aster*}

BAD QUALITY
-of little merit
-leaves much to be desired

BAD SITUATION
-plight
-predicament

BAD SMELLING
-noisome odor
-putrid
-fetid

BAD TASTE
-in bad form
-off color
-in poor form
-indecorous

Your comments were in bad taste.

Your comments were in poor form.

BAD TEMPERED
-ill-humored
-ill-tempered
-irascible
-morose
-querulous
-snarky
-cantankerous

BAD TIMING
-untimely

BAD WEATHER
-inclement weather {*in-CLEM-ent*}

BADLY AFFECTED BY
-adversely affected
-were subjected to

BADLY AFFECTED THE
-cast a pall over
-put a terror on

"...but there were dry years too, and they put a terror on the valley." John Steinbeck, *East of Eden*

BADLY CONCEIVED
-misbegotten

BAG OF TRICKS
-repertoire {French, *REH-per-twahr*}

BALANCE
-equilibrium

BALANCE (TO BALANCE)
-strike a balance

BALCONY
-gallery

BANDITS
-outlanders
-marauders

"Long ago it wasn't just a road, following the high ground, away from the woods and swamps lower down, but a defensive barrier, a bulwark against marauders from the north, whomever they may have been." Henry Shukman, *New York Times*, Nov. 1, 2009

BANKER
-financier
-investment banker
-merchant banker

BARE
-spartan
-unembellished
-austere

BARELY
-narrowly
-scarcely
-by a tiny margin
-it was all they could do to

BARELY KNOW HER
-we're on short acquaintance

BARELY PERCEPTIBLE
-liminal

BARGAINING
-horse-trading
-negotiating

BARK IS WORSE THAN HIS BITE
-he's just blustering
-not as formidable as his words

His bark is worse than his bite.

He is not as formidable as his words.

BARRICADE
-cordon {French, *KOR-dn*}

BARTENDER
-barkeep [humorous]
-barmaid [humorous]

BASED ON
-founded on
-rests in part on
-predicated on
-informed by
-built on

"Love built on beauty, soon as beauty, dies." John Donne {pronounced *Dun*}

BASED IN
-rooted in

BASIC
-underlying
-framework upon which
-basic to our understanding of

BASIC INSTINCT
-primal urge

BATHROOM
-washroom

BATTING AVERAGE BELOW .200
-the Mendoza line

BATTLE (A BATTLE)
-firestorm

"The measure has ignited a political firestorm."
-flashpoint
-standoff
-maelstrom {*MALE-strum*} (turbulent confusion)
-melee {*may-lay*}
-bitter wrangling

BATTLE (TO BATTLE)
-take the fight to
-have at
-join the fray

BE
-remain

BE CAREFUL
-tread carefully
-take care what you do
-take care to

"Take care to select the proper ratios and flavors."

BE DISCOURAGED
-lose heart

BE GOOD ENOUGH
-should suffice

BE HOSPITABLE
-extend hospitality

BE INFLUENCED BY
-fall into the hands of

BE LIKED
-find favor
-prove acceptable

BE MY GUEST
-by all means

BE OFFENDED BY
-take umbrage
-take exception to
-recoil from

BE OPTIMISTIC
-strike an optimistic tone

BE PRESENTED TO
-come before

BE PRICED AT
-will fetch
-should command

BE QUIET
-hold your peace
-keep your counsel

A good lawyer knows when to speak, and when to be quiet.

A good lawyer knows when to speak, and when to keep her counsel.

BE SEEN AS
-constitute
-amount to

BE SO BAD
-fall into error

"How can you fall into such error?"

BE SURE
-rest assured

BE THERE
-be on hand

BEAR MOST OF IT
-bear the brunt of it

BEAR-LIKE
-ursine

BEAT (1)
-overcome
-best the competition
-bested

BEAT (2)
-bludgeon

BEAT AROUND THE BUSH
-flutter round it

BEAT IT
-clear off

"...you get some who blow kisses or try to get hold of your arm, but then they are definitely knocking at the wrong door. I get off my bicycle and refuse to go further in their company, or I pretend to be insulted and tell them in no uncertain terms to clear off."

Anne Frank, *Anne Frank: The Diary of a Young Girl*

BEATEN
-equaled
-surpassed

BEATEN BADLY
-routed
-schooled

BEATING
-drubbing
-shellacking

BEAUTIFUL
-breathtaking
-exquisite
-striking
-stunning
-handsome

"New London, in southeastern Connecticut about midway between New York and Boston, seems on paper a lot like Mystic, its neighbor to the east—all sea views, seafood, and seafaring history. But unlike that quaint (or perhaps faux quaint) town, New London is becoming as recognized for its independent art scene as for its handsome harbor." Laura Siciliano-Rosen, *New York Times*, Nov. 1, 2009

BEAUTIFUL WOMAN
-belle {French, *bell*}
-love runs after her like puppies (said of a beautiful woman)

BECAME
-came to be
-grew to be more
-gave way to
-came to be regarded as
-came to have significant

BECAME FAMOUS
-first rose to prominence
-gained wide recognition
-won notoriety

BECAME GOOD AT
-mastered the art of

BECAME POPULAR
-found favor with

BECAME PRESIDENT
-assumed office

BECAUSE OF
-owing to
-as a consequence of

"This is a tale of a meeting between two lonesome, skinny, fairly old white men on a planet which was dying fast. One of them was a science fiction writer named Kilgore Trout. He was a nobody at the time, and he supposed his life was over. He was mistaken. As a consequence of the meeting, he became one of the most beloved and respected human beings in history." Kurt Vonnegut, *Breakfast of Champions*

-in light of
-as (so young as I was,)
-in that
-for reasons
-for the purposes of
-substantially owing to
-what with the
-on her account
-by virtue of
-in consequence
-for fear of
-for the sake of

"There was a girl named Flora, who paid Mrs. Sucksby a penny to take me begging at a play. People used to like to take me begging then, for the sake of my bright hair; and Flora being also very fair, she would pass me off as her sister." Sarah Waters, *Fingersmith*

-by dint of
-in view of
-for the reason that
-on account of

"My parents, Lord and Lady Amberley, were considered shocking in their day on

account of their advanced opinions in politics, theology, and morals." Bertrand Russell, *On God and Religion*

BECAUSE I WAS SO YOUNG
-so young as I was

BECAUSE OF A LACK OF
-for want of

> It died because of a lack of water and sun.
>
> It died for want of water and sun.

BECAUSE OF THAT
-by that very fact
-ipso facto {Latin, *IP-soe FACT-oh*, lit. by the fact itself}

BECAUSE OF YOUR
-that's what comes of your

BECAUSE THAT'S ALL WE HAVE
-for want of something better

BECOME
-grow to be
-lead to
-grow
-cross the border into

"*I enjoyed such moments—but only in brief. If the talk began to wander, or cross the border into familiarity, I would soon find reason to excuse myself. I had grown too comfortable in my solitude, the safest place I knew.*" Barack Obama, *Dreams from My Father*

BECOME A VICTIM OF
-fall victim to

BECOME ANNOYED WITH
-chafe under the leadership style of

BECOME FULLY EFFECTIVE
-come into one's own

BECOME MORE ACCEPTED
-gain currency with

> In recent years, the possibility of extra dimensions has become more accepted by physicists.
>
> In recent years, the possibility of extra dimensions has gained currency with physicists.

BECOME MORE PROMINENT
-claim more attention

BECOME PUBLIC
-see the light of day
-come to light

BECOMES
-is rendered
-assumes
-manifests

"*My fingers are mated into a mirrored series of what manifests, to me, as the letter X.*" David Foster Wallace, *Infinite Jest*

BECOMES FRIENDS WITH____
-finds a friend in _____

BECOMING EXTINCT
-in dramatic decline

BEEHIVE
-swirl of activity

BEEN (MIGHT HAVE BEEN)
-might have proved

"*I took up my coat and carpet-bag, and went into the next room to change my linen, and dress for dinner. Any distress at the termination of my intrigue with Betty was amply compensated for by my joy at the happy ending of a troublesome affair which might have proved fatal for me.*" Jacques Casanova, *Volume 6c—Rome: The Memoirs of Jacques Casanova*

BEFORE
-beforehand
-formerly

BEFORE MENTIONED
-aforementioned

BEFORE NOW
-heretofore [academic]

BEFORE THE REVOLUTION
-ancien regime {French, *ahn-syohn
   ray-ZHEEM*}

BEG
-plead
-implore
-supplicate [academic]

BEGAN
-we got down to it
-established
-embarked on
-begun its course

*"The planet Mars, I scarcely need remind
the reader, revolves about the sun at a
mean distance of 140,000,000 miles, and
the light and heat it receives from the sun
is barely half that received by this world. It
must be, if the nebular hypothesis has any
truth, older than our world; and long before
this earth ceased to be molten, life upon its
surface must have begun its course."* H. G.
Wells, *The War of the Worlds*

BEGAN AGAIN
-resumed

BEGAN LIVING IN
-took up residence in

BEGAN TO
-set about

BEGAN TO COLLECT
-came to collect

BEGAN TO CRY
-fell to crying

*"And all at once, though I had remained
dry-eyed through all the insults done me on
board ship and through the hours of despair
when I was alone on the waves with the
captain lying dead at my feet, a handspike
jutting from his eye-socket, I fell to crying."*
J.M. Coetzee, *Foe*

BEGAN TO PLAY (MUSIC)
-the band struck up
-a dozen voices caught up the refrain

BEGAN TO THINK ABOUT
-her thoughts turned to

BEGIN
-arise
-commence
-establish
-inaugurate
-set about
-take up
-embark upon
-enter upon
-launch into
-begin the task of
-fire the opening salvo
-get to the business of
-begin its course
-there are the beginnings of

BEGINNER
-novice
-neophyte

BEGINNING (ARE BEGINNING)
-incipient
-emergent
-nascent

BEGINNING (THE BEGINNING)
-the inception
-the onset
-the emergence

BEGINNING AND END OF
-birth and death of

*"I always found in myself a dread of west
and a love of east. Where I ever got such*

an idea I cannot say, unless it could be that the morning came over the peaks of the Gabilans and the night drifted back from the ridges of the Santa Lucias. It may be that the birth and death of the day had some part in the feeling about the two ranges of mountains." John Steinbeck, *East of Eden*

BEGINNING STAGES
-in ovo {Latin, *in oh-voe*}

BEGINNINGS OF
-inklings of

BEGS THE QUESTION [INCORRECT USAGE]
-raises the question
-leads to the question of

BEGUN HANGING OUT WITH
-taken up with

> He's begun hanging out with the wrong crowd.
>
> He's taken up with the wrong crowd.

BEHAVE
-conduct oneself
-comport oneself
-remain within the bounds of decorum
-act with regard to

BEHAVIOR
-decorum
-conventions
-composure
-governance
-_____ in her manner
-demeanor
-severity of demeanor
-with playfully exaggerated ceremony
-tone
-poise
-carriage

BEHIND IT IS
-it is informed by

BEHIND CLOSED DOORS
-à huis clos {French, *uh-wee KLOE*}

BEHIND THE SCENES
-the inner workings of
-the inner counsels of

BEING ATTACKED
-embattled
-beset upon
-much maligned

BEING POLITE
-from politeness

BELIEF
-notion
-conviction
-sentiment
-thoughts on the matter
-faith

"We need more humanity, more care, more love. There are those who expect a political system to produce that; and others who expect the love to produce the system. My own faith is that the truth of the future lies between the two and we shall behave humanly and a bit humanely, stumbling along, haphazardly generous and gallant, foolishly and meanly wise until the rape of our planet is seen to be the preposterous folly that it is." William Golding

-tenet
-axiom
-doctrine
-dogma
-ideology
-ethos

BELIEF IN ONLY ONE GOD
-the monotheistic creed

BELIEVABILITY
-credence
-plausibility

BELIEVABLE
-plausible
-well-founded

BELIEVE
-accept
-subscribe to
-embrace the theory of
-partial to the view that
-suppose
-presume

BELIEVE IN
-hew
-adhere to
-favor
-hold to

"Augustus held to a more leisurely philosophy. He believed in giving creatures a little time to think, so he stood in the sun a few minutes until the rattler calmed down and crawled out a hole." Larry McMurtry, *Lonesome Dove*

BELIEVE IT OR NOT
-unbelievable as it may seem

BELIEVE ME
-rest assured

BELIEVED TO BE
-thought on good grounds to be
-have it on good authority that

BELIEVERS
-advocates of

BELL RINGING
-bell tolling
-tolling

BELONGED TO
-were those of

BENEATH ONE'S DIGNITY
-infra dig {Latin, *in-fruh DIG*}
  [academic]

"Most professors consider the grading of papers to be infra dig."

BENEFICIAL
-salutary

BENEFIT
-would profit by
-enjoy the fruits of
-favor

"The political winds favor their chances."

BENEFITS
-dividends
-profits
-gifts

"There must be acceptance and the knowledge that sorrow fully accepted brings its own gifts. For there is an alchemy in sorrow. It can be transmuted into wisdom, which, if it does not bring joy, can yet bring happiness." Pearl S. Buck, *The Child Who Never Grew*

BESIDES
-quite apart from

BEST
-unparalleled
-in a class by itself
-unrivaled
-unsurpassed
-of the first order
-beyond compare
-incomparable
-a___ like no other
-preeminent
-nonpareil {French, *non-puh-REL*}
-the noblest of
-of the highest quality
-sets a standard of
-the foremost
-a hallmark of
-the crown princess of
-the dean of
-the maestro of
-transcendent
-rarely equaled

BEST CASE SCENARIO
-at best

BEST EXPRESSED
-most notably expressed

BEST OF THE BEST
-crème de la crème {French, *KREM de la KREM*, lit. cream of the cream}

BEST PART (SHOWPIECE)
-pièce de résistance {French, *pee-ESS duh ruh-zee-STAHNCE*}

BEST WAY TO
-how best to

> There is considerable debate over the best way to prevent future oil spills.
>
> There is considerable debate over how best to prevent future oil spills.

BEST WE CAN DO IS
-we can do no better than to

BET ME
-Who will take a bet with me?

BETRAYAL
-duplicity

BETRAYED
-broke faith with

BETTER
-better suited for
-a more perfect
-preferable
-to be preferred

BETWEEN
-among

"There is little agreement among party leaders."

BETWEEN THEMSELVES
-inter se {Latin, *inter SAY*}

BETWEEN YOU AND I (INCORRECT USAGE)
-between you and me

BIASED
-partisan
-predisposed
-tendentious

BIG DECLINES
-sharp declines

BIG SHOT
-grandee {Spanish, *gran-DEE*}

"'Don't worry,' Bill said to Sheba, 'you'll get used to the gloom.' He smiled at her magnanimously, the grandee allowing her into the little enclosure of his bonhomie." Zoe Heller, *Notes on a Scandal*

BIG WORD
-lofty word
-pretentious word

BIOGRAPHICAL MOVIE OR TV SHOW
-a biopic

BIRDS SINGING (LISTEN TO THE BIRDS SINGING)
-birdsong

BIRTH
-genesis
-nascence

BIRTHING (PLACE OF BIRTHING)
-accouchement {French, *a-koosh-MAH*}

"The royal family attended the accouchement of the queen, and did behold their future king."

BIRTHPLACE
-cradle of
-spawning ground of
-provenance

"No matter what its name or provenance, it is believed that the arrival of the Europeans

on Hispaniola unleashed the fukú on the world, and we've all been in the shit ever since." Junot Diaz, *The Brief Wondrous Life of Oscar Wao*

BITING
-acerbic

BITTER
-acrid

BITTERNESS
-rancor {RANG-ker}

BLACK
-raven black
-sable
-obsidian

BLACK AND WHITE VIEW OF THE WORLD
-Manichean view of the world {man-i-KEE-uhn}

"As political analysis, there's something to be said for Krugman's Manichean view of the world. But Krugman is also an economist—a very good one—and the economics of what is proposed bear inspection." John Cassidy, *The New Yorker*, Nov. 4, 2009

BLACK COMEDY [ANTIQUATED]
-gallows humor

BLACK SHEEP [ANTIQUATED]
-pariah

BLACK SLAVERY IN THE U.S.
-that peculiar institution

BLAME
-implicate
-point an accusatory finger
-apportion blame
-the fault lay in part with
-hold to account for
-find fault with

"She had bonny children, yet she felt they had been thrust upon her, and she could

not love them. They looked at her coldly, as if they were finding fault with her. And hurriedly she felt she must cover up some fault in herself." D. H. Lawrence, "The Rocking-Horse Winner"

You are blaming others when you are to blame.

You are finding fault when the fault is your own.

BLAMING YOURSELF
-self reproach
-much of this is my own doing

BLAND
-insipid
-vapid
-nondescript
-weary, flat, stale, and unprofitable [Shakespeare]

BLANK SLATE
-tabula rasa {Latin, TAB-you-la RAH-zah}

BLATANT
-overt
-patent

BLEACHER BUMS
-groundlings

BLEND INTO
-assimilate

BLESSINGS
-mercies
"Let's be glad for small mercies."

BLEW
-gave forth a blast of wind

BLINDLY DEVOTED FOLLOWER
-an apparatchik {Russian, op-er-RAH-chick}

BLOCK
-stymie
-thwart
-frustrate
-check

BLOCKED HIM
-prevented his passing
-barred him from

BLOOD BATH
-a bath of blood

BLOOD FEUD
-vendetta

BLOOD MONEY
-filthy lucre {LOO-ker}

BLOOM
-come into its own

BLOW A KISS
-waft a phantom kiss

BLOWN
-driven

"Driven on the wind that sweeps the gloomy hills of London." T. S. Eliot, *Four Quartets*

BLUE
-vishnu blue

BLUE SKIES
-azure skies {AZH-er} [poetic]

BLUFFING
-posturing

BOARD OF DIRECTORS
-the directorate

BOAST
-lord it over
-trumpet

BOASTFUL
-vaunting

BODILY
-corporeal

BODY
-his whole person rose up
-the figure of a man could be seen

BODY OF WORK
-oeuvre {French, OHV-ruh}

BOGUS
-without merit

BOLD
-brazen
-nervy
-audacious
-brassy

BOLDNESS
-bravado
-temerity
-audacity

BOMBARD
-barrage

BOND
-a rapport

BOOK
-work
-tome (large and scholarly) {rhymes with *home*}
-source

BOOMERANG
-recoil

"Violence does, in truth, recoil upon the violent." Arthur Conan Doyle

BOONDOCKS
-the hinterland
-in some far corner
-outlands

BOOS
-a chorus of disdain
-full-throated boos

BOOST
-shot in the arm

BORED OF [INCORRECT USAGE]
-bored with
-bored by

BOREDOM
-tedium
-ennui {French, *ahn-WEE*}

BORING
-tedious
-mundane
-hackneyed
-warmed over retreads of
-fairly sleepy
-not a show-stopper
-not electrifying

"If his performance was not electrifying, at least it was believable."

BORING AND OVERSIMPLIFIED WRITING
-pabulum

BORING PARTS OF A BOOK
-longueurs {French, *lon-GUERZ*}

BORN WITH
-graced with

BORROWS FROM
-draws upon
-is informed by

BOSSY
-imperious
-magisterial
-officious
-high-handed

BOTH
-both of which
-either
-respectively
-the two
-it is at once ____ and ____

"Everything about her was at once vigorous and exquisite, at once strong and fine." Edith Wharton, *The House of Mirth*

BOTH ENDS
-opposite ends

BOTH OF THEM
-both
-both these persons
-the two
-them both

"There are only two extant copies, and we own them both."

BOTHERED BY
-burdened by
-subjected to
-encumbered by
-subject to
-we have no rest from it
-it's a source of much distress to her
-we are plagued by

BOTHERS (IT BOTHERS)
-it pains me to
-it weighs on me
-it grieves me
-troubles

"Nevertheless, when her children were present, she always felt the center of her heart go hard. This troubled her, and in her manner she was all the more gentle and anxious for her children, as if she loved them very much." D. H. Lawrence, "The Rocking-Horse Winner"

BOTTOMLESS PIT
-abyss

BRAG
-lord it over them
-vaunt
-boast

"You can boast about anything if it's all you have. Maybe the less you have, the more you are required to boast." John Steinbeck, *East of Eden*

> She came from a prominent family, but she wouldn't brag about it.
>
> She came from a prominent family, but she wouldn't lord it over us.

BRAINWASH
-inculcate a sense of
-instill a sense of

BRANCH OF
-arm of
-wing of
-organ of

BRANCHED
-took different courses
-diverged

BRAVE
-unflinching
-undaunted
-plucky

BREAK APART
-fracture
-disband
-splinter
-rupture

BREAK OPEN
-breach

BREAK-UP
-a parting of the ways
-part company

BREAK UP
-fragment

BREAK THROUGH
-breach

BREATHED IN
-drew breath

BREATHING HARD
-breath comes fast

"*His nostrils are dilated and his breath comes fast—his demons are driving him.*" Upton Sinclair, *The Jungle*

BRIBERY
-graft

BRIEF
-cursory
-momentary
-fleeting
-short-lived
-ephemeral

BRIEFLY
-in passing
-in a word
-in brief

"*I enjoyed such moments—but only in brief. If the talk began to wander, or cross the border into familiarity, I would soon find reason to excuse myself. I had grown too comfortable in my solitude, the safest place I knew.*" Barack Obama, *Dreams from My Father*

BRIGHT LIGHT
-brilliant light

BRIGHTNESS
-luminosity

BRIMMING WITH
-alive to the sultry sounds of

BRING ABOUT
-engender
-raise

"*The competing viewpoints have raised debate among both wings of the Democratic party.*"
-conjure up
-summon
-invite
-effect
-elicit

-give cause for
-arouse
-occasion

"The coverage of Fort Hood will, rightfully, be extensive in the next few days. But it will be a pity if it completely overshadows how significant a story the killing of the British soldiers has become in their country. What the incidents may have most in common is that they occasion a reckoning of the costs of war." Amy Davidson, *The New Yorker*, Nov. 6, 2009

BRING BACK
-resurrect

BRING DOWN A NOTCH
-depose you of your lofty perch

BRING ME A
-produce a

BRING TO LIFE
-animate

"He had a way of animating the past like no other history teacher could."

BRING TOGETHER
-draw together
-assemble

BRING UP FOR DISCUSSION
-broach the subject

BRINGS BACK MEMORIES
-it's Proustian {*PRUE-stee-un*}
(after Marcel Proust, which is pro-
  nounced *Proost*, not *Proust*)

BRINGS OUT
-accents

BRITISH GOVERNMENT
-Whitehall

BROAD RANGE OF
-eclectic

BROKE THROUGH
-breached

BROKEN DOWN
-in disrepair
-derelict

BROTHERS
-brethren

BROUGHT ABOUT
-kindled

_____**BROUGHT BACK**
-_____ redux {French, *ree-DUCKS*}

"Upon its release in 2001, Francis Ford Coppola's 1979 film Apocalypse Now *was aptly re-titled* Apocalypse Now Redux*."*

BROUGHT OUT
-drew
-elicited
-incurred

BROUGHT THEM TOGETHER
-assembled them

"Nightfall assembled them, as it did the stars. With nothing in common but their destitution, they mustered to sleep together in the Porch of Our Lord, cursing, insulting and jostling each other, picking quarrels with old enemies, or throwing earth and rubbish, even rolling on the ground and spitting and biting with rage." Miguel Angel Asturias, *The President*

BROUGHT TO MIND
-aroused in his mind the idea of

BROWN
-chestnut
-sepia
-tawny

BROWN-NOSER
-sycophant {*SICK-uh-fnt*}
-toady
-lackey
-obsequious person
-unctuous person

BROWN-NOSING
-fawning

BRUSH ASIDE
-think no more of
-discount
-dismiss

BRUTAL (DEPRAVED)
-bestial {BEES-chel}

BUFFER (A BUFFER)
-hedge against
-cordon sanitaire {French, *kawr-dawn
sahn-ee-TAIR*} (as in buffer states
between two countries)

BUILDUP
-groundswell

BUILT A CAREER
-having fashioned a career

BUILT FROM
-built of

"*We were sitting in the blind that
Wanderobo hunters had built of twigs
and branches at the edge of the salt-lick
when we heard the truck coming.*" Ernest
Hemingway, *The Green Hills of Africa*

BUILT-IN
-inherent
-deep-seated
-innate
-resident

BUILT ON
-rests in part on
-is predicated on
-is informed by
-built on

"*Love built on beauty, soon as beauty,
dies.*" John Donne {pronounced *Dun*}

BUILT WITH
-built of

BULL
-PR

"*My main ambition as a journalist is to cut
through the PR and find the truth in what
politicians are saying.*" Chris Matthews,
2010 *Hardball* promo

I want it straight, without
the bull.

I want it straight, without
the PR.

BULLIED
-hectored

BULLY
-tormentor
-tyrant

BUM
-indigent
-layabout
-wastrel {*WAY-struhl*}

BUM-LOOKING
-unkempt
-bedraggled
-harried

BUNCH OF
-accumulation of
-assemblage of
-repository of
-trove of

BURDEN (A BURDEN)
-an albatross
-a tax on
-an encumbrance

"*This was still the era—it would end
later in that famous decade—when to
be young was a social encumbrance, a
mark of irrelevance, a faintly embarrassing condition for which marriage was
the beginning of a cure.*" Ian McEwan,
Chesil Beach

BURDEN (TO BURDEN)
-to saddle with

-to encumber
-to weigh heavy on
-to subject to

BUREAUCRAT
-a functionary
-government official

BURNING AT THE STAKE
-auto-da-fé {Portuguese,
 out-oh-da-FAY}

BURYING YOUR HEAD IN THE SAND
-a fool's paradise

BUSHES SHAPED LIKE ANIMALS
-topiary sculptures {*TOE-pee-AIR-ee*}

"*The whimsical theme is carried through from topiary sculptures to 'reinvented' takes on classic cocktails, like the Blackforest mojito, which is made with Chambord.*" Christine Chow, *New York Times*, Nov. 1, 2009

BUSY
-preoccupied
-engaged in
-absorbed in
-not a moment to spare

I'm busy thinking.
I'm absorbed in thought.

BUSY PLACE
-swirl of activity

BUSY THINKING (SHE'S BUSY THINKING)
-pensive

BUSYBODY
-a yenta

BUT
-with the caveat

BUT AGAIN
-but here again

"*I proceeded, as I have said, to question Weena about this Under-world, but here again I was disappointed.*" H. G. Wells, *The Time Machine*

BUT NOT
-if not

BUT NOT YOU
-not so you

BUTT IN
-horn in

BUYER BEWARE
-caveat emptor {Latin, *CAV-ee-ot EMP-tor*}

BY
-by means of
-by the hands of
-by way of
-the work of
-through the agency of
-by virtue of
-on the part of
-by nothing less than

"*Man is explicable by nothing less than all his history. Without hurry, without rest, the human spirit goes forth from the beginning to embody every faculty, every thought, every emotion, which belongs to it, in appropriate events. But the thought is always prior to the fact; all the facts of history preexist in the mind as laws.*" Ralph Waldo Emerson, "Essay on History"

BY CHANCE
-happenstance
-serendipity

BY DOING THAT, SHE
-in so doing, she

BY FORCE
-in high-handed fashion

-by force of arms

BY ITSELF
-in and of itself
-of its own accord
-intrinsically
-in its own right
-per se {Latin, *per say*}
-of itself

BY ME
-on my part

BY THAT I MEAN...
-by which I mean...

BY THAT VERY FACT
-ipso facto {Latin, *IP-soe FAK-toe*}

BY-THE-BOOK KIND OF PERSON
-a strict textualist
-does not live upon instinct

BY THE END OF THE WEEK
-by week's end

BY THE POWER OF
-by dint of

BY THE SAME TOKEN
-in the same way
-for the same reason

BY THE WAY
-incidentally
-if I may say
-it may be added that

BY USING
-by the use of
-by means of

BY YOUR OWN DECISION
-of your own accord
-by your own volition
-take it upon yourself to

Cc

CALCULATE
-assess

CALL (NAME)
-refer to as
-have a name for

"We have a name for that sort of thing."

-christen
-dub
-what one could term

"It has been recorded that during his studies he particularly relished psychology; this is amply borne out by his writings. St. John was not what one could term a scholar. He was, however, intimately acquainted with the 'Summa' of St. Thomas Aquinas, as almost every page of his works proves..."
St. Thomas Aquinas, *On Prayer and a Contemplative Life*

CALL ATTENTION TO
-feature

CALL ON
-call forth
-summon
-beckon

CALL OUT FOR
-hail

CALL TOGETHER
-convene
-summon
-assemble

CALLED (IS CALLED)
-known as
-dubbed by such adjectives as
-what is commonly called
-takes its name from
-heralded as

CALLED EVERYONE'S ATTENTION
-called for the attention of all

CALLS HIMSELF
-is a self-described ___

CALM
-serene
-placid
-philosophical (in the face of
  disappointment)

> He was surprisingly calm after
> the biggest disappointment of his
> career.
>
> He was philosophical.

CALM BEHAVIOR
-composed
-unflappable
-poised
-sangfroid {French, *sah-FWAH*}
-self-possessed

CALM DOWN
-compose oneself
-put at ease
-defuse the situation
-grow calmer

"He reached out and with the back of his hand touched my arm. He is trying my flesh, I thought. But by and by my breathing slowed and I grew calmer." J.M. Coetzee, *Foe*

CALM YOUR FEARS
-dispel your fears

CALMNESS
-composure
-equanimity
-presence of mind
-tranquility

CAME
-there came

"From a distance there came the sound of tanks."

CAME BEFORE
-a forerunner
-a precursor

CAME FROM
-issued from

CAME NEAR
-drew near

"In the first days of December the birds, after frequent biting frosts, flew into villages and towns, and even wild beasts came out of dense forests and drew near the houses of people." Henryk Sienkiewicz, *On the Field of Glory*

CAME ON HER OWN
-came of her own accord
-on his own volition

> Have you come here on
> your own?
>
> Have you come of your
> own accord?

CAME THROUGH FOR ME
-I expected nothing less

CAME TO A
-came in sight of
-happened upon
-chanced upon

CAME TO REALIZE
-was borne in upon her [poetic]

CAME UP
-arose

CAMPAIGN
-barrage
-blitz
-part of the latest effort to

CAN AT LEAST BRING
-can yet bring

"There must be acceptance and the knowledge that sorrow fully accepted brings its own gifts. For there is an alchemy in sorrow. It can be transmuted into wisdom, which, if it does not bring joy, can yet bring happiness." Pearl S. Buck, *The Child Who Never Grew*

CAN BE SEEN IN
-is reflected in

CAN GET
-is to be had

CAN ONLY BE
-cannot be other than

CAN SPEAK GERMAN
-fluent in German

CAN STILL BRING
-can yet bring

CAN YOU BELIEVE IT?
-can you even conceive of it?

CANCEL
-abrogate the contract
-redline
-rescind

CANDY
-confections
-confectionery

CANNOT
-can no more

"I can no more disown him than I can disown the black community." Barack Obama, 2009 presidential speech

CANNOT AFFORD TO
-can ill afford to

CANNOT BE
-is incapable of being

CANNOT BE STOPPED
-is inexorable

CANNOT DO ANYTHING ABOUT
-it's inescapable

CANNOT EXPLAIN
-it's inexplicable
-cannot account for

CANNOT HAVE
-deprived of

CANNOT MAKE UP YOUR MIND
-undetermined in your choice of

CANNOT SEE IT
-is indiscernible

CANNOT THINK OF
-escapes me

> I can't think of it.
>
> The words escape me.

CAN'T FIND _____
-there has been no trace of _____
-_____ are nowhere to be found

CAN'T SEE HER
-have lost sight of her

CAN'T STAND
-can't bear

CAN'T WE
-can we not

"Can we not come to some kind of agreement?"

CAPITAL
-seat of government

CARE (GOD'S CARE)
-God's keeping
-providence

CARE [SARCASTIC]
-tender mercies

"They were abandoned to the tender mercies of the SS."

CARE ABOUT
-sympathetic to
-mindful of
-give importance to

"The young man, whose name was Robert Jordan, was extremely hungry and he was worried. He was often hungry but he was not usually worried because he did not give any importance to what happened to himself and he knew from experience how simple it was to move behind the enemy lines in all this country." Ernest Hemingway, *For Whom the Bell Tolls*

CARE FOR
-nurture
-nurture and perpetuate
-minister to

CAREFREE
-capricious
-blithe

CAREFREE ATTITUDE
-insouciance {French, *in-SUE-see-ance*}

CARED FOR
-had the care of

"His sister Lizzie, too young to hem sheets but old…enough to carry a baby on her hip, had the care of the little ones." Kate Grenville, *The Secret River*

CAREFUL
-mindful
-prudential
-solicitous
-circumspect
-studied
-prudent
-guarded
-assiduous
-chary {*CHAIR-ee*}

CAREFUL NOT TO
-on guard against

CAREFULLY
-tread with caution

-tread gingerly
-take great pains to
-with care
-I use that word advisedly
-guardedly

CARELESS
-indifferent
-remiss

CARRY
-shoulder
-ferry
-labor under
-bear
-schlep

CARRY OUT
-perpetrate

CARRYING OUT OF A PLAN
-the pursuance of

CARTOON
-caricature

CARVE
-inscribe
-incise

CARVED (SCULPTED OR INSCRIBED)
-graven

CARVED DESIGN
-a design in intaglio {Italian, *in-TAL-yoe*}

CAST OF CHARACTERS
-dramatis personae {Latin, *DRAH-ma-tis per-SAWN-eye*}

CASTRATED
-gelded

CASUAL
-cavalier
-haphazard
-perfunctory
-leisurely

"*Augustus held to a more leisurely philosophy. He believed in giving creatures a little time to think, so he stood in the sun a few minutes until the rattler calmed down and crawled out a hole.*" Larry McMurtry, *Lonesome Dove*

CASUALTIES
-blood and treasure

CATCH
-ensnare
-snare

CATCH PHRASE
-mantra {MAHN-truh}

"*In 2008, 'Drill Baby Drill!' became the mantra of the conservative party.*"

CATCH UP TO
-overtake

CATEGORIZE
-catalog

CATEGORY
-rubric of
-species
-of its kind
-genre

> This vintage falls under the category of table wine.
>
> This vintage falls under the rubric of table wine.

CAUGHT BETWEEN
-hemmed in by

CAUGHT IN THE ACT
-in flagrante {Latin, *in fla-GRAHN-tay*}

CAUGHT IN THE ACT OF ADULTERY
-in flagrante delicto {Latin, *in fla-GRAHN-TAY de-LICK-toe*}

CAUGHT ON
-took a firm hold throughout the country
-it seems to have gained currency

CAUGHT UP IN
-enmeshed
-entangled

CAUGHT UP TO
-overtook her

CAUSE (TO CAUSE)
-give rise to
-engender
-foster
-prompt
-excite
-inspire
-elicit
-induce
-rouse

"*It was characteristic of her that she always roused speculation, that her simplest acts seemed the result of some far-reaching intentions.*" Edith Wharton, *The House of Mirth*.

-bring about
-impel
-drive the decision to
-fuel
-move to
-invite
-precipitate
-provoke
-arouse
-awaken
-evoke
-hasten a desire for
-spawn
-effect
-spark discussion
-sow
-compel
-occasion

"*This measure it was desirable to avoid, because it would occasion much public inconvenience and a considerable public expense and add to the calamities of the inhabitants of this city…"* John Adams, *State of the Union address*

CAUSE (A CAUSE)
-basis for
-precipitant

CAUSE HIM TO FEEL
-inspire in him thoughts of

CAUSE OF
-the author of

"The terror and hurt in my story happened because when I was young I thought others were the authors of my fortune and misfortune; I did not know that a person could hold up a wall made of imaginary bricks and mortar against the horrors and cruel, dark tricks of time that assail us, and be the author therefore of themselves." Sebastian Barry, *The Secret Scripture*

CAUSE PROBLEMS FOR
-hamper

CAUSE SUSPICION
-excite suspicion

CAUSED BY
-was prompted in part by
-stems from

> Obesity is caused by a disregard for healthy food.
>
> Obesity stems from a disregard for healthy food.

CAUSED HER TO
-moved her to
-produced in her a
-produced upon her a

"She had never been pretty; her whole life, which had been but a succession of pious works, had produced upon her a kind of transparent whiteness, and in growing old she had acquired what may be called the beauty of goodness." Victor Hugo, *Les Misérables*

CAUSING A SERIOUS PROBLEM WITH
-exacting a serious toll

CAUSING _____ TO
-so that

"He lit fires in several locations so that the entire house was engulfed in flame."

CAUSING TROUBLE
-making mischief

"It was the jackal—Tabaqui the Dish-licker—and the wolves of India despise Tabaqui because he runs about making mischief, and telling tales, and eating rags and pieces of leather from the village rubbish-heaps." Rudyard Kipling, *The Jungle Book*

CAUTIOUS
-circumspect
-prudent
-assiduous
-mindful
-prudential
-studied
-solicitous
-guarded
-chary {CHAIR-ee}

CAVE
-grotto

CAVEMAN DAYS
-Paleolithic times

CELEBRATE
-commemorate
-memorialize
-mark

CELEBRATE NOISILY
-roister

CELEBRATION (ELABORATE OUTDOOR PARTY)
-fête {French, *fate*}

"The event was an Empire Day fête: I stood with a line of other village children making a Boy Scout salute while Mrs. Ayres and the Colonel went past us, handing out commemorative medals; afterwards we sat to tea with our parents at long tables on what I suppose was the south lawn." Sarah Waters, *The Little Stranger*

CELEBRITIES
-personages
-luminaries

CENSORED
-pasteurized
-bowdlerized

CENTER OF
-the bastion of
-the locus of
-the still point of the turning world [T. S. Eliot]
-the mecca of

CENTERS AROUND [INCORRECT USAGE]
-centers on

CERTAIN
-beyond dispute
-doubtless
-assured

CERTAIN AREAS
-select areas

CERTAIN WAY
-given manner

CERTAINLY
-doubtless
-no doubt

"No one even knows I have a story. Next year, next week, tomorrow, I will no doubt be gone, and it will be a small size coffin they will need for me, and a narrow hole.

There will never be a stone at my head, and no matter." Sebastian Barry, *The Secret Scripture*

CHALLENGE THE TRUTH OF
-take to task
-impugn
-call into question

> Scientists have begun to challenge the truth of BP's estimates.
>
> Scientists have begun to call into question BP's estimates.

CHALLENGING
-interrogating

"Month after month he sets, collects, reads, and annotates their assignments, correcting lapses in punctuation, spelling and usages, interrogating weak arguments, appending to each paper a brief, considered critique." J. M. Coetzee, *Disgrace*

CHAMPIONED
-hailed

CHANCE
-a sporting chance that
-contingency

"Nothing was left to contingency."

CHANGE (TO CHANGE)
-adapt
-modify
-reform
-threaten established precedent
-make wholesale renovations
-amend
-transfigure
-transition
-undergo yet another

CHANGE (A CHANGE)
-departure from
-gradation of
-metamorphosis

-turning point
-transmutation [academic]

CHANGE COURSE
-deviate from the prescribed heading
-turn the compass needle
-take a new turn

CHANGE THE SUBJECT
-turn our attention to

> Let's change the subject to something that isn't often discussed.
>
> Let's turn our attention to something that isn't often discussed.

CHANGE YOUR POSITION
-backpedal
-roll that one back

CHANGEABLE
-protean

"Because the senator is more than willing to switch parties to survive the primary, you could safely characterize his political convictions as protean."

CHANGES
-vagaries

CHANGES OF FORTUNE
-vicissitudes

CHANNEL (A CHANNEL)
-a conduit

CHANT IN MONOTONE
-intone

CHARACTERISTIC OF
-by nature
-peculiar to
-as his habit was to
-as she was given to

CHARACTERIZED BY
-marked by

CHARISMA
-stage presence

CHARITABLE
-benevolent
-altruistic

CHARM (APPEAL)
-open and easy air
-allure

CHARM (CAPTIVATE)
-endear
-beguile

CHARM (ORNAMENT)
-talisman
-amulet

CHARMING
-beguiling
-disarming
-engaging

CHASE
-give chase

CHEAP (STINGY)
-miserly
-frugal [euphemism]

"You're not a cheap bastard—you're a frugal bastard."

CHEAT
-bilk

CHECK OUT
-case

"Oh come take my hand, we're riding out tonight to case the promised land." Bruce Springsteen, "Thunder Road"

CHEER UP
-hearten
-take heart

CHEERFUL
-blithe
-sanguine

CHEERFUL READINESS
-alacrity

CHEERFULLY SELF-CONFIDENT
-jaunty

CHEMISTRY
-alchemy

"There must be acceptance and the knowledge that sorrow fully accepted brings its own gifts. For there is an alchemy in sorrow. It can be transmuted into wisdom, which, if it does not bring joy, can yet bring happiness." Pearl S. Buck, *The Child Who Never Grew*

CHIEF ADVOCATE
-high priest of
-dean of
-doyen of

CHILD
-a creature so charming

CHILD PRODIGY
-wunderkind {German, *VUHN-der-kint*}

CHILDHOOD FRIEND
-the friend of her childhood

CHILDISH
-infantile
-puerile
-pettish
-petulant

CHOICE
-of one's own choosing

CHOICE BETWEEN ____ AND ____
-have the choice to ____ or ____

CHOOSE
-favor
-opt for

CHOOSE WHATEVER YOU WANT
-choose what you will

CHOSE POORLY
-made a poor choice of

> She chose the wrong husband.
>
> She made a poor choice of husband.

CHOSEN TO
-empowered to
-tapped to be

CHRISTIAN (IN A BROAD SENSE)
-ecumenical

CHRISTIAN WORLD
-Christendom

"I have it here before me on my bed, with his name in black ink inside, Joe Clear, and the date 1888, and the town Southampton, for in his extreme youth he had been a sailor, sailing into every port of Christendom before he was seventeen." Sebastian Barry, *The Secret Scripture*

CHURCH LEADER
-prelate

CHURCH RELATED
-ecclesiastical

CIRCLE
-encircle
-gird
-envelope

CIRCUMSTANCES
-state of affairs

CITE
-invoke

CITIZEN
-denizen of
-inhabitant

"And the tall walls of the commercial heart of an American city of perhaps 400,000 inhabitants—such walls as in time may linger

as a mere fable." Theodore Dreiser, *An American Tragedy*

CITY
-metropolis
-megalopolis
-the sprawl of _____

CITY FOLKS
-urbanites

CLAIM (TO CLAIM)
-assert
-contend
-lay claim to
-profess to favor
-purport (often falsely)
-make no pretentions

> I'm not claiming to be the most virtuous person.
>
> I make no pretensions to virtue.

CLAIM (A CLAIM)
-contention
-pronouncement
-assertion

CLAMOR
-alarums and excursions {*uh-LAR-ums*}

CLARIFY
-illuminate
-bring into sharper focus

CLASS
-standing
-station
-social strata

CLASSIFIED
-classed as

CLEAN SLATE
-tabula rasa {Latin, *TAB-you-luh RAW-zuh*}

CLEAR
-incisive
-with clarity
-coherent
-well defined
-explicit
-lucid
-unequivocal
-unambiguous
-doubly plain
-clear and present
-clear, logical, and convincing
-abundantly clear

CLEAR THINKING
-incisive

CLEARLY
-there can be little doubt
-without question
-markedly
-in no uncertain terms
-decidedly
-manifestly
-patently
-without doubt
-assuredly
-acutely
-incontrovertibly

CLEVER REMARK
-sally
-bon mot {French, *bon MOE*, lit. good word}

"Common Sense and Education: The more you think you have of one, the less you think you need of the other."

CLEVER BUT UNSOUND DEBATER
-a sophist {*SOHF-ist*}
-a casuist {*KAZH-oo-ist*}

CLEVERNESS
-guile
-cunning

CLICHÉ
-truism

-platitude
-bromide
-vulgarism
-as the cliché will have it,

CLIFF
-precipice
-bluff
-palisade

CLIFF OVERLOOKING THE SEA
-promontory
-headland {HEAD-lund}

CLIMATE CHANGE [ORWELLIAN]
-global warming

CLIMAX
-height of
-pinnacle
-zenith

CLIMB
-ascend
-clamber up

CLIMB DOWN
-scurry down

CLIMBING
-ascendant

CLIMBING OF
-ascendancy of
-ascent of

CLIQUE
-coterie {French, KOE-ter-ee}

CLOSE (AFFECTIONATE)
-close in spirit

"We are a family that has always been close in spirit. Our father was drowned in a sailing accident when we were young, and our mother has always stressed the fact that our familial relationships have a kind of permanence that we will never meet with again." John Cheever, The Stories of John Cheever

CLOSE (NEAR IN DEGREE)
-closely contested

> It's turning out to be a close race.
>
> It's proving to be a closely contested race.

CLOSE (SHUT)
-enclose
-hedge in

CLOSE BY
-within earshot

CLOSE DOWN
-shutter
-disband
-dissolve

CLOSE TO
-on the brink of

CLOSE TO BECOMING
-came very near being

CLOSENESS
-proximity

CLOSER TO
-nearer the
-nearer to

CLOSEST
-near most
-immediate
-proximate [academic]

CLOSING DOWN (BREAKING UP)
-disbanding
-dissolving

CLOTH BACKDROP
-scrim

"Mr. Wilson underscores the point by dividing his characters with scrims and pools of light that seem to confine them to inescapably *separate orbits*." Ben Brantley, *New York Times*, Nov. 6, 2009

CLOTHED
-clad

CLOTHING
-attire
-garb
-finery
-regalia
-trappings
-apparel

CLOUD
-nebula
-islands on a dark blue sea [Shelly]

CLOUDY
-nebulous

CLOWNING AROUND
-buffoonery

CLUB (TO CLUB)
-bludgeon

CLUELESS
-feckless

COACH (TO COACH)
-mentor

COAT WITH GOLD
-gild

CODE OF SILENCE
-omerta {Italian, *ah-MAIR-tah*}

COFFEE AND CONVERSATION
-kaffeeklatsch {German, *coffee-clach*}

COFFEE WITH MILK
-café au lait {French, *ka-FAY oh LAY*}

COINCIDENCE
-happenstance
-by the strangest of chances

COLD AND DAMP
-dank

COLDHEARTED
-dispassionate
-callous
-indifferent
-changed to me

COLLATERAL DAMAGE [MILITARY JINGOISM]
-civilian deaths

COLLECT
-marshal
-stockpile
-amass
-assemble

COLLECTION
-assemblage
-assortment
-family
-amalgam
-congregation
-panoply [academic]
-distillation
-compilation
-anthology
-body of work
-repertoire
-compendium

COLLECTION OF WRITINGS OR PAINTINGS
-corpus
-oeuvre {French, *OH-vruh*}

COLOR
-hue
-complexion

COLOR (COLORIZE)
-lay on color
-imbue with

COLOR QUALITY
-chroma

COLORFUL
-in technicolor
-polychrome

COLORS
-color scheme
-tapestry of color
-kaleidoscope

COLORS OF FALL
-autumnal colors

COMBINATION
-mix of
-tapestry of
-ultimate marriage of
-composite
-synthesis

COMBINE
-coalesce
-assimilate

COME
-come hither [playful]
-draw near

COME ABOUT
-emerge

COME ACROSS AS
-cast himself as

He likes to come across as the dad in charge.

He likes to cast himself as the family patriarch.

COME BACK
-resurface

COME BEFORE
-precede

COME BETWEEN
-intervene

COME CLOSE TO
-verge close to

"Depression is a disorder of mood, so mysteriously painful and elusive in the way it becomes known to the self—to the mediating intellect—as to verge close to being beyond description." William Styron, *Darkness Visible*

COME FROM (THAT COME FROM)
-draw on
-spring from
-lie in

"His own opinion, which he does not air, is that the origins of speech lie in song, and the origins of song in the need to fill out with sound the overlarge and rather empty human soul." J.M. Coetzee, *Disgrace*

Like all animals, humans come from a preexisting species.

Like all animals, humans are descended from a preexisting species.

COME FROM MONEY
-from a moneyed background

COME OUT
-emerge
-come to light
-materialize

COME TO A BOIL
-culminate in

COME TO AN AGREEMENT
-broker a deal

COME TO OUR ATTENTION
-have come under our attention

COME TO THE AID OF
-intercede on her behalf

COME TOGETHER
-consolidate
-coalesce
-bridge the differences that divide
-close ranks

COME UP WITH
-muster

COMEDY ROUTINE
-shtick

COMES BEFORE
-is prior to
-preexists

"Man is explicable by nothing less than all his history. Without hurry, without rest, the human spirit goes forth from the beginning to embody every faculty, every thought, every emotion, which belongs to it, in appropriate events. But the thought is always prior to the fact; all the facts of history preexist in the mind as laws." Ralph Waldo Emerson, "Essay on History"

COMES CLOSE (NOTHING COMES CLOSE)
-nothing even touches it

COMES FROM
-born out of
-stems from

COMFORT (TAKE COMFORT IN)
-take solace in
-sustained by the

COMFORTABLE
-at ease
-at home with

COMFORTS
-creature comforts
-amenities

COMICAL
-farcical

COMING SOON
-oncoming
-impending

COMING TOGETHER OF
-a confluence of

COMMENDABLE
-deserving of praise
-laudable

COMMENTED
-remarked
-spoke of
-made mention of

COMMIT
-commend

COMMIT A CRIME
-perpetrate

COMMITTED
-devout
-undaunted

COMMON
-customary
-familiar

COMMON LANGUAGE
-lingua franca {Italian, *LEEN-gwuh FRANK-uh*}

COMMON SENSE MOTIVES
-prudential motives

COMMONPLACE
-prosaic
-in an all-to-typical fashion

COMMOTION
-astir over the news of

COMMUNICATE
-correspond
-share your thoughts
-betray (unwittingly)
-convey

"If the eyes could lie, his troubles might be over. If the eyes were not such well behaving creatures, that spent their time trying their best to convey the world and all its gore to him, good portions of life might not be so dismal." Sarah Hall, *The Electric Michelangelo*

COMPARED TO
-by way of comparison, it stands as a
-by comparison
-invited comparisons to
-likened it to
-I prefer the latter, as being the more _____
-as compared with
-in comparison with
-vis-à-vis (pretentious)
-compared with that of
-at the expense of

> Certain aspects were exaggerated compared to others.
>
> Certain aspects were exaggerated at the expense of others.

COMPATIBLE
-simpatico

COMPENSATING
-compensatory

COMPETE
-joust
-vie for
-rival

COMPETENCY EXAMINATION FOR COURT
-voir dire {French, *vwar dear*}

COMPLAIN
-grouse about
-venture to complain
-lodge a complaint
-express concern about
-kvetch {Yiddish, *k-VETCH*}

COMPLAINER
-a malcontent

COMPLAINING
-bemoaning
-grumbling

COMPLAINT
-grievance

COMPLETE
-comprehensive
-wholesale

COMPLETE AUTHORITY
-supreme authority

COMPLETE NONSENSE
-arrant nonsense

COMPLETELY
-wholly
-entirely
-altogether
-thoroughly

"I got masses of things from Mummy and Daddy, and was thoroughly spoiled by various friends." Anne Frank, *Anne Frank: The Diary of a Young Girl*

-well and truly
-in all respects
-in full force
-to its full extent
-in its entirety
-in every respect

COMPLETELY ABSORBED
-rapt

COMPLETELY DEPENDABLE
-unfailing

> Her love and support is something I can count on.
>
> Her love and support is unfailing.

COMPLETELY EXPLAIN
-do justice to

COMPLICATED
-abstruse
-convoluted
-defies comprehension

COMPLICATED DEVICE FOR SIMPLE THINGS
-a Rube Goldberg device

COMPLIES WITH
-in keeping with

COMPOSURE UNDER PRESSURE
-sangfroid {French, *sahn-FRAW*}

COMPREHEND COMPLETELY
-grok

"When Chevy Chase said to 'be the ball,' he was groking the game of golf."

COMPREHENSIVE
-overarching

COMPROMISE ON
-accommodate

"Can we not accommodate both positions?"

CONCERN
-center on
-speak to

CONCERN FOR ONE'S OWN INTERESTS ONLY
-particularism

CONCERNED ABOUT
-solicitous of

"How is it that Americans, so solicitous of the animals they keep as pets, are so indifferent to the ones they cook for dinner? The answer cannot lie in the beasts themselves. Pigs, after all, are quite companionable, and dogs are said to be delicious." Elizabeth Kolbert, *The New Yorker*, Nov. 9, 2009

CONCERNING
-with respect to
-with regard to
-in light of
-we look to
-apropos of

"In later years, holding forth to an interviewer or to an audience of aging fans at a comic book convention, Sam Clay liked to declare, apropos of his and Joe Kavalier's greatest creation, that back when he was a boy, sealed and hog-tied inside the airtight vessel known as Brooklyn, New York, he had been haunted by dreams of Harry Houdini."* Michael Chabon, *The Amazing Adventures of Kavalier & Clay*

-as for
-as to
-for his part
-in his case
-pointing to
-on matters concerning
-of this issue
-in discussing
-hereto
-as regards
-touch on
-relating to
-apply to
-subject being

"Our subject being Poetry, I propose to speak not only of the art in general but also of its species and their respective capacities; of the structure of plot required for a good poem…" Aristotle, *The Poetics*

CONCERNS (DOUBTS)
-having reservations

CONCERNS (RELATES TO)
-speaks to
-pertains to
-centers on

CONCISE
-terse
-succinct

CONCISE AND EXPRESSIVE
-pithy
-taut

CONCLUDE (TO DEDUCE)
-arrive at such a conclusion
-fair to conclude that

-presume
-reckon
-suppose

CONCLUDE (TO FINISH)
-come to fruition
-culminate in

CONCLUSIONS
-findings

CONCOCTION
-a confection

"The accusation of wrongdoing was dismissed as nothing more than a partisan confection."

CONDEMN
-decry
-denounce

CONDESCEND
-deign to

CONDITION
-proviso {*pruh-VIE-soh*}

> He had been hired so long as he bring his clients with him.
>
> He had been hired with the proviso that he bring his clients with him.

CONDITION OF
-the state of

CONDITIONED RESPONSE
-Pavlovian response

CONDUCT ONESELF WELL
-bear oneself with dignity
-acquit oneself well

CONDUCT THE WAR
-prosecute the war

CONFIDENTIALLY
-entre nous {French, *ahn-tre NEW*, lit. between us}

CONFUSED
-bemused
-nonplussed

CONFUSED WITH
-confounded with

"A serious writer is not to be confounded with a solemn writer. A serious writer may be a hawk or a buzzard or even a popinjay, but a solemn writer is always a bloody owl." Ernest Hemingway

CONNECTING
-adjoining

CONNECTION
-nexus

CONFERENCE
-colloquy [academic] {*CALL-uh-kwee*}
-symposium
-forum
-summit

CONFIDENT
-in no doubt
-self-assured

CONFIRM
-attest to
-bear witness to
-substantiate
-corroborate

CONFIRMED BY
-borne out by

CONFLICT
-dissention
-factious infighting
-amid a vortex of
-clamor
-ferment
-tumult
-upheaval
-whenever battle is joined over

CONFLICT WITH
-run counter to
-run afoul of
-put at odds with
-at variance with

CONFUSE
-bewilder
-befuddle
-perplex
-discombobulate
-confound
-obfuscate

CONFUSED
-convoluted
-in a condition of such mental
 confusion
-muddled
-drug-addled

CONFUSED HER
-left her at a loss

CONFUSED LANGUAGE
-turbid language

CONFUSED MISUNDERSTANDING
-imbroglio {Italian, *im-BROE-yoe*}

CONFUSED MIXTURE
-hodgepodge of

CONFUSION
-bedlam
-disorder
-disarray

CONGRATULATIONS
-kudos {*KOO-doze*}

CONGRESSIONAL BILL
-a measure

CONGRESSIONAL LOBBYISTS
-the Gucci gulch

CONNECTION
-liaison

CONNECTION BETWEEN
-correlation

CONNIVE
-inveigle one's way into {*in-VAY-gul*}

CONNOISSEUR
-epicure

CONQUER
-subdue
-quell
-level

CONSCIENCE
-super-ego

CONSCIOUS
-sentient

CONSCIOUS MIND
-your waking mind

**CONSERVATIVE AND
UNADVENTUROUS**
-staid

CONSERVATIVE EXTREMIST
-reactionary
-troglodyte

CONSERVE
-husband

"The Master once observed that to rule well one of the larger States meant strict attention to its affairs and conscientiousness on the part of the ruler; careful husbanding of its resources, with at the same time a tender care for the interests of all classes; and the employing of the masses in the public service at suitable seasons." Confucius, *The Analects*

CONSIDER
-you would do well to consider
-entertain the idea that
-take into account
-take into consideration
-to consult and consider
-indulge

"Good writers indulge their readers; great writers know better."

CONSIDERATE
-mindful of
-complaisant
-accommodating
-attentive to

> I am aware of our environmental responsibilities.
>
> I am mindful of our environmental responsibilities.

CONSIDERED (IS CONSIDERED)
-acknowledged to be
-looked upon as
-is reckoned a
-is deemed to be
-is regarded as
-is seen to be

CONSIDERED ONE OF
-was counted among the

CONSIDERING
-given the

CONSISTENT WITH
-remain faithful to
-in keeping with
-in accordance with
-accordingly

CONSISTS OF
-comprises

CONSOLATION
-compensatory factors

CONSPIRING
-colluding
-in league with
-in league together

CONSTANT
-invariable
-habitual
-continual
-incessant

CONSTANT CHANGING
-mutability

CONTACTED
-can be reached at

CONTEMPTUOUS
-pejorative

CONTINUAL
-unremitting

CONTINUATION OF
-the progression of

CONTINUE
-perpetuate
-persist
-stretch past
-endure

CONTINUES
-persists
-endures

"As the sesquicentennial of Fort Sumter approaches in 2011, the enduring problem for neo-Confederates endures: anyone who seeks an Edenic Southern past in which the war was principally about states' rights and not slavery is searching in vain, for the Confederacy and slavery are inextricably and forever linked." Jon Meacham, "Southern Discomfort," *New York Times*, April 10, 2010

CONTINUING
-unending
-enduring

CONTINUOUSLY
-incessantly
-without pause
-unabated

CONTRADICT
-belie {bu-LIE}

His rough outer shell contra-
dicted a soft heart.

His rough outer shell belied a
soft heart.

CONTRADICTION
-paradox
-discrepancy in logic
-inconsistency

CONTRARY TO
-inconsistent with

CONTRAST (TO CONTRAST)
-draw a distinction
-distinguish
-juxtapose

CONTRAST THAT WITH
-by contrast

CONTRASTED WITH
-formed the most striking contrast to

CONTRIBUTING
-contributory

CONTROL (TO CONTROL)
-rein in
-manage
-harness
-establish dominion over
-wield control
-restrain
-subdue your instinct to
-curb
-govern
-hold in check
-hold sway
-command

CONTROLLED BY
-governed by
-under the sway of

*"Each step in the development of the bour-
geoisie was accompanied by a corresponding
political advance of that class. An oppressed
class under the sway of the feudal nobility."*
Karl Marx, *The Communist Manifesto*

CONTROVERSIAL
-contentious
-polarizing
-provocative
-divisive
-volatile
-polemical

CONVENTIONAL BEHAVIOR
-propriety

CONVERSATION
-discourse
-repartee {French, *re-par-TAY*}

CONVINCE
-prevail upon

CONVINCING
-cogent

COOK
-rustle up

COOKING
-the culinary arts

**COOKING STOCK (HIGHLY
CONCENTRATED)**
-demi-glace {French, *DEM-ee-glass*}

COOL
-unflappable

COOPERATION
-compliance
-entente {French, *ahn-TAHNT*}

COOPERATIVE
-forthcoming
-informative

> The witness has not been very cooperative.
>
> The witness has been less than forthcoming.

COORDINATED
-concerted

COPIED FROM OTHERS
-derivative

COPY (TO COPY)
-mimic
-emulate
-parrot

COPY OF
-draft of
-facsimile of

COPYCAT
-copyist

CORRECT
-remedy
-redress
-disabuse

"Allow me to disabuse you of that notion."

-rectify
-correct for the fact that
-right the error
-set them right

"Alexander the Grammarian taught me not to be ruggedly critical about words, nor find fault with people for improprieties of phrase or pronunciation, but to set them right by speaking the thing properly myself, and that either by way of answer, assent, or inquiry, or by some such other indirect and suitable correction." Marcus Aurelius, *Meditations*

CORRECTLY
-rightly

CORRODED
-fretted

"The mist took pity on the fretted structures of earlier generations: the Post Office with its shingle-tortured mansard, the red brick minarets of hulking old homes, factories with stingy and sooted windows, wooden tenements colored like mud." Sinclair Lewis, *Babbitt*

CORRUPT (IS CORRUPT)
-not exactly a paragon of virtue
-venal

CORRUPT (TO CORRUPT)
-undermine the legitimacy of
-lead someone astray
-bastardize
-adulterate
-vitiate {VISH-ee-ate}

COSIGNER OF A TREATY
-cosignatory

COUGHING ALL THE TIME
-tubercular

COULD
-should

"The Utopians wonder how any man should be so much taken with the glaring doubtful lustre of a jewel or stone, that can look up to a star, or to the sun himself." Sir Thomas More, *Utopia*

COULD BE
-it's conceivable

COULD NOT BELIEVE
-reacted with dismay

COULD NOT EVEN
-could not so much as

"But we had scarcely begun to climb when I felt a sharp hurt, and drew from my heel a long black-tipped thorn. Though I chafed it, the heel quickly swelled till I

could not so much as hobble for the pain."
J. M. Coetzee, *Foe*

COULD NOT SLEEP LAST NIGHT
-slept little last night

COULD NOT STOP
-could not restrain

COULD STILL BE
-were still to be

"A city where American faces were still to be seen upon all its streets, a cleaner and a kindlier town, with more courtesy in its life, less of the vulgar scramble." Ernest Poole, *His Family*

COULDN'T ROW ANY FURTHER
-could row no further

"At last I could row no further. My hands were blistered, my back was burned, my body ached." J.M. Coetzee, *Foe*

COULDN'T STAND IT ANY LONGER
-could bear it no longer

"On Friday, June 12, I woke up at six o'clock and no wonder; it was my birthday. But of course I was not allowed to get up at that hour, so I had to control my curiosity until a quarter to seven. Then I could bear it no longer and went to the dining room, where I received a warm welcome from Moortje (the cat)." Anne Frank, *Anne Frank: The Diary of a Young Girl*

COUNTER ACCUSATIONS
-recriminations

COUNTERACT
-countervail

COUNTRY LIFE
-pastoral

COURAGE
-valor
-pluck
-grace under pressure [Hemingway]

COURAGE IN PAIN
-fortitude

COURAGEOUS
-plucky

COURT
-tribunal

COVER YOUR EYES
-avert your eyes

COVERED
-veiled

"Light struggled in through small panes of cracked glass and the soot from the smoking fireplace veiled the walls." Kate Grenville, *The Secret River*

COVERED IN
-enveloped in

COVERED WITH
-festooned with
-adorned with

COWARD
-invertebrate
-spineless jellyfish

COWARDLY
-craven

CO-WORKER
-colleague
-people with whom I work

> They are my co-workers.
> They are my colleagues.

CRAFTINESS
-guile

CRAFTSPERSON
-artisan

CRAP
-PR

CRATER
-caldera

CRAZY
-certifiable
-unsound
-out of one's senses

"It's enough to drive one out of one's senses."

CREATE
-fashion
-render
-give rise to
-shape
-draft
-form
-formulate
-inspire
-manifest
-manufacture
-popularize
-devise
-carve out
-evolve
-engender
-conceive
-construct
-forge

CREATOR
-driving force behind
-architect
-author

CREDENTIALS
-bona fides {French, *BONE-uh FIDE-ees*}

CREDIBLE
-well-founded
-well-grounded
-carefully considered

CRIME
-vice
-misdeed
-transgression

CRIME STORY
-police procedural

CRIMINAL BEHAVIOR
-illicit
-nefarious
-felonious

CRINGE
-wince
-blanch

CRIPPLED
-hamstrung

CRITICAL
-pejorative
-captious

CRITICAL HUMOR
-biting
-mordant

CRITICISM (NEGATIVE)
-aspersion
-criticisms leveled at
-has provoked criticism
-the critical reception of

CRITICIZE
-fault
-chastise
-rebuke
-be highly critical of
-deliver a harsh critique of
-come under intense criticism
-be not without detractors

CRITICIZE SEVERELY
-flay
-assail
-lambaste
-lampoon [comically]
-light into

CRITICS
-detractors

> She has a few critics.
> She is not without her detractors.

CROOKED
-awry {a-RYE}

CROSS
-traverse

CROSSED HIS MIND
-entered his mind
-entered his consciousness

CROWD
-throng
-onlookers
-bystanders

CROWDED WITH
-chockablock with

CRUDE
-coarse
-bawdy
-gauche
-base
-boorish

CRUDE POEM
-doggerel {DOG-er-ul}

CRUEL
-inhuman
-draconian
-depraved

CRUEL CRITICISM
-vitriol

CRY
-become emotional
-give way to tears
-fall to weeping
-move to tears
-dissolve in tears

"Her itinerary provided for two weeks in Paris, and she had suffered through one week of it when, like an angel from heaven, an Englishman called Tippy Akenside showed up at her hotel at the very moment when she was about to dissolve in tears and book passage home." Katherine Anne Porter, "Maria Concepción"

-bemoan
-lament
-bray

CULTURAL ATTITUDE
-ethos

CURE ALL
-panacea
-philosopher's stone
-elixir

CURIOUS
-inquisitive

CURRENT
-prevailing
-topical

CURRENTLY (IS CURRENTLY)
-is

CURSE
-a pox on _____
-malediction

CURTAINS
-draperies

"The two big windows were open; their limp and listless draperies showed that there was not the least motion in the stifling humid air of the July afternoon." David Graham Phillips, *Susan Lenox: Her Fall and Rise*

CURVED
-aquiline

CUSTARD
-crème brûlée {French, *krem brue-LAY*, lit. scorched cream}

CUSTODY (IN HER CUSTODY)
-in her charge

CUSTOM
-convention
-wont

CUSTOM MADE ATTIRE
-bespoke attire {beh-SPOKE}

CUSTOMS
-folklore
-mores {MOR-ayz}

CUSTOM OF
-practice of

CUSTOMERS
-patrons
-clientele

CUT (IS CUT)
-cropped

CUT DOWN (A TREE)
-fell a tree

CUT TO PIECES
-eviscerate

CUTTING BACK
-retrenchment

CUTTING EDGE
-vanguard
-avant-garde {French, AH-vahnt-GUARD, lit. vanguard}

"Humboldt was just what everyone had been waiting for. Out in the Midwest I had certainly been waiting eagerly, I can tell you that. An avant-guard writer, the first of a new generation, he was hand-some, fair, large, serious, witty, he was learned. The guy had it all." Saul Bellow, *Humboldt's Gift*

CUT OUT
-excise

CYNICAL
-sardonic
-hard-boiled

Dd

DAILY BASIS [INCORRECT USAGE]
-daily

DAILY BATHS
-daily ablutions [poetic]

DAMAGING
-delivering a setback to

DAMAGING EFFECTS
-ravages of

DAMPEN
-cast a pall over
-suppress

DAMSEL IN DISTRESS
-The Perils of Pauline

DANCING AROUND
-frolicking
-cavorting
-waltzing about

DANGEROUS
-not to be trifled with
-looms as a threat
-fraught with danger
-perilous
-treacherous
-precarious

> That chick is dangerous.
>
> That chick is not to be trifled with.

DANGEROUS SITUATION
-powder keg

DANGEROUS THING
-widow maker

DANGEROUSLY HIGH
-precipitous (steep)

DANGERS
-hazards
-inherent dangers

DARED TO
-hazarded to

"No one had hazarded to discover whether the speech of the known empires, khanates, emirates, hordes and kingdoms was intelligible to him." Michael Chabon, *Gentlemen of the Road*

DARK RED
-crimson
-scarlet
-vermillion

DARK YELLOW (ORANGE YELLOW)
-ocher {*OAK-er*}

DARKNESS
-darkishness [poetic]

DAWN
-at first light

DAYDREAMING
-lost in reverie

DAYDREAMS
-waking dreams
-reveries

DAYS GO BY
-as the days unwind

DEAD ANIMALS
-carrion

Vultures eat roadkill.

Vultures eat carrion.

DEAD PERSON
-departed
-decedent [legal]

DEADENED
-benumbed

"She carried about a dozen living fowls slung over her right shoulder, their feet fastened together. Half of them fell upon the flat of her back, the balance dangled uneasily over her breast. They wriggled their benumbed and swollen legs against her neck, they twisted their stupefied eyes and peered into her face inquiringly. She did not see them or think of them." Katherine Anne Porter, "Maria Concepción"

DEADLOCK
-impasse

DEADLY
-pestilent
-pernicious
-virulent

DEAL WAS ALMOST DONE
-the deal was almost in hand

DEAL WITH
-contend with
-attend to
-address
-negotiate
-endure this
-take in stride
-take stock of
-make a virtue of necessity

DEATH (1)
-the hereafter
-beyond the veil
-the great divide

DEATH (2)
-your demise
-your end

DEATHBLOW
-coup de grâce {French, *koo de GRAHS*}

DEBATE
-vigorous discussion
-verbal volley
-repartee {French, *re-par-TAY*}
-little agreement among
-sword play
-barbed exchanges

DEBATE WITH
-quarrel with

DEBATABLE
-open to dispute
-a matter for debate
-arguable
-still in dispute

DECEIT
-subterfuge
-duplicity
-guile

DECENCY
-propriety
-within the pale of decency

DECENT PERSON
-a mensch {Yiddish, *a mensh*}

"A mensch is the very opposite of a schmuck."

DECEPTION
-subterfuge
-sleight of hand
-artifice
-ruse
-pretext

DECEPTIVE
-illusory

DECIDED NOT TO
-did not think fit to
-thought better of

> I was about to, but then I decided not to.
>
> I was about to, but then I thought better of it.

DECIDED TO
-resolved to
-brought myself to

"Quite inadvertently, I brought myself to tell him about an idea I had now and then entertained. 'My husband has to be someone who can afford a two-bedroom apartment, since Eeyore will be living with us. And I want to live a quiet life there.'" Kenzaburo Oe, *A Quiet Life*

-reached a conclusion
-opted to
-settled on
-determined to
-elected to
-took it into his head to
-ventured to
-took it upon yourself to
-saw fit to
-made the resolve to

"Either we live by accident and die by accident, or we live by plan and die by plan. And on that instant Brother Juniper made the resolve to inquire into the secret lives of those five persons, that moment falling through the air, and to surprise the reason of their taking off." Thornton Wilder, *The Bridge of San Luis Rey*

DECIDED ALREADY
-preordained

DECIDING WHETHER OR NOT TO
-weighing whether or not to

DECISION HAS BEEN MADE
-decision has been taken

DECLARATION
-fiat
-dictum [academic]

DECLARE
-avow
-profess
-aver
-maintain

DECLARE SACRED
-consecrate
-sanctify

DECLINE
-downturn in
-is at an ebb

DECORATED WITH
-adorned with
-garnished
-embellished with

"The wine was from France, though no particular region was mentioned on the label, which was embellished with a solitary darting swallow." Ian McEwan, *Chesil Beach*

DECORATION
-flourish
-embellishment

DECORATIVE DESIGN (OR THEME)
-motif {*moe-TEEF*}

DECREASE (IT WILL DECREASE)
-subside
-abate

DECREASE (TO DECREASE)
-scale back
-draw down

DEDICATED
-deeply anchored in the tradition of
-devout
-dyed-in-the-wool

DEDUCTION
-a corollary

DEEP (DIFFICULT TO COMPREHEND)
-rarified
-abstruse

"It was only toward the middle of the twentieth century that the inhabitants of many European countries came, in general unpleasantly, to the realization that their fate could be influenced directly by the intricate and abstruse books of philosophy." Czeslaw Milosz, *The Captive Mind*

DEEP DOWN
-at heart

DEEP IN THOUGHT
-pensive

DEEP-ROOTED
-inherent
-deep-seated
-innate
-congenital

DEFEAT
-topple
-vanquish
-dispatch

DEFEATED
-finished
-done for
-met his Waterloo

DEFECATION
-evacuation

DEFECTOR
-apostate

DEFEND AGAINST
-turn aside repeated questions
-deflect criticism
-mount a defense
-rally in defense

DEFENDER OF
-apologist for

> I'm not here to defend that; however...
>
> I'm no apologist for that; however...

DEFENSE
-deterrent
-preventative

DEFENSIBLE
-tenable

DEFENSIVE BARRIER
-rampart
-bulwark

DEFINITELY
-profoundly
-you may be sure that
-without doubt
-categorically
-undoubtedly
-by any measure
-unmistakably
-in no measured terms
-in every respect
-decidedly
-invariably
-indeed
-in every respect
-without question

"This is without question the best beer on the menu."

DEGREE
-the full scope of
-the extent to which
-to the extent that we have
-the degree to which
-a measure of
-scale
-the scope and reach of
-the magnitude

-a flavor of

"Unpretending mediocrity is good, and genius is glorious; but a weak flavor of genius in an essentially common person is detestable." Oliver Holmes, *The Autocrat of the Breakfast-Table*

DELAY (TO DELAY)
-defer
-postpone

DELAY (A DELAY)
-a postponement

DELAYING STRATEGY
-dilatory strategy

DELIBERATE
-willful

DELIBERATED
-given careful consideration

DELICATE
-ethereal

DELICIOUS
-delectable
-succulent

DELIGHTFUL
-delicious
-enchanting

DELIVER
-render

DELIVERING OBJECTIVES [INCORRECT USAGE]
-achieving our goals

DEMAND
-call for
-clamor for

DEMANDING
-exacting

DEMONSTRATED
-has shown himself to be

DEMONSTRATES
-underscores
-highlights

DEMOTE
-consign
-relegate

DENIED RIGHTS
-disenfranchised

DENY AN ACCUSATION
-disavow any knowledge of
-gainsay
-disclaim
-flatly reject
-repudiate
-disavow
-forswear

> He denied any knowledge of the affair.
>
> He disavowed any knowledge of the affair.

DENY ONESELF
-abstain from
-deprive oneself of

DEPARTMENT
-proper channels

DEPENDING ON EACH OTHER
-interdependent

DEPENDS ON
-leans on
-contingent upon
-depends to some degree on

DEPICT
-portray
-render

DEPICTION
-a rendering

DEPRESSED
-despondent

DEPRESSION
-malaise {ma-LAYZ}

DEPRIVED OF
-bereft of

DERIVED FROM
-owes its existence to

DESCENDANTS
-lineage
-progeny

DESCRIBE
-characterize
-draw a portrait
-tell of
-articulate
-depict
-portray
-convey
-cast it as
-lay out
-paint

DESCRIPTION
-characterization
-portraiture

DESCRIPTION OF EVENT
-account of
-rendering of

DESERT
-badlands

DESERTED
-desolate

DESERVED
-warranted

DESERVED AND RECEIVED
-commanded

"She was an extremely handsome and well-kept woman of the beauty and social position which had, five years before,

commanded five thousand dollars as the price of endorsing, with photographs, a beauty product which she had never used." Ernest Hemingway, "The Short Happy Life of Francis Macomber"

DESERVES MY
-commands my
-merits a

DESERVING
-worthy of merit

DESIGN
-motif {*moe-TEEF*}

DESIRABLE
-much sought after

DESIRE (A DESIRE)
-an impulse
-a craving
-an appetite for

DESIRE (TO DESIRE)
-covet
-long for
-pine for
-want for
-bay after
-have designs on
-long to

> I've wanted that for quite some time now.
>
> I've had designs on that for quite some time now.

DESIRE FOR TRAVELING
-wanderlust {German, *WOHN-der-lust*}

DESIRES (HER DESIRES)
-wants

DESPICABLE
-beneath contempt

DESSERTS
-entremets {French, *AWN-tre-mays*}

DESTINATION
-at journey's end

DESTINED BY BIRTH
-to the manner borne

DESTINY
-serendipity

DESTROY
-put an end to
-eradicate
-obliterate
-lay waste to
-vanquish
-bring low

DESTRUCTION
-demise
-vastation

"Next fell the stars, tinkling about him like the ornaments of heaven shaken loose. Finally, the black vastation itself came untacked and draped over the entire heap, covering George's confused obliteration." Paul Harding, *Tinkers*

DETAIL
-delicacy

"You could see it in the delicacy of the drawing."

DETAILS
-minutiae
-intricacies
-niceties
-particularities
-nuances
-particulars

DETAIL ORIENTED
-meticulous
-fastidious

DETERIORATE
-calcify

-devolve into
-erode
-lose ground
-degenerate

DETERMINATION
-grit
-resolve
-dogged style

DETERMINE (DECIDE)
-resolve

DETERMINE (FIND OUT)
-establish
-assess

DETERMINED TO
-bent on
-resolute
-resolved to
-intent upon its business

"The man sinks and reappears, flings up his arms and shouts, but no one hears. The ship, heeling in the wind, is intent upon its business, and passengers and crew have lost sight of him, a pinpoint in the immensity of the sea." Victor Hugo, *Les Miserables*

DETESTED BY
-is anathema to

"Racism is anathema to me."

DETESTED THING
-a bête noire {French, betn-WAHR}

DEVELOP
-nurture
-evolve
-cultivate

DEVELOPING
-formative

DEVELOPMENT
-progression
-gestation

DEVICE
-contrivance

DEVIL
-fiend

"I can forgive Alfred Nobel for having invented dynamite, but only a fiend in human form could have invented the Nobel Prize." George Bernard Shaw

DEVIOUS
-aberrant
-wayward

DEVOTED
-ardent
-fervent

DIAGNOSED WITH [INCORRECT USAGE]
-diagnosed as having

DICTATE
-ordain

DID
-did serve to
-did so
-fared well

DID ANY GOOD
-made little impression

DID ANYONE EVER
-did ever anyone

DID GOOD
-expected nothing less

> You did good.
>
> I expected nothing less.

DID IT DIFFERENTLY THIS TIME
-made a departure from his ordinary
 routine

DID IT TO YOURSELF
-it was self-imposed

DID NOT
-failed to
-neglected to
-kept himself free from
-had not
-never did she

DID NOT ANSWER
-made no answer

DID NOT EVEN HAVE TO SPEAK
-had not even to speak

DID NOT EXIST
-was nonexistent

DID NOT EXPECT
-didn't bargain for

DID NOT GET TO SEE
-got no audience with

DID NOT HAVE
-if we had not
-had not a

"He felt as if he hadn't a friend in the world."

DID NOT KNOW HOW
-knew not how [poetic]

DID NOT LIKE IT
-did not think a lot of it
-didn't particularly warm to that

DID NOT MATTER
-mattered not at all
-mattered little
-was of no consequence

DID NOT MEAN TO SAY THAT
-I misspoke

DID NOT MENTION
-made no mention of

DID NOT PARTICIPATE
-took no part in

DID NOT REPLY
-made no reply

DID NOT SEE
-saw not one

DID NOT THINK ANYTHING OF IT
-didn't think anymore of it

DID NOT THINK IT WAS
-had not thought it

DID NOT USE
-made no use of

DID NOT WANT TO
-declined

DIDN'T CARE ABOUT
-cared nothing for

"Robert Cohn was once middle-weight boxing champion of Princeton. Do not think that I am very much impressed by that as a boxing title, but it meant a lot to Cohn. He cared nothing for boxing, in fact he disliked it, but he learned it painfully and thoroughly to counteract the feeling of inferiority and shyness he had felt on being treated as a Jew at Princeton." Ernest Hemingway, *The Sun Also Rises*

DIDN'T DARE TO
-dared not open her eyes

DIDN'T SEE HIM AGAIN FOR A LONG TIME
-didn't see any more of him for a long time

DIDN'T USED TO BE [INCORRECT USAGE]
-never was before now

> He didn't used to be.
>
> He never was before now.

DIE
-perish
-yield to death
-expire

DIET
-regimen

DIFFER WITH
-at odds with

DIFFERENCE
-disparity
-divergence
-distinguished by the fact that
-draw a distinction between
-varying degrees of

> I don't see much of a difference between them.
>
> I wouldn't draw a distinction between the two.

DIFFERENT
-far removed from
-contrasted with
-distinct
-different from that of
-in contrast to that of
-disparate (markedly different)
-stand in marked contrast to
-a far cry from
-departs from
-dissimilar
-runs counter to
-quite changed
-differing
-quite a contrast

DIFFERENT FORM OF
-a variant of
-different order of
-diversities of

DIFFERENT TAKE ON A TEXT
-a variant reading

"Religious texts in particular tend to inspire many variant readings."

-varia lectio {Latin, *WAHR-ee-ah LEK-tee-oh*}

DIFFERENT TASTES
-diversities of taste

DIFFERENT THAN
-different from
-different from that of
-draw a distinction between

DIFFICULT
-daunting
-trying
-strained
-arduous
-onerous
-unenviable
-formidable

DIFFICULT CONDITIONS
-rigors of

DIFFICULT PROBLEM
-a Gordian knot
-arduous problem

DIFFICULT TO UNDERSTAND
-abstruse
-convoluted
-opaque

DIG
-excavate
-unearth
-uncover
-exhume

DIGNIFY
-ennoble {*eh-NO-ble*}

DIGNIFIED
-venerable
-stately

DILIGENT
-assiduous

DILUTE
-adulterate

DIPLOMACY
-discretion
-quiet diplomacy

DIRECT A DEPARTMENT
-oversee

DIRECT (FRANK)
-pointed
-forthright
-forthcoming

DIRECTED BY
-under the direction of

DIRECTION
-trajectory
-precise course of

DIRECTLY
-squarely

DIRECTOR OF
-overseer of

DIRECTOR OF AN OPERA HOUSE
-the intendant

DIRTY (TO DIRTY)
-sully
-defile

DIS
-belittle
-speak harshly of
-disparage
-denigrate
-express contempt for
-throw aspersions at
-deride
-refer to derisively
-debase
-libel

"You cannot libel the dead, I think, you can only console them." Anne Enright, *The Gathering*

DISABLED (OUT OF ACTION)
-hors de combat {French, *or de come-BAH*}

DISADVANTAGE
-drawback

DISAGREE
-take issue with
-dispute
-are sharply divided
-not everyone shared their admiration for
-at odds with
-take exception

I disagree with her strict ways.

I take issue with her draconian ways.

DISAGREEING
-discordant
-at variance with
-run counter to

DISAGREEMENT
-bone of contention
-fundamental divide
-schism
-rift
-discord
-dissention

DISAPPEAR
-melt away
-vanish from the scene
-wane
-ebb
-melt, thaw and dissolve itself [Shakespeare]
-pass from sight
-fade from view

"He calls despairingly, gazing in agony after the receding sail as, ghostlike, it fades from view. A short time ago he was on board, a member of the crew busy on deck with the rest, a living being with his share of air and sunlight. What has become of him now? He slipped and fell, and this is the end." Victor Hugo, *Les Miserables*

DISAPPOINT
-underwhelm

DISAPPOINTED
-despondent
-crestfallen

DISAPPOINTING
-disheartening

DISAPPOINTMENT
-dashed hopes
-false dawns

DISAPPROVAL
-under the frowning eyes of

DISAPPROVED OF
-looked askance at

DISAPPROVING
-reproachful

DISASSOCIATE
-distance oneself

DISASTER
-debacle
-calamity

DISASTROUS
-fateful
-dreadful
-ruinous

DISCONNECTED
-divorced from reality
-untethered

DISCONTINUE
-dispense with

DISCOURAGE
-dissuade
-deter

DISCOURAGED
-disheartened
-downhearted

DISCOURAGING
-dispiriting

DISCOVER
-happen upon
-chance upon
-turn over
-unearth
-uncover

DISCRETIONS
-diplomatic delicacies

DISCUSS CASUALLY
-bandy about

DISEASE
-contagion
-affliction

DISGRACEFUL
-reprehensible
-opprobrious [academic]

DISGRUNTLED
-disaffected

DISGUISED
-in the guise of
-incognito [male]
-incognita [female]
-assumed a disguise

DISGUST
-revulsion
-antipathy

DISGUSTING
-abhorrent
-repugnant
-reprehensible
-vile
-odious

DISHONEST
-less than forthcoming
-disingenuous
-insincere
-mendacious [academic]

DISINTEGRATION
-dissolution of

DISLIKE
-have contempt for
-frown on
-hold in low regard

> They don't like her political views.
>
> Her politics are held in very low regard.

DISMISS
-attach no importance to
-relegate
-consign to
-discount

DISOBEDIENT
-badly behaved
-wayward
-insubordinate

DISPLAY
-bear
-exhibit
-showcase
-radiate
-exude

DISPLAYED
-bore the markings of
-was embellished with

"The wine was from France, though no particular region was mentioned on the label, which was embellished with a solitary darting swallow." Ian McEwan, *Chesil Beach*

DISREGARD
-indifference
-wonton disregard

DISREGARD FOR THE LAW
-nonfeasance

DISREPUTABLE
-unsavory

DISRESPECT
-belittle
-spurn
-rebuff
-discount
-marginalize
-dismiss
-disparage
-make light of
-heap scorn on
-desecrate
-deride
-slight
-speak slightingly of
-depreciate
-trample over the rights of

> He disrespects anyone he disagrees with.
>
> He is quick to belittle anyone with whom he disagrees.

DISRESPECTFUL
-impertinent
-impudent
-insolent
-dismissive
-contemptuous

DISRUPT
-play havoc with

DISTANCE BETWEEN
-gulf between

DISTANT
-seemed far removed from

DISTINGUISH BETWEEN
-draw a distinction

DISTINGUISHED
-illustrious
-inspires respect

DISTORT THE TRUTH
-sugarcoat

DISTRACTING
-diversionary

DISTRACTION
-a red herring

DISTRESSING
-vexing
-disquieting

DISTURBING
-unsettling
-disquieting

DISTRUSTFUL
-baneful
-cynical

DIVERSION
-a red herring

DIVIDE
-dissect

DIVIDED INTO
-comprised of

DIVIDED UP
-apportioned
-asunder [poetic]

DIVISION
-dichotomy
-discord

DIVISIVE
-separative
-polarizing

DO
-carry out
-accomplish
-effect

DO AN ABOUT-FACE
-backpedal
-roll that one back

DO I NEED TO SAY MORE?
-need I say more?

DO IT ANYWAY
-think nothing of doing it

DO IT FOR
-do this for

DO NOT
-be not [poetic]

DO NOT AGREE
-cannot agree with

DO NOT BELIEVE
-find hard to accept

DO NOT BELONG
-out of my element

DO NOT CLAIM TO BE
-make no pretensions to

DO NOT CRY OVER SPILLED MILK
-steel yourself

DO NOT DISAGREE
-make no objection to

DO NOT DISMISS
-there's something to be said for

"As political analysis, there's something to be said for Krugman's Manichean view of the world. But Krugman is also an economist—a very good one—and the economics of what is proposed bear inspection." John Cassidy, The New Yorker, Nov. 4, 2009

DO NOT DO ANY GOOD
-are ineffectual
-are of no use to us

DO NOT DO THAT
-do not think of such a thing
-you can dispense with the
-what do you hope to accomplish by

DO NOT EVEN HAVE
-have not even

DO NOT FEAR
-fear not [poetic]

"Fear not the tyrant; fear the tyrant's wake."

DO NOT FORGET
-let it not be forgotten

DO NOT GET ALONG
-do not get on

DO NOT GIVE UP HOPE
-do not despair

DO NOT GO TOGETHER
-are incompatible

DO NOT HAVE
-have not
-haven't many

DO NOT KEEP ME FROM
-do not deprive me of

DO NOT KNOW
-cannot say
-could not say
-know little of these matters myself
-know not [poetic]

DO NOT LIKE
-take a dim view of
-take no pleasure in
-don't care for
-won't hear it spoken of
-have a particular dislike for
-hold in low regard

DO NOT LIKE TO HAVE TO
-take no pleasure in

> I don't like doing it.
>
> I take no pleasure in it.

DO NOT NEED
-have no need of such
-have no use for

DO NOT NEED TO
-need not
-needn't

DO NOT SAY ANYTHING
-say no more

DO NOT SAY NO
-do not refuse me [humorous]

DO NOT UNDERSTAND
-the distinction is lost on
-the point escapes me

DO NOT WANT THAT
-want nothing of the sort

DO NOT WANT TO
-do not care to
-would rather not
-if it's all the same to you
-disinclined to
-averse to
-loath to

DO NOT WORRY ABOUT IT
-think nothing of it
-don't trouble yourself
-it needn't concern you
-don't give it another thought
-it's no matter

DO THAT
-do so

DO THAT TO SOMEONE
-subject someone to that

DO THE BEST YOU CAN
-do your utmost

DO THE SAME
-do likewise

DO THIS
-do so

DO WE HAVE TIME TO?
-have we time to?

DO WHAT THEY WANT
-have their own will
-have a will all their own

DO WHATEVER IT TAKES
-are expedient

DO WITHOUT
-forswear
-forgo

DO YOU HAVE A MINUTE
-can you spare a moment

DO YOU LIKE
-how does it sit with you
-is it to your liking

DO YOU THINK
-do you suppose

DO YOUR BEST
-make every effort to

DOABLE
-feasible
-viable

DODGE
-circumvent

DODGE THE QUESTION
-prevaricate

DOCUMENTARY STYLE
-cinéma vérité {French, *SIN-em-uh
veer-i-TAY*}

DOCUMENTS (PROVES)
-gives proof
-evidences

DOES THAT
-indulges in

**DOES IT ALWAYS HAVE TO BE
THAT WAY**
-must it always be

DOES NOT
-fails to

DOES NOT BELONG
-is out of keeping with
-is inconsistent with
-is incongruous

DOES NOT DRINK ALCOHOL
-she is a self-described teetotaler

DOES NOT JIVE
-does not bear close examination
-does not bear inspection
-does not bear scrutiny

DOES NOT LACK MOTIVATION
-does not lack for motivation

DOES NOT LOOK GOOD ON YOU
-does not become you

DOES NOT MATTER
-it matters not [poetic]

*"We shall be sentenced to ten years in
the Palace of Corrective Detention if it be
discovered. But this matters not. It matters only that the light is precious and we
should not waste it to write when we need
it for that work which is our crime. Nothing
matters save the work, our secret, our evil,
our precious work."* Ayn Rand, *Anthem*
{Ayn rhymes with *vine*}

-extraneous
-neither here nor there
-of little consequence
-a moot point

DOES NOT OFFEND YOU
-I hope it gives no offense

DOES NOT RESENT
-is ungrudging
-does not begrudge her success

DOES NOT TOLERATE
- is not one to suffer fools gladly

She does not tolerate nine-to-
five types.

She is not one to suffer fools
gladly.

DOES WITHOUT
-forgoes

"His curiosity is boundless but also disciplined, and he forgoes explanation in favor of a visual version of what anthropologists call thick description." A. O. Scott, *New York Times*, Nov. 4, 2009

DOESN'T CARE
-apathetic
-indifferent to
-nonchalant

DOING
-engaged in
-indulging in

DOING A NUMBER ON
-wreaking havoc on

DOING EVERYTHING SHE COULD
-doing her utmost

DOING HIS THING
-he's out and about

DOING IT DIFFERENTLY
-departing from his regular routine

DOING THIS TO YOU
-inflicting this upon you

DOMINANCY
-primacy

DOMINANT MALE
-alpha male

DOMINATE
-impose
-hold sway

DOMINATE A DEBATE
-hold the stage

DOMINATING (IN AN UNSEEMLY WAY)
-_____uber alles {German, *oo-bur AL-es*, lit. above all}

"'Apple Uber Alles' would be a good title for an article on how this giant computer company has trouble playing with others."

DOMINEERING
-autocratic
-imperious

DONE
-undertaken

DONE BECAUSE
-was prompted in part by

DONE OPENLY
-overt

DONE QUICKLY JUST FOR THE MONEY
-a potboiler

DONE THAT
-done such a thing
-done anything of the sort

DON'T BE AFRAID
-you need not be afraid

DON'T BELONG
-have no place

"The world is what it is; men who are nothing, who allow themselves to become nothing, have no place in it." V. S. Naipaul, *A Bend in the River*

DON'T DO THAT (THEY DON'T DO THAT)
-are not in the business of

DON'T EVER SAY
-never let it be said

DON'T GIVE ENOUGH
-give insufficient

"Man always tends to avoid physical contact with anything strange. In the dark, the fear of an unexpected touch can mount to panic. Even clothes give insufficient security; it is easy to tear them and pierce through to the naked, smooth, defenseless flesh of the victim." Elias Canetti, *Crowds and Power*

DON'T HAVE
-are without

DON'T HAVE ONE
-have not one

DON'T HAVE TO PUT UP WITH
-I am not bound to put up with

DON'T KNOW ANYTHING ABOUT
-you know nothing of

> You don't know anything about this country.
>
> You know nothing of this country.

DON'T LET THE BASTARDS GET YOU DOWN
-illegitinati non carborundum {mock Latin, *il-eh-JIT-uh-my non car-bor-UN-dum*}

DON'T LOOK LIKE
-bear little resemblance to

DON'T MENTION IT
-think nothing of it

DON'T PAY ANY ATTENTION TO
-take no notice of

> I didn't pay any attention to it.
>
> I took little notice of it.

DON'T YOU THINK IT WOULD
-do you not think it would

DON'T WORRY ABOUT IT
-don't give the matter another thought

DOOMED
-fated

"We'll choke on our vomit, and that will be the end, we were fated to pretend."

Andrew VanWyngarden and Ben Goldwasser, "Time to Pretend"

DOUBLE MEANING
-double entendre {French *DOO-blu ahn-TAHN-druh*}
-innuendo

DOUBT
-call into question

DOUBTFUL
-dubious
-raising doubts
-equivocal

DOUBTFUL STORIES
-apocryphal tales

DOUBTING
-incredulous

DOUBTS
-misgivings
-reservations

DOUGHY (UNDERCOOKED)
-sodden

DOWN IN THE DUMPS
-in a malaise

DOWN TO EARTH
-has few pretensions

DOWNER
-depressant

DOWNGRADE
-consign
-relegate

DOWNSIZING [CORPORATE EUPHEMISM]
-laying off

DRAFTED
-conscripted

"They conscripted me for the Russo-Japanese War but it was over before I got

in. *Thank God."* Jonathan Safran Foer, *The Fixer*

DRAIN A POND
-draw a pond

DRAMATIC
-melodramatic
-affected
-mannered

DRAMATICALLY
-with a flourish

DRAW A BOUNDARY
-demarcate

DRAW OUT
-elicit

DRAWING (A DRAWING)
-a rendering

DREAM (A FANCIFUL THOUGHT)
-a conceit

DREAM ON
-isn't it pretty to think so
  [Hemingway]

DREAMED OF
-harbored the ambition

"He possessed an incorrect but fervent understanding of the workings of television, atom power, and antigravity, and harbored the ambition—one of a thousand—of ending his days on the warm sunny beaches of the Great Polar Ocean of Venus." Michael Chabon, *The Amazing Adventures of Kavalier & Clay*

DREAM-LIKE
-chimerical
-surreal

DREAM-LIKE IMAGES
-phantasmagoria

DRESS CODES
-sartorial codes

DRESS HERSELF IN
-array herself in
-adorn herself in

DRESSED IN
-in the dress of
-attired in
-fitted out with

"…and above it there hung a picture that he had recently cut out of an illustrated magazine and housed in a nice, gilded frame. It showed a lady fitted out with a fur hat and fur boa who sat upright, raising a heavy fur muff that covered the whole of her lower arm towards the viewer." Franz Kafka, *Metamorphosis*

DRESSED UP
-gussied up

"Many seaside towns make much of their location. Their shops are gussied up with nautical décor—rigging, buoys, mounted fish—and their restaurants often have the word 'captain' in the name." Sarah Maslin Nir, *New York Times*, Oct. 29, 2009

DRESSED UP AS
-guised as

DRIED OUT
-parched

DRIFTERS
-transients

DRINK
-soak up

DRINK LIQUOR
-commune with the spirits
-drink one's fill

DRINKABLE
-potable

DRIVE OFF
-dispel

DRIVE OUT
-oust

-expel
-exorcise

"A spectre is haunting Europe—the spectre of Communism. All the Powers of old Europe have entered into a holy alliance to exorcise this spectre: Pope and Czar, Metternich and Guizot, French Radicals and German police-spies." Karl Marx, The Communist Manifesto

DRIVES THEM CRAZY
-gives them fits

DRIVE THROUGH THE CURVE
-negotiate the curve

DRIVING FORCE
-the impetus for

DROWNED
-was drowned

"We are a family that has always been close in spirit. Our father was drowned in a sailing accident when we were young, and our mother has always stressed the fact that our familial relationships have a kind of permanence that we will never meet with again." John Cheever, The Stories of John Cheever

DRUGS
-contraband

DRUNK
-heady
-intoxicated

DRUNKENNESS
-insobriety

DRY
-arid

DRY LAND
-terra firma

DUE TO
-by dint of
-owing to

DUG
-bore

DULL
-pedestrian
-trite
-insipid
-vapid
-banal
-lackluster
-pallid
-prosaic {*pro-ZAY-ick*}

DULL LANGUAGE
-prosy

DULLED
-lobotomized

DUMB
-of questionable intellect
-benighted
-obtuse
-inane
-bovine
-none-too-bright
-unenlightened

> Her reading tastes could be described as pretty dumb.
>
> Her reading tastes could be described as fairly benighted.

DUMB IDEA
-ill-advised
-ill-conceived
-lacks the intellectual sophistication of

DUMB MOVE
-faux pas {French, *foe PAH*}
-gaff
-howler

DUMBED-DOWN
-lobotomized

DURING
-throughout
-over the course of
-in the span of
-in the midst of
-in the space of

DUTIES OF
-functions of

DUTIFUL
-resolute in the performance of her
  duty

DYING TO
-spoiling for
-can scarcely contain her

Ee

EACH OTHER
-among themselves
-one another
-each to each

EAGER
-keen to
-avid for

EAGER AND EXCITED
-aflame with

EAGER TO PLEASE
-complaisant (not to be confused with
  complacent)
-showing alacrity
-servile [derogatory]
-obsequious [derogatory]

EAGERLY
-with relish

EAGERNESS
-alacrity

EARLIEST EXAMPLES OF
-precedents of

EARLY
-formative
-preliminary
-nascent
-early on
-premature (too early)

EARLY DEVELOPMENT
-gestation

"I consider the process of gestation just as important as when you're actually sitting down putting words to the paper." Wole Soyinka

EARLY EXAMPLE OF
-forerunner of
-precedent

EARLIER PEOPLE
-predecessors

EARNED
-garnered

EARNING A SPOT
-cementing its position as

EARTH
-spaceship earth
-this goodly frame, the earth
  [Shakespeare]

EASE YOUR FEARS
-allay
-assuage {a-SWAYZH}

EASIER
-might have made easier going of this

EASILY
-with little opposition
-readily
-with ease
-without difficulty
-with facile movements
-sail through
-it's nothing for you to

> You could easily look the
> other way.
>
> It is nothing for you to look the
> other way.

EASILY AVAILABLE
-readily available

EASILY GOTTEN
-easily had
-there for the taking

EASILY IRRITATED
-fractious

EASING OF DIPLOMATIC TENSION
-détente {French, *day-TAWNT*}

EASY
-a very simple matter to
-facile victory

EASY PICKINGS
-ripe for the taking
-low hanging fruit

EAT
-dine
-feast
-break bread
-dispatch
-dispose of
-have one's fill
-devour
-partake
-let's take breakfast
-take some lunch
-polish off

EATS
-feeds on
-dines on

ECONOMICS
-the dismal science

ECSTASY
-elation

EDGES
-contours

EDUCATED (THE EDUCATED)
-the learned
-the intelligencia
-the clerisy {*CLAIR-uh-see*}
-the literati

EFFECTIVE
-effectual
-of use
-profitable

EFFECTIVENESS
-potency
-the efficacy of [academic]

EFFECTS
-implications
-repercussions
-reverberations
-consequences

EFFICIENCY
-with rare economy

EFFORT
-campaign
-bid
-expenditure of energy

EGGING ON
-a provocation

EGO
-to feed their vanity
-the care and feeding of her vanity

EGYPTIAN KINGS
-Ptolemies {*TALL-u-mees*} (323–30
 BCE)

EITHER OR
-it's binary

EITHER WAY
-in any case

ELATED
-could scarcely contain their delight

ELBOWING
-jostling

"Nightfall assembled them, as it did the stars. With nothing in common but their destitution, they mustered to sleep together in the Porch of Our Lord, cursing, insulting and jostling each other, picking quarrels with old enemies, or throwing earth and rubbish, even rolling on the ground and spitting and biting with rage." Miguel Angel Asturias, *The President*

ELEGANT
-soigné {French, *swan-YAY*}

ELEGANTLY EXPRESSED
-well turned

ELEPHANT LIKE (LUMBERING)
-elephantine {*el-la-FAN-teen*}

ELEVATED REPUTATION (BOASTFUL)
-vaunted reputation

"My two days at the Canadian branch of the Paris Cooking School, its only outpost in North America, provided an opportunity to sample the teaching techniques that earned Cordon Bleu its vaunted reputation. It also taught me the highs and, sadly, the lows that the professional kitchen can provoke." Micheline Maynard, *New York Times*, Nov. 1, 2009

ELSEWHERE
-in other quarters

ELUSIVE
-elusory

EMBARRASSED BY
-abashed by

EMBARRASSING
-compromising

EMBARRASSING SITUATION
-an imbroglio {*im-BROLE-yoh*}
-a contretemps {French, *KAHN-tru-taw*}

EMBARRASSMENT
-chagrin

EMBASSY
-ministry
-consulate

"A nation may have many consulates in a foreign country, but only one embassy."

EMBODIMENT
-personification
-incarnation
-avatar

EMBRACING
-holding her in his embrace

EMBROIDERED WITH
-inwrought with

EMERGE
-come to the fore

EMERGING
-emergent

EMOTION
-sentiment
-an outpouring of emotion

EMOTIONAL
-moving
-visceral
-emotive

EMOTIONAL APPEAL
-pathos {Greek, *PAY-thos*}

EMOTIONAL RELEASE
-catharsis

EMOTIONLESS
-impassive
-stoic

EMPHASIZE
-accentuate

-drive home
-underscore

"*Mr. Wilson underscores the point by dividing his characters with scrims and pools of light that seem to confine them to inescapably separate orbits.*" Ben Brantley, *New York Times*, Nov. 6, 2009

EMPHASIZED
-stressed the fact that

"*We are a family that has always been close in spirit. Our father was drowned in a sailing accident when we were young, and our mother has always stressed the fact that our familial relationships have a kind of permanence that we will never meet with again.*" John Cheever, *The Stories of John Cheever*

EMPLOY
-put to the task of
-commission
-in the pay of

EMPTY
-vacuous
-vacant

"*But true mercy only arrived at night, a breeze chilled by the vacant desert, moistened by the humming sea, a reluctant guest silently passing through the empty streets, vague about how far it was allowed to roam in this realm of the absolute star.*" Hisham Matar, *In the Country of Men*

EMPTY COMPLIMENTS
-flummery

EMPTY THE ____ OUT OF THE ____
-empty the ____ of ____

> Empty the soil out of the pot.
>
> Empty the pot of soil.

ENABLES
-clears the way for

ENCOUNTERED (EXPERIENCED)
-witnessed

"*This period also witnessed the emergence of the Nazi Party.*"

ENCOURAGE
-invite
-welcome
-embrace
-embolden
-exhort
-stoke
-is conducive to [academic]
-perpetuate
-rouse
-enjoin
-oblige

END
-put an end to

END JUSTIFIES THE MEANS
-where means are matched with ends

END OF
-downfall
-marked the end of

END OF THE CENTURY
-fin de siècle {French, *fahn duh SYEK-luh*}

"*Fashion is currently obsessed with a redux of the new wave '80s, which, for the most part, has also been sanitized for your re-consumption. The sleazy, over-stimulated parts were left on the old side of the fin de siècle, and only the off-shoulder Tiffany tops and 'Flashdance' leggings were welcomed back to the future.*" Cintra Wilson, *New York Times*, Nov. 3, 2009

END OF THE WORLD
-the apocalypse
-end of days

END RESULT (OF A STORY)
-denouement {French,
 day-new-MAHN}

"Well, the denouement is, they lived happily ever after."

ENDANGER
-imperil the safety of
-compromise

ENDED
-was exhausted
-brought to a close

ENDING
-putting a close to

ENDLESS
-interminable
-enduring
-perennial
-without end
-unfailing

"Because he takes pleasure in her, because his pleasure is unfailing, an affection has grown up in him for her." J.M. Coetzee, *Disgrace*

ENEMY
-foe
-nemesis
-detractors
-no friend to

ENERGETIC
-industrious
-kinetic

"She was already a recognized writer of kinetic, tough-corded prose, both beguiling and dangerous. Her manner was to take the reader by surprise. In the middle of a flattened rambling paragraph, deceived by warm stretches of reflection, you came upon hard cartilage." Carol Shields, *Unless*

ENERGIZE
-help bolster
-enliven

ENERGY
-vigor
-verve
-gusto
-élan {ay-LAHN}

ENERGY EXPLORATION [ORWELLIAN]
-oil drilling

ENFORCE
-impose

ENGAGE IN
-indulge in

ENGROSSED IN
-glued to
-preoccupied
-immersed his whole being in

ENJOY
-indulge in
-gobble up
-enjoy the fruits of
-enjoy the blessings of
-revel in
-relish
-luxuriate
-take great delight in

> The bees enjoyed taking nectar from the flowers.
>
> The bees took great delight in depriving the flowers of their fruit.

ENJOYING
-indulging oneself

ENOUGH
-sufficiency of
-sufficient

ENOUGH WITH THE
-let's dispense with the
-enough said

ENSLAVE
-subjugate

"They have no iron, their spears are made of cane…They would make fine servants… With fifty men we could subjugate them all and make them do whatever we want."
Christopher Columbus

ENTERTAIN
-hold captive
-fend off the boredom

ENTHUSIASM
-infectious enthusiasm
-contagious enthusiasm
-verve
-élan {French, *ay-LAHN*}

ENTHUSIAST
-disciple
-fancier of
-connoisseur
-aficionado

ENTHUSIASTIC
-spirited
-ardent
-fervent

ENTRANCE
-vestibule

ENTRENCHED POWER IN WASHINGTON
-the iron triangle

"…the iron triangle, that incestuous relationship which exists between Congress, government agencies, and lobbyists."

ENVIRONMENT
-hotbed
-habitat
-landscape
-in your element
-a medium

ENVY
-begrudge

> I don't envy her success.
> I don't begrudge her success.

EQUAL IN CLASS
-egalitarian

EQUAL TO
-on a par with
-commensurate with [academic]
-in parity with
-comparable with

EQUALLY AS [INCORRECT USAGE]
-equally

EQUALS
-constitutes
-rivals

EQUIVALENT TO
-tantamount to

ERASE
-efface

ERECT PENIS [ART WORLD]
-ithyphallic

"Ithyphallic dancers adorn the fresco."

ERODE
-abrade

ERROR FREE
-inerrant {*in-AIR-unt*}

ESCAPE (AN ESCAPE)
-exodus
-hegira {*hi-JIE-ruh*}

ESCAPE FROM
-elude
-steal away
-affect one's escape
-abscond

ESCAPED (HAS ESCAPED)
-is at large
-is a fugitive

ESCORT
-see your guest out
-conduct [formal]

ESOTERIC
-rarified

ESPECIALLY
-most strikingly
-particularly
-not the least of which is
-and above all

"What is reported of men, whether it be true or false, may play as large a part in their lives, and above all in their destiny, as the things they do." Victor Hugo, *Les Miserables*

ESPIONAGE
-the great game

ESSENCE OF
-fabric of
-alpha and omega
-epitome of

ESSENTIAL
-intrinsic
-invaluable
-indispensable
-integral
-a lynchpin

ESSENTIAL THING
-it's a sine qua non {Latin, *SIN-ih kwah NON*}

ESTABLISHED (ARE ESTABLISHED)
-are now well in place
-ingrained
-entrenched
-enshrined
-ensconced
-installed
-long standing
-deeply rooted

ESTABLISHED CUSTOMS
-use and wont

"People naturally tend to follow the use and wont of the culture in which they live."

ESTABLISHMENT
-the existing order

ESTIMATE
-appraise
-judge

"The stranger's eyes were green, his hair burnt to a straw colour. I judged he was sixty years of age." J.M. Coetzee, *Foe*

ETCETERA
-and so forth
-and what have you
-and the like
-and such

EUPHEMISM
-genteelism

EUPHORIA
-rapture
-elation

EVALUATE
-appraise
-assess

EVEN ____ER (AS IN, EVEN POORER)
-____er still

"There was poverty in every province in the country, and in every face. But Lola's province, whether you saw it in her cheekbones or around her mouth or smack in the middle of her eyes, was perhaps poorer still. More land than landscape." Herta Müller, *The Land of Green Plumbs*

EVEN IF IT WAS
-however

"The outfit was acceptable by any theological and geometrical standards, however abstruse, and suggested a rich

inner life." John Kennedy Toole, *A Confederacy of Dunces*

EVEN MORE
-still more
-all the more
-to a greater extent

EVEN SO
-be that as it may

> Even so, I cannot support this measure.
>
> Be that as it may, I cannot support this measure.

EVEN THOUGH
-that being said
-suffice to say
-____ as she is
-however painful
-and yet
-nevertheless
-albeit

EVENING PRAYERS
-vespers

EVENT
-a moment
-the event unfolded amid

EVENTUALLY
-ultimately
-in due course
-by and by

"He reached out and with the back of his hand touched my arm. He is trying my flesh, I thought. But by and by my breathing slowed and I grew calmer." J. M. Coetzee, *Foe*

EVER
-ever and at any time

"We are alone here under the earth. It is a fearful word, alone. The laws say that none among men may be alone, ever and at any time, for this is the great transgression and the root of all evil."* Ayn Rand, *Anthem*

EVER ____
-famously ____

EVER PRESENT
-enduring
-prevailing

EVERY MAN FOR HIMSELF
-it's war of all against all [Thomas Hobbes]

EVERY NOW AND THEN
-now and again
-on occasion
-by and by
-intermittently
-at times
-from time to time
-upon occasion

"He taught me also to put my own hand to business upon occasion, to endure hardship and fatigues, and to throw the necessities of nature into a little compass; that I ought not to meddle in other people's business, nor be easy in giving credit to informers." Marcus Aurelius, *Meditations*

EVERY POSSIBILITY
-every contingency

EVERY TIME
-at every turn

EVERYBODY KNOWS
-universally acknowledged

"It is a truth universally acknowledged, that a single man in possession of a good fortune, must be in want of a wife." Jane Austen, *Pride and Prejudice*

EVERYDAY
-customary
-quotidian [academic]
-commonplace
-workaday

-prosaic {pro-ZAY-ick}

EVERYDAY LANGUAGE
-colloquial

EVERYDAY-LIFE PAINTING
-a genre painting {ZHAWN-ruh}

EVERYONE
-all without exception
-the whole cry of voices

EVERYTHING THAT IS GOOD
-all that is good

EVERYTHING IS OK
-God's in heaven; all's right with the
 world. [Robert Browning]

EVERYWHERE
-common to
-pervasive
-near and far
-ubiquitous
-in all quarters
-the world over
-in all creation
-in every corner of
-widespread
-prevalent

EVERYWHERE ELSE
-elsewhere

EVIDENCE
-a clear source of evidence for this is
-there is little to suggest that
-all trace of evidence
-a thread of evidence

EVIDENT
-conspicuous
-in evidence

EVIDENTLY
-presumably
-it would seem so
-seemingly
-is said to be
-reportedly

-purportedly
-every reason to believe that
-so it was held
-is known to have

EVIL
-unhallowed
-unholy
-depraved
-heinous

EVILNESS
-depravity
-depraved indifference
-malevolence
-malice
-moral turpitude

EVOLVING
-was being evolved

EXACT
-scrupulous

EXACT OPPOSITE
-on the contrary
-the very opposite of

EXACT WORDS
-ipsissima verba {Latin, ip-SIS- ih-muh
  VER-buh}
-verbatim {Latin, ver-BAY-tim}
-word for word

EXACTLY
-necessarily
-as such

EXACTLY OPPOSITE
-diametrical
-diametrically opposed

EXAGGERATE
-embellish
-lay it on thick
-aggrandize

> Do not exaggerate the story.
>
> Do not embellish the story.

EXAGGERATED
-a caricature of
-over-the-top

EXAGGERATED MANNER
-self-dramatizing

EXAGGERATED PRAISE
-puffery

EXAGGERATION
-hyperbole {Greek, *high-PER-bu-lee*}

EXAMINATION
-scrutiny
-careful screening of
-consideration of

EXAMINE
-appraise
-plumb
-take inventory of
-probe
-scrutinize

"I'm talking about the girl that the guards took away in chains…Yes, the one they say casts spells and enchantments…has her own pitchforks…sticks pins into puppets…strangles cats and scrutinizes their intestines to foretell the future…" Dario Fo, *Johan Padan and the Discovery of the America*

EXAMINE THEIR DIFFERENCES
-distinguish their subtler differences

EXAMPLE OF
-in this treatment of
-this exemplar is
-in this case study in
-an instance of
-an exercise in
-a display of

-it exemplifies

EXCEED
-go far beyond
-surpass
-outpace

EXCELLENT
-brilliant
-stellar
-superb

EXCEPT FOR
-apart from
-exclusive of
-save for

"The room is about thirty foot square, with whitewashed walls, bare save for a calendar, a picture of a race-horse, and a family tree in a gilded frame." Upton Sinclair, *The Jungle*

-but for
-excepting

"We are alone, absolutely alone on this chance planet; and, amid all the forms of life that surround us, not one, excepting the dog, has made an alliance with us." Maurice Maeterlinck

EXCEPT TO
-save to

EXCEPTION
-aberration

EXCESSIVE AMOUNT
-surfeit {SUR-fit}

EXCESSIVE POLITENESS
-an Alphonse and Gaston routine

EXCESSIVELY
-unduly

EXCESSIVELY CONCERNED WITH MINOR DETAILS
-pedantic

EXCITE
-titillate
-work them up

EXCITED
-fevered
-afire over

EXCITEMENT
-with great fanfare
-hoopla

EXCITING
-intoxicating
-rousing
-stirring
-an excitement

"They were hungry for breakfast which they ate at the café, ordering brioche and café au lait and eggs, and the type of preserve that they chose and the manner in which the eggs were to be cooked was an excitement."
Ernest Hemingway, *Garden of Eden*

EXCLUDE
-ostracize

EXCUSABLE
-pardonable
-venial {VEEN-ee-ul}

EXCUSE (DON'T EXCUSE THAT BEHAVIOR)
-make allowances for
-apologize for

EXCUSE FOR
-a pretext for

"Her being seemed composed of shadow, with too little substance for it to possess sex. It was a shred of matter harboring a light, with large eyes that were always cast down; a pretext for a soul to linger on earth."
Victor Hugo, *Les Miserables*

EXCUSE ME
-pardon me
-if I may
-beg your pardon

EXECUTE
-carry out
-undertake

EXHAUSTED
-haggard
-spent

EXILED
-in the wilderness

EXIST
-occur
-are widespread
-are prevalent
-are most in evidence
-lie in
-abound
-prevail

EXISTENCE OF
-presence of
-undercurrent of
-prevalence of

EXISTING
-in existence

EXISTING EVERYWHERE
-ubiquitous

EXISTS
-prevails
-is in evidence in a number of
-takes the form of
-stands as a

EXOTIC THINGS
-exotica

EXPECT
-rely upon

EXPECTED
-not surprising
-to be expected

EXPECTING
-expectant of [academic]

EXPENSES
-expenditures

EXPENSIVE
-far beyond her means
-do not come cheap

EXPENSIVE CLOTHES
-finery

EXPERIENCE
-undergo
-are subject to
-sustain

EXPERIENCE (A TOUGH EXPERIENCE)
-an ordeal

EXPERIENCED
-a veteran_____
-a long-time _____
-a seasoned_____
-schooled in the art of_____
-a_____ maven
-practiced in the art of_____

EXPERT
-something of an authority on

I am an expert on imported beers.

I am something of an authority on imported beers.

EXPLAIN THIS
-shed some light on
-expound on
-attribute that to
-give an account of
-account for
-elucidate
-illuminate

EXPLAINABLE
-explicable

"Man is explicable by nothing less than all his history. Without hurry, without rest, the human spirit goes forth from the beginning to embody every faculty, every thought, every emotion, which belongs to it, in appropriate events." Ralph Waldo Emerson, "Essay on History"

EXPLORE
-plumb the depths of

EXPOSE
-bring out

"I want to write, but more than that, I want to bring out all kinds of things that lie buried deep in my heart." Anne Frank, *Anne Frank: Diary of a Young Girl*

-lay bare

"The disclosure that the United States ambassador in Kabul has expressed written opposition to deploying more American troops to Afghanistan lays bare the fierce debate within the Obama administration over the direction of the war, even after weeks of deliberations and with the president on the verge of a decision." Mark Landler and Jeff Zeleny, *New York Times*, Nov. 12, 2009

EXPOSE A SCANDAL
-rake up a scandal

EXPOSE AS FALSE
-debunk
-discredit

EXPOSE HIMSELF AS A
-show himself to be a

"He was dressed in the same sort of safari clothes that Wilson wore except that his were new, he was thirty-five years old, kept himself very fit, was good at court games, had a number of big game fishing records, and had just shown himself, very publicly, to be a coward." Ernest Hemingway, "The Short Happy Life of Francis Macomber."

> He has exposed himself as someone we can't trust.
>
> He has shown himself to be unworthy of our trust and support.

EXPRESS
-give voice to

EXPRESS IN A CERTAIN WAY
-couch what you say in

EXPRESSED
-enunciated in

EXPRESSES
-conveys
-captures
-conveys a sense of
-gives the general impression of

EXPRESSION OF
-token of

EXTEND
-prolong
-protract

EXTENDED METAPHOR
-conceit

EXTENSIVE
-vast
-wholesale
-wide range of
-whole range of

EXTRAORDINARY
-transcendent

EXTREME
-the boggier reaches of
-severe
-ungodly

EXTREMELY
-fearfully
-exceedingly
-most
-terribly
-to an extreme

EXTREMELY WASTEFUL
-profligate

EXTREMIST
-zealot
-ideologue

EYE CATCHING
-arresting

"Perhaps the most arresting piece is 'Nomade,' by the Spanish sculptor Jaume Plensa, a 27-foot-tall hollow human form made of a latticework of white steel letters, which looms over Locust Street, the one-way eastbound thoroughfare through Des Moines's compact business district." Betsy Rubiner, New York Times, Oct. 30, 2009

EYE SORES
-grotesqueries

"The mist took pity on the fretted structures of earlier generations: the Post Office with its shingle-tortured mansard, the red brick minarets of hulking old homes, factories with stingy and sooted windows, wooden tenements colored like mud. The city was full of such grotesqueries, but the clean towers were thrusting them from the business center, and on the farther hills were shining new houses, homes—they seemed—for laughter and tranquility." Sinclair Lewis, *Babbitt*

EYE-OPENING
-edifying

Ff

FACE
-come to grips with
-confront

FACIAL EXPRESSION
-visage
-countenance
-the smile which played continually
  about her face
-he wore a look of
-her face expressed _____
-with faces that seemed to say
-her face assumed the expression it
  had worn
-the smile was instantly reflected on
-her face was full of
-a smile on her lips

FACTOR
-determinant [academic]

FACTS
-considerations
-circumstances
-gleanings
-credible information
-unassailable truths
-verities
-gospel
-holy writ
-factors
-realities

FADDISH
-modish

FADE
-wane

FADE AWAY
-evanesce
-turn to dust

FADING
-waning
-evanescent
-failing

"Mr. Hacket turned the corner and saw, in the failing light, at some little distance, his seat. It seemed to be occupied." Samuel Beckett, *Watt*

FAIL
-buckle under the strain of
-have a bad time of it

FAILED
-has not enjoyed any great measure of
  success
-found wanting
-fared poorly
-fell short of
-come up dry
-success has been elusive
-success remains out of reach
-his efforts were not entirely successful

> They have failed
>
> They have enjoyed little success.

FAILURE
-abject failure
-fiasco
-debacle

FAINT
-swoon

FAIR
-equitable

FAKE (IMITATION)
-pseudo
-so-called
-ersatz {German, *AIR-sahts*}
-faux {French, *foe*, lit. false}

"A good 96 percent of the Penney's inventory is made of polyester. The few clothing items that are made of cotton make a sincere point of being cotton and tell you earnestly about their 100-percent cottonness with faux-hand-scribbled labels so obviously on the green bandwagon they practically spit pine cones." Cintra Wilson, *New York Times*, Aug. 13, 2009

-contrived
-highly mannered

FAKE (TO FAKE)
-to feign

FAKE ATTACK
-feint

FAKE DIAMOND
-ersatz diamond {German, *AIR-sahts*}

FAKING AN ILLNESS
-malingering

FALL
-descent

FALL APART
-fall into ruin
-fragment

FALL BACK INTO
-lapse into

FALL GUY
-left to twist slowly in the wind

FALL INTO THE HANDS OF
-fall into their clutches

"When we walked across our little square together a few days ago, Daddy began to talk of us going into hiding. I asked him why on earth was he beginning to talk of that already. 'Yes, Anne,' he said, 'you know that we have been taking food, clothes, furniture to other people for more than a year now. We don't want our belongings to be seized by the Germans, but we certainly don't want to fall into their clutches ourselves.'" Anne Frank, *Anne Frank: The Diary of a Young Girl*

FALLOUT
-serious implications
-consequences

FALSE
-dubious
-suspect
-fallacious
-groundless
-patently false

-spurious
-proved baseless
-run counter to
-faux {French, *foe*, lit. false}

FALSE APPEARANCE
-façade {*fuh-SAHD*}

FAME
-celebrity
-renown
-the statusphere [Tom Wolfe]

FAMILIAR WITH
-acquainted with
-hauntingly familiar
-conversant

FAMILIARIZED HERSELF WITH
-made herself familiar with
-acquainted herself with

> You need to get to know the facts related to the merger.
>
> You need to acquaint yourself with the facts surrounding the merger.

FAMILIES WITH STEPCHILDREN
-blended families

FAMILY HISTORY
-descent
-lineage
-parentage

FAMILY LIFE
-domestic life

FAMILY MEMBER
-relation

FAMILY RELATED
-familial

FAMOUS
-famed for its
-renowned

-fabled
-eminent
-noted
-immortalized in
-infamous
-notorious
-celebrated

FAMOUS PERSON
-luminary

FAN
-disciple of
-devotee {dev-uh-TEE}

FANCY
-more elaborate
-extravagant
-stately
-pretentious [pejorative]
-pompous [pejorative]
-grandiose
-ornate

> These are more fancy.
>
> These are more extravagant.

FAR AWAY
-remote
-out on the peripheries
-in the hinterland
-out on the farthermost
-on the outskirts of
-the outlands
-the outlying
-the outmost
-outermost
-afar [poetic]

FARMING
-cultivation

FASCINATED
-enthralled
-enraptured
-rapt

FASHION BUSINESS
-Seventh Avenue

FASHION DESIGNER
-couturier {French, koo-TOUR-ee-er}

FASHION OF THE DAY
-in the mode of the day

FASHIONABLE PERSON
-fashion plate
-fashionista

FAST
-fleet-footed
-expeditious
-at a breakneck pace

FAST TRACK (WE ARE GOING TO FAST TRACK THIS)
-expedite

FAT
-stout
-plethoric
-well nourished
-Ruebenesque
-corpulent
-vente {Italian, VEN-tay} [humorous
   when said of a guy]

"Dude, you're not fat, you're vente."

FAT AND JOLLY
-Falstaffian

"It has been three centuries since Dr. [Samuel] Johnson was born, on Sept. 7, 1709. He died on Dec. 13, 1784, still struggling for the mixed blessing of more life. His Falstaffian vitalism is always my first thought when I reread, teach again or continue brooding upon the canonical critic of Western literature." Harold Bloom, New York Times, Nov. 5, 2009

FATAL FLAW
-tragic flaw

FATE
-divine intervention
-providence

FATHERLY
-paternal

FATIGUE
-fatigues

"He taught me also to put my own hand to business upon occasion, to endure hardship and fatigues, and to throw the necessities of nature into a little compass; that I ought not to meddle in other people's business, nor be easy in giving credit to informers." Marcus Aurelius, *Meditations*

FAULTS
-human frailties
-failings
-deficiencies
-shortcomings

FAVORABLE
-auspicious
-propitious

FAVORITE
-favored
-beloved
-darling of

"Who can foretell for what high cause / This darling of the gods was born?" Andrew Marvell

FAVORITISM
-partiality

FEAR
-angst
-worry
-foreboding
-dread
-apprehension
-unholy dread
-alarm
-trepidation [poetic]

"On the morning of the day that the young couple were to arrive, Princess Mary entered the antechamber as usual at the time appointed for the morning greeting, crossing herself with trepidation and repeating a silent prayer. Every morning she came in like that, and every morning prayed that the daily interview might pass off well." Leo Tolstoy, *War and Peace*.

FEAR MONGER
-scare baby
-alarmist

FEAR OF
-dread of

"I always found in myself a dread of west and a love of east." John Steinbeck, *East of Eden*

FEATHERS
-plumage

FEATURES
-amenities

FED UP
-disillusioned
-disgruntled

FEEL (THINK)
-entertain
-nurture a feeling
-harbor a feeling
-entertain a feeling
-find in myself
-intuit

"...a film that often dazzles during its quietest moments, as when Max sets sail, and you intuit his pluck and will from the closeups of him staring into the unknown." Manohla Dargis, *New York Times*, Oct. 16, 2009

> I think he's hiding his feelings of resentment.
>
> I think he harbors feelings of resentment.

FEEL (TOUCH)
-_____ to the touch

FEEL BETTER
-it would be of comfort to me
-to allay feelings of

FEEL IT THE WORST
-bear the brunt of

FEEL SORRY FOR
-commiserate
-study your pain

"…you can hide 'neath your covers and study your pain, make crosses from your lovers, throw roses in the rain…" Bruce Springsteen, "Thunder Road"

FEELING OF
-air of
-expression of
-in agonies of
-in a state of
-atmosphere of

FEELINGS
-sentiments
-give free play to your feelings

FEELS GOOD
-heartwarming
-uplifting
-touching

FELL ASLEEP
-dozed off

FELL ON DEAF EARS
-had no resonance with either of them

FELLOW CITIZEN
-compatriot

FELT
-found in myself

"I always found in myself a dread of west and a love of east. Where I ever got such an idea I cannot say, unless it could be that the morning came over the peaks of the Gabilans and the night drifted back from the ridges of the Santa Lucias." John Steinbeck, *East of Eden*

FEMALE LOVER
-inamorata {Italian, *i-nam-ah-RAW-tah*}

FEMININE
-kittenish

FEMININE HANDWRITING
-addressed in a feminine hand

> It was in a woman's handwriting.
>
> It was addressed in a feminine hand.

FERTILE LAND
-arable land

FESTIVE
-convivial {*cun-VIV-ee-ul*}

FEW
-smattering of
-select few
-minority of
-the _____s are few

FIANCÉ
-betrothed

FICTITIOUS NAME (PEN NAME)
-pseudonym
-nom de guerre {French, *nom dih-GARE*}
-nom de plume {French, *nom dih-PLUME*}

FIDGETY
-restive

FIGHT (A FIGHT)
-a roe
-a ruckus
-a melee

FIGHT (TO FIGHT)
-rail against
-do battle against
-contend with
-vie with

-square off against
-take the fight to
-join the fray
-wage a battle for
-jockey for

FIGHTING
-discord
-bloodletting
-strife

FIGHTING EACH OTHER
-at loggerheads
-amid bitter wrangling

FIGHTING OFF
-embattled
-beset by
-subject to

FIGURE
-surmise
-infer
-ascertain
-assess
-appraise
-calibrate
-deduce
-divine
-presume
-reason

FIGURE OUT
-gather
-appreciate
-grasp

"Hence, this diary. In order to enhance in my mind's eye the picture of the friend for whom I have waited so long, I don't want to set down a series of bald facts in a diary like most people do, but I want this diary itself to be my friend, and I shall call my friend Kitty. No one will grasp what I'm talking about if I begin my letters to Kitty just out of the blue, so, albeit unwillingly, I will start by sketching in brief the story of my life." Anne Frank, Anne Frank: Diary of a Young Girl

FIGURED IT
-deemed it

FILE (ON A PERSON)
-dossier {French, dos-ee-AY}

FILLED WITH
-awash in
-bathed in
-marbled with
-instilled with
-dense with
-suffused with
-took and held

"It took and held her with fear."

-rich in
-leavened with
-invested with
-imbued with
-laden with

"For the traveler we see leaning on his neighbor is an honest and well-meaning man and full of melancholy, like those Chekhov characters so laden with virtues that they never know success in life." Orhan Pamuk, Snow

-fraught with
-steeped in
-freighted with
-rife with
-infused with

"The fragrant pilaf is a kind of savory fish-cake, made out of small hamsi filets wrapped around a thick bed of rice that is infused with herbs, currants and pine nuts." Yigal Schleifer, New York Times, Nov. 1, 2009

-infested with
-replete with
-garnished with
-permeated with a sense of
-brimming with
-possessed of

"All day, the colors had been those of dusk, mist moving like a water creature across *the great flanks of mountains possessed of ocean shadows and depths."* Kiran Desai, *The Inheritance of Loss*

FILLED WITH PEOPLE
-peopled with

> Her childhood was filled with a succession of stepfathers.
>
> Her childhood was peopled with a succession of stepfathers.

FILMMAKER WHO EXERCISES CREATIVE CONTROL
-auteur {French, *oh-TUR*}

FILTH
-squalor

FILTHY
-squalid

FINAL
-irrevocable
-the omega _____

FINAL BID
-the hammer price

FINAL BLOW
-coup de grâce {French, *koo de GRAHS*}

FINAL DEFEAT
-your Waterloo

FINAL OUTCOME
-denouement {French, *day-new-MAH*}

"In Paris, I am able to see now, I was at a critical stage in the development of the disease, situated at an ominous way station between its unfocused stirrings earlier that summer and the near-violent denouement of December, which sent me into the hospital." William Styron, *Darkness Visible*

FINAL REMARK
-parting shot

FINAL STRAW
-beginning of the end
-death knell

FINAL TRY
-last ditch effort to

FINALIZE
-consummate

FINALLY
-at last

"At last I could row no further. My hands were blistered, my back was burned, my body ached." J.M. Coetzee, *Foe*

FINANCIAL MOTIVES
-pecuniary motives [academic]

FIND
-reveal
-come upon
-chance upon
-unearth

FIND A LOOPHOLE
-circumvent

FIND A WAY TO
-a way had to be found to

FIND INNOCENT
-exonerate
-absolve

FIND IT (YOU WILL FIND IT IN)
-it is to be found in

FIND OUT
-an accounting of
-ascertain

FIND THE DIFFERENCE
-draw a distinction
-differentiate between the two

FIND YOUR WAY AROUND
-find your way about

"Now, thanks to the energy and the imagination of one of the greatest of colonial

administrators, the country, at least in the French zone, is as safe and open as the opposite shore of Spain. All that remains is to tell the traveler how to find his way about it." Edith Wharton, In Morocco

FINE
-exquisite

FINISHED
-over and done with

FIRED (FIRED HIM)
-presided over his resignation

FIRED (WAS FIRED)
-was dismissed
-received his walking papers

FIRM FACTS
-unassailable truths

FIRMLY
-rooted fast in
-steadfastly
-doggedly

FIRST
-for openers
-first and foremost
-to begin with

FISH OUT OF WATER
-amid the alien corn

FIT FOR
-suitable for

FIVE OF SOMETHING IN ONE DAY
-a Full Ginsburg

FIX
-resolve
-remedy

FIX THE PROBLEM
-set it right

FLABBY
-flaccid

FLAGRANT
-egregious

FLAKY
-idiosyncratic
-eccentric
-peculiar

FLASH OF INSIGHT
-epiphany

FLASHY
-tawdry
-meretricious [academic]

FLATTERING (SHAMELESSLY SO)
-unctuous
-smarmy

FLATTERY
-flummery
-puffery

FLAVORED WITH
-leavened with
-imbued with
-laced with [derogatory]

FLAVORFUL
-sapid [academic]

FLAWED ARGUMENT
-specious argument

FLAWS
-failings
-shortcomings
-deficiencies

FLEE
-abscond

FLIGHTY
-capricious

FLIRT (A FLIRT)
-coquette {French, kaw-KET} [feminine]

FLIRTY
-coquettish [feminine]

FLOOD (A FLOOD)
-a torrent
-a deluge

FLOOD (TO FLOOD)
-to inundate with

FLOODED
-awash in

FLOURISHING
-burgeoning

FLOWERY LANGUAGE
-purple prose
-purple patch

FLOWING IN
-an influx of

FLUKE
-aberration
-irregularity

FOCUS (A FOCUS)
-a single-mindedness
-a preoccupation with

FOCUSED ON
-centered on
-engrossed in
-aimed at
-preoccupied with
-turned her attention to

FOLLOW
-trace
-pursue

FOLLOW THE RULES
-abide by
-act in accordance with
-adhere to

FOLLOWED BY
-succeeded by
-was in turn

FOLLOWERS
-rank and file
-disciples
-acolytes
-adherents

FOOD
-fare
-sustenance
-cuisine {qua-ZEEN}

FOOLISH
-misbegotten
-ill-conceived

FOOLISH ACTIONS
-fooleries

FOOLISHNESS
-foolhardiness
-folly

"We need more humanity, more care, more love. There are those who expect a political system to produce that; and others who expect the love to produce the system. My own faith is that the truth of the future lies between the two and we shall behave humanly and a bit humanely, stumbling along, haphazardly generous and gallant, foolishly and meanly wise until the rape of our planet is seen to be the preposterous folly that it is." William Golding

FOOTSTEPS
-footfalls

"Outside, on peaceful-morning Cleveland Street, I hear the footfalls of a lone jogger, tramping past and down the hill toward Taft Lane and across to the Choir College, there to run in the damp grass." Richard Ford, *Independence Day*

FOR
-these

"She has been dead these twenty years." Henry James, *The Turn of the Screw*

FOR (I AM FOR____)
-in favor of

> I am for free speech.
>
> I am in favor of free speech.

FOR ___ HOURS
-for all of ___ hours

"When he, Moses, finally freed himself of the ancient and brittle harness that connected him to the oldest mule his master owned, all that was left of the sun was a five-inch-long memory of red orange laid out in still waves across the horizon between two mountains on the left and one on the right. He had been in the fields for all of fourteen hours." Edward P. Jones, *The Known World*

FOR A LIVING
-for his living

"Nearly seventy years before George died, his father, Howard Aaron Crosby, drove a wagon for his living." Paul Harding, *Tinkers*

FOR A LONG TIME (HAS FOR A LONG TIME)
-has long collected names
-she had been a long while out of the public eye
-it has long been
-friend of long standing
-have been a long time

"I have been a long time making up my mind to write this story. It is a true one, and that makes it hard to tell. Pearl S. Buck, *The Child Who Never Grew*

FOR A MOMENT
-for an instant

FOR A REASON
-for good reason

FOR A SPECIFIC PURPOSE
-ad hoc

FOR A WHILE
-for the time being
-for a time
-for some time now
-for a space in time

FOR EXAMPLE
-for instance
-case in point
-such as
-exemplified in
-a prime example is
-to name but a few
-to illustrate
-this is particularly true of
-to take an example

FOR GOOD (PERMANENTLY)
-irrevocably
-irretrievably

FOR HER AGE
-for her years

FOR HIM
-at his disposal

FOR MOST OF
-for the greater part of

FOR NO REASON
-without cause

FOR NOW (TEMPORARILY)
-for the time being
-pro tem {Latin, *pro-TEM*}
-for the foreseeable future
-for the near-term

FOR PRACTICAL PURPOSES
-for all intents and purposes
-in effect
-for our purposes

FOR REASONS
-on the grounds that

FOR SURE
-it's a certainty

FOR THAT REASON
-to that end

"Only to that end has he continued to fight."

FOR THE BENEFIT OF
-in the interest of

FOR THE MOST PART
-effectively
-in large measure
-predominantly
-on the whole
-by and large
-most is of

"Some are authentic, but most are of dubious origin."

FOR THE PURPOSE OF
-for the sake of
-in the interest of
-so as to
-intended to ensure
-used as a means of

FOR THE REST OF THE DAY
-all the day after

FOR THE SAME REASON THAT
-for the same reason as did

FORBIDDEN
-verboten {German, *ver-BOAT-un*}

FORCE
-compel
-foist on
-by force of
-bring pressure to bear on
-dislodge
-impose

FORCE ONESELF TO
-bring oneself to

I can't force myself to tell her.

I can't bring myself to tell her.

FORCED TO
-were made to

FORCEFUL
-muscular

FORCES
-dynamics
-tectonic plates of

FOREHEAD
-brow

FOREIGN AND DANGEROUS
-outlandish

"Lavrans had four men with him, and they were all well armed; for at this time there were many kinds of outlandish people lying up among the mountains." Sigrid Undset, *Kristin Lavransdatter*

FOREVER
-lasting
-enduring
-perennial
-eternal
-abiding
-ad infinitum {Latin, *ad in-fi-NIGHT-um*}
-immortal
-everlasting
-imperishable
-forevermore
-in perpetuity
-timeless
-undying

FORESHADOWED
-prefigured the rise of

FOREWARNING
-premonition
-foreboding
-presentiment

FORGET ABOUT IT
-think no more of it

FORGIVE
-absolve
-indulge
-willing to put the incident behind me

FORGIVENESS
-clemency
-forbearance

FORGIVING
-forbearing
-stoic
-indulgent to

FORGOT ABOUT
-passed out of her thoughts
-lost all memory of

FORGOT TO
-neglected to

FORGOTTEN
-near-forgotten
-long forgotten

FORM
-take the form of

FORMAL
-a soup-and-fish affair

FORMAL NAME
-an appellation

FORMAL SPEECH
-oratory

FORMALITY
-done pro forma
-a nicety

FORMER
-erstwhile

"His erstwhile friends have become an issue in the campaign."
-quondam [academic]

FORMLESS
-un-fashioned

FORMS
-manifestations

FORTIFICATION
-citadel
-redoubt {ri-DOUT}

FORWARD
-onward

FOUGHT OVER
-contested

FOUND
-detected
-came upon
-chanced upon
-fell upon
-came on

> We found a cabin in the woods
>
> We came upon a cabin in the woods.

FOUND A FRIEND
-found favor with
-found a friend in

FOUND IN
-implicit in
-endemic to

FOUND OUT ABOUT
-it became known
-caught wind of

FOUND WAYS TO
-found means to

FOUNDATION
-underpinning
-underlying support
-basis for
-lay the foundation for
-amid the ruins of
-cornerstone

FOUR-LETTER WORD
-a pejorative
-colorful language
-an expletive

FOYER
-vestibule
-portico

FRANK AND OPEN
-ingenuous {in-JEN-you-us}

FRANK LLOYD WRIGHT [IN THE STYLE OF]
-Usonian {you-SONE-ee-un}

> The library has a Frank Lloyd Wright feel to it.
>
> The library has a Usonian feel to it.

FRANKLY
-in no uncertain terms

FRANTIC
-frenetic

FREAK OUT
-come unglued
-having undue concern
-ride off in all directions

FREE FROM
-independent of

FREE GIFT [INCORRECT USAGE]
-gift
-endowment

FREE OF CHARGE
-gratis {Latin, GRAT-is}

FREE-RANGE CHICKEN
-abuse-free chicken

"Five minutes of FDA-mandated 'roaming time' per day does not a free-range chicken make."

FREEDOM
-carte blanche
-not bound by
-free rein
-autonomy
-latitude
-license to
-open season on

FREELY
-with impunity

FRENCH
-Gallic {GAL-ick}

FRENCH EXPRESSION, WORD, OR TRAIT
-a Gallicism {GAL-ih-sih-sum}

FRENZIED
-madding

FRIEND
-accomplice [playful]
-friend and confidant
-cohort

FRIENDLY
-affable
-genial
-kindly
-amiable
-congenial
-approachable
-hospitable
-jovial
-cordial
-good-humored
-personable
-benevolent

FRIENDLY [OF ANIMALS]
-docile
-companionable

"How is it that Americans, so solicitous of the animals they keep as pets, are so indifferent to the ones they cook for dinner? The answer cannot lie in the beasts themselves. Pigs, after all, are quite companionable,

and dogs are said to be delicious." Elizabeth Kolbert, *The New Yorker*, Nov. 9, 2009

FRIENDLY FIRE
-accidental fire

FRIENDS WITH
-on friendly terms with

FRIENDSHIP
-intimacy

FROM
-from which
-wherefrom
-derived from
-borne by
-of

"Year by year, slowly but inexorably, his spirit had withered. Dry of heat and dry-eyed. During his nineteen years imprisonment he had not shed a tear." Victor Hugo, *Les Miserables*

FROM (SHE IS FROM AUSTRALIA)
-of Australian origin
-Mrs. Jones, a native of Australia
-born and bred there

> Her family comes from Germany.
> Her family is of German origin.

FROM A DISTANCE
-from afar [poetic]

FROM A GOOD FAMILY
-of good family
-well descended
-born into a noble family

FROM A POOR FAMILY
-of modest family origins

FROM NOW ON
-from this time on
-hereafter
-henceforth

FROM PLACE TO PLACE
-hither and thither
-from somewhere to elsewhere

"He stopped at a bench where people could catch buses from somewhere to elsewhere." John Crowley, *Little, Big*

FROM THE BEGINNING
-early on
-from the outset

FROM THE PAST
-_____ of old

FROM THEN ON
-ever after

FROM WITHIN
-within its ranks

FRONT
-frontal
-fore
-in the foremost
-at the forefront

FRONT (OF A BUILDING)
-façade {fe-SAWD}

FRONT DESK
-concierge {French, kohn-SEE-AIRZH}

FRONT ROW SEAT
-ringside seat

FROWN ON
-look askance at

FROWNING
-glancing severely at

FRUITLESS LIFE
-a hardscrabble life

FRUSTRATE
-bedevil
-exasperate

FULL OF
-rife with
-chock-full of

-rich in
-fraught with
-replete with
-endowed with
-teeming with
-peppered with
-immense in

"Of Life immense in passion, pulse, and power, Cheerful, for freest action form'd under the laws divine, The Modern Man I sing." Walt Whitman, Leaves of Grass, Book I, "Inscriptions"

FULLY AWARE
-under no illusion

FULSOME APOLOGY [INCORRECT USAGE]
-full apology

FUN
-rollicking fun

FUNDAMENTALS OF
-rudiments of

FUNERAL PROCESSION
-cortege {French, *cor-TEZH*}

FUNNY
-antic
-jocular
-riotous

FURNITURE
-furnishings
-appointments

FUTURE
-what is to come
-_____ to be
-the foreseeable future
-succeeding ages
-in future times
-forthcoming events

FUTURE GENERATIONS
-posterity

Gg

GAIN
-secure

GAIN CONTROL
-assert control
-reassert control

GAIN ON A SHIP
-draw on

GAINED MORE ACCEPTANCE
-played better

"Conservative ideals have traditionally played better in southern states."

GAINS
-spoils

GALL
-effrontery
-audacity
-temerity

GAP
-fissure

GAPING
-yawning

"It also has a wealth of greenery—residents proudly claim more trees per capita than any city in the world besides Paris. It's enough to make you forget about the state's yawning budget gap." Beth Greenfield, New York Times, Nov. 1, 2009

GARBAGE
-refuse

GATHER
-assemble
-congregate

GATHERED
-mustered

"Nightfall assembled them, as it did the stars. With nothing in common but their

destitution, they mustered to sleep together in the Porch of Our Lord, cursing, insulting and jostling each other, picking quarrels with old enemies, or throwing earth and rubbish, even rolling on the ground and spitting and biting with rage." Miguel Angel Asturias, *The President*

-resorted

"There was a black river that flowed through the town, and if it had no grace for mortal beings, it did for swans, and many swans resorted there, and even rode the river like some kind of plunging animals, in floods." Sebastian Barry, *The Secret Scripture*

GATHERING (A GATHERING)
-an assembly
-a vigil

GAUDILY ORNATE
-baroque

GAVE IN
-gave myself up to it

GAVE ME
-committed to me

GAVE ME EXPERIENCE IN
-seasoned me in

GAVE OUT
-dispensed

GAVE THE IMPRESSION THAT
-conveyed the impression
-gave a sense of
-suggested

"The outfit was acceptable by any theological and geometrical standards, however abstruse, and suggested a rich inner life." John Kennedy Toole, *A Confederacy of Dunces*

GAVE UP
-despaired of trying

GENERALITY (A GENERALITY)
-a banality
-a platitude

GENERALLY SPEAKING
-on balance
-all things considered
-is, in the main

> It was, generally speaking, the wrong decision.
>
> It was, all things considered, the wrong choice to make.

GENERATED
-elicited

GENEROUS
-altruistic
-beneficent
-philanthropic
-benevolent
-liberal

"I have to thank my great-grandfather that I did not go to a public school, but had good masters at home, and learned to know that one ought to spend liberally on such things." Marcus Aurelius, *Meditations*

GENTLE
-clement
-pacific

GENUINE DEMEANOR
-unaffected

GERMAN ARMY
-the Wehrmacht {German, VAIR-mahkt} [between 1921 and 1945]

GERMS
-pathogens

GET
-come by
-glean
-acquire

-elicit
-derive
-procure
-receive
-draw a lot of self-satisfaction from
-find
-attain
-gain
-garner
-assume control of
-capture
-secure

GET A GRIP
-steel yourself
-take hold of your senses

GET ALONG WITH
-mix easily
-get along famously
-get on with

GET AROUND
-circumvent

> She tried to get around the
> regulations.
>
> She tried to circumvent the
> regulations.

GET BETTER
-hone

GET ENOUGH SUPPORT TO
-garner enough support to

GET GOING
-swing into action
-mobilize
-marshal

GET HERE
-appear on the scene

GET HOLD OF
-lay hold of

GET IN
-gain admission

GET IN THE WAY
-encumber
-intervene

"But whenever I start to talk about the South Pacific, people intervene. I try to tell somebody what the steaming Hebrides were like and first thing you know I'm telling about the old Tonkinese woman who used to sell human heads. As souvenirs. For fifty dollars!"
James Michener, *Tales of the South Pacific*

GET INVOLVED
-become embroiled
-wade into
-traffic in

"Like good aunts the world over, she dispenses the info that moms and dads are too squeamish to traffic in, beginning with a factoid that would delight any red-blooded child: the death by boiling of one Margaret Davy in 1542 for poisoning her employer."
David Kirby, *New York Times*, Nov. 5, 2009

GET IT BACK
-retrieve it

GET MAD
-stew

GET OFF
-disembark

GET ON
-mount

GET OUT OF
-extricate yourself

GET OVER THE
-overcome the

GET READY FOR
-gird for
-ready yourself

GET RID OF
-divorce oneself of

-divest
-dispense with
-dispose of
-eradicate
-rid them of
-be rid of
-purge
-do away with
-cast off

GET THEIR (THEY GET THEIR...)
-owe their

GET TIRED OF
-tire of

"When Zarathustra was thirty years old he left his home and the lake of his home and went into the mountains. Here he enjoyed his spirit and his solitude and for ten years did not tire of it." Friedrich Nietzsche, *Thus Spoke Zarathustra*

GET TO KNOW
-make acquaintances

GET TO YOUR
-attend to your

GET UNDRESSED
-disrobe
-doff
-shed

GET UPSET
-distress yourself

GET USED TO
-become accustomed to
-accustom oneself to

"Do not accustom yourself to use big words for little matters." Samuel Johnson

-become inured
-acclimate yourself to

GET WELL
-convalesce

GET WHAT YOU DESERVE
-be held to account for

-receive your comeuppance

> She will get what she deserves.
> She will be held to account for her actions.

GET WORSE
-left to fester

GET YOUR WAY
-impose your will

GETS ME EXCITED
-stirs my blood

GETTING CLOSER TO
-nearing
-coming nearer

"Now we, and the carts, are coming nearer to the noble city..." Edith Sitwell, *Fanfare for Elizabeth*

GETTING DARK
-growing dark

GETTING INTO
-warming into

GETTING READY TO
-making ready to

GHOST
-apparition
-phantasm
-manifestation

GIANT (A GIANT)
-a goliath
-a behemoth
-a gargantua

GIFT GIVING
-largess
-gifting

GIFTED WITH
-endowed with
-bestowed with

GIGANTIC
-Brobdingnagian
{*brahb-dig-NAG-ee-uhn*}

GIST
-the crux
-its measure

"I read enough to get its measure."

GIVE
-render
-afford
-bestow
-lavish
-extend
-imbue
-infuse
-contribute
-convey
-dispense
-allot
-apportion
-it lends a
-grant
-allow
-confer
-endow
-entrust
-accord
-assign
-provide
-deliver
-impart

GIVE AN APOLOGY
-tender an apology

> You should give a formal apology.
>
> You should tender a formal apology.

GIVE AN OPINION
-weigh in
-opine
-sermonize [derogatory]

GIVE AND TAKE
-symbiosis

GIVE ASSISTANCE
-render assistance

GIVE AWAY SECRETS
-betray
-reveal

GIVE CREDIBILITY
-lend credible substance to

GIVE EXAMPLES
-cite
-point to
-speak specifically of

GIVE IN TO
-cede a little ground
-capitulate
-acquiesce

"To fill rooms, hotels are offering special sales on their own Web sites, turning to third-party sites like Expedia.com to sell excess inventory and even quietly acquiescing to travelers who call up or walk in and haggle." Michelle Higgins, *New York Times*, Nov. 1, 2009

-accede to
-bow to
-succumb to

"It was dark by the time I reached Bonn, and I forced myself not to succumb to the series of mechanical actions which had taken hold of me in five years of traveling back and forth: down the station steps, up the station steps, put down my suitcase, take my ticket out of my coat pocket, pick up my suitcase, hand in my ticket, cross over to the newsstand, buy the evening papers, go outside, and signal for a taxi." Heinrich Böll, *The Clown*

-yield to
-waver
-surrender

"The foolish read to escape reality; the wise surrender to it."

GIVE IT TO ME
-give it here

GIVE ME NO CHOICE
-leave me no choice

GIVE ORDERS
-issue orders

GIVE OUT
-dispense
-disclose

GIVE THE BENEFIT OF THE DOUBT
-view it in the light most favorable

GIVE THEM CREDIT
-credit them with

GIVE UP (GIVE IN)
-capitulate
-resign oneself to
-lay down arms

GIVE UP (HAND OVER)
-forfeit
-cede
-relinquish

GIVE UP (STOP)
-forswear

GIVEN
-entrusted with
-invested with
-accorded
-delivered
-extended
-endowed
-apportioned
-favored with
-blessed with

GIVEN ORDERS
-issued orders

"She had left the church last of all, and, desiring to arrive first at the hall, had issued orders to the coachman to drive faster." Upton Sinclair, *The Jungle*

GIVEN OUT
-apportioned
-dispensed

GIVEN TO ME
-given me

"It is silence all about. My hand is good and I have a beautiful biro full of blue ink, given me by my friend the doctor..." Sebastian Barry, *The Secret Scripture*

GIVES A GOOD IMPRESSION
-conducts himself well
-acquits himself well

He gave a very good impression.

He acquitted himself brilliantly.

GIVES CREDIBILITY
-lends credence to

GIVES THE IMPRESSION
-conveys the impression
-gives a sense of
-suggests

"The outfit was acceptable by any theological and geometrical standards, however abstruse, and suggested a rich inner life." John Kennedy Toole, *A Confederacy of Dunces*

GIVING IN
-succumbing to

GIVING US INFORMATION
-yielding information

GLAD
-glad of it

"Longstreet was not asleep. He lay on the cot watching the lightning flare in the door

of the tent. It was very quiet in the grove and there was the sound of the raindrops continuing to fall from the trees although the rain had ended. When Sorrel touched him on the arm he was glad of it; he was thinking of his dead children." Michael Shaara, *The Killer Angels*

GLADLY
-with pleasure

GLEAMING
-resplendent

GLOOMY
-dour
-sullen
-somber
-stygian (hellish) {STIH-jee-un}
-leaden
-dreary

GLORIFICATION OF
-deification of
-apotheosis of [academic]

GLORIFY
-lionize
-deify

GLOSS OVER
-varnish over

GO
-set out
-go about
-venture to

GO AFTER
-pursue

GO AHEAD
-do what you will
-do what you must

GO ALL THE WAY
-carry through to the end

GO AROUND
-circumnavigate

-circumvent

GO BACK TO
-date from prehistoric times

GO BEYOND
-transcend

GO DOWN
-recede
-descend

GO EASY ON
-has shown little desire to go for the jugular

GO HAYWIRE
-go awry

GO OUT IN PUBLIC
-go about among people [poetic]

"The repugnance to being touched remains with us when we go about among people; the way we move in a busy street, in restaurants, trains or buses, is governed by it." Elias Canetti, *Crowds and Power*

GO PAST
-go beyond

GO THERE
-frequent

GO TO
-attend
-frequent

GO WITH
-accompany
-attend

GO WITHOUT
-forgo

You will go without any more luxuries.

You will forgo any more luxuries.

GOAL
-aspiration
-ambition

"My main ambition as a journalist is to cut through the PR and find the truth in what politicians are saying." Chris Matthews, 2010 *Hardball* promo

GOD'S CARE
-God's keeping
-providence

GOES BEYOND
-transcends
-escapes
-extends far beyond

GOES WITH (AGREES WITH)
-compliments
-goes hand in hand with
-is in keeping with
-comports with
-is consistent with the views of
-echoes
-reflects
-accords with

"It is not because the truth is too difficult to see that we make mistakes...we make mistakes because the easiest and most comfortable course for us is to seek insight where it accords with our emotions—especially selfish ones." Alexander Solzhenitsyn

My views on this agree with the administration's position.

My views are consistent with those of the administration.

GOES WITH THE TERRITORY
-is inevitable
-is part and parcel

GOING
-off to

GOING AFTER
-chasing
-pursuing
-giving chase to

GOING BACK TO
-dating back to

GOING HOME
-homeward bound
-returning homewards

GOING ON FOR A LONG TIME
-longstanding

GOING OUT OF STYLE
-falling out of fashion

GOING TO
-in danger of
-disposed to
-inclined to

GONE
-exhausted

GONE CRAZY
-taken leave of one's senses

GONE FOR GOOD
-irretrievable

"The last moments slipped by, one by one, irretrievable. 'The earth is the Lord's and the fullness thereof, the earth and everything that dwells therein.' The priest, with a gesture of a cross, scattered earth over the body of Maria Nikolaevna." Boris Pasternak, *Doctor Zhivago*

GOOD
-well

"It is well to read everything of something, and something of everything." Joseph Brodsky

GOOD AT
-gifted
-has an eye for
-accomplished

GOOD AT SEX
-lively in bed

"Women desire six things: They want their husbands to be brave, wise, rich, generous, obedient to wife, and lively in bed." Geoffrey Chaucer

GOOD BEHAVIOR
-exemplary behavior

GOOD-BYE (A GOOD-BYE)
-a proper sendoff

GOOD CHANCE OF SUCCESS
-propitious

GOOD ENOUGH
-to your liking
-sufficient
-should suffice

GOOD ENOUGH BUT NOT GREAT
-palatable
-admissible
-such as it is

GOOD EXCUSE
-extenuating circumstances
-mitigating circumstances

GOOD FOR
-lends itself to
-suitable for
-well-suited for

GOOD FOR ME
-did me good to

GOOD FOR THE SOUL
-redemptive

GOOD FRIEND
-intimate friend

GOOD JOB (DOING A GOOD JOB)
-exact in the discharge of his duties [formal]

GOOD JUDGMENT (HAS GOOD JUDGMENT)
-is discerning

-is shrewd
-is sagacious [academic]

GOOD LUCK
-wish you every success

GOOD OLE DAYS
-the halcyon days {HAL-see-on}
-the bygone era of
-of bygone days
-my salad days

GOOD OMEN
-a good harbinger

GOOD PART OF
-a goodly part of [poetic]

"The world begins anew with every birth, my father used to say. He forgot to say, with every death it ends. Or did not think he needed to. Because for a goodly part of his life he worked in a graveyard." Sebastian Barry, *The Secret Scripture*

GOOD REASON
-compelling reason

GOOD SIGN
-harbinger of good

GOOD THING
-godsend

GOOD WISHES
-Godspeed [humorous when melodramatic]

GOOD-HEARTED INCOMPETENCE
-a regular Bertie Wooster

GOODNESS
-her better nature
-arête {Greek, ahr-i-TAY}
-virtues

"For the traveler we see leaning on his neighbor is an honest and well-meaning man and full of melancholy, like those Chekhov characters so laden with vir-

tues that they never know success in life."
Orhan Pamuk, *Snow*

GOSSIP
-hold court
-tell tales

GOT (SEE "GET")

GOT BACK UP
-he righted himself

GOT CLOSER
-drew near

GOT OFF
-dismounted

GOT QUIET
-he fell silent

GOT SICK
-was taken ill
-fell ill

GOT TO KNOW
-acquainted herself with
-made herself familiar with

GOT TO WORK
-set to work

GOT UP
-drew himself up
-rose

GOURMET
-epicure

GOURMET COOKING
-haute cuisine {French, *oat-kwi-ZEEN*}

GOVERNMENT
-affairs of state

GOVERNMENT OF THE WEALTHY
-plutocracy

GRAB
-lay hold of
-lay hold upon

*"Since the world was sure to misunderstand
everything, mere defensive instinct prompted him to give it as little as possible to lay
hold upon."* Booth Tarkington, *Penrod*

-get hold of

*"…you get some who blow kisses or try to
get hold of your arm, but then they are definitely knocking at the wrong door. I get off
my bicycle and refuse to go further in their
company, or I pretend to be insulted and
tell them in no uncertain terms to clear off."*
Anne Frank, *Anne Frank: The Diary of a
Young Girl*

GRABBED
-took hold of
-clutched
-caught hold of

GRABBING
-clasping
-clutching

GRADE
-evaluate
-critique
-appraise

GRANT
-bestow
-confer
-accord

*"The voyage will not teach you any-
thing if you do not accord it the right to
destroy you—a rule as old as the world
itself. A voyage is like a shipwreck, and
those whose boat has never sunk will never
know anything about the sea. The rest is
skating or tourism."* Nicolas Bouvier, *Le
Vide et le Plein*

GRAPE HARVEST
-the vendange {French, *von-DONJ*}

GRASS
-grasses

"When June came the grasses headed out and turned brown, and the hills turned a brown which was not brown but a gold and saffron and red—an indescribable color." John Steinbeck, *East of Eden*

GRATEFUL
-effusive
-beholden to

GRATEFUL FOR THE WAY YOU TREATED ME
-grateful for past kindnesses

GRAY
-gun metal gray
-charcoal

GREAT
-profound
-monumental
-remarkable
-glorious

"Unpretending mediocrity is good, and genius is glorious; but a weak flavor of genius in an essentially common person is detestable." Oliver Holmes, *The Autocrat of the Breakfast-Table*

GREAT CARE
-elaborate care

GREAT DEAL
-fair amount of

GREAT JOB (WAY TO GO)
-kudos

GREAT TO SEE YOU
-no one I could have been more pleased to see

GREATER THAN THE SUM OF ITS PARTS
-a synergism
-gestalt {German, *gih-STAHLT*}

"The Well-Spoken Thesaurus *is gestalt-like in the sense that it is more than the words it contains.*"

GREATEST (THE GREATEST)
-as great a _____ as any age ever produced

"As I could never hope to write anything myself, worthy to be laid before YOUR MAJESTY; I think it a very great happiness, that it should be my lot to usher into the world, under Your Sacred Name, the last work of as great a Genius as any Age ever produced..." Sir Isaac Newton, *The Chronology of Ancient Kingdoms Amended*

GREATEST WORK
-magnum opus {Latin, *MAG-num OH-pus*}

GREATLY
-in no small measure

GREATNESS
-grandeur

GREED
-excesses
-avarice
-cupidity [academic]

GREEDY
-covetous
-rapacious
-acquisitive
-avaricious
-esurient [academic]

GREEK SCULPTURE (NUDE)
-a kouros {Greek, *CORE-ahs*}

GREEK THREE HANDLED WATER VESSEL
-hydria {Old French, *HIGH-dree-uh*}

GREEN
-verdant

GREENHOUSE
-conservatory

GREET
-receive

GREET WARMLY
-glad-hand

GREW (THEY GREW VEGETABLES)
-cultivated

GRID
-lattice

GRIMACED
-gave her one pained look

GRIPE
-grievance

GROCERIES
-provisions

GROPE
-flounder

GROSS INJUSTICE
-iniquity

GROUCH
-curmudgeon

GROUCHY
-ill-tempered
-morose
-ill-humored
-irascible
-querulous
-snarky
-cantankerous

GROUP
-entourage
-camp
-inner circle
-coterie
-cabal
-tribe
-cluster
-bevy
-faction
-arm of
-detail
-cadre of
-contingent of
-throng

-business of ferrets
-clutch of eggs
-coven of witches
-collective of artists
-guild of writers
-gaggle of girls
-assembly of churches
-consortium of companies
-complement of soldiers

GROUP OF HONORED PERSONS
-a pantheon

GROUPED
-clustered

GROUPIES
-entourage
-retinue
-claque

GROUPINGS
-enclaves

GROW
-ferment
-evolve
-flourish
-thrive
-prosper
-burgeon
-proliferate
-mushroom
-intensify
-take root
-gather force
-mount

"Favored by the favorable dream. I shall listen to the authority of the dream that mounts within me." Saint-John Perse

GROWING
-in ascendance

GRUESOME
-macabre

GUARANTEE
-assurance

GUARDIANSHIP
-tutelage
-wardship

GUARDS HIS TERRITORY
-holds his purchase on

> He guards his territory over a wide swath of the executive branch.
>
> He holds his purchase on a wide swath of the executive branch.

GUERILLA WARFARE
-Fabian tactics

GUESS
-speculate
-venture a guess
-extrapolate
-surmise

"She stood apart from the crowd, letting it drift by her to the platform or the street, and wearing an air of irresolution which might, as he surmised, be the mask of a very definite purpose." Edith Wharton, *The House of Mirth*

GUESS (A GUESS)
-conjecture

GUIDE
-shepherd
-mentor
-herd
-usher

GUIDED BY
-governed by

GUILTY
-complicit
-culpable
-blameworthy

GULF
-chasm

GULLIBILITY
-credulity

GUT (TO GUT)
-eviscerate

GUTS
-entrails
-viscera

Hh

HABIT
-convention
-bent
-proclivity
-idiosyncrasy
-second nature
-peculiarity
-inclination

HABIT OF
-given to
-has a propensity for

HAD
-enjoyed
-had at her disposal a

HAD A SCAR
-bore a scar

HAD A CHILD
-has borne a child

"Of her life outside Windsor Mansions Soraya reveals nothing. Soraya is not her real name, that he is sure of. There are signs she has borne a child, or children." J. M. Coetzee, *Disgrace*

HAD A CONFUSING EFFECT ON
-played havoc with

HAD A DOG
-kept a dog

"Their splendour lasted throughout all the years that saw their Midland town spread

and darken into a city, but reached its topmost during the period when every prosperous family with children kept a Newfoundland dog." Booth Tarkington, The Magnificent Ambersons

HAD AN IDEA
-the idea struck him
-she hit on a novel solution

HAD DONE TO ME
-what she had produced in me

HAD NO ANSWER
-could find no reply

HAD NO APPEAL TO
-had no grace for [poetic]

"There was a black river that flowed through the town, and if it had no grace for mortal beings, it did for swans, and many swans resorted there, and even rode the river like some kind of plunging animals, in floods." Sebastian Barry, The Secret Scripture

HAD NOTHING TO DO WITH
-played no role in

Drugs had nothing to do with his death.

Drugs played no role in his death.

HAD SOMETHING TO DO WITH
-had some part in
-played a role in

HAD TAUGHT HER TO
-had accustomed her to

HAD TO HAPPEN
-was inevitable

HAIR CUT SHORT
-hair cropped short

HALF OF WHAT IS
-half of that

"The planet Mars, I scarcely need remind the reader, revolves about the sun at a mean distance of 140,000,000 miles, and the light and heat it receives from the sun is barely half of that received by this world. It must be, if the nebular hypothesis has any truth, older than our world; and long before this earth ceased to be molten, life upon its surface must have begun its course." H. G. Wells, The War of the Worlds

HALLWAY
-corridor

HAND OVER TO
-entrust to your care
-commend to your care

HANDED DOWN
-bequeathed
-bestowed

HANDLED HERSELF WELL
-acquitted herself well

HANDLERS (POLITICAL HANDLERS)
-the Praetorian Guard

"If you want to interview the president, you've got to get past the Praetorian Guard."

HANDS OFF APPROACH
-laissez-faire {French, lay-zay-FAIR}
-benign neglect

HANDSOME
-rakish

HANDWRITING
-script
-in the most beautiful hand
-in the hand of

HANG OUT WITH THAT CROWD
-the circles in which they move

HANG OVER
-drape

HANGING OUT WITH
-going about with

HANGOUTS
-usual haunts

HANGOVER REMEDY
-prairie oyster

HAPPEN
-ensue
-befall
-come about
-is borne out
-come to pass
-take place

HAPPEN AT THE SAME TIME
-coincide

HAPPENED AGAIN
-the scene replayed itself in

HAPPENED TO
-what became of
-why such a thing had fallen on
-befallen

"There is one mind common to all individual men. Every man is an inlet to the same and to all of the same. He that is once admitted to the right of reason is made a freeman of the whole estate. What Plato has thought, he may think; what a saint has felt, he may feel; what at any time has befallen any man, he can understand. Who hath access to this universal mind is a party to all that is or can be done, for this is the only and sovereign agent." Ralph Waldo Emerson, "Essay on History"

> Whatever happened to the child?
>
> What became of the child?

HAPPENED TO SEE HER ONE DAY
-chanced to see her one day

HAPPENS EVERY DAY
-an everyday occurrence

HAPPINESS
-cheer
-felicity
-elation

HAPPY
-blithe
-elated
-sanguine
-scarcely able to contain his joy

HAPPY-GO-LUCKY
-improvident [academic]
-devil-may-care

HAPPY WITH
-encouraged by
-contented with

HARASSED
-hampered
-bedeviled
-beleaguered
-beset
-dragooned

HARD
-difficult
-onerous
-like herding cats
-arduous

HARD LINE (TAKEN A HARD LINE)
-has not softened her view

HARD TO CATCH
-elusive

HARD TO HANDLE
-cumbersome

HARD TO SEE
-imperceptible

HARD TO UNDERSTAND
-abstruse
-recondite [academic]

HARD TO USE
-unwieldy

HARD TO TAKE
-bitter pill to swallow

HARD WORK
-heavy lifting

HARD WORKER
-workhorse

HARDBOILED CRIME DRAMA
-film noir {French, *film nwar*}

HARDEN
-calcify

HARDLY
-scarcely

"The planet Mars, I scarcely need remind the reader, revolves about the sun at a mean distance of 140,000,000 miles, and the light and heat it receives from the sun is barely half of that received by this world." H. G. Wells, *The War of the Worlds*

-little

"We little know the things for which we pray." Geoffrey Chaucer

HARDLY ANY
-scant
-next to no experience
-next to nothing
-negligible

HARDLY SLEPT
-slept little

HARDSHIPS
-travails
-wants
-privations

"The French nuns might hardly recognize their former quarters. Austerity and privations have given way to a classy, comfortable small hotel." Seth Sherwood, *New York Times*, Nov. 1, 2009

HARDWORKING
-assiduous
-untiring
-laborious

HARM
-grievous harm
-does violence to

HARMFUL
-adverse
-injurious
-pernicious
-deleterious [academic]
-nocuous

HARMLESS
-benign
-innocuous

HARSH
-discordant
-unforgiving
-acidulous {a-SIJ-eh-lus} [academic]
-strident

HARSH AND SIMPLE
-austere
-spartan
-ascetic
-puritanical
-utilitarian
-institutional

HARSH LAWS
-draconian laws

HARSH QUALITIES
-asperities {as-PARE-ih-tees}

HARSH SOUNDING
-strident
-enough to set the teeth on edge
-braying

HARSH STATEMENT
-strongly worded statement
-speaking less diplomatically

HARSH WORDS
-caustic commentary

HARSHNESS OF TEMPER
-asperity

HARSHNESS OF OPINION
-tyranny of opinion

HAS
-presents
-displays
-is endowed with
-enjoys
-suffers from
-is blessed with
-boasts
-commands
-occupies
-retains

HAS ALWAYS ARGUED
-has long argued

HAS ANYTHING TO DO WITH
-seldom trades in the currency of

HAS BEEN FOR A LONG TIME
-has long been

HAS BEEN WATCHED
-has come under greater scrutiny

HAS BEGUN
-is in full swing

HAS CONTROL OVER
-has purchase on

HAS MORE TO DO WITH
-has greater relevance to

HAS NO IDEA
-cannot account for

> She had no idea what happened to the money.
>
> She could not account for the discrepancy in funds.

HAS NOTHING TO DO WITH
-bears little relationship to
-has no direct bearing on

"Although it has no direct bearing on the tale we have to tell, we must nevertheless give some account of the rumours and gossip concerning him which were in circulation when he came to occupy the Diocese."
Victor Hugo, *Les Miserables*

HAS POSSIBILITIES FOR
-presents possibilities for

HAS RUN OUT
-has been exhausted

HAS VALUE
-is a commodity

HASTY
-brash
-impudent

HATE
-hold in contempt
-abhor
-loathe
-have no liking for

HATEFUL
-odious
-contemptuous
-invidious

HATRED
-enmity
-animosity
-antipathy
-aversion
-contempt
-deep antagonism
-ill-will

HATRED OF PEOPLE
-misanthropy

HATRED OF WOMEN
-misogyny

HAVE
-are endowed with
-come equipped with

"In Texas, in the good ol' days, I spent lots of time riding around in trucks with complete maniacs who liked to talk about kicking ass, and especially minority ass, (Alexie's stories frequently explore this dynamic) and sometimes they acted on it. In real life these dudes all pretty much lacked the ability to reflect on their behavior, no matter how dire the consequences, but Alexie's come equipped with souls." Macy Halford, *The New Yorker*, Nov. 5, 2009

-are in receipt of
-carry with them
-possess

"Her being seemed composed of shadow, with too little substance for it to possess sex. It was a shred of matter harboring a light, with large eyes that were always cast down; a pretext for a soul to linger on earth." Victor Hugo, *Les Miserables*

-hold
-bear

HAVE A NEGATIVE EFFECT ON
-impinge on

HAVE A PROBLEM WITH
-have a quarrel with
-bristle at
-take umbrage to
-take issue with

> They will have a problem with that.
>
> They will take issue with that.

HAVE AN EFFECT ON
-take hold of
-arouse a feeling in
-impress upon
-strike home

-inform
-reverberate

HAVE ANY PROBLEMS
-encounter any problems

HAVE BECOME IMPORTANT
-have gained increasing importance
-have gained currency

HAVE CONFIDENCE IN
-have every confidence in

HAVE FOR A LONG TIME
-have long been

HAVE GOTTEN USED TO
-have grown accustomed to

HAVE HATRED
-bear malice
-harbor ill-will

> I don't hate him.
>
> I bear him no ill-will.

HAVE IN COMMON
-a common thread underlies

HAVE LITTLE TO DO WITH
-have only indirect bearing upon

HAVE MY REVENGE
-exact revenge

HAVE NO
-am free from
-own no

"I suppose each of us must be guilty of certain sins. We'd be less than human if we weren't blemished a bit. And I strive earnestly not to envy, not to grow little snips and slips and buds and seeds of jealousy. I deplore cruelty, and own no avarice—at least none I'm conscious of." MacKinlay Kantor, *Andersonville*

HAVE NOT COME TRUE
-have proved hollow

"The predictions of war have proved hollow."

HAVE POWER
-hold sway

HAVE QUALITIES
-exhibit qualities

HAVE SECOND THOUGHTS
-think better of

HAVE SEX
-to couple
-to bed

HAVE THE OPPORTUNITY
-have the occasion to

HAVE THE RIGHT
-are entitled
-have just claim to

HAVEN'T YOU EVER SEEN IT
-have you never seen it

HAVING AN EFFECT
-reverberating

HAVING DIFFICULTIES
-hard-pressed
-burdened
-beset with

HAZY
-nebulous

HE
-for his part
-he, on his part

HE DIDN'T SEEM TO MIND
-he was philosophical

HE IS
-I have found him to be
-he may suffer from spells of
-his ___ manner never abandoned him
-he is given to

-he has shown himself to be
-he is the product of
-he has a taste for
-he is learned in
-he could easily be classified as

HE IS GOOD AT
-he is learned in
-he was suited for nothing so well as
 for the study of

HE LITERALLY HAD TO
-he had literally to

"Until he was almost ten the name stuck to him. He had literally to fight his way free of it." Edna Ferber, *So Big*

____ HE SAID
-_____said he [poetic]

"'And Satin has a tail, Broader than a large ship's sail. Hold up your tail, Satin!' said he." Geoffrey Chaucer

HE THOUGHT OF HIMSELF AS A
-he thought himself a

HEAD BOWED
-with downcast head

HEAD OF HAIR
-mane
-thatch

HEAD UP
-preside over

HEALING
-curative
-restorative

HEALTHY
-the picture of health

HEAR
-get wind of

HEAR IT FROM
-have it from

HEARD IT THROUGH THE GRAPEVINE
-have it on good authority

HEARD OF
-the only instance she had ever met was that of

HEARING WHAT WAS SAID, HE
-at these words, he

HEAVEN
-the heavens

HEAVENLY
-ethereal
-otherworldly

HEAVY
-ponderous
-leaden

HEAVY DRINKER
-prodigious drinker

HEDGE
-equivocate

HEIGHT
-stature

HEIR TO A PROMINENT FAMILY
-scion

HELD BACK
-checked her first impulse
-kept his counsel

HELD ON TO IT
-kept hold of it
-held to it

HELD PRISONER (NOT ALLOWED TO COMMUNICATE)
-held incommunicado

HELD RESPONSIBLE
-held accountable
-being called to account

HELL
-perdition

-inferno
-nether world

HELLO-HOW-ARE-YOU (EXCHANGING HELLO'S)
-exchanging pleasantries

HELP
-cater to
-enable
-facilitate
-accommodate
-address the needs of
-ease the workload of
-be of service to
-come to the aid of
-render aid
-minister to
-empower
-ease the job of
-be of help
-offer some assistance
-intervene

HELPFUL
-accommodating
-obliging
-conducive to
-effectual
-salutary
-helpful to your cause

> The concierge was very helpful.
>
> The concierge was more than accommodating.

HELPLESS
-impotent

HELPS ME
-has served me well

HELPS TO
-serves to

HELPS TO PROMOTE
-makes for a better

HER OPINIONS ARE
-in her general opinions she is

"In her general opinions she is surprisingly moralistic. She is offended by tourists who bare their breasts ('udders,' she calls them) on public beaches; she thinks vagabonds should be rounded up and put to work sweeping the streets." J.M. Coetzee, *Disgrace*

HERE
-at hand
-upon us
-accounted for
-in attendance

HERE AND THERE
-about and about

"It was bandaged about and about with dirty white tape, tied in a neat bow." A. S. Byatt, *Possession*

HERE LIES (GRAVESTONE)
-hic jacet {Latin, *heek YAH-kit*}

HESITATE
-dither
-waver

HIDDEN
-cloaked
-harbored
-ensconced
-latent
-dormant
-smoldering
-vestigial
-veiled
-obscured by
-secluded from
-indistinguishable from
-masked by

HIDDEN TRAITORS
-the fifth column

HIDE
-obscure
-ensconce
-enshroud
-belie
-cloak
-sequester
-conceal

HIDE FROM
-lie in wait
-take refuge in
-escape the notice of
-sequester
-conceal

HIDE MONEY
-salt it away

HIGH
-lofty
-from on high

HIGH CLASS
-privately bred

"She was a woman privately bred."

HIGH FASHION
-couture {French, *koo-TOUR*}

HIGH PRESSURE TACTICS
-coercive tactics

HIGH SOCIETY
-haut monde {French, *oh MOND*}

HIGHER STANDARD
-a new pitch of perfection

HIGHEST
-loftiest

HIGHEST POINT
-zenith
-apex
-culmination
-pinnacle

HIGHLIGHTS (IT HIGHLIGHTS)
-it underscores

HIGHLY SPECIALIZED
-esoteric

HIGH-PITCHED
-falsetto

HIMSELF
-his whole person
-his ungainly person
-his self

"Carbolic soap, that would have cleaned a greasy floor, he agitated it into a suit of suds, that fitted him well, and he scraped at his self with a piece of greystone, that he stuck into the wall in a particular niche when he was done—from where it poked out like a nose." Sebastian Barry, *The Secret Scripture*

HINDSIGHT'S 20/20
-in retrospect

> Hindsight's 20/20.
>
> In retrospect, we should have exercised more caution.

HINT AT
-allude to
-signal
-make intimations of

HINTS OF
-traces of
-reminiscences of
-remnants of

HIRED
-engaged
-commissioned

HIS ____ WAS
-his was a ____ that could

HIS ____ WERE LIKE A ____
-his ____ were the ____ of a ____

"The skin of his wrinkled brown face had a dry and scaly look; his hands were the hands of a crocodile. His movements were marked by the lizard's disconcertingly abrupt

clockwork speed; his speech was thin, fluty, and dry." Aldous Huxley, *Chrome Yellow*

HISTORY OF
-in the annals of
-in the ledgers of
-the chronology of
-the evolution of

HIT BY
-struck by

HIT HOME
-it came home to me when

HOBBY
-my ruling passion

HOLD
-harbor

HOLD BACK
-check
-refrain from
-restrain

HOLD OFF
-keep at bay
-stave off

> There are ways to hold them off.
> There are ways to keep them at bay.

HOLD ON TO
-keep hold of
-hold to them

"His sentiments are, he is aware, complacent, even uxorious. Nevertheless he does not cease to hold to them." J.M. Coetzee, *Disgrace*

HOLD UP
-bear scrutiny
-bear inspection

"As political analysis, there's something to be said for Krugman's Manichean view

of the world. But Krugman is also an economist—a very good one—and the economics of what is proposed bear inspection." John Cassidy, *The New Yorker*, Nov. 4, 2009

HOLD UP TO
-bear the weight of

HOLDING BACK
-withholding

HOLDING BACK FEELINGS
-reticent

HOLE
-aperture [technical]

HOLINESS
-sanctity

HOME
-dwelling
-habitat
-abode

HOMELAND [THIS WORD HAS A FASCIST CONNOTATION]
-the country

HOMELAND SECURITY
-National Security
-Civil Defense

HOMELESS
-destitute
-dispossessed

HOMELESSNESS
-destitution

"Nightfall assembled them, as it did the stars. With nothing in common but their destitution, they mustered to sleep together in the Porch of Our Lord, cursing, insulting and jostling each other, picking quarrels with old enemies, or throwing earth and rubbish, even rolling on the ground and spitting and biting with rage." Miguel Angel Asturias, *The President*

HONEST
-principled
-forthright
-candid

HONESTY
-veracity
-candor
-probity [academic]

HONOR (TO HONOR)
-pay homage to {HAW-mij}

HONORARY
-titular {TI-chuh-ler} (in title only)

HOOKED OR CURVED
-aquiline

HOPE
-hold out the possibility that
-trust that
-aspire to

HOPE TO GOD THAT
-God grant that you never

HOPELESS
-an exercise in futility
-incorrigible
-irredeemable
-tilting at windmills

HOPELESS ACT
-fool's errand

HOPELESSLY
-irredeemably

HORIZONTAL
-prone
-supine
-recumbent

HOSPITAL-LIKE
-utilitarian
-institutional

"Get some plaster, he said, propped up in the bed, which looked odd and institutional among the Persian rugs and Colonial

furniture and dozens of antique clocks."
Paul Harding, *Tinkers*

HOSTILE
-acrimonious

HOSTING
-playing host to

HOT
-torrid
-sultry
-oppressive

HOT-TEMPERED
-irascible
-choleric

HOUR (IN AN HOUR)
-in an hour's time

HOVER

-LOOM HOW
-however did you
-the way in which
-the ___ by which
-the means whereby control of

HOW ARE YOU NOT
-how is it you're not

HOW CAN
-how is it that

"How is it that Americans, so solicitous of the animals they keep as pets, are so indifferent to the ones they cook for dinner? The answer cannot lie in the beasts themselves. Pigs, after all, are quite companionable, and dogs are said to be delicious."
Elizabeth Kolbert, *The New Yorker,*
Nov. 9, 2009

HOW DO I
-how does one go about

HOW DO YOU EXPECT HER TO
-how is she to

HOW DO YOU EXPLAIN
-how to explain

HOW DO YOU MEAN
-in what respect

HOW FAR
-to what extent

HOW HE DOES IT
-how he goes about it

HOW IT IS (THAT'S HOW IT IS)
-that's the nature of the beast

HOW IT IS DONE
-as is standard practice when
-it is the custom of

HOW IT WILL TURN OUT
-what may come of

HOW MANY ___ DO YOU HAVE
-how many ___ have you

HOW MUCH
-to what extent

HOW SHOULD I TAKE THAT
-how am I to take that

HOWEVER
-nevertheless
-nonetheless
-howbeit
-howsoever
-that said
-then again
-notwithstanding

HUGE
-beyond measure
-immeasurable
-monumental
-commanding
-elephantine
-prodigious
-ponderous

HUGE AMOUNT OF
-torrent of

-considerable amount of
-wealth of
-host of
-extensive amount of
-goodly number of
-fair amount of
-fuming not a little
-hordes of
-profuse amount of
-great many
-litany of
-galaxy of
-legion of

"The number of secretly gay anti-gay activists is legion."

HUGE THING
-leviathan

HUMAN RESOURCES [INCORRECT USAGE]
-people

HUMBLE
-unassuming
-inglorious
-innocuous
-self-effacing
-deferential

HUMILIATE
-abase

HUMILIATING
-ignominious {ig-nu-MIN-ee-us}
-abject

HUMILIATION
-indignity

HUMOR SOMEONE
-indulge someone

HUMOROUS
-jesting
-jocular

HUNG OUT AT
-frequented

-habituated

"Years ago, my clique habituated a lower east-side restaurant called Hat (translated from El Sombrero for N.Y.C. natives). The enchiladas were O.K.; the main attractions were the cheap margaritas, the salsa jukebox and the nervy, unreasonable mood of the place, largely delivered by the indifferent Goth waitress who always wore an enormous black turban." Cintra Wilson, *New York Times*, Nov. 3, 2009

HUNGRY
-ravenous
-an appetite for
-peckish (somewhat hungry) [British]
-ravening {RAV-en-ing}
-voracious

HURRY
-hasten
-must not linger
-make haste

HURT (FEEL PAIN)
-suffer
-endure
-pains me to
-gives me much pain

HURT (INFLICT PAIN)
-aggrieve
-afflict

HURT RELATIONS WITH
-sour relations with

HURTING
-feeling the sting

HYMEN
-maidenhead

HYPNOTIC
-mesmeric

HYPOCRITE
-a whited sepulcher {*WHITE-ed SEP-ul-ker*}

HYPOTHESIZE
-theorize

I i

I ACCEPT THAT
-I am resigned to
-I will allow that
-I have come to terms with

I ACCUSE!
-J'accuse! {French, *zhu-CUSE*}
[often playful in a melodramatic way]

I ADMIT THAT
-I make no secret of
-I will allow that
-I will grant you
-I recognize
-I must come to terms with
-by my own account

I AGREE
-yes, that it is
-my sentiments exactly
-I'm inclined to agree
-I consent to
-I subscribe to
-I am of like mind
-I will allow that
-I am in support of
-I have reached an accommodation
-I am in complete accord

I AGREE WITH _____
-I'm with _____ on this

I AM
-I remain

I AM AFRAID THAT IT WOULD
-I fear it would

I AM GOING TO
-I have a mind to

I AM NOT HERE TO DEFEND
-I'm no apologist for

I AM NOT SURE IF
-it's not clear to me whether

I AM PROUD OF
-they do me honor

I AM STILL YOUNG
-I am young still

I AM SURE
-I have no doubt
-of this I'm sure

I AM TELLING YOU
-I tell you

I BEGAN TO CRY
-I fell to crying [poetic]

"And all at once, though I had remained dry-eyed through all the insults done me on board ship and through the hours of despair when I was alone on the waves with the captain lying dead at my feet, a handspike jutting from his eye-socket, I fell to crying." J.M. Coetzee, *Foe*

I BELIEVE THEY WOULD DO THAT
-I believe that of them

I CAN THINK OF MANY ____
-many ____ come to mind

I CAN USE
-I have use for

"'I can use dynamite,' said the man with the carbine. He handed back the paper to Robert Jordan and looked him over. 'Yes, I have use for dynamite. How much have you brought me.'" Ernest Hemingway, *For Whom the Bell Tolls*

I CANNOT
-I regret that I cannot
-normally I would be delighted, but

-it puts me in something of a dilemma
-I remain unconvinced of the value of
-I find that I cannot
-your idea has merit, but

I CAN'T TALK, BECAUSE I'M JUST AS GUILTY
-I'm not exactly in a position to criticize

I COULD BE WRONG
-nothing I have said is immune to scrutiny

I DID NOT
-I had not the

I DID NOT KNOW SHE DID THAT
-it happened unbeknownst to me

I DO NOT HAVE
-I have not the [poetic]

I DO NOT KNOW
-I cannot say

I DO NOT UNDERSTAND HOW
-I cannot comprehend how

I DON'T BELIEVE IT
-I find that hard to accept

I DON'T CARE
-it's of no consequence to me
-it's a matter of indifference to me

I DON'T HAVE TIME FOR THIS
-I've no time for this

I DON'T HAVE YOUR SENSE OF
-I haven't your sense of

I DON'T KNOW WHY
-it is not at all clear why

I DON'T LIKE IT
-it's not to my liking

I DON'T LIKE TO
-I take no pleasure in
-I'm not one to

I don't like to complain.

I'm not one to complain.

I DON'T MEAN TO
-it is not my intention to

I DON'T THINK IT WILL WORK
-I'm skeptical that it will work

I DON'T THINK SO
-there is little to suggest that
-I think not

I DON'T WANT
-I'm not comfortable with

I ENCOURAGE
-it is to be encouraged
-it is to be welcomed

I FELT
-there came to me a

I GIVE YOU MY WORD
-here is my hand on it

I HAVE ALSO SEEN
-so have I seen

I HAVE BEEN
-I am

"A dark shadow fell upon me, not of a cloud, but of a man with a dazzling halo about him. 'Castaway,' I said with my thick dry tongue. 'I am cast away. I am all alone.' And I held out my sore hands."
J.M. Coetzee, *Foe*

I HAVE DECIDED TO
-I have resolved to
-I have taken it upon myself to
-I have thought it well to

I HAVE NEVER
-never have I

I HAVE NEVER SEEN
-I have never encountered

I HAVE NO IDEA HOW
-I cannot account for
-I can give no account of how

I HAVE SEEN THIS
-this I have seen

I HAVE WANTED FOR A LONG TIME TO
-I have long wanted to

I HEARD IT THROUGH THE GRAPEVINE
-I have it on good authority

I HOPE THAT
-it is my hope that

I HOPE THIS WILL HELP
-I hope this will be of some help
-I hope this information will be of use to

I HOPE YOU'VE LEARNED YOUR LESSON
-let this be a lesson to you

I HOPED
-I was not without hope

I JUST MIGHT
-I have a mind to

I KNOW WHAT IT'S LIKE TO
-I know what it is to

> I know what it's like to be young and foolish.
>
> I know what it is to be young and foolish.

I KNOW YOU VERY WELL
-I know you only too well

I ONLY NEED TO SEE
-I need only see

I MEAN WHAT I SAY
-so help me God

I MIGHT BE PERSUADED
-I could take an interest

I MUST ADMIT
-truth be told

I REMEMBER THE
-I remember well the

I REPLIED
-I returned

I SHOULD SAY
-I hasten to add

I STAND HERE
-here I stand [poetic]

I STILL LOVE HER
-I love her still

"Granny died in January, 1942; no one will ever know how much she is present in my thoughts and how much I love her still."
Anne Frank, *Anne Frank: The Diary of a Young Girl*

I SWEAR
-upon my word

I THINK
-in my judgment
-I am of the opinion that
-to my thinking
-it strikes me as
-as I see it
-I should think
-I should imagine
-my own feeling is

I THINK, BUT I'M NOT ENTIRELY SURE
-it is ostensibly

I THINK I'LL
-I've a mind to

I THOUGHT
-I reasoned

I THOUGHT TO MYSELF
-I figured to myself

I WAS BORN IN
-I was born at

"I was born at Geneva in 1712, the son of Isaac Rousseau, a citizen of that town, and Susann Bernard, his wife." Jean-Jacques Rousseau, *The Confessions*

I WAS LUCKY ENOUGH TO
-I had the good luck to

"I had the great luck one summer of studying the three-toed sloth in situ in the equatorial jungles of Brazil." Yann Martel, *Life of Pi*

I WAS SURPRISED TO
-I was struck by

I WILL
-I will do so

I WILL ALWAYS REMEMBER
-I will long remember

I WILL BE THE ____
-I will take on the job of ____

I WON'T
-who am I to

I WOULD LIKE TO
-I am happy to
-I take genuine pleasure in
-I should like to

"...my bed is a goal attained at last, it is my consolation and might become my faith if the management allowed me to make a few changes: I should like, for instance, to have the bars built up higher, to prevent anyone from coming too close to me." Günter Grass, *Tin Drum*

I WOULD NEVER
-far be it from me to _____

I WOULD NOT CARE IF
-I would care little if

IDEA
-conception
-construct
-sentiment
-abstraction
-notion

IDEA I HAD
-an idea I had entertained

"Quite inadvertently, I brought myself to tell him about an idea I had now and then entertained. 'My husband has to be someone who can afford a two-bedroom apartment, since Eeyore will be living with us. And I want to live a quiet life there.'" Kenzaburo Oe, *A Quiet Life*

IDEA OF
-prospect of
-brainchild of
-notion of

IDEA OF BEAUTY
-his aesthetic

IDEAL MODEL
-exemplar

IDEALISTIC
-quixotic (impractically idealistic)

IDENTIFY
-pinpoint
-establish
-distinguish

IDEOLOGICAL
-doctrinaire {dock-trin-AIR}

IDIOT
-troglodyte

IDOLIZATION OF
-deification of
-apotheosis of [academic] {Greek, uh-POTH-ee-OH-sis}

IDOLIZE
-deify

IF
-should
-whether
-if presumably
-were it

"I have taken this subject on a former occasion; and were it left to my own will, I should prefer to repeat it almost every year..." Michael Faraday, *The Chemical History of a Candle*

IF ANYTHING HAPPENS TO HIM
-if any harm comes to him
-should any harm come to him

IF I EVER HELD
-if I came to hold

IF I THOUGHT IT WOULD WORK
-if I knew anything would come of it

IF I WANTED TO
-if I were so inclined
-should I be so inclined
-had I so willed it

IF IT IS TRUE
-if it has any truth

"The planet Mars, I scarcely need remind the reader, revolves about the sun at a mean distance of 140,000,000 miles, and the light and heat it receives from the sun is barely half of that received by this world. It must be, if the nebular hypothesis has any truth, older than our world; and long before this earth ceased to be molten, life upon its surface must have begun its course." H. G. Wells, *The War of the Worlds*

IF NECESSARY
-if need be

IF SHE WERE TO
-were she to

IF THERE ARE
-if there be [poetic]

IF THEY WERE ALSO
-if they too were

IF YOU LIKE THIS ONE
-if you think well of this one

IF YOU SAY SO
-as you please

IF YOU WANT TO
-if you like

IF YOU WERE TO
-were you to

IFFY
-in doubt
-open to question

IGNORANT
-unenlightened
-poorly informed
-unacquainted with affairs of the world
-uninitiated
-uninstructed in

"By the year 1536, this nation had been joined by the helpless, needy wretches, unused to dolour, and uninstructed in business, who were turned abroad following the overthrow of the monasteries." Edith Sitwell, *Fanfare for Elizabeth*

-benighted

"Thirty years ago, modern methods of farming, even methods that were modern in the benighted eighteen-nineties, had not penetrated to this thinly settled part of Virginia." Ellen Glasgow, *Barren Ground*

IGNORE
-dismiss
-give short shrift
-take little notice of

"As soon as a boy asks if he may bicycle home with me and we get into conversation, nine out of ten times I can be sure that he will fall head over heels in love immediately and simply won't allow me out

of his sight. After a while it cools down of course, especially as I take little notice of ardent looks and pedal blithely on."
Anne Frank, *Anne Frank: The Diary of a Young Girl*

-discount
-put aside

"But neither he nor she can put aside what has happened. The two little boys become presences between them, playing quiet as shadows in a corner of the room where their mother and the strange man couple."
J. M. Coetzee, *Disgrace*

I'LL BET THAT
-I would go so far as saying

ILLEGAL
-illicit

ILLEGAL DETENTION LAWSUITS
-habeas corpus suits {Latin, *HAY-be-us COR-pus*}

ILLEGITIMATE
-questionable
-of dubious origins

ILLOGICAL CONCLUSION
-non sequitur {Latin, *non SECK-wuh-tor*}

ILLUSION
-sleight of hand

ILLUSTRATED
-exemplified
-brought home
-served as an example of
-embodied

I'M AWARE OF
-I'm well acquainted with

I'M NOT IN A POSITION TO [CORPORATE CLICHÉ]
-I would rather not

IMAGE
-persona
-posture

IMAGINARY
-fictitious
-fictive
-chimerical {*ky-MARE-i-cal*}

IMAGINATION
-in my mind's eye

IMAGINE
-conjure up
-envisage
-call up
-conceived an image in her mind

IMITATION
-ersatz
-pseudo
-so-called
-faux {French, *foe*, lit. false}

"A good 96 percent of the Penney's inventory is made of polyester. The few clothing items that are made of cotton make a sincere point of being cotton and tell you earnestly about their 100-percent cottonness with faux-hand-scribbled labels so obviously on the green bandwagon they practically spit pine cones." Cintra Wilson, *New York Times*, Aug. 13, 2009

IMITATIVE ART
-derivative art

> Her ideas went over well, but they were unoriginal.
>
> Her ideas were well-received, if a bit derivative.

IMMEDIATELY
-there and then
-at once

"He has always been a man of the city, at home amid a flux of bodies where eros

stalks and glances flash like arrows. But this glance between himself and Soraya he regrets at once." J.M. Coetzee, *Disgrace*

IMMORAL
-depraved
-profligate

IMMORTAL
-deathless

IMPATIENT
-does not suffer fools gladly
-could not endure inaction
-chafing at
-un-forbearing

IMPLIED
-implicit
-told in so many words

IMPLY
-purport
-intimate
-color the conversation with

IMPORTANCE
-import
-with an air of gravity

IMPORTANT
-pressing
-of the highest distinction
-figure prominently in
-worthy of note
-deserving special mention
-central to
-notable
-far-reaching
-integral
-of considerable importance
-of some importance
-substantive
-substantial
-of great consequence
-no small factor in
-consequential
-of huge significance
-imperative

-prominent
-pivotal
-looms large
-crucial to

IMPORTANT ACHIEVEMENT
-significant point of arrival

IMPORTANT LESSON
-affecting lesson

IMPORTANT MOMENT
-singular moment

IMPORTANT PERSON
-personage

IMPOSSIBLE
-out of the question
-untenable

IMPOSSIBLE TO DENY
-irrefutable

IMPOSSIBLE TO OVERCOME
-insurmountable
-insuperable [academic]

IMPOSSIBLE TO SATISFY
-insatiable

IMPOSSIBLE TO SEPARATE
-inextricable

IMPOSSIBLE TO STOP
-inexorable

IMPOSSIBLE TO UNDERSTAND
-inscrutable

IMPRESS
-awe
-command the respect of

IMPRESSED WITH
-was taken with

IMPRESSIVE
-striking
-considerable
-noteworthy

-worthy of note
-lofty
-imposing
-distinguished

IMPROPER
-untoward
-unseemly
-in poor form

IMPROVE
-make great strides in
-shore up
-further burnishes the beauty of
-bolster

IMPROVEMENT
-betterment

IN
-within
-among
-in and among
-amid
-embodied in
-contained in
-where it resides
-at

"He likes giving her presents. At New York he gave her an enameled bracelet, at Eid a little malachite heron that caught his eye in a curio shop. He enjoys her pleasure, which is quite unaffected." J.M. Coetzee, *Disgrace*

IN A BIGGER OR STRONGER WAY
-writ large

> Conceptually speaking, an observatory is nothing more than a very big telescope.
>
> Conceptually speaking, an observatory is nothing more than a telescope writ large.

IN A BOOK
-in print

IN A CERTAIN WAY
-in a given manner

IN A LIVING BODY (AS OPPOSED TO A TEST-TUBE)
in vivo {Latin, *in VEE-voe*}

IN A LONG TIME
-in recent memory

IN A NUT SHELL
-it is, in a word

IN A TEST-TUBE (AS OPPOSED TO A LIVING BODY)
-in vitro {Latin, *in VEE-troe*}

IN A TIMELY FASHION [CORP. CLICHÉ]
-with deliberate speed
-with all deliberate speed
-expedited

IN A TRANCE
-catatonic
-in a fugue state

IN A WAY
-in some sense

IN ACCORDANCE WITH
-pursuant to [formal]

IN ADDITION
-parenthetically
-at that
-furthermore
-for good measure

IN AGREEMENT
-of common mind
-congruent [academic]

IN AGREEMENT WITH
-in accordance with

"The day had gone by just as days go by. I had killed it in accordance with my primitive

and retiring way of life." Hermann Hesse, *Steppenwolf*

-in keeping with
-in sympathy with
-in obedience to

"She glanced with interest along the new brick and limestone house-fronts, fantastically varied in obedience to the American craving for novelty, but fresh and inviting with their awnings and flower-boxes." Edith Wharton, *The House of Mirth*

IN AN ACT OF
-in a gesture of

IN CAHOOTS WITH
-in league with

IN CASE YOU
-lest you

IN CHARGE OF
-over which she will preside
-preside over
-reign
-hold court
-oversee
-command over

> The agency is in cahoots with the very industry it oversees.
>
> The agency is in league with the very industry it oversees.

IN CONCLUSION
-it remains the recommendation that

IN DETAIL
-at length

IN EVERY WAY
-in all respects
-in every respect
-on all counts

IN EXISTENCE
-extant [academic]

IN EXTREME DIFFICULTY
-in extremis {Latin, *in ex-TREEM-is*}

IN FACT
-in truth

IN FRONT OF YOU
-before you

IN FULL
-in its entirety
-in extenso {Latin, *in ex-TEN-so*} [academic]

IN GENERAL
-as a whole
-on the whole
-by and large
-in the usual course of events

IN ITS NATURAL PLACE
-in situ {Latin, *in SIGH-too*}

"I had the great luck one summer of studying the three-toed sloth in situ in the equatorial jungles of Brazil." Yann Martel, *Life of Pi*

IN JANUARY OF 1940
-in the January of 1940 [poetic]

IN LINE WITH
-accords with

IN LOVE WITH
-enamored with
-taken with

"The Utopians wonder how any man should be so much taken with the glaring doubtful luster of a jewel or stone, that can look up to a star, or to the sun himself." Sir Thomas More, *Utopia*

IN MANY WAYS
-in many respects

IN MOURNING
-bereaved

IN MY OPINION
-to my mind

IN NEED OF
-in want of

"It is a truth universally acknowledged, that a single man in possession of a good fortune, must be in want of a wife." Jane Austen, *Pride and Prejudice*

IN NO WAY ARE YOU TO
-on no account are you to

IN ON
-privy to

> I was not in on the conversation.
>
> I was not privy to the conversation.

IN ORDER FOR THIS TO OCCUR
-to this end

IN ORDER TO
-so as to

IN OTHER COUNTRIES
-abroad

IN OTHER WORDS
-that is to say

IN OUR CUSTODY
-in our charge

IN PAIN
-hobbled by pain
-pained

IN PASSING
-en passant {French, *ah pa-SAHn*}

IN RESPONSE TO
-in consequence of

"I had at one time, when I was thirteen, a very orthodox Swiss tutor, who, in consequence of something I had said, stated with great earnestness: 'If you are a Darwinian I pity you, for one cannot be a Darwinian and a Christian at the same time.' I did not then believe in the incompatibility, but I was already clear that, if I had to choose, I would choose Darwin." Bertrand Russell, *On God and Religion*

IN ROUGH DRAFT FORM
-roughed out

IN SEARCH OF
-in pursuance of [academic]

IN SECRET
-sub rosa

IN SOME OF THE MOST
-in certain of the most

IN SOME WAYS
-in some respects

IN SPIRIT
-in mindset

IN SPITE OF
-notwithstanding
-nonetheless
-nevertheless
-irrespective of

IN THAT CROWD
-of that crowd

IN THAT SITUATION
-under those circumstances

IN THE BEST LIGHT POSSIBLE
-sympathetically

"The artist has treated her sympathetically."

IN THE END
-in the final analysis

IN THE MIDDLE OF
-amid
-in the midst of
-in the throes of a

IN THE PLACE OF
-in the stead of [poetic]

IN THE PLACE OF A PARENT
-in loco parentis {Latin, *in loco pa-RENT-is*}

IN THE PRESENCE OF
-in the face of
-at the center of

IN THE REAL WORLD
-in practice

IN THE SAME WAY
-in kind
-much as

IN THE STATE THAT IT'S IN, WHICH IS NOT SO GOOD
-such as it is

IN THE STYLE BACK THEN
-in the style of the day

IN THE STYLE OF
-à la {French, *ah-lah*, short for *a la mode de*, lit. in the manner of}

IN THE WAY IT IS USED
-in its application

IN THE WAY THEY DRESSED
-in their dress

IN THE WORLD
-of all this world

"The foremost man of all this world." Shakespeare on Caesar

IN THE WOMB
-in utero {Latin, *in YOU-ter-oh*}

IN THEIR DAY
-in their day and place

"Magnificence, like the size of a fortune, is always comparative, as even Magnificent Lorenzo may now perceive, if he has happened to haunt New York in 1916; and the Ambersons were magnificent in their day and place." Booth Tarkington, *The Magnificent Ambersons*

IN THIS BOOK
-herein

IN TOTAL
-all told
-en masse
-in toto {Latin, *in TOE-TOE*}

IN TROUBLE
-in some danger
-in a compromising position

IN YOUR BEST INTEREST TO
-you have much to gain from
-you have little to lose by

IN YOUR MIND
-psychosomatic

INABILITY
-incapacity

INACTIVE
-hibernating
-standing idly by
-sedentary
-torpid

INADEQUATE
-falls short of
-tinkering around the edges
-half-measures

INANIMATE
-insentient

"Of the few fair complexioned Jewish students in our preponderantly Jewish public high school, none possessed anything remotely like the steep-jawed, insentient Viking mask of this blue-eyed blond born into our tribe as Seymour Irving Levov." Philip Roth, *American Pastoral*

INAPPROPRIATE
-out of keeping with
-untoward
-unseemly

INAPPROPRIATE HUMOR
-facetious {fuh-SEE-shus}
-flippant

INCIDENTALLY
-parenthetically
-as an aside

INCITE
-foment
-stir the embers

INCLINATION (A MERE INCLINATION)
-velleity {veh-LEE-uh-tee}

"As it happens, her wish to become a marine biologist was no more than another passing velleity."

INCLUDE
-extend to
-incorporate
-embrace
-comprise

INCLUDING
-comprising
-encompassing
-extending from
-complete with
-replete with
-embracing

INCOME
-means of support

INCOMPETENT
-feckless

INCONSEQUENTIAL EVENT
-dalliance

INCONSPICUOUS
-unobtrusive
-nondescript

> The buildings were plain and average looking.
>
> The buildings were nondescript.

INCORRECT
-erroneous
-flies in the face of

INCREASE
-bolster
-intensify
-heighten
-expand
-augment
-accrue
-mount to

"Man always tends to avoid physical contact with anything strange. In the dark, the fear of an unexpected touch can mount to panic. Even clothes give insufficient security; it is easy to tear them and pierce through to the naked, smooth, defenseless flesh of the victim." Elias Canetti, *Crowds and Power*

INCREASE (AN INCREASE IN)
-accession of

INCREASING
-mounting
-swelling the ranks of

INCREDIBLE
-defied description

INDEPENDENCE
-autonomy

INDEPENDENT
-autonomous
-sovereign

INDESCRIBABLY
-ineffably

INDESTRUCTIBLE
-impregnable
-unassailable
-impervious
-invulnerable

INDICATES
-is suggestive of

INDICATION OF
-a clear measure of how
-marks a new phase in

INDIFFERENCE
-insouciance {in-SUE-see-ence}

INDIFFERENT
-perfunctory

"He gave me a perfunctory hey-how-ya-doin' as he passed me in the hall."

INDIRECT
-roundabout
-circuitous
-oblique

INDISPUTABLE
-incontrovertible
-uncontroversial [academic]

> The facts are the facts.
>
> The facts are incontrovertible.

INDIVIDUAL
-singular

INEFFECTIVE
-unavailing
-feckless

INEFFECTIVE LINE OF DEFENSE
-a Maginot line {French, MAZH-ih-no}

INEQUALITY
-disparity between

INEXPENSIVE
-on the cheap

INEXPERIENCED
-unfledged

INFERIOR
-subservient
-lesser

INFLUENCE (TO INFLUENCE)
-inform the work of
-shape
-play a part
-inspire
-impose a more _____ stamp on
-make his imprint clear
-make his presence felt
-make itself felt
-reverberate
-spill over
-leave its mark
-govern the appearance of
-find many echoes in

INFLUENCED BY
-informed by
-wrought by
-subject to
-absorbed by
-fell into the hands of

INFORM
-apprise

INFORMAL EXPRESSION
-colloquialism

INFORMED (I AM WELL INFORMED)
-I am acquainted with
-I am articulate on the subject of
-I am schooled in the art of

INFORMED (I HAVE BEEN INFORMED)
-given to understand that
-kept abreast of
-kept apprised of

> We were informed that partici-
> pation would be optional.
>
> We were given to understand
> that participation would be
> optional.

INHABITANT
-denizen of

INHALED
-drew a deep breath

INHERITOR OF
-heir to

INITIALS
-the initialism

"The initialism SPQR attested her alle-giance to Rome."

INNER THOUGHTS
-interior monologue

INSANITY
-psychosis
-dementia

"He is the witness in his death-throws of the immeasurable dementia of the sea, and, tormented by this madness, he hears sounds unknown to man that seem to come from some dreadful place beyond the bounds of earth." Victor Hugo, *Les Miserables*

INSENSITIVE
-callous
-crass
-indelicate

INSERT BETWEEN
-interpose

INSIDE
-inhabiting
-within
-internal
-inner recesses
-innermost

INSIDES (GUTS)
-viscera

INSIGNIFICANT
-negligible
-of little significance

"This story at no point becomes my own. I am in it—good heavens, I'm in it to the point of almost never being out of it!—but the story belongs, all of it, to the Carmodys, and my own part, while substantial enough, was never really of any great sig-nificance at all." Edwin O'Connor, *The Edge of Sadness*

INSINCERE
-glib
-disingenuous

INSIST ON RESPECT
-stand on one's dignity

INSPECT
-scrutinize

INSPECTION
-under close scrutiny
-under a watchful eye

INSPIRE
-enkindle

INSPIRE HER TO
-inspire in her thoughts of

INSTEAD
-in place of
-in the place of
-sooner than
-in her stead [poetic]
-as opposed to
-in lieu of {French, *lue*}
-rather than
-otherwise

INSTIGATE
-foment

INSTIGATING
-incendiary

INSTINCTIVE
-visceral
-intuitive

INSTINCTIVELY UNDERSTAND
-intuit

INSTINCTS
-imperatives

INSTRUCTION
-tutelage

INSULT (TO INSULT)
-belittle
-disparage

INSULT (AN INSULT)
-slight
-that was the unkindest cut
[Shakespeare]

INSULTING
-insolent
-pejorative

INSULTING LANGUAGE
-invective
-vitriol
-injurious attack

INSULTS THROWN AT ME
-insults done me

"And all at once, though I had remained dry-eyed through all the insults done me on board ship and through the hours of despair when I was alone on the waves with the captain lying dead at my feet, a handspike jutting from his eye-socket, I fell to crying." J.M. Coetzee, *Foe*

INSURE
-indemnify

INTELLECTUAL ELITE
-literati

"At other times, SWAT police awkwardly balanced machine guns outside the restaurant's doors while military helicopters buzzed overhead—all rather incongruous to the atmosphere that Ms. Garnaut aimed for at her restaurants, where diplomats, power brokers, and literati mingled over Champagne and caviar." Jen Lin-Liu, *New York Times*, Oct. 31, 2009
-the illuminati
-the intelligentsia

INTELLECTUAL PURSUITS
-cerebral pursuits

INTELLECTUAL, RATIONAL, AND CREATIVE
-Apollonian (as opposed to Dionysian)

INTELLECTUALS
-intelligentsia

INTENSE UNDERSTANDING OF
-intimate knowledge of

INTENSIFY
-heighten the effect
-compound

INTENSITY
-severity

INTERDEPENDENT
-symbiotic
-obliging

INTEREST
-concern
-engage the attention of
-vested interest

INTERESTED IN
-keen on
-taking a close interest in

INTERESTING
-of interest
-compelling
-engrossing

-likely to be of interest
-arresting

INTERESTS OF
-preoccupations of

INTERPRET
-construe
-view the issue through the lens of

INTERPRETATION OF
-rendition of

INTERRUPTED
-interjected
-interposed [academic]

INTERRUPTED BY
-punctuated by

INTERVENE
-intercede

INTERVENING RESOLUTION
-deus ex machina {Latin, *deh-oose ex MAHK-in-uh*}

INTIMATE AND PRIVATE
-intime {French, *ahn-TEEM*}

INTIMIDATE
-buffalo

INTIMIDATED BY IT
-cowed by it

INTIMIDATING
-daunting
-imposing

INTO VIEW
-to the fore

INTRODUCE
-unveil

INTRODUCE INTO
-infuse
-inject a dose of

INTRODUCING
-let me direct your attention to

INTRODUCTION
-preamble
-prelude
-exordium [academic]

INTRUDE
-encroach
-trespass on your privacy

INTRUDER
-interloper

INTRUDING
-intrusive
-invasive

INVASION
-incursion

INVENTION
-innovation

INVESTIGATION
-inquest
-inquiry
-review

INVISIBLE
-vaporous
-ethereal
-veiled

INVITES
-provides fertile ground for

INVOLVE
-entail
-embroil

INVOLVED
-played a key role in
-is immersed in
-is at the center of
-may be a party to
-will take part in
-will partake in
-is a participant in

INVOLVED ILLEGALLY
-complicit

INVOLVED IN AN ONGOING FIGHT
-embattled

INVOLVEMENT
-what role he may have played

IRRATIONAL, DESTRUCTIVE, UNINHIBITED
-Dionysian (as opposed to Apollonian)

IRRELEVANT
-beside the point
-neither here nor there
-of no consequence

> It doesn't matter.
>
> It's of no consequence.

IRRITABLE
-peevish

IRRITATE
-pique
-vex
-gall

IRRITATING
-grating
-galling

IS
[consider dropping this word in special circumstances]

"Good-bye—if you hear of my being stood up against a Mexican stone wall and shot to rags please know that I think that [ ] a pretty good way to depart this life. It beats old age, disease, or falling down the cellar stairs. To be a Gringo in Mexico—ah, that is euthanasia!" Ambrose Bierce in a letter to his niece Lora

-remains
-constitutes
-is by far
-is, if nothing else

-as is standard practice when
-qualifies as
-is proving to be
-is subject to
-survives
-is of course
-serves as
-has tendencies towards
-is that of
-finds itself
-is of great importance
-is the personification of
-personifies
-is the product of
-amounts to no more than
-is at once apparent in

> At least he's entertaining.
>
> He is, if nothing else, entertaining.

____ IS A
-what is ____ but a

IS A LOT LIKE
-has the more general character of

IS A SIGN OF
-denotes
-indicates

IS A STORY ABOUT
-tells the story of

IS ABOUT
-concerns itself with

IS AS GOOD AS
-can take its place alongside

IS AT
-stands at

IS BECAUSE OF
-stems from
-is owing to
-is governed by

IS BEING USED FOR
-is occupied by

"The soil is fertile, the rains plentiful, and a considerable proportion of ground is occupied by cultivation, and amply supplies the wants of the inhabitants." Winston Churchill, *The Story of the Malakand Field Force*

IS BOTH
-is at once _____ and _____

IS CALLED
-is known by the name of

"...there lies a small market town or rural port, which by some is called Greensburgh, but which is more generally and properly known by the name of Tarry Town." Washington Irving, *The Legend of Sleepy Hollow*

IS COMPOSED OF
-comprises

IS CONSIDERED
-is seen as

IS DESTRUCTIVE
-is a destroyer

IS DUE TO
-owes something to

IS EQUAL TO
-constitutes

IS FOR (IS FOR TWO WEEKS)
-provides for

"Her itinerary provided for two weeks in Paris, and she had suffered through one week of it when, like an angel from heaven, an Englishman called Tippy Akenside showed up at her hotel at the very moment when she was about to dissolve in tears and book passage home." Jean Stafford, *The Collected Stories of Jean Stafford*

IS FOR THE READER TO DECIDE
-is left to the reader to decide

IS FOUND
-is to be found

IS FROM _____
-is a native of _____

IS GOING TO
-intends to

IS GONE
-gone is the

IS HERE
-is at hand

IS IMPORTANT
-figures prominently in

IS IN THE
-lay in the
-lies in the

IS INTERESTING
-is of some interest

IS IT
-can it be

IS IT ACCEPTED
-does it have currency

IS LUCKY (HE IS LUCKY)
-lucky is he who [poetic]

IS MADE UP OF
-is comprised of

IS MUCH LIKE
-it recalls

IS NO LONGER
-has ceased to be

IS NO LONGER A FOOL
-is a fool no more

IS NO LONGER ACCEPTED
-fell out of favor

IS NOT A BATTLE BETWEEN
-is a battle not between

"Life—the way it really is—is a battle not between Bad and Good but between Bad and Worse." Joseph Brodsky

IS NOT IN THE
-lies not in the

IS OBVIOUS
-is hardly to be questioned

IS ONE OF
-is among

IS ONLY
-remains at best no more than

IS PROOF OF
-is testament to

IS RESPECTED
-carries great weight

IS SO FAR THE BEST
-is yet unequalled

IS SOMEWHERE IN BETWEEN
-lies between the two

IS STILL THE
-remains the

IS THE BASIS OF
-underlies

IS UNLIMITED
-is unending
-knows no bounds
-has no bounds

"His arrogance has no bounds by day or night." Anonymous, *Gilgamesh*

IS USUALLY AT THE
-can often be found at the

ISOLATE
-insulate
-sequester

ISOLATED
-insular

IT
-the matter (after looking into the matter)
-the thing

IT DIDN'T SCARE HIM
-it gave him no fear

IT IS A GOOD IDEA
-the idea is appealing

IT IS ABOUT TIME
-it was so long in coming

IT IS AMAZING
-it is a wonder

IT IS BECAUSE
-it is that

"Yet one cannot say with equal certainty just why the difficulty was peculiar to Memphis, unless it is that Memphis, unlike other Tennessee cities, remains to this day a 'land-oriented' place." Peter Taylor, A *Summons to Memphis*

IT IS IMPORTANT
-it bears repeating

IT IS IMPOSSIBLE TO KNOW
-there is no saying

IT IS LIKE
-it recalls a certain
-it is reminiscent of
-it is akin to
-it is much the same as
-it's _____ian

IT IS NO USE
-it is to no avail

IT IS NOT EVEN PART OF
-it is outside the realm of

IT IS NOT SURPRISING THAT
-it may come as no surprise that

IT IS THE RESPONSIBILITY OF
-the onus is on

IT IS TOO BAD
-more's the pity
-what a pity

IT IS TRUE THAT
-there is no question that
-it's the truth I'm telling you

IT IS UP TO YOU
-it's at your discretion

IT JUST SO HAPPENS THAT
-as it happens

IT MAKES HER CRAZY
-it gives her fits

IT NO LONGER
-it has ceased to

IT ONLY NEEDS TO BE
-it need only be

IT REMINDS ME OF
-I am reminded that
-it recalls

> It reminds me of my childhood.
> It recalls my childhood.

IT SEEMS
-it has an element of
-it has a strain of
-it strikes me as

IT SEEMS THAT
-it often appears that
-we are left with the impression that

IT SEEMS THAT WAY
-it seems so

IT SOLD FOR
-it brought

IT TOOK ONLY _____ MINUTES
-it took all of _____ minutes

IT WAS _____
-_____ as it was

IT WAS A
-it made for a

IT WAS CERTAIN THAT
-certain it was that

IT WAS FRIDAY
-the day was Friday

IT WAS LIKE HER TO
-it was characteristic of her that

"It was characteristic of her that she always roused speculation, that her simplest acts seemed the result of some far-reaching intentions." Edith Wharton, *The House of Mirth*

IT WAS LOVE AT FIRST SIGHT
-she loved right from the first sight
  [Geoffrey Chaucer]

IT WAS NAMED
-the name was given

"...there lies a small market town or rural port, which by some is called Greensburgh, but which is more generally and properly known by the name of Tarry Town. This name was given, we are told, in former days, by the good housewives of the adjacent country, from the inveterate propensity of their husbands to linger about the village tavern on market days." Washington Irving, *The Legend of Sleepy Hollow*

IT WAS THOUGHT
-it was held to be certain that

IT WOULD BE GOOD IF YOU
-you would do well to

IT WOULD HAVE BEEN GOOD IF
-it would have been well if

IT WOULD NOT BE GOOD FOR THE
-it would not do for the

IT'S ABOUT TIME
-it's high time

IT'S ALL I KNOW HOW TO DO
-I know no other way

"I love you without knowing how, or when, or from where. I love you straightforwardly, without complexities or pride; so I love you because I know no other way." Pablo Neruda

IT'S GOOD FOR YOU
-it does one good

IT'S LOGICAL
-it stands to reason

IT'S NOT EASY FOR ME TO
-I find it difficult to

I'VE NEVER UNDERSTOOD THAT
-that I've never understood

"I'm not one of those writers I learned about who get up in the morning, put a piece of paper in their typewriter machine and start writing. That I've never understood." Wole Soyinka

Jj

JARGON
-dialect
-vernacular

JEALOUS
-with jaundiced eye

JERK
-enfant terrible {French, *ahn-fawn tair-EEB-la*}

JET SET
-glitterati

JOB
-undertaking

-pursuit
-post
-position

JOINED
-conjoined

JOKE
-farce

JOKING
-in jest

JOKING AROUND
-playful banter

JOURNEY
-sojourn

JOY OF LIVING
-joie de vivre {French, *zhwa duh VEEV-ruh*}

JUDGE (A JUDGE)
-an arbiter
-an umpire

"Those who are esteemed umpires of taste are often persons who have acquired some knowledge of admired pictures or sculptures, and have an inclination for whatever is elegant; but if you inquire whether they are beautiful souls, and whether their own acts are like fair pictures, you learn that they are selfish and sensual." Ralph Waldo Emerson, "The Poet"

JUDGE THEM
-pass judgment on
-render judgment
-form assumptions
-judge of them

JUDGED
-deemed

JUDGES (THE JUDGES)
-the judiciary

JUDGMENT
-reckoning

JUDGMENT DAY
-day of reckoning
-a day you will rue

JUDICIAL BRANCH OF GOVERNMENT
-the judiciary

JUMP
-bound

JUMP IN
-intervene

JUNK
-debris
-detritus [academic]

JURY IS STILL OUT ON THAT ONE
-it's a matter of dispute

JUST
-simply

JUST ABOUT
-nearly

JUST AS
-just as _____, if not more so
-with the same ferocity it reserves for
-is equally well suited for
-no less

"*No less destructive are the insidious ways in which he enables her addiction to painkillers.*"

JUST AS GOOD AS
-yields the same in terms of

JUST AS IMPRESSIVE
-no less impressive is
-not less capable than

JUST AS MUCH
-no less
-_____ no less

JUST BEGUN
-nascent
-incipient
-inchoate {in-KOE-it}

JUST DESERTS
-poetic justice

JUST FOR THIS PURPOSE
-ad hoc

JUST IN CASE YOU
-lest you
-if by chance you

JUST IN TIME
-heaven sent
-a godsend

JUST LIKE
-likewise
-true of all such
-might be mistaken for
-in the style of

"*Reflections on politics, though, take a back seat to the practicalities of surviving on the road and, in the style of Herodotus, collecting dubious bits of lore.*" Richard B. Woodward, *New York Times*, Nov. 1, 2009

JUST LIKE THIS
-rather like this

JUST SHOOT ME
-finish me off entirely why don't you

JUST THE RIGHT WORD
-le mot juste {French, *lay moe* ZHOOST}

JUST TO BE ON THE SAFE SIDE
-for good measure

JUSTICE
-an accounting
-a reckoning

JUSTIFICATION
-rationale
-grounds
"*You have no grounds for saying so.*"
-under the banner of
-done in the name of

-on what basis
-pretext for
-warrant for

JUSTIFY
-account for
-warrant
-provide a basis for

Kk

KEEN
-acute
-incisive
-penetrating

KEEP
-retain
-hold in abeyance [formal]

KEEP AN OPEN MIND
-leave the door open to

KEEP FROM
-refrain from
-forbear from

"As for my mother, she taught me to have regard for religion, to be generous and open-handed, and not only to forbear from doing anybody an ill turn, but not so much as to endure the thought of it. By her likewise I was bred to a plain, inexpensive way of living, very different from the common luxury of the rich." Marcus Aurelius, *Meditations*

KEEP GOING
-stop at nothing
-persist in
-sustain a level of

KEEP IN MIND
-bear in mind

KEEP IT AWAY
-keep it at bay

KEEP IT FRIENDLY
-remain in good graces

KEEP IT TO YOURSELF
-don't breathe a word

KEEP QUIET
-keep your peace
-keep your counsel

KEEP WATCH OVER
-ride herd on

KEPT
-retained
-preserved

KEPT FROM IT
-deprived of it

"But when you're deprived of it for a lengthy period then you value human companionship. But you have to survive and so you devise all kinds of mental exercises and it's amazing." Wole Soyinka

KEPT SECRET
-closely held

KEPT SILENT
-he preserved a _____ silence

KEY
-fundamental

KEY TO
-passport to
-instrumental in

KICK THE HABIT
-cure oneself of

KID
-jest

KILL
-dispatch
-slay

"Clocks slay time…time is dead as long as it is being clicked off by little wheels; only

when the clock stops does time come to life." William Faulkner

KILL TIME
-while away the hours

KILLED THEM
-claimed more than a thousand lives
-felled them all
-dealt a fatal blow
-made an end of them

"*Some she pursued over the moors and assailed with her sword, and brightly flashed the blade as she made an end of them.*" Halldór Laxness, *Independent People*

KILLED BY
-died at the hand of
-was slain by

KIND
-the likes of
-of that nature
-of the _____ persuasion
-of a certain bent
-a form of
-specimen
-a species of

"*Grief, sir, is a species of idleness.*" Saul Bellow

KIND OF
-to some extent
-quasi
-pseudo
-a _____ of sorts
-something of a

KINDER
-kindlier

"*A city where American faces were still to be seen upon all its streets, a cleaner and a kindlier town, with more courtesy in its life, less of the vulgar scramble.*" Ernest Poole, *His Family*

KINDLY
-benevolent

-benign

KINDS OF
-modes of
-varieties of
-species of

KING
-_____ rex

KNEW
-knew full well

KNICK KNACK
-tchotchke {Yiddish, CHAUCH-*kuh*}
-bric-á-brac {French, BRICK-*a-brack*}
-bauble

KNOW
-acquainted with
-well informed of
-mindful of
-surprised to find

KNOW AHEAD OF TIME
-have foreknowledge of

KNOW MY WAY AROUND
-know my way about

KNOW NO MORE THAN BEFORE
-be none the wiser

> She'll never know.
> She'll be none the wiser.

KNOW WHAT IT'S LIKE TO
-know what it is to be

"*I lost my own father at 12 yr. of age and I know what it is to be raised on lies and silences my dear daughter you are presently too young to understand a word I write but this history is for you and will contain no single lie may I burn in Hell if I speak false.*" Peter Carey, *True History of the Kelly Gang*

KNOWLEDGE
-mastery
-sound understanding
-learning

"There, as it should be, the druggist is a councilor, a confessor, an advisor, an able and willing missionary and mentor whose learning is respected, whose occult wisdom is venerated and whose medicine is often poured, untasted, into the gutter." O. Henry, "The Love-Philtre of Ikey Schoenstein"

KNOWLEDGEABLE ABOUT
-learned in {LER-ned}
-conversant in
-erudite {AIR-you-dite}
-well informed

KNOWN AS
-celebrated as

KNOWN FOR
-renowned for
-widely described as
-noted for their

L l

LABELED
-classed as
-dismissed as [derogatory]

LACK
-require
-are short of
-want

LACK OF
-dearth of
-shortness of
-paucity of
-scarcity of
-want of

LACKING
-wanting
-bereft of
-deficient in
-impoverished
-devoid of

"And yet when I take a look at my inner identity it impresses me as being precisely the same as it was thirty or forty years ago. My present station, power, the amount of worldly happiness at my command, and the rest of it, seem to be devoid of significance." Abraham Cahan, *The Rise of David Levinski*

LACKING RESPECT
-irreverent

LACKING SELF-CONTROL
-intemperate

LACKING SELF-CONFIDENCE
-diffident

LACKLUSTER WISH
-a velleity {vuh-LEE-uh-tee}

LAME ARGUMENT
-unconvincing argument

That's a lame argument.
That's an unconvincing argument.

LAND
-landscape
-terrain

LANGUAGE
-in the parlance of
-dialect
-in the vernacular
-jargon
-idiom
-prose

LARGE AMOUNT OF
-wealth of
-serious application of

"From the freezer she pulled out a bottle and poured herself a serious application of vodka." Tim Winton, *Dirt Music*

-legion of
-preponderance of

LARGE AREA
-wide swath
-vast region
-expanse

LARGE GROUP
-throng
-horde

"In this diminished form the words rush out of the cornucopia of my brain to course over the surface of the world, tickling reality like fingers on piano keys. They're an invisible army on a peacekeeping mission, a peaceable horde." Jonathan Lethem, *Motherless Brooklyn*

LARGE SIZE
-mammoth proportions
-some size
-considerable

LARGER-THAN-LIFE
-of epic proportions
-Homeric {home-AIR-ik}

LAST LINE OF DEFENSE
-thin red line

LAST PERFORMANCE OF HER CAREER
-her swan song

LAST STAND
-my Thermopylae {Greek, thir-MOP-uh-lee}

LAST STRAW
-the drop of water that makes the glass run over
-all I can bear

LASTING
-abiding
-enduring

LASTING A LONG TIME
-protracted
-prolonged

LATE
-belated
-late in arriving
-slow to

"It happened at the end of winter, in a year when the poppies were strangely slow to shed their petals; for mile after mile, from Benares onwards, the Ganga seemed to be flowing between twin glaciers, both its banks being blanketed by thick drifts of white-petalled flowers." Amitav Ghosh, *Sea of Poppies*

LATELY
-of late
-in recent years

LATER ____
-____s of later date

LATEST FAD
-____ du jour {French, *du ZHOOR*, lit. of the day}

"Drilling for off-shore oil became the Republican cause du jour of 2008."

-dernier cri {French, *den-yay CREE*}

LAUGH ALL YOU WANT
-think what you will of it

LAUGHTER
-mirth [poetic]
-cackling
-hilarity

LAW
-jurisprudence
-rule of law
-body of law

LAW (A LAW)
-an injunction
-an ordinance
-a statute

LAYERS (IN THICK LAYERS)
-impasto {Italian, *im- PASS- toe*} [art world]

LAZINESS
-indolence

LAZY
-indolent
-in a persistent vegetative state
-torpid
-languid

LEAD
-spearhead

LEAD UP
-prelude

"Theatergoers who use plays as mood-setting preludes to romantic evenings had better look elsewhere. 'Quartett,' which opened Wednesday night and runs through Nov. 14, may well be the sexually frankest play in New York this side of a backroom peephole. But with a cast led by the formidable French actress Isabelle Humpert in a magnificently mannered performance, it is the very opposite of an aphrodisiac." Ben Brantley, *New York Times*, Nov. 6, 2009

LEADER
-pacesetter
-standard bearer

LEADERS
-the vanguard
-captains

"But the truck moved on and the limits of mere privilege became visible, for here now came the acres of truly prestigious death; illustrious men and women, captains of life without their diamonds, furs, carriages, and limousines, but buried in pomp and glory, vaulted in great tombs built like heavenly safe deposit boxes, or parts of the Acropolis." William J. Kennedy, *Ironweed*

LEADING
-foremost

LEADING EDGE
-in the vanguard of

LEAN TO ONE SIDE
-list

LEARN
-glean
-gather
-acquire an understanding of
-familiarize oneself with
-unearth
-stumble upon
-increase your knowledge beyond
-gain a better understanding of

LEAVE
-tear myself away
-exit stage left
-depart from
-quit
-go forth from here [poetic]

LEAVE ALONE
-leave undeterred
-let play out
-let him be
-let run its course
-left to her own devices
-let him have a moment's peace

LECTURE (A SELF-RIGHTEOUS LECTURE)
-a diatribe
-a sermon
-a treatise {*TREAT-is*}

LEEWAY
-latitude

LEFT
-withdrew

-parted
-parted from
-departed

"In early times, say the Icelandic chronicles, men from the Western Islands came to live in this country, and when they departed, left behind them crosses, bells, and other objects used in the practice of sorcery." Halldór Laxness, *Independent People*

LEFT FOR
-set out

LEFTOVER FROM
-remnant of
-trace of
-relic of
-residual
-residue

LEGAL
-forensic
-judicial

LEGAL ACTION
-adjudication

LEGEND
-lore

"Reflections on politics, though, take a back seat to the practicalities of surviving on the road and, in the style of Herodotus, collecting dubious bits of lore." Richard B. Woodward, *New York Times*, Nov. 1, 2009

LEGEND HAS IT THAT
-it is said that

LEGITIMACY
-credence

LEGITIMATE
-well-founded
-well-established
-sound

LEGITIMATE ARGUMENT
-sound argument

LENGTH
-measure
-span

LENGTH OF TIME
-in the space of

LENGTHENED (TIME)
-prolonged
-protracted

LENGTHY
-interminable
-without end
-ad infinitum {Latin, *add in-fih-NIGHT-um*}
-ad nauseam {Latin, *add NAUS-ee-um*}

LENIENT WITH
-indulgent towards

LESS
-fewer in number

LESS OFFENSIVE
-more palatable

LESS RECKLESS
-a more measured approach

> Let's be less reckless in the future.
>
> Let's take a more measured approach.

LESS THAN
-fewer in number

LESSON LEARNED
-cautionary tale

LESSON NOT LEARNED
-lesson not fully absorbed

LET
-enable
-play host to
-perpetuate

> You continue to let him be offensive.
>
> You continue to play host to his offensive behavior.

LET GO OF
-relinquish
-cease to hold to them

"His sentiments are, he is aware, complacent, even uxorious. Nevertheless he does not cease to hold to them." J.M. Coetzee, *Disgrace*

LET GO OF MY HAND
-let go my hand

LET IT BE KNOWN
-it should be noted that

LET ME THINK FOR A MINUTE
-let me collect my thoughts

LETTER (A WRITTEN MESSAGE)
-a missive

LETTER HAD BEEN SENT TO
-letter had gone off to

LEWD
-prurient

LIBERAL
-catholic tastes
-Gladstonian

LIE (A LIE)
-a contrivance
-an artifact
-a fabrication
-a fiction

LIE (TO LIE)
-to be less than forthcoming
-to be disingenuous
-to be economical with the truth
-to fabricate
-to be less than candid
-to speak false

"I lost my own father at 12 yr. of age and I know what it is to be raised on lies and silences my dear daughter you are presently too young to understand a word I write but this history is for you and will contain no single lie may I burn in Hell if I speak false." Peter Carey, *True History of the Kelly Gang*

LIFE AND DEATH ISSUES
-existential issues

LIFE IS MEANINGLESS
-nihilism {*NIE-uh-li-zum, nie* as in Nile}

LIGHTHEARTED
-breezy
-blithe

LIKE (I LIKE IT)
-I welcome it
-is it to your liking
-it resonates with me
-I'm leaning towards the view
-it has found favor among
-I find her agreeable
-I favor
-I have an affinity for
-it was well received
-they are responding well to the
-it appeals to many
-I'm partial to
-I have an affection for
-I'm fond of
-I took pleasure in
-I was taken with her
-she speaks well of him
-there's something to be said for

LIKE ALL
-as with all

LIKE (SIMILAR)
-recalls a certain
-much like
-reminiscent of
-marked by

"His movements were marked by the lizard's disconcertingly abrupt clockwork speed; his speech was thin, fluty, and dry." Aldous Huxley, *Chrome Yellow*

-akin to
-much the same as
-it's _____ian
-has the character of
-calls to mind
-reflects
-captures the elegance of
-epitomizes
-is suggestive of

"He is in shirt sleeves, with a vest figured with faded gold horseshoes, and a pink-striped shirt, suggestive of peppermint candy." Upton Sinclair, *The Jungle*

-conveys
-evokes
-is akin to
-reminds me of nothing so
-rather like
-along the lines of
-bears a resemblance to
-bears the stamp of
-is not dissimilar to
-is in the nature of
-is analogous to
-corresponds with
-is in the manner of
-is characteristic of
-it's not my nature to
-is typical of
-is evocative of
-is similar to that of
-is an echo of
-as

"The walls are cracked and water runs upon them in thin threads without sound,

black and glistening as blood." Ayn Rand, *Anthem*

-is in the form of
-as expressed in
-such as one might expect from
-in a way that suggests
-much as
-of the sort
-with the air of
-wore the stamp of

*Consider dropping "like" altogether: "The young man reveres men of genius, because, to speak truly, they are more [ ] himself than he is." Ralph Waldo Emerson, "The Poet"

LIKE HE DID
-as he did

LIKE I SAID
-as I said

LIKE IN
-as in

LIKE NEVER BEFORE
-in memorable fashion

LIKE THESE
-along these lines

LIKE THIS
-of this kind

LIKE TO
-take pleasure in

LIKE YOU
-as you are

"He was fair, as you are, but not as tall but with large hands and a broken nose." Ernest Hemingway, *For Whom the Bell Tolls*

LIKED BY
-appeals to

LIKED TO
-was in the habit of
-took pleasure in
-was given to

LIKELIHOOD
-promise

"I don't think about the family much, but when I remember its members and the coast where they lived and the sea salt that I think is in our blood, I am happy to recall that I am a Pommeroy—that I have the nose, the coloring, and the promise of longevity—and that while we are not a distinguished family, we enjoy the illusion, when we are together, that the Pommeroys are unique." John Cheever, *The Stories of John Cheever*

LIKELY SUCCESSOR
-heir apparent

LIKELY TO BE
-disposed to
-prone to
-given to
-inclined to
-liable to be

LIKES TO
-is quick to
-is given to
-is a practitioner of
-is so fond of studying

LIKES TO COME ACROSS AS
-likes to portray himself as
-fancies herself a

LIMBER
-supple
-lithe

LIMIT
-curtail
-frame it as narrowly as possible
-confine ourselves to the study of
-qualify
-constrain

LIMITATIONS
-constraints
-strictures
-proscriptions [academic]
-bounds

"He is the witness in his death-throws of the immeasurable dementia of the sea, and, tormented by this madness, he hears sounds unknown to man that seem to come from some dreadful place beyond the bounds of earth." Victor Hugo, *Les Miserables*

LIMITED
-measured
-narrow
-only so much
-to the extent that it does exist
-sparing in the use of

LIMITED IN APPEAL
-esoteric

LIMITED TO
-peculiar to

LIMITING FACTOR
-determinant

LIMITLESS
-unbounded
-knows no bounds

> Your ambition is limitless.
>
> Your ambition knows no bounds.

LIMITS
-bounds
-confines
-verges
-periphery

LINE
-queue
-procession

"She had seen the fish clearly from above and his length and the shine of him in the water and her husband with the bamboo

pole bent almost double and the procession of people following." Ernest Hemingway, *Garden of Eden*

LINE BETWEEN
-demarcation

LINED UP
-queued

LION-LIKE
-leonine {*LEE-uh-nine*}

LIQUOR
-spirits

LIST (TO LIST)
-enumerate
-reel off
-spell out
-catalog

LISTEN
-take note
-give audience to

LIT THE CANDLE
-lighted the candle

LIT UP
-illuminated
-bathed in light

LITERAL MEANING OF A WORD
-denotation
-lexical meaning

LITTLE KNOWN
-undistinguished

LIVE A LONG TIME
-long-lived

LIVE IN
-inhabit
-dwell in

LIVE YOUR LIFE
-make your way in life

LIVED UP TO HIS REPUTATION
-lived up to his billing

LIVELY
-vibrant
-buoyant

LIVESTOCK
-beasts

"As always, we continued to grow more crops and beasts than we needed, and exchanged these with other near planets for their surpluses." Doris Lessing, *The Making of the Representative for Planet 8*

LIVING IN
-dwelling in
-abiding in

LOADED WITH
-laden with
-fraught with

LOANED TO US BY
-on loan from

LOBBYISTS
-the Gucci gulch

LOCAL
-insular
-indigenous
-native-born
-ambient
-parochial
-topical
-provincial

LOCAL LANGUAGE
-vernacular

LOCATED (IS LOCATED)
-it bears due south

LOCATED IN
-centered in

LOCATION
-whereabouts
-locale

LOCK UP
-detain

LOCKED (IT LOCKED)
-locked against him

"He rushed to the door but to his amazement it was locked against him." Sebastian Barry, *The Secret Scripture*

LONDON PRESS
-Fleet Street

LONG
-prolonged
-protracted
-ongoing
-longstanding
-lengthy

We're trying to avoid a long legal battle.

We're trying to avoid a protracted legal battle.

LONG AGO
-days of yore
-in antiquity
-long since
-in early times

"In early times, say the Icelandic chronicles, men from the Western Islands came to live in this country, and when they departed, left behind them crosses, bells, and other objects used in the practice of sorcery." Halldór Laxness, *Independent People*

LONG DINNER TABLE (LIKE IN HARRY POTTER)
-refectory table

LONG LASTING
-enduring
-long standing
-abiding

LONG TIME
-for a long while
-a lengthy period

LONGER PERIOD OF EXISTENCE
-longer measure of existence

LONG-WINDED
-prolix

LOOK
-behold
-never lose sight of

LOOK AROUND
-look about

LOOK AT
-consider
-address
-take up a central question
-eye
-set my gaze on
-distinguish

"And so, plainly, we must distinguish plots not by their skeletons but by their full bodies; for they are embodiments, little worlds. Here is another: let us try to distinguish it as if it were literally a little world, and spinning closely now into our vision." Eudora Welty, *On Writing*

LOOK BACK AT THE CAREER OF
-a retrospective

LOOK DOWN ON
-treat with disdain

LOOK FAR AND WIDE
-cast a wide net

LOOK FOR (ASK FOR)
-inquire about

LOOK FOR (SEARCH FOR)
-pursue

LOOK LIKE
-resemble
-recall

-bear a resemblance to
-have every appearance of

> The Shroud of Turin looks like a photographic negative.
>
> The Shroud of Turin bears a striking resemblance to a photographic negative.

LOOK OF (A LOOK OF)
-an air of

LOOK ON HER FACE
-expression
-visage

LOOK OVER
-scrutinize

LOOKED
-bore the look of
-looked to be

LOOKED AT
-looked upon
-gazed
-eyes rested upon
-fixed my gaze

LOOKED AT ALL OF US AGAIN
-he looked us round again

LOOKED AT ME
-met my eyes

LOOKED AT ME AS THOUGH
-regarded me as

"'Agua,' I said, trying Portuguese, and made a sign of drinking. He gave no reply, but regarded me as he would a seal or a porpoise thrown up by the waves, that would shortly expire and then be cut up for food." J.M. Coetzee, *Foe*

LOOKED AWAY
-took his eyes from me
-averted her eyes

LOOKED YOUNG
-she preserved the appearance of youth

LOOKING _____
-wearing an air of

"She stood apart from the crowd, letting it drift by her to the platform or the street, and wearing an air of irresolution which might, as he surmised, be the mask of a very definite purpose." Edith Wharton, *The House of Mirth*

LOOKING AT
-all eyes were fixed upon
-fixing his eyes intently on her
-casting a keen eye over

LOOKING BACK
-in retrospect

LOOKING DOWN
-cast down

"Her being seemed composed of shadow, with too little substance for it to possess sex. It was a shred of matter harboring a light, with large eyes that were always cast down; a pretext for a soul to linger on earth." Victor Hugo, *Les Miserables*

LOOKING ELSEWHERE
-attention shifting to

LOOKING FOR
-in search of
-out for
-trolling for
-in pursuit of
-in want of

"It is a truth universally acknowledged, that a single man in possession of a good fortune, must be in want of a wife." Jane Austen, *Pride and Prejudice*

LOOKING FOR REVENGE
-determined on revenge

LOOKING FOR TROUBLE
-making mischief

"It was the jackal—Tabaqui the Dish-licker—and the wolves of India despise Tabaqui because he runs about making mischief, and telling tales, and eating rags and pieces of leather from the village rubbish-heaps." Rudyard Kipling, *The Jungle Book*

LOOKS
-gives the eye

"The rice fields along both banks of the stream display a broad, winding strip of vivid green, which gives the eye its only relief from the somber colours of the mountains." Winston Churchill, *The Story of the Malakand Field Force*

LOOKS LIKE
-looks to be

LOSE MOMENTUM
-falter

LOSER
-an also-ran

LOSERS GET NOTHING
-vae victis {Latin, *why WICK-tees*}

LOSING MONEY QUICKLY
-hemorrhaging

LOSS OF MEMORY
-defect of memory

"Here is what I have done, and if by chance I have used some immaterial embellishment it has been only to fill a void due to a defect of memory. I may have taken for fact what was no more than probability, but I have never put down as true what I knew to be false." Jean-Jacques Rousseau, *The Confessions*

LOST
-shed

LOST CAUSE
-fool's errand

LOST FOCUS ON
-lost attention for

LOST HIM
-lost sight of him

LOT OF LAND
-parcel

LOUD
-clamorous
-raucous
-vociferous
-resounding

LOUD AND CLEAR
-clarion

LOUD NOISE
-yammer
-din

LOUD-VOICED
-full-throated

LOVE
-relish
-treasure

LOVE FOR HUMANITY
-agape {Greek, *uh-GAH-pay*}

LOVE HER TO DEATH
-love her to distraction

LOVE TO
-delight in

> You love it that I'm tormented.
> You delight in my torment.

LOVED
-beloved

LOW-NECKED (OF A GARMENT SHOWING CLEAVAGE)
-décolleté {French, *day-kol-TAY*}

LOW-PAID
-ill-paid

LOW POINT
-a low ebb

LOW PROFILE (KEEP A LOW PROFILE)
-be inconspicuous
-be nondescript

LOW CLASS
-lowbrow
-ill-bred
-downscale

LOWER CLASSES
-lower orders
-hoi polloi

LOWER END
-nether end

LOWER LEVELS
-lower reaches
-lower echelons

LOWERS HIMSELF TO
-condescends to

"The spirit of the occasion takes hold of the stately bartender, who condescends to a plate of stewed duck; even the fat police-man—whose duty it will be, later in the evening, to break up the fights—draws up a chair to the foot of the table." Upton Sinclair, *The Jungle*

LOYAL
-stalwart

LUCK
-providence

LUCKILY
-as luck would have it

LUCKY ENOUGH TO
-privileged to

"Those privileged to be present at a fam-ily festival of the Forsytes have seen that

charming and instructive sight—an upper middle-class family in full plumage." John Galsworthy, *Forsyte Saga*

LUCKY FIND
-a chance find
-fortuitous

LUKEWARM
-tepid

LUNCH
-the noon dinner [poetic]

"The fire on the kitchen hearth was dying down. His mother was hanging up pots and pans after the noon dinner." Marjorie Kinnan Rawlings, *The Yearling*

LURK
-lie in wait
-skulk

LUSTFUL
-salacious
-lecherous

LUXURIES
-creature comforts
-amenities

LUXURIOUS
-opulent

LUXURIOUS PLACE
-a Xanadu {ZAN-uh-doo}

LUXURY
-indulgence
-opulence

LUXURY-LOVING
-hedonistic
-self-indulgent
-epicurean

LYING DOWN [OF STATUES OR SCULPTURES]
-recumbent statues

LYING FACE DOWN
-prostrate

Mm

MACHINE
-contrivance

MADE
-produced
-rendered
-crafted

MADE A FOOL OF HIMSELF
-has exposed himself to ridicule

You will make a fool out of yourself.

You will expose yourself to ridicule.

MADE A POINT TO
-was careful to

MADE A REMARK
-put it by

"He put it by without the slightest hint of anger."

MADE AWARE OF
-attuned to

MADE BY LOCAL CRAFTSMEN
-the work of local craftsmen

MADE FAMOUS
-popularized

MADE HER EVEN MORE
-rendered her even more

MADE HER FEEL GOOD
-cheered her

MADE HER SICK
-afflicted her

MADE HIM A HERO
-made a hero of him

MADE HIM LOOK BAD
-did not reflect well on him

MADE IT GO AWAY
-dispelled
-dispersed

MADE IT KNOWN
-had it given out

"She carried his bones home to her scaffold, but the flesh and the bowels she left behind for the ravens, and had it given out in the district that he had perished while searching the mountains for sheep that had strayed." Halldór Laxness, *Independent People*

MADE OF
-composed of

"Her being seemed composed of shadow, with too little substance for it to possess sex. It was a shred of matter harboring a light, with large eyes that were always cast down; a pretext for a soul to linger on earth." Victor Hugo, *Les Miserables*

-comprised of
-the stuff of
-of brick

MADE PUBLIC (WAS MADE PUBLIC)
-was disclosed

MADE RESPECTABLE
-lent respectability to

MADE SENSE
-was intelligible to

"No one had hazarded to discover whether the speech of the known empires, khanates, emirates, hordes and kingdoms was intelligible to him." Michael Chabon, *Gentlemen of the Road*

MADE TO FIT HIM
-made to his measure

MADE UP
-a contrivance
-contrived
-apocryphal
-pure invention
-wholesale falsification
-fictitious
-dubious
-spurious

> That's a made up lie.
>
> That's pure invention.

MADE UP FOR
-atoned for

MADE UP OF
-comprised of

MADE UP STORIES
-apocryphal tales
-fabrications

MADE WHITE
-whited

MADHOUSE SITUATION
-theater of the absurd

MAFIA BOSS
-padrone

MAGICAL
-phantasmagoric

MAIN
-dominant
-leading
-principal
-foremost

MAIN ARGUMENT
-core argument

MAIN CHARACTER
-protagonist

MAIN EVENT
-pièce de resistance {French, *pee-ESS duh ruh-zee-STANCE*}

MAIN PART
-brunt of

MAINLY
-primarily
-largely
-predominantly
-in large measure
-in the main
-principally

MAINTAIN (DECLARE)
-aver

"The defendant was said to aver innocence on all counts."

MAJESTIC
-august {*au-GUST*}

MAJOR
-concentration in
-academic specialty

"He had graduated from Princeton in 1941 with high marks in all subjects except mathematics and sciences. His academic specialty had been comparative literature. But his real career at Princeton had consisted of playing the piano and inventing bright little songs for parties and shows." Herman Wouk, *The Caine Mutiny*

MAJOR CHANGE
-tectonic shift
-marked changes

MAJORITY
-lion's share of
-preponderance of

MAJORITY BELIEFS (VOICE OF THE PEOPLE)
-vox populi {Latin, *vox POP-you-lie*}

MAKE
-render
-leave

MAKE (FORCE)
-compel to

MAKE A BIG DEAL ABOUT
-make much of

"Many seaside towns make much of their location. Their shops are gussied up with nautical décor—rigging, buoys, mounted fish—and their restaurants often have the word 'captain' in the name." Sarah Maslin Nir, *New York Times*, Oct. 29, 2009

MAKE A DEAL
-broker a deal

MAKE A GOOD LIVING
-get a good living

"They did get a good living regularly, even in times when stock-raisers elsewhere were wearing patched clothes, shooting home-reloaded cartridges, and making biscuits out of hand-pounded wheat." Harold Lenoir Davis, *Honey in the Horn*

MAKE A NAME FOR HERSELF
-make her mark

MAKE A SCENE
-make an exhibition of oneself
-throw off all appearance of decorum

MAKE AMENDS FOR
-atone for

MAKE AN IMPRESSION
-impress upon

MAKE ANGRY
-infuriate
-rouse the ire of

MAKE CLEAR
-leave little doubt

MAKE DINNER
-rustle something up

MAKE EVERYBODY MAD
-set off a furor

MAKE FRIENDS
-forge a close bond
-befriend
-ingratiate
-curry favor
-find favor among
-make acquaintances

MAKE FUN OF
-poke fun at
-make light of
-caricature
-ridicule

MAKE GO AWAY
-ward off

MAKE HER CRY
-reduce her to tears

MAKE HER FEEL SORRY
-reduce her to repentance

"Already he was polishing a few carefully worded accusations designed to reduce his mother to repentance or, at least, confusion. He often had to keep her in her place." John Kennedy Toole, *A Confederacy of Dunces*

MAKE HER MAD
-incur her displeasure

MAKE HIM
-compel him

MAKE ILLEGAL
-proscribe [academic]
-disallow
-forbid

MAKE IMPOSSIBLE
-preclude

> Your employment at this company makes it impossible for you to take part in the sweepstakes.
>
> Your employment at this company precludes you from taking part in the sweepstakes.

MAKE INFERIOR
-adulterate

MAKE IT
-render it

MAKE IT CLEAR
-provide clear indications

MAKE IT MORE LIKE
-bring it more into line with

MAKE IT SEEM
-characterize it as

MAKE IT WORSE
-exacerbate

MAKE IT YOUR BUSINESS
-insinuate yourself into

MAKE KNOWN
-disclose
-convey
-divulge
-impart
-bring to light
-air

"His own opinion, which he does not air, is that the origins of speech lie in song, and the origins of song in the need to fill out with sound the overlarge and rather empty human soul." J.M. Coetzee, *Disgrace*

MAKE LAWS
-enact legislation
-sponsor a bill

MAKE LESS SEVERE
-mitigate

MAKE MYSELF USEFUL
-make myself of some use

MAKE NECESSARY
-necessitate

MAKE NO MISTAKE
-to be sure

MAKE POSSIBLE
-render possible

MAKE RESERVATIONS
-book passage

MAKE ROOM FOR
-accommodate

MAKE SACRED
-consecrate

MAKE SURE
-see that
-take pains to see that
-make it my business to

MAKE SUSPICIOUS
-cast a veil of suspicion over
-excite the suspicions of

MAKE THE MOST OF
-leverage

MAKE THE POINT
-stress that
-advance the point

"I don't say any of this because I'm interested in family history or because this sense of uniqueness is deep or important to me but in order to advance the point that we are loyal to one another in spite of our differences, and that any rupture in this loyalty is a source of confusion and pain." John Cheever, *The Stories of John Cheever*

MAKE THINGS WORSE
-further compound
-exacerbate

MAKE US THINK OF
-call to mind
-evoke
-summon up images of
-recall

MAKE YOU FEEL GUILTY
-accuse the conscience

"If the more sensitive among those she served or addressed failed to look at Rose, it was because her manner seemed to accuse the conscience, or it could have been, more simply, that they were embarrassed by her hair lip." Patrick White, *Voss*

MAKE YOU REALIZE
-dispel the notion that
-disabuse you of the notion that

MAKE YOU SEEM
-cast you as

MAKE YOU UNDERSTAND
-impress upon you

MAKE YOUR WAY THROUGH
-navigate
-negotiate

MAKES A POINT TO
-is careful to
-pointedly avoids

MAKES ME
-compels me

MAKES ME FEEL
-leaves me

"It leaves me wanting more."

MAKES SENSE
-is a coherent argument
-stands to reason

MAKES YOU FEEL GOOD INSIDE
-it's very heartening

MAKING FRIENDS
-befriending
-glad handing

MAKING FUN OF
-jesting banter at
-mocking

MAKING NO DIFFERENCE
-tilting at windmills

MAKING THE ROUNDS
-circulating

MAN BEHIND THE CURTAIN (OR THRONE)
-éminence grise {French, *ay-mee-nahs GREEZ*}

MAN OF FEW WORDS
-laconic

"He's so laconic it's a little creepy."

MANAGE WITHOUT
-dispense with

MANAGED BY
-syndicated to

MANAGEMENT OF
-stewardship of

MANEUVER
-gambit

MANIPULATE
-orchestrate

MANKIND [ARCHAIC]
-humankind

MANNER
-air of
-bearing
-demeanor
-presence

MANNERS
-decorum
-deportment
-social niceties

MANY
-any number of
-innumerable
-untold numbers of
-wealth of
-host of
-considerable
-goodly number of
-fair amount of
-hordes of
-legions of
-profuse
-abundant
-multitudes of
-many a

"Many a true word is spoken in jest."
Geoffrey Chaucer

MANY DIFFERENT KINDS OF
-all manner of

MANY REASONS
-competing reasons

MANY TIMES
-on numerous occasions

MARCH (A MARCH)
-a procession

MARCH ON
-forge ahead

MARK OFF
-circumscribe
-demarcate

MARRIED
-wed

MASTER
-impresario

MASTERPIECE
-tour de force {French, *tour de FORCE*}

MATCH
-correspond

MATCH IT TO
-pair it to

MATCHLESS
-inimitable
-incomparable

MATERIALISTIC
-acquisitive

MATURING
-coming of age

MAXIMUM AMOUNT
-its capacity

MAY
-may be compelled to
-appears to have

MAY BE (IT MAY BE)
-it may well be

MAY END UP BEING
-may prove to be

> It may end up being your
> undoing.
>
> It may prove to be your undoing.

MAYBE
-perhaps
-weather permitting [humorous]

MAYBE A LITTLE
-somewhat
-in part
-to some degree
-to some extent

*"Perhaps to some extent, but I think her
judicial decisions are based less on politics
than on natural justice."*

MAYBE EVEN
-if not

ME?
-Moi? {French, *mwah*, lit. me} (often as an ironic reply to an accusation)

"Chauvinistic? Moi?"

ME AS I REALLY AM
-me in the rough

ME NEITHER
-neither do I

MEANINGFUL
-appreciable
-substantive

MEANINGLESS
-academic
-moot
-merely decorative
-mere embellishment

MEANINGLESS MESSAGES
-white noise

MEANS NOTHING TO ME
-is of no consequence to me
-is a matter of complete indifference to me

MEANS THAT
-raises concerns that
-carries with it the possibility that

MEANS WELL
-is well intentioned
-is well intended

MEAN-SPIRITED
-caustic
-ignoble {ig-KNOW-bul}
-blood-drawing

MEANT FOR
-caters to
-intended for

MEANT TO
-was by design
-was aimed at
-intended to be so

-was consciously chosen

> It's supposed to be that way.
>
> It's that way by design.

MEAT-EATER
-carnivore

MEAT-EATING
-carnivorous

MEDIA
-the fourth estate

MEDIATE
-conciliate
-intercede

MEDIATOR
-intermediary

MEDICINE
-elixir

MEDITATING
-absorbed in thought

MEET
-fulfill
-satisfy

MEET FOR THE FIRST TIME
-make the acquaintance of

MEET HER
-receive her [formal]

MEETING
-encounter

MEETING BETWEEN TWO OPPOS-ING SIDES
-a parley

MEETING-PLACE (SECRET)
-a place of assignation

MELT DOWN
-render

MELTING OF GLACIAL ICE
-ablation

MELTING POT
-ethnic stew

MEMBER
-member in good standing
-charter members of

MEMORIZE
-register in your mind
-commit to memory

MEMORY
-remembrance
-recollection

MEN'S FASHION
-sartorial conventions

MENTAL CONCEPT
-precept

MENTAL DISORDER
-dementia
-neurosis
-psychosis

MENTAL PERCEPTION
-ken

MENTALLY DISTURBED
-pathological

MENTION
-allude to
-make mention of

MENU
-bill of fare

MERCY
-clemency

MERE BEGINNINGS OF
-rudiments of

MERGE
-coalesce

MERGING
-confluent

MESMERIZED
-enthralled
-spellbound
-transfixed

MESS
-this disorder

"Everybody had washed before going to bed, apparently, and the bowls were ringed with a dark sediment which the hard, alkaline water had not dissolved. Shutting the door on this disorder, he turned back to the kitchen, took Mahailey's tin basin, doused his face and head in cold water, and began to plaster down his wet hair." Willa Cather, *One of Ours*

MESSENGER
-intermediary
-emissary
-consul
-attaché
-internuncio

MET
-made the acquaintance of [formal]

METAPHOR
-trope
-conceit

METHOD
-mechanism
-vehicle
-mode
-modus operandi {Latin, *MODE-us op-er-AND-ee*}
-modality [academic]
-means
-approach

METICULOUS
-exacting
-fastidious

MID NINETEENTH CENTURY
-the middle years of the nineteenth
 century

MIDDLE AGES
-antiquity

MIDDLE CLASS
-bourgeois {French, *boor-ZHWAH*}

MIDDLE OF SUMMER
-height of summer

MIDDLE OF THE NIGHT
-into the small hours of the night

MIDDLEMAN
-intermediary

MIDNIGHT
-in the midnight hour [poetic]

MIGHT HAVE
-is thought to have

MIGHT HAVE BEEN
-might have proved

"I took up my coat and carpet-bag, and went into the next room to change my linen, and dress for dinner. Any distress at the termination of my intrigue with Betty was amply compensated for by my joy at the happy ending of a troublesome affair which might have proved fatal for me." Jacques Casanova, *Volume 6c—Rome: The Memoirs of Jacques Casanova*

MILD
-temperate

MILES AND MILES
-league upon league

"He could not make out even the black ground in front of him, and he was aware of the vast, flat horizon only from the March wind blowing in broad, sweeping gusts as though across a sea, bitterly cold after its passage over league upon league of marsh and bare earth." Emile Zola, *Germinal*

MILITARISTIC LANGUAGE
-martial language

"Like many talk-show hosts, he [Limbaugh] uses martial language to rouse the faithful: 'The enemy camp is the White House right now,' he says." Evan Thomas and Eve Conant, "Hate." *Newsweek*, April 19th, 2010

MIND READER
-clairvoyant

MINDLESS
-vacuous

MINIMAL
-nominal

MINIMUM AMOUNT NEEDED
-critical mass

MINOR
-of minor status

MINOR DISAGREEMENT
-differ only on the margins

We don't disagree that much on this issue.

We differ only on the margins.

MINOR EVENTS
-small happenings

MISBEHAVIOR
-impropriety

MISCELLANEOUS COLLECTION
-an olio {*OH-lee-oh*} [academic]

MISCHIEVOUS
-impish
-cheeky
-puckish

MISCHIEVOUSNESS
-devilry
-diablerie {French, *dee-AH-blu-ree*}
-villainy

MISINTERPRET
-misconstrue

MISSING
-conspicuous by its absence
-bereft of
-gone missing

MISTAKES
-lapses in

"Month after month he sets, collects, reads, and annotates their assignments, correcting lapses in punctuation, spelling and usages, interrogating weak arguments, appending to each paper a brief, considered critique. J. M. Coetzee, *Disgrace*

-miscues
-miscalculations
-improprieties of

"Alexander the Grammarian taught me not to be ruggedly critical about words, nor find fault with people for improprieties of phrase or pronunciation, but to set them right by speaking the thing properly myself, and that either by way of answer, assent, or inquiry, or by some such other indirect and suitable correction." Marcus Aurelius, *Meditations*

MIXED FEELINGS
-ambivalent
-of two minds

MIXED WITH
-laced with

MIXTURE
-miscellany
-collage of
-potpourri of
-hodgepodge of
-mélange {French, *may-LONZH*}

MOCKING
-derisive
-dismissive

MOCKING OF CHRISTIANITY
-how many divisions has the Pope

MOCKING OF SOCIETY
-Swiftian

"In a Swiftian mood, Foer even throws in a Filipino recipe for 'Stewed Dog, Wedding Style.' 'Can't we get over our sentimentality?' he asks. 'Dogs are plentiful, good for you, easy to cook and tasty, and eating them is vastly more reasonable than going through all the trouble of processing them into protein bits to become the food for the other species that become our food.'" Jennifer Schuessler, *New York Times*, Nov. 13, 2009

MODE OF TRANSPORTATION
-conveyance

MODEL
-paradigm
-held her up as template for
-an exemplar

MODEL OF PERFECTION
-paragon of

MODERATE (TO MODERATE)
-mitigate
-temper

MODERATE IN EATING AND DRINKING
-temperate in diet
-abstemious [academic]

MODERATES
-centrists

MODERATION
-temperance

MODERN
-nouveau {French, *new-VOH*}

MODEST
-unassuming
-without ceremony
-self-effacing {*uh-FAY-sing*}
-demure

MOMENT OF INSIGHT
-epiphany

MOMENTARY
-fleeting

MONEY (WEALTH)
-wherewithal
-means

MONEY SPENT
-expenditures
-outlays

MONK
-an ascetic

MONOPOLY
-cartel

MONOTONE (TO SPEAK IN A MONOTONE VOICE)
-intone

MONTHS AND MONTHS
-months on end

MOOD (COLLECTIVE MOOD)
-atmosphere of
-ambiance
-color
-with an air of
-with a note of
-with distinct ____ undertones
-flavor
-aura
-prevailing winds

MOOD (INDIVIDUAL MOOD)
-frame of mind
-temper

MOODY
-capricious
-mercurial

MORAL DEFECT
-blemish
-failing

MORAL WEAKNESS
-human frailty

MORALISTIC
-didactic

MORALIZING
-edifying
-sanctimonious
-sententious [academic]

MORALLY LAX
-dissolute
-licentious

MORE
-all the more
-further

MORE ____ THAN NORMAL
-more ____ than was his custom

MORE ACCURATE
-nearer the truth

MORE APPROPRIATE FOR
-better suited for

MORE CAREFULLY
-with greater care

MORE IMPORTANT
-takes precedence

MORE LIKE ____ THAN ____
-more worthy of ____ than ____
-nearer to

MORE SERIOUS
-carries more weight than

MORE SPECIFIC
-narrower notion of

MORE THAN
-better than

"There are better than twenty in every batch."
-more so than

MORE THAN ANYTHING ELSE
-above all

MORNING
-at first light
-in the small hours of the morning
-daybreak

MORTAL LIFE (AS OPPOSED TO THE AFTERLIFE)
-this veil of tears [Shakespeare]
-more worldly matters

MOST (DEGREE)
-are among the most
-utmost

MOST (NUMBER)
-most of which
-the bulk of
-the lion's share
-the better part of

MOST IMPORTANT
-foremost of these
-above all
-seminal
-more so than anything else
-central to
-overriding
-salient
-chief
-most noted
-pre-eminent
-_____ of the first rank
-of the greatest consequence

MOST IMPORTANT FEATURE
-pièce de resistance {French, *pee-ES duh ruh-zee-STANCE*}

MOST IMPORTANT POINT
-the crux

MOST LIKELY POSSIBILITY
-most plausible

MOST LIKELY TO
-odds on favorite to

MOST OF THE REVENUE
-bulk of the revenue

MOST RELEVANT WORD
-the operative word being

> "Possibly" is the relevant word.
>
> The operative word being "possibly."

MOSTLY
-in large part
-to a great extent
-primarily
-largely
-principally
-chiefly

"He was aware that the qualities distinguishing her from the herd of her sex were chiefly external, as though a fine glaze of beauty and fastidiousness had been applied to vulgar clay." Edith Wharton, *The House of Mirth*

-for the most part
-in large measure
-preponderantly

"Of the few fair complexioned Jewish students in our preponderantly Jewish public high school, none possessed anything remotely like the steep-jawed, insentient Viking mask of this blue-eyed blond born into our tribe as Seymour Irving Levov." Philip Roth, *American Pastoral*

-in great measure
-predominantly
-above all

"Self-discovery is above all the realization that we are alone: it is the opening of an impalpable, transparent wall— that of our consciousness—between the world and ourselves." Octavio Paz, *The Labyrinth of Solitude*

MOTIVATE
-provoke

-whet the appetite for
-rally behind
-actuate
-determine

"What determined me was the look she gave me."

MOTIVATED BY
-driven by

He is motivated by greed.

He is driven by greed.

MOTIVATION
-inclination
-impetus
-incentive
-inducement

MOTIVATOR
-catalyst for

MOURNFUL
-plaintive

MOURNFUL SONG
-dirge

MOVE AWAY
-draw away

MOVE BACK
-stand aside
-draw off

MOVE INTO POSITION
-deploy
-assemble
-martial

MOVED
-darted
-ambled up
-trooped in
-sauntered in
-gamboled up to
-legged it

MOVED FROM
-migrated from

MOVEMENT
-animation
-stirring
-locomotion

MOVING (EMOTION)
-affecting

"This was by far her most affecting performance."

-striking to the heart

MOVING (MOTION)
-kinetic

"The atmosphere at the New York Stock Exchange is kinetic."

MUCH LONGER THAN
-far longer than

MUCH MORE
-vastly more

MUCH OF
-good portions of

"If the eyes could lie, his troubles might be over. If the eyes were not such well behaving creatures, that spent their time trying their best to convey the world and all its gore to him, good portions of life might not be so dismal." Sarah Hall, *The Electric Michelangelo*

MUDDY WATER
-turbid water

MULTI-COLORED
-varicolored

MULTI-DIMENSIONAL
-operates on several levels

MULTI-LINGUAL NEIGHBORHOODS
-polyglot neighborhoods

MULTIPLY
-proliferate

MULTI-TALENTED
-versatile

MUSCLES
-musculature

MUSICAL CONDUCTOR
-intendant {in-TEN-dent}

MUST
-cannot help but
-have no choice but to

MUST BE
-must count as
-must rank as one of the most

MUSTY
-fusty

MUTUAL
-concerted

MUTUALLY DESTRUCTIVE
-internecine {in-ter-NEH-scene}

MY OWN FAULT
-of my own making

MY WAY OR THE HIGHWAY STYLE
-a high-handed approach

MYSTERIES
-arcana {ar-KANE-uh}

MYSTERIOUS
-enigmatic
-inscrutable
-arcane

MYSTERY
-enigma
-paradox

MYSTICISM
-quietism

N n

NAG
-plague
-chivvy

"Her political strategy was to chivvy Governor Palin with lawsuit after petty lawsuit."

NAME OF
-the name given to
-taking its name from

NAME SOMETHING
-christen
-dub

NAME THEM ALL
-give account of them all

NAMED INCORRECTLY
-is something of a misnomer

NARROW-MINDED
-parochial
-provincial
-dogmatic

NARROW, PETTY TEACHER
-pedagogue

NASTY
-nasty, brutish, and short [Thomas Hobbes]

NATIONALISM
-jingoism

NATIONALISTIC
-has insular characteristics

NATIONALLY KNOWN
-as he steps on to the national stage

NATIONS AT WAR
-belligerents

NATIVE TO
-indigenous

-endemic
-aboriginal

NATURAL
-innate
-instinctual
-the nature of the beast
-at home in it

NATURAL INCLINATION FOR
-a tropism toward

NATURALLY
-by nature

NATURALLY CURLY HAIR
-curl natural to it

"General Beal removed this object and hung it on the microphone. He began to rub his brown hair, cropped in order to conceal the unmilitary curl natural to it." James Gould Cozzens, *Guard of Honor*

NATURALLY EXISTING
-innate

NEAR
-at hand
-looming
-forthcoming soon
-an intimate distance

The funds never got here.

The funds were not forthcoming.

NEAR FUTURE
-foreseeable future

NEARBY
-near

"As always, we continued to grow more crops and beasts than we needed, and exchanged these with other near planets for their surpluses." Doris Lessing, *The Making of the Representative for Planet 8*

NECESSARY
-indispensable
-requisite
-integral to
-of necessity

NECESSARY FOR THE
-necessary to the

NEED
-require
-in need of

"For all men live by truth and stand in need of expression. In love, in art, in avarice, in politics, in labor, in games, we study to utter our painful secret. The man is only half himself, the other half is his expression." Ralph Waldo Emerson, "The Poet"

-in want of
-have a need for

NEEDED
-requisite
-sine qua non {Latin, SIN-uh qua non}
-indispensable

NEEDLESS REPETITION
-a tautology

"Django was a ponytailed visionary—if that's not a tautology—who, following an epiphany in Vietnam, founded the New Earth Army in order to establish whether love and peace can win wars." Anthony Lane, *The New Yorker*, Nov. 9, 2009

NEEDS (THE NEEDS OF)
-wishes
-wants

"The soil is fertile, the rains plentiful, and a considerable proportion of ground is occupied by cultivation, and amply supplies the wants of the inhabitants." Winston Churchill, *The Story of the Malakand Field Force*

NEEDY PEOPLE
-the necessitous

NEGATIVELY EFFECT
-impinge on

NEGLECTED (WAS NEGLECTED)
-languished

> The bill has been neglected in the senate for months.
>
> The bill has languished in the senate for months.

NEGLECTFUL
-derelict

NEGLIGENT
-remiss
-derelict

NEGOTIATING WITH
-negotiating opposite

NEITHER DID
-nor did
-not either

NERDY
-bookish

NERVE
-audacity
-effrontery
-moxie
-metal
-pluck
-temerity
-impertinence
-impudence
-chutzpah {Yiddish, *HUT-spuh*}

NERVOUS
-pensive
-flurried
-on edge
-ill at ease

NERVOUSNESS
-consternation
-angst

-apprehension

NEVER
-on no occasion
-having never
-never anything of the sort
-hardly
-seldom

NEVER AGAIN
-nevermore

NEVER ASK
-never send to know [poetic]

"Any man's death diminishes me, because I am involved in Mankind; and therefore never send to know for whom the bell tolls; it tolls for thee." John Donne {pronounced *Dun*}

NEVER CHANGING
-abiding
-invariant
-invariable

NEVER ENDING
-interminable
-inexhaustible
-incessant
-unremitting
-abiding
-imperishable

NEVER FIND
-never meet with

"We are a family that has always been close in spirit. Our father was drowned in a sailing accident when we were young, and our mother has always stressed the fact that our familial relationships have a kind of permanence that we will never meet with again." John Cheever, *The Stories of John Cheever*

NEVER IN HIS ENTIRE LIFE
-never in the whole course of his life

NEVER SEE HIM AGAIN
-will see no more of him

NEVER SEEN SO
-seldom seen such

NEW
-novel
-fledgling
-newly minted
-newfangled
-recent

"At that time Macondo was a village of twenty adobe houses, built on the bank of a river of clear water that ran along a bed of polished stones, which were white and enormous, like prehistoric eggs. The world was so recent that many things lacked names, and in order to indicate them it was necessary to point." Gabriel Garcia Marquez, *One Hundred Years of Solitude*

NEW OPPORTUNITIES
-new pastures

NEW WAYS OF
-new approaches to

NEWS FLASH
-communiqué
-dispatch

NEXT
-then followed
-from here, we move to the question of

NEXT FEW DAYS
-in the coming days

NEXT ONE OVER
-adjacent

NEXT TO
-flanked by
-bounded by

NEXT TO THE LAST
-penultimate

NICE
-appealing
-pleasant

"They lived in a pleasant house, with a garden, and they had discrete servants, and felt themselves superior to anyone in the neighborhood." D. H. Lawrence, "The Rocking-Horse Winner"

NICE WAY OF SAYING SOMETHING
-euphemism
-being politically correct
-putting it charitably

NICKNAME
-pet name
-sobriquet {French, SO-bri-kay}

NIGHT
-nightfall

NIGHTMARE
-trial by ordeal

NITPICK
-to cavil at {KAV-uhl}
-to chivvy

NIXED
-derailed

NO
-far from it
-I think not [confrontational]
-no such
-not by any means
-not in the least
-in principle, yes [diplomatic]
-no _____ to speak of
-not the slightest
-I won't allow it
-you'll do nothing of the sort
-to the contrary
-quite the contrary
-none among

"We are alone here under the earth. It is a fearful word, alone. The laws say that none among men may be alone, ever and at any time, for this is the great transgression and the root of all evil." Ayn Rand, *Anthem*

NO GOOD
-leave much to be desired

NO IDEA THAT
-no notion why
-no inkling

NO LONGER
-have ceased to

NO LONGER A ROOKIE
-a rookie no more

NO LONGER MEANS ____
-that meaning is gone out of it

NO MATTER HOW ____
-however much
-however many ____

"However many holy words you read, however many you speak, what good will they do you if you do not act upon them?" Guatama Buddha {GAW-tuh-muh}

-however ____

"However hard he threw himself onto his right, he always rolled back to where he was." Franz Kafka, *Metamorphosis*

NO MATTER WHAT HAPPENS
-come what may

NO MORE THAN
-at most

NO NEED TO WORRY
-no cause for concern
-no cause for alarm

NO ONE
-not a blessed soul

NO ONE HAS BEEN HERE FOR FOUR DAYS
-no one has been here these four days

NO ONE KNEW WHICH
-no one could have said which

NO PROBLEM [IN POOR FORM AS A RESPONSE TO THANK YOU]
-you're welcome
-say nothing of it

NO PUN INTENDED
-pardon the pun
-as it were

"Taking a page, as it were, from the detective novels he loves, he decides to become a detective himself, and puts an ad on Craigslist offering his services." Nancy Franklin, *The New Yorker*, Sept 28, 2009

NO USE
-to no avail

NO WAY
-by no means
-nothing doing
-out of the question
-far from it

NO WILLPOWER
-intemperate

NO WONDER
-small wonder

NOBLE
-high-minded
-lofty

NOBLE GESTURE
-beau geste {French, *boh ZHEST*, lit. beautiful gesture}

NOBODY CARES TOO MUCH ABOUT
-nobody much cares

NOISE
-din
-uproar
-hue and cry

NOISY
-resounding
-deafening

-in full cry
-atonal

NONDISCRIMINATORY
-making not the slightest distinction
  between

NONE OF THIS MATTERS
-none of this need concern
-this is inconsequential
-it's of no consequence

NONENTITY (A NOBODY)
-a cipher

*"He considers the interns mere ciphers, and
treats them accordingly."*

NON-INTERFERENCE
-laissez-faire {French, *lez-ay-FARE*}

*"The government's laissez-faire attitude
contributed to the BP disaster."*

NONRELIGIOUS
-secular
-profane [pejorative]
-nonsectarian

NONSENSE
-blather

NONVIOLENT PROTEST DOCTRINE
-ahimsa {Sanskrit, *uh-HIM-suh*}

*"Martin Luther King's political strategies
owe much of their success to the concept
of ahimsa."*

NORM (THE NORM)
-prescribed form

NORMALITY
-normalcy

NORTHERN FOREST
-the boreal forest {*BORE-ee-ul*}

NOSY
-inquisitive
-inquisitorial

NOT
-by no means
-not by any means
-not gone so far as to
-not for a moment
-not so much as
-nary a
-a far cry from
-not in the least
-on no account
-in no respect
-God forbid
-nothing doing
-anything but

NOT A CHEAPSKATE
-free with her money

NOT A GOOD THING
-not exactly cause for celebration
-does not bode well for

NOT ABLE TO COMMUNICATE
-incommunicado

NOT AFFECTED BY
-impervious to

NOT ANYONE'S BUSINESS
-an internal matter

NOT APPROPRIATE
-inopportune
-unbecoming

NOT AS ____ AS YOU THINK
-not so ____ as might be imagined

NOT AS GOOD AS
-not so good as
-less admirable

NOT AS MUCH OF A
-far less of a

NOT AS SIMPLE AS THAT
-not so simple as that

NOT ASHAMED
-unabashed

NOT AT ALL
-by no means
-not even in the remotest degree
-not-in-the-least

NOT CURIOUS
-incurious

NOT DECIDED
-remains to be seen

NOT DOABLE
-infeasible

NOT EASILY
-not very well

"The news had not come to us directly from our neighbors, but authoritatively from a friend of theirs, who was also a friend of ours, and we could not very well hold back." William Dean Howells, *The Whole Family*

NOT EASY
-no mean feat
-a difficult matter
-no easy task
-that's a tall order
-hard-won battles

NOT EASY TO SAY
-a great effort for him to say

NOT EDIBLE
-inedible
-unpalatable

NOT ENOUGH
-too little

NOT EQUIPPED TO
-ill-equipped to

NOT FAIR
-inequitable

NOT GIVING IN
-unbowed

NOT GOOD (OF A PERSON)
-perverse
-wayward
-wretched
-deplorable
-unredeeming

NOT GOOD AT
-inept
-not well suited for

"It's not a game in which I'm particularly well-suited."

NOT GOOD FOR
-do not lend themselves easily to
-ill suited for
-is unconducive to [academic]

NOT GOOD QUALITY
-of little merit
-leaves much to be desired

NOT HAPPENING
-nothing doing

NOT HERE
-unaccounted for
-elsewhere
-in absentia {Latin, *in ab-SENT-shee-ya*}

"He was wrongfully tried and convicted in absentia."

NOT HESITATE
-think nothing of

NOT IMPORTANT
-of little use
-expendable

NOT IMPRESSIVE
-has a modest history in that area

NOT IN LINE
-out of step

NOT INCLUDED
-excepted

NOT INCLUDING
-apart from

-notwithstanding
-excepting
-exclusive of

NOT INTERESTED IN
-indifferent to
-listless

NOT LIKE
-not at all like
-atypical of other
-bears no resemblance to

NOT LITERALLY
-figuratively
-metaphorically speaking
-in a manner of speaking

NOT MANY
-scant

NOT MUCH
-nothing to speak of
-little to be had
-if at all

NOT NEEDED
-unwarranted
-redundant
-superfluous

NOT NORMAL BEHAVIOR
-atypical behavior

NOT NOTICEABLE
-unobtrusive
-nondescript
-inconspicuous

NOT OFTEN
-seldom

NOT ORIGINAL
-derivative

NOT PAYING ATTENTION
-inattentive

NOT PERFECT
-fallible

NOT PRACTICAL
-academic
-idealistic

NOT PRESENT
-in absentia

NOT REAL
-illusory

NOT REALLY MEANING IT
-tongue-in-cheek

> She didn't really mean it seriously.
>
> She said it with tongue firmly in cheek.

NOT RELEVANT
-inapplicable

NOT RIGHT
-something is awry

NOT SAYING
-cagey

NOT SHOWING EMOTION
-stoic
-impassive

NOT SHY
-unretiring

NOT SPECIFIC
-generic

NOT SPIRITUAL
-temporal
-secular

NOT TAKEN INTO ACCOUNT
-unreckoned

NOT THOUGHT OUT
-arbitrary

NOT TO MENTION
-to say nothing of

NOT UNDERSTANDABLE
-inexplicable

NOT USED TO
-unaccustomed to
-not in the habit of

NOT VERY GOOD
-ill-suited for
-of little merit
-leave much to be desired

NOT WANTING TO
-not seeing fit to

NOT WELL
-indisposed

NOT WELL KNOWN
-too little known

NOT WHAT HAPPENED
-that's not an accurate reflection of

> That's not the way it happened and you know it.
>
> That's not an accurate reflection of what happened.

NOT WILLING
-disinclined to

NOT WORKING
-idle
-ineffectual

NOT YET DECIDED
-an open question
-a matter of opinion
-that remains to be seen

> We're not sure yet.
>
> That remains to be seen.

NOTE HOW
-consider

-witness
-take note of

NOTHING COULD
-hardly anything had the power to

NOTHING I CAN REMEMBER
-nothing to be remembered

NOTHING THAT I KNOW ABOUT
-nothing to speak of

NOTHING THERE
-there's no meat on the bone
-there's no there there [Gertrude Stein]

NOTHING TO DO WITH
-divorced from

NOTHINGNESS
-vacancy

NOTICE
-consider
-witness
-take note of

NOTICEABLE
-pronounced
-conspicuous
-marked
-salient

NOTICEABLY
-conspicuously

"There was something disturbingly like hypocrisy about it all, though it was meant only to compensate for Jack, who was so conspicuously not good as to cast a shadow over their household." Marilynne Robinson, *Home*

NOVEL (ABOUT REAL PERSONS UNDER FICTITIOUS NAMES)
-roman à clef {French, *raw-MAHN ah KLAY*}

NOVEL (COMING OF AGE)
-bildungsroman {German, *BILL-dunks-roe-MAHN*}

NOW
-at this point
-here and now
-at once
-forthwith
-at present
-at this moment

NOW AND THEN
-periodically
-now and again
-off and on

Oo

OBEDIENCE
-compliance
-deference

OBEDIENT
-compliant
-subservient
-obsequious (excessively so)

OBEY
-adhere to
-are in accordance with
-are in obedience to
-heed
-abide by

OBJECT
-take issue with
-demur {di-MUR}
-take exception to (often in an
  offended way)

OBJECTS
-figures

OBLIGATED TO
-feel it incumbent upon me to
-liable to
-obliged to
-bound to

OBNOXIOUS
-repellent
-invidious

OBSCENITIES
-colorful language
-expletives

Try not to use too many bad
words.

Try to keep the colorful language
to a minimum.

OBSCURE
-cryptic
-arcane
-Derrida would be proud
  {dear-ee-DAH}

OBSERVANT
-acute

OBSERVER
-onlooker
-beholder

OBSESSED
-preoccupied
-fixated
-consumed by

OBSESSED WITH DETAIL (IN AN ANNOYING WAY)
-anal retentive

OBSESSION
-fixation
-preoccupation

OBSESSIVE
-pathological
-an obsessional search for

OBSTACLE
-hazard

OBSTRUCT
-hinder

-hamper
-impede
-encumber
-fetter
-derail
-blunt
-foil
-bedevil
-forestall
-impair
-inhibit
-daunt

"Stained glass will daunt intruding light."

OBSTRUCTION
-impediment

OBTAIN
-secure

OBVIOUS
-evident
-conspicuous
-goes without saying
-axiomatic
-explicit
-manifest
-a forgone conclusion
-patent
-well-pronounced
-plain

"It's plain the woman cares deeply."

-only too evident
-palpable
-all too clear
-unmistakable
-patently obvious

OBVIOUS REMARK
-truism
-trite remark

OBVIOUSLY
-needless to say

OCCASIONALLY
-on occasion

OCCUPATION
-your calling

OCCUPIED TERRITORY
-irredenta {Italian, *ear-ri-DEN-ta*}

"Irredentas are literal breeding grounds for extremism."

OCCUPY
-inhabit
-reside
-abide

OCCUR
-appear
-arise
-come to pass
-befall you
-are borne out
-ensue
-come about

OCCURRED BEFORE
-predated

OCCURRENCE
-occasion
-first installment of

OCCURRING
-prevalent
-unfolding
-arising
-in the making

OCEAN LINER
-leviathan

ODD
-peculiar

ODD THINGS OR HABITS
-peculiarities

ODDS
-however slight may be the hope
-likelihood

OF ALL TYPES
-in every variety

-of every sort
-of any sort

OF COURSE
-by all means
-to be sure
-it goes without saying

OF THE (SEVEN OF THE BOOKS EXIST)
-such

"Seven such books exist."

OF THE DAY
-du jour {French, *doo-ZHER*}

"It seems like every day there's another cause du jour."

OF THE PAST
-of things past

OF THE SAME TIME PERIOD
-of similar date

OF UPPER CLASS BIRTH
-to the manner born

OFF
-askew

OFF LIMITS
-the third rail—touch it and you die

OFF OF [INCORRECT USAGE]
-off

OFF SEASON PLAY
-hot stove league

OFF THE CUFF
-impromptu
-in passing
-perfunctory
-extemporaneous

OFFENDED BY
-take exception to
-take issue with
-take umbrage to

OFFENSIVE
-boorish

OFFER
-hold out to
-extend
-make available to
-proffer

"His father proffered a Life Saver, courteously, man to man; he took it with a special sense of courtesy. It sealed their contract." James Agee, *A Death in the Family*

OFFER AN OPINION
-air an opinion

"His own opinion, which he does not air, is that the origins of speech lie in song, and the origins of song in the need to fill out with sound the overlarge and rather empty human soul." J.M. Coetzee, *Disgrace*

OFFERINGS
-fare
-creature comforts
-amenities

OFFICE
-bureau
-desk

OFFICES
-executive suites

OFFICE-SEEKER
-aspirant

OFFICIAL
-functionary

OFFICIAL ORDER
-mandate
-directive

OFFSETTING
-countervailing

"A political party without a strong countervailing opposition is a sick thing."

OFTEN
-customary
-at frequent intervals
-as often as not

OK (FINE)
-no worse for wear
-everything in order

OKAY
-very well then
-very good

OKAY TO
-there is no harm in

> Would it be okay if we continued?
>
> Is there any harm in continuing?

OLD (AN OLD THING)
-archaic
-dated
-timeworn
-a dusty remembrance of
-aged
-elderly

"She had her check all ready and the manager said the keys were in the car, so in no time she was free to go. The car was parked toward the rear of the shop, an elderly grey-blue Dodge." Anne Tyler, *Breathing Lessons*

OLD (IS VERY OLD)
-dates from _____ BCE
-dates from _____ times
-of the _____ century

OLD AGE
-at a late age
-advanced age

"The late owner of this estate was a single man, who lived to a very advanced age, and who for many years of his life, had a constant companion and housekeeper in his sister." Jane Austen, *Sense and Sensibility*

OLD-FASHIONED AND OUTDATED
-fusty
-antediluvian
-outmoded
-old school

OLD LADY
-matriarch

OLD PERSON
-elder

OLDEST
-eldest

OMEN
-portent
-premonition

ON
-upon

"A dark shadow fell upon me, not of a cloud but of a man with a dazzling halo about him." J.M. Coetzee, *Foe*

ON A DAILY BASIS [INCORRECT USAGE]
-daily

ON A NIGHT LIKE THIS
-on such a night as this

ON A REGULAR BASIS [INCORRECT USAGE]
-regularly
-habitually

ON ACCOUNT OF
-in consideration of

ON AND ON
-ad infinitum {Latin, *add in-fih-NIGHT-um*}
-ad nauseam {Latin, *add NAUS-ee-um*}
-without end

ON DISPLAY
-in full plumage

"*Those privileged to be present at a family festival of the Forsytes have seen that charming and instructive sight—an upper middle-class family in full plumage.*" John Galsworthy, *Forsyte Saga*

ON FIRE
-alight
-ablaze

ON FIRST APPEARANCE (OBVIOUS)
-on prima facie evidence {Latin, *prime-uh FAY-shya*}

"*Initially it looked to be a prima facie case, but it was later determined that no crime occurred.*"

ON HER MIND
-what was in her mind

ON HER ORDERS
-at her behest

The new policy was implemented on her orders.

The new policy was implemented at her behest.

ON MY OWN (MYSELF)
-of my own accord

"'*Your father is preparing to set off on a long journey. Have you prayed for him?' There was a hint of severity in his gaze, and it may have been this that awakened in me a keen sense of negligence toward my father, because, to be sure, I would never have thought of that of my own accord.*" Imre Kértesz, *Fateless*

ON ONE CONDITION
-under the proviso that {*pruh-VIZE-oh*}

ON PURPOSE
-by design
-the calculated use of

-far from haphazard

ON THE AVERAGE
-all things considered

ON THE DAY HE
-the day on which he

ON THE FENCE
-noncommittal

ON THE OTHER HAND
-conversely
-but then again
-by comparison,
-per contra [academic]

ON THE SAME PAGE
-working from the same script
-simpatico

"*One sign that they are simpatico is that Madeleine wears chic noise-making clothes whose crackle is similar to sounds made by Adrian's group.*" Stephen Holden, *New York Times*, Oct. 23, 2009

ON THE SIDELINES
-on the periphery

ON THE SURFACE
-on the face of
-at first sight

"*Mansfield Park is a fairy tale, but then all novels are, in a sense, fairy tales. At first sight Jane Austen's manner and matter may seem to be old fashioned, stilted, unreal. But this is a delusion to which the bad reader succumbs. The good reader is aware that the quest for real life, real people, and so forth is a meaningless process when speaking of books.*" Vladimir Nabokov, *Lectures on Literature*

ON THE TIP OF MY TONGUE
-the word escapes me

ON THE WAY
-en route

ON THIS DAY
-on this, one of the great days in

ON TOP OF
-atop
-upon

ON VACATION
-on holiday [humorous]

ON YOUR OWN
-of your own accord
-left to your own devices
-by your own discretion

ONCE AGAIN
-yet again

ONCE IN A WHILE
-every now and again
-on occasion

ONCE SHE HAD ESTABLISHED HER
-having established her

ONE
-one such
-sole
-the singular notion that

ONE AFTER ANOTHER
-in rapid fire succession
-in turn
-seriatim {Latin, *sear-ee-AY-tum*}

ONE AT A TIME THEY
-one behind the other they

ONE BY ONE
-they came in continual succession
-a procession of
-one behind the other they

ONE IN FRONT OF THE OTHER
-in tandem

ONE OF THE
-among the

ONE OF A KIND
-rare find

ONE OF THE GREATEST ____
-one of the greatest of _____

"Now, thanks to the energy and the imagination of one of the greatest of colonial administrators, the country, at least in the French zone, is as safe and open as the opposite shore of Spain. All that remains is to tell the traveler how to find his way about it." Edith Wharton, *In Morocco*

ONE OF THEM
-there is one among the

ONE-EIGHTY
-a significant turnabout

ONE'S SELF
-the self

"Depression is a disorder of mood, so mysteriously painful and elusive in the way it becomes known to the self—to the mediating intellect—as to verge close to being beyond description." William Styron, *Darkness Visible*

ONLY
-is but
-is merely
-is scarcely
-is all of

"It took all of five minutes."

-is a mere
-it alone is
-it is little more than
-it is nothing but

"Ultimately, literature is nothing but carpentry. With both you are working with reality, a material just as hard as wood." Gabriel Garcia Marquez

---

There is only one.

There is but one.

ONLY HAVE
-I have only

> I only have three.
> I have only three.

ONLY A FEW
-a meager number of
-just a smattering of

ONLY GO SO FAR
-go only so far

ONLY HUMAN
-all-too-mortal

ONLY NEED TO
-need only to

ONLY ONE
-there was but one

ONLY OPTION
-only recourse

ONLY THING I'M GOOD AT IS
-I'm no good for anything except

ONLY THINKS ABOUT HIMSELF
-he thinks of nothing but himself

ONLY WANT (THEY ONLY WANT TO)
-they want nothing but to

ONLY WITH
-peculiar to

"Yet one cannot say with equal certainty just why the difficulty was peculiar to Memphis, unless it is that Memphis, unlike other Tennessee cities, remains to this day a 'land-oriented' place." Peter Taylor, *A Summons to Memphis*

OPEN
-lay open
-undo

"Soon after seven I went to Mummy and Daddy and then to the sitting room to undo my presents." Anne Frank, *Anne Frank: The Diary of a Young Girl"*

OPEN AIR (OF A CAFÉ)
-alfresco

"Tonight we dine alfresco!"

OPENLY DISREGARD A CONVENTION
-to flout

OPEN-MINDED
-amenable
-catholic
-liberal

OPINION
-commentary
-sentiment
-your take on

OPINION OF (MY OPINION OF HER)
-I found her to be

OPINIONATED
-outspoken

OPINIONS
-sentiments
-surmises
-assumptions

OPPONENT
-rival
-counterpart
-detractor
-gainsayer
-adversary
-antagonist
-naysayer

OPPORTUNITIES
-prospects

OPPORTUNITY
-occasion

OPPOSE
-contravene

"You dare to contravene police protocol?"

OPPOSED TO
-averse to
-not one to

OPPOSITE OF
-the very opposite of

"Theatergoers who use plays as mood-setting preludes to romantic evenings had better look elsewhere. 'Quartett,' which opened Wednesday night and runs through Nov. 14, may well be the sexually frankest play in New York this side of a backroom peephole. But with a cast led by the formidable French actress Isabelle Humpert in a magnificently mannered performance, it is the very opposite of an aphrodisiac." Ben Brantley, *New York Times*, Nov. 6, 2009

-far from it
-in stark contrast to
-the antithesis of

OPPRESSED (THE OPPRESSED)
-the downtrodden

OPTIMISTIC
-to strike an optimistic tone
-to be guardedly optimistic
-sanguine
-irrepressible
-Panglossian (excessively optimistic)

OPTIMISTIC IN SPEECH
-ebullient

ORDER (IN ORDER)
-in proper sequence

ORDER
-edict
-decree
-precept
-dictate

ORDERED
-he gave orders for the

ORDERED TO
-adjured to

"You have been adjured to tell the whole truth and nothing but the truth."

ORDINARY
-mundane
-pedestrian

ORDINARY PEOPLE
-ordinary beings
-the nothing in particular

"Nowadays, as long as they are still able to travel, they flock back home, even from the other side of the Pacific, arriving in cars or big air-conditioned coaches. The rich, the famous and the nothing in particular all hurry back because they are getting old. After all, who doesn't love the home of their ancestors?" Gao Xingjian, *Soul Mountain*

ORGANIZATION
-a concern
-an apparatus
-an enterprise
-a collective

ORGANIZED
-ordered
-ordered within a hierarchy of
-in good order

ORIGIN
-provenance
-genesis of

ORIGINAL
-archetypal {ark-ih-TYPE-ul}

"Achilles is the archetypal hero from which so many come."

ORIGINAL AND HIGHLY INFLUENTIAL
-seminal

ORIGINAL MODEL
-archetype

ORIGINALLY WRITTEN
-conceived

ORIGINATE FROM
-stem from
-origins lie in

"His own opinion, which he does not air, is that the origins of speech lie in song, and the origins of song in the need to fill out with sound the overlarge and rather empty human soul." J.M. Coetzee, *Disgrace*

ORIGINATED (WORDS)
-the term was coined back in

ORIGINATING FROM
-indebted to
-derived from
-owing to
-come by way of
-owes something to

ORIGINATOR OF
-progenitor of {*pruh-JEN-uh-ter*} [academic]

OSTENTATIOUS DISPLAY
-éclat {French, *ay-KLAH*}

"As soon as the bacon was well under way, and Millie, her lymphatic aid, had been brisked up a bit by a few deftly chosen expressions of contempt, she carried the cloth, plates, and glasses into the parlour and began to lay them with the utmost éclat." H. G. Wells, *The Invisible Man*

OSTENTATIOUS GIFT GIVING
-largess {*lar-JESS*}

OSTENTATIOUS IN ONE'S LEARNING
-pedantic
-turgid

OTHER
-peripheral

OTHER PLACES
-elsewhere

OTHER SIDE
-the reverse

OTHER SIMILAR THINGS
-and what have you

OTHERS OF THAT TIME
-contemporaries

OUR
-ours is a

OUT AND OUT
-unmitigated

OUT IN PUBLIC
-about among people

OUT IN THE MIDDLE OF NO WHERE
-in some lost corner of

OUT LOUD
-aloud

OUT OF ACTION
-incapacitated
-hors de combat {French, *or de cohm-BAH*}

OUT OF CONTROL
-overzealous
-a little

OUT OF ITS PROPER HISTORICAL TIME
-an anachronism
-anachronistic

OUT OF LINE
-outside the bounds of acceptable behavior

OUT OF NECESSITY
-where, of necessity, we
-of necessity

OUT OF PLACE
-among the alien corn

-incongruous

OUT OF REACH
-beyond reach

OUT OF REGARD FOR
-in a nod to

OUT OF THE BLUE
-quite by chance

OUT OF THE RUNNING (OF A COMPETITION)
-hors concours {French, *or* kawn-COOR}

OUT OF TUNE
-discordant
-dissonant

OUTCAST
-pariah

OUTDO
-best

OUTDOOR
-alfresco settings

OUTER LIMITS
-periphery

OUTLINE IT
-contour
-delineate

OUTRAGE
-indignation

OUTRAGEOUS
-beyond the pale
-outside the bounds of acceptable behavior
-outlandish

OUTSIDE (1)
-out-of-doors

OUTSIDE (2)
-outside the boundaries of
-outside the confines of

OUTSTANDING
-a banner _____

OUTWARD APPEARANCE
-guise

OUTWARD SIGNS OF
-trappings of

OUTWARDLY VIRTUOUS, BUT INWARDLY CORRUPT
-a whited sepulcher {*WHITE-ed SEP-uhl-ker*}

OUTWIT
-outflank
-outfox

OVER
-ended

"When the killing was ended, the postbellum government enacted measures to lessen the likelihood of another war."

OVER ALL
-all things considered
-on the whole
-by and large

OVER TIME
-in time
-with the lapse of time
-over the expanse of

OVER USED
-hackneyed
-trite

OVER WITH
-at an end
-no more

OVERALL
-on balance

OVERBEARING
-overweening

OVERCONFIDENCE
-hubris
-complacency

-an act of presumption

OVERCONFIDENT BUT POORLY INFORMED
-sophomoric

OVER-DO
-egg the pudding

"Don't egg the pudding with needless adjectives and adverbs."

OVERDOING A GOOD THING
-cloying

"It wasn't long before my 3-D glasses became a cloying annoyance."

OVERFLOWING (A STREAM FROM THAWING SNOW)
-full-freshet

"In the winter of wet years the streams ran full-freshet, and they swelled the river until sometimes it raged and boiled, bank full, and then it was a destroyer." John Steinbeck, *East of Eden*

OVERLOOKED
-commanded a view

OVERLY CRITICAL
-ruggedly critical

"Alexander the Grammarian taught me not to be ruggedly critical about words, nor find fault with people for improprieties of phrase or pronunciation, but to set them right by speaking the thing properly myself, and that either by way of answer, assent, or inquiry, or by some such other indirect and suitable correction." Marcus Aurelius, *Meditations*

OVERLY SENTIMENTAL
-mawkish
-maudlin
-cloying

OVERPROTECT
-coddle

OVER-REFINED AND DAINTY
-precious

OVER-REFINEMENT IN WORD CHOICE
-preciosity {presh-ee-AU-sih-tee} [academic]

"If you find yourself using words like preciosity, then you are likely engaged in precisely that."

OVERSAW
-ushered in

OVER-USED
-hackneyed
-trite

OVERWHELMED
-inundated
-harried

OVERWHELMING FAVORITE TO WIN
-the prohibitive favorite

OWED
-had been indebted to

OWNER
-proprietor
-keeper of [poetic]

Pp

PACING BACK AND FORTH
-toing and froing

PAID ATTENTION TO
-concerned themselves with

PAID OFF
-bore fruit

PAIN (A PAIN)
-a hurt

"But we had scarcely begun to climb when I felt a sharp hurt, and drew from my heel a long black-tipped thorn. Though I chafed it, the heel quickly swelled till I could not so much as hobble for the pain." J.M. Coetzee, Foe

PAIN (IN PAIN)
-in distress

PAIN IN THE NECK
-annoyance

PAINTED (OR PHOTOGRAPHED)
-captured

PAINTING OF MADONNA AND CHILD IN AN ENCLOSED GARDEN
-hortus conclusus {Latin, *hor-tus cun-CLUE-sus*}

PALE FROM POOR HEALTH
-pallid
-having a pallor about her
-a deathly hue
-sallow

PALE WITH FEAR
-ashen

PALENESS
-pallor

PAMPER
-cosset
-coddle

PANGS OF GUILT
-scruples

"Her scruples kept her from accepting the bribe."

PANIC
-hysteria

PAPAL AUTHORITY OVER NATIONAL AUTHORITY
-ultramontane {*ul-truh-MON-tane*} adj.

"When the Pope asserts that matters relating to pedophilia should fall outside the purview of any state government, he is asserting an ultramontane legal position."

PAPAL SUBSERVIENCE TO NATIONAL AUTHORITY
-gallican {*GAL-ih-ken*} adj.

"A gallican legal argument would support the rights of nation states to assert their authority over the Vatican."

PAPER
-thesis
-tract
-treatise {*TREET-is*}
-manuscript

PAR FOR THE COURSE
-standard fare
-prescribed form
-the norm and standard

> These are par for the course.
>
> These are pretty standard fare.

PARADISE-LIKE
-Edenic {*ee-DEN-ik*}

"As the sesquicentennial of Fort Sumter approaches in 2011, the enduring problem for neo-Confederates endures: anyone who seeks an Edenic Southern past in which the war was principally about states' rights and not slavery is searching in vain, for the Confederacy and slavery are inextricably and forever linked." Jon Meacham, "Southern Discomfort," New York Times, April 10, 2010

PARADOXICAL QUESTION OR STATEMENT
-a koan {*KOE-on*}

"If freedom had no defenders, it might actually begin to catch on."

PARDONED HIM OF HIS SINS
-absolved him of his sins

PARISIAN BOULEVARD (MOST FAMOUS)
-Champs Élysées {French, *shawnz ay-lee-ZAY*}

PARODY
-a send-up

PART
-component of
-arm of
-element of
-constituent of [academic]
-involved in

"Any man's death diminishes me, because I am involved in Mankind; and therefore never send to know for whom the bell tolls; it tolls for thee." John Donne {pronounced *Dun*}

PART (PLAYS A PART IN)
-her role in

PART _____ AND PART _____
-equal parts _____ and _____

PART OF A PLAN TO
-part of an effort to

PARTICIPATING IN
-taking part in
-engaging in
-being complicit in [derogatory]
-weighing in
-as part of a

"The CEO was in New York, as part of a three day conference on mergers."

PARTLY
-to the extent that
-in part
-to a certain extent
-in some measure
-appreciably
-in a manner
-to some extent

"To some extent yes, that's true."
-in part

"It is in part psychological, but also physiological."

PARTNER IN CRIME
-accomplice
-abettor
-accessory
-fellow traveler

PARTNERED WITH
-found a marriage of convenience with

PARTNERS
-associates
-brethren

PARTNERSHIP
-alliance

PARTY (TO PARTY)
-revel

PARTYING
-revelry

PASS
-overtake
-draw ahead

PASSIONATE
-fervent
-impassioned
-passional
-vehement
-emphatic
-torrid [sexual]

PASSIONATE ABOUT A CAUSE
-a firebrand

PASSIVE
-diffident

PASSIVITY
-quietism

PAST (LOCATION)
-beyond

PAST (THE PAST)
-those bygone days
-storied past
-those departed days

PATTERNED IN
-adorned with
-figured with

"He is in shirt sleeves, with a vest figured with faded gold horseshoes, and a pink-striped shirt, suggestive of peppermint candy." Upton Sinclair, *The Jungle*

PATIENCE
-forbearance

PATIENT
-forbearing
-indulgent

PAY ATTENTION TO
-take note of
-attend to
-address
-take notice of
-pay heed to
-heed
-devote considerable attention to
-concern ourselves with

PAY NO ATTENTION TO
-take no notice of

> I didn't pay any attention to it.
>
> I took little notice of it.

PAY OUT
-disburse

PAYMENT
-remittance [formal]

PEACE
-a moment's rest

"All the gold that lies beneath the moon, or ever did, could never give a moment's rest to any of these wearied souls." Dante's *Inferno, Canto VII*

PEACEFUL
-pacific [poetic]
-serene
-peaceable

"In this diminished form the words rush out of the cornucopia of my brain to course over the surface of the world, tickling reality like fingers on piano keys. They're an invisible army on a peacekeeping mission, a peaceable horde." Jonathan Lethem, *Motherless Brooklyn*

PEACEFUL PLACE
-far from the madding crowd

PEANUT GALLERY
-Greek chorus

PEERS
-counterparts
-cousins

PEN NAME
-pseudonym
-nom de guerre {French, *nom dih GARE*}
-nom de plume {French, *nom dih PLUME*}

PENALTY
-sanction
-censure
-punitive action

PENIS
-phallus

PENIS LIKE
-phallic

PEOPLE
-beings
-inhabitants
-distant figures
-personages
-persons

"Either we live by accident and die by accident, or we live by plan and die by plan. And on that instant Brother Juniper made the resolve to inquire into the secret lives of those five persons, that moment falling through the air, and to surprise the reason of their taking off." Thornton Wilder, *The Bridge of San Luis Rey*

-the populace
-interested parties
-mortals
-mortal beings

"There was a black river that flowed through the town, and if it had no grace for mortal beings, it did for swans, and many swans resorted there, and even rode the river like some kind of plunging animals, in floods." Sebastian Barry, *The Secret Scripture*

-we
-to some
-peoples
-voices
-things

"'Those white things have taken all I had or dreamed,' she said, 'and broke my heartstrings too. There is no bad luck in the world but white folks.'" Toni Morrison, *Beloved*

PEOPLE LIKE TO
-it is the way with people to [poetic]

PEOPLE OF A NATION
-the body politic
-the commonwealth
-inhabitants

"It was only toward the middle of the twentieth century that the inhabitants of many European countries came, in general unpleasantly, to the realization that their fate could be influenced directly by the intricate and abstruse books of philosophy." Czeslaw Milosz, *The Captive Mind*

PEOPLE SAY THAT I
-it may be said of me that

PEOPLE WALKING BY
-passers-by

PEOPLE WHO ARE LIKELY TO
-people given to

PEOPLE WHO LIVE THERE
-inhabitants

PER PERSON
-per capita

PER YEAR
-per annum

PERCENTAGE OF
-proportion of

PERFECT
-idyllic
-ideal
-infallible
-made to order
-irreproachable
-consummate
-impeccable
-quintessential

PERFECT EXAMPLE
-a paragon
-an exemplar
-the consummate _____
-the archetype of

PERFECT FOR
-it lends itself to
-it's particularly well suited for
-it suits you

> It's perfect for you.
>
> It suits you well.

PERFECT TIMING
-the stars are finally aligned in his favor
-opportune
-providential

PERFECTLY
-to brilliant effect
-ideally

PERFORM
-fare

"How did I fare?"

PERFORM WELL
-perform to strong reviews
-rise to the occasion

PERFORMANCE
-rendering
-rendition
-portrayal

PERIOD AFTER
-aftermath

PERIOD EXPERIENCED A
-this period saw a growth in
-this period witnessed

PERIOD OF TIME
-interval
-chapter
-interlude
-span of years

PERMANENT
-indissoluble [academic]
-lasting
-irrevocable

PERMANENT DAMAGE
-irreparable harm

PERMANENTLY
-indelibly

PERMEABLE
-pervious

PERMISSION
-consent
-license to
-carte blanche

PERPETUAL
-perennial

PERSECUTED
-put upon
-beset with
-beleaguered

PERSECUTION
-a pogrom

PERSECUTOR
-grand inquisitor

PERSISTENCE
-tenacity
-doggedness

PERSISTENT
-unrelenting
-relentless
-assiduous
-unremitting

PERSON
-a soul
-personage
-creature
-being
-a living being

"He calls despairingly, gazing in agony after the receding sail as, ghostlike, it fades from view. A short time ago he was on board, a member of the crew busy on deck with the rest, a living being with his share of air and sunlight. What has become of him now? He slipped and fell, and this is the end." Victor Hugo, *Les Miserables*

PERSON YOU'RE TALKING TO
-interlocutor

PERSONAL
-first-hand

PERSONAL ATTACKS (IN A DEBATE)
-ad hominem attacks {Latin, *add HAW-mih-num*}

> Personal attacks do nothing to further your point.
>
> Ad hominem arguments do nothing to further your point.

PERSONALITY
-persona
-nature

PERSONIFICATION OF
-_____ incarnate
-it is the embodiment of

PERSPECTIVE
-frame of reference
-in the eyes of
-from a _____ standpoint
-through the prism of their own culture

PERSUADE
-prevail upon
-strike a sympathetic chord
-cajole

PERSUADE NOT TO
-dissuade

PERSUADE TO SPEAK
-draw him out

PERSUADED ME TO
-moved me to

PETTY
-penny ante

PETTY OBJECTIONS
-cavils

PETTY THING
-trifling matter

PHILOSOPHY
-movements of thought

"Until I went to Cambridge I was almost wholly unaware of contemporary movements of thought." Bertrand Russell, On God and Religion

PHONY
-affected
-contrived
-highly mannered

> Stop sounding so phony.
>
> Stop sounding so affected.

PHOTOGRAPHS OF KNOWN CRIMINALS
-the rogues gallery

PHRASES
-expressions
-verbiage

PHYSICAL
-corporeal [academic]

PICK
-appoint
-assemble

PICK THROUGH
-rifle through

PICK UP
-retrieve

PICKED UP
-took up

"I took up my coat and carpet-bag, and went into the next room to change my linen, and dress for dinner." Jacques Casanova, Volume 6c—Rome: The Memoirs of Jacques Casanova

PICKY
-discriminating
-finical

PICTURE
-tableau {TA-blow}
-depiction
-portrait

PICTURES
-tableaux {TA-blows}
-portraiture

PICTURESQUE
-idyllic

PIECE
-fragment
-remnant

PIECE OF ART
-a work
-this piece

PIECE OF CLOTH
-swatch from

PIECES
-elements
-remnants
-components
-traces
-fragments
-smithereens

"Nothing much was left of her but charred smithereens." Margaret Atwood, *The Blind Assassin*

PIG-LIKE
-porcine

PILGRIMAGE
-hajj {HADJ}

PIONEER
-forerunner

PISS HER OFF
-embitter her
-rouse her ire

PITHY SAYING
-aphorism
-adage

"The educated don't get that way by memorizing facts; they get that way by respecting them."

PIVOTAL EVENT
-watershed moment

PLACE
-forum
-arena
-venue

PLACE OF CORRUPTION
-Augean stables {au-JEE-un}

"ACORN is regarded by many to be the Augean stables of the Democratic Party."

PLACE OF STORAGE
-repository

PLACE TO SLEEP
-accommodations

PLACED IN
-housed in

"A collection of textile samples lay spread out on the table—Samsa was a travelling salesman—and above it there hung a picture that he had recently cut out of an illustrated magazine and housed in a nice, gilded frame." Franz Kafka, *Metamorphosis*

PLACES
-quarters

PLAIN
-nondescript
-unprepossessing

PLAN
-agenda
-intent
-stratagem
-scheme

PLAN ON
-foresee
-intend on
-have every intention

PLANNED
-drew their plans against us

PLANT LIFE
-flora

PLAY WITH
-toy with

PLAYFUL TALK
-banter

PLAYING DUMB
-laying on the Socratic irony

> She's playing dumb to make you look ridiculous.
>
> She's using Socratic irony to make you look ridiculous.

PLEASANT
-not disagreeable

PLEASE
-would you be good enough to
-won't you come over to our table
-if you please
-I will thank you to [hostile]
-would you be so good as to
-if you think it might be possible
-it would be most helpful
-I would be grateful if

PLEASE DON'T
-I will thank you not to [hostile]

PLEASURE DERIVED FROM ANOTHER'S MISFORTUNE
-schadenfreude {German, SHAHD-n-froid}

PLEASURE SEEKER
-hedonist
-voluptuary
-bon vivant {French, bone vee-VAHN}
-epicure

PLEDGE OF SUPPORT
-avowal of support

PLENTY OF
-ample

PLOT
-scheme
-contrivance

POETIC
-poetical

"The Greek Antiquities are full of Poetical Fictions, because the Greeks wrote nothing in Prose, before the Conquest of Asia by Cyrus the Persian." Sir Isaac Newton, *The Chronology of Ancient Kingdoms*

POINT ME TO THE APPROPRIATE
-direct me to the appropriate

POINT OF NO RETURN
-crossing the Rubicon

POINT TO
-draw attention to
-cite

POISONOUS
-virulent

POLICY
-course

"As a matter of course, we no longer accept unsolicited submissions."
-protocol

"Contrary to popular belief, there is no legal requirement, nor is there even police protocol which requires officers to use stilted, overly formal language in their reports."

POLISH
-burnish
-smooth over

"It took a few weeks to smooth over the cracks in his English."

POLITICALLY INCORRECT
-off-color

> His joke was politically incorrect.
>
> His joke was off-color.

POLITICIAN
-politico
-demagogue (uses fear as a tactic)

POLITICS
-the body politic
-polity

"The aftermath of the First World War resulted in a new kind of German polity."

POLLUTE
-befoul
-defile

POMPOUS TALK OR WRITING
-bombast
-turgid prose
-grandiloquence {gran-DILL-uh-quence}

POMPOUSLY LEARNED
-pedantic
-turgid

POOR
-impoverished
-of small means
-of reduced circumstances
-indigent

POPULAR
-widely accepted
-the darling of
-an object of much attention
-much in demand
-highly valued

PORCH
-veranda

PORNOGRAPHIC
-salacious

PORTRAIT
-likeness

POSITION (ADMINISTRATIVE)
-post
-in her capacity as

POSITION (PHYSICAL)
-pose
-stance
-posture

POSITIVE
-complimentary

"Can't you say anything complimentary about her?"

POSSIBILITY
-contingency

POSSIBILITY FOR
-prospects for
-prospect of
-specter of

POSSIBLE
-plausible
-conceivable

POSSIBLE OUTCOMES
-contingencies

> We've prepared for all possible outcomes.
>
> We've prepared for all contingencies.

POSSIBLY
-perhaps
-presumably
-is said to be
-is arguably

POSSESSED HIM
-took possession of him

POSSESSES (HAS)
-harbors

POUR INTO
-decant

POVERTY
-want

"Even if perfect social justice and complete freedom from want were to prevail in a world at peace, rebels would still be needed wherever the world is out of joint, which now means everywhere." René Dubose, So Human an Animal: How We Are Shaped by Surroundings and Events

POWER
-influence
-agency
-means
-auspices
-instrumentality
-within the orbit of Roman power

POWERFUL
-formidable
-high octane

POWERFUL ENTITIES
-vested interests
-the powers that be

POWERFUL FORCE
-juggernaut

POWERFUL PERSON
-a _____ magnate
-mogul

POWERLESS
-inert
-impotent

PRACTICAL
-more firmly tethered to reality
-applicative [academic]

PRACTICAL ASPECTS
-practicalities

PRACTICAL POLITICS
-realpolitik {German, ray-AL-pol-uh-TEEK}

"It wasn't long before the newly elected ideologue learned her first lesson in realpolitik."

PRACTICALLY
-he all but made a

PRACTICING
-polishing

"Already he was polishing a few carefully worded accusations designed to reduce his mother to repentance or, at least, confusion. He often had to keep her in her place." John Kennedy Toole, A Confederacy of Dunces

PRAISE
-extol praise on
-sing her praises
-kudos
-hail
-speak well of
-vaunt
-applaud
-give praise to

PRAISES OF THE CRITICS
-plaudits of the critics

PRECEDES
-heralds

PRECEDING
-foregoing
-precursory [academic]
-antecedent [academic]

PREDATORY
-predacious

PREDICT
-foresee
-foretell
-bode
-portend
-had the forethought to
-venture to predict
-presage something evil
-prognosticate

-extrapolate
-preordain
-prefigure
-betoken [poetic]

PREDICTABLE
-formulaic
-foreseeable
-so paint-by-numbers

PREDICTING DISASTER
-apocalyptic

"He would scare his way to higher ratings with apocalyptic conspiracy theories."

PREDICTIONS OF
-prophecies

"The prophecies of impending doom have proved hollow."
-prognostications

PREDICTOR
-bellwether

PREDITORIAL BEHAIVOR
-predation

PREFER
-favor

PREFERENCE
-predilection
-proclivity
-penchant

PREGNANT
-in a delicate condition

PREJUDICE
-preconceived view
-provincialism
-xenophobia (against foreigners)
-intolerance

PRELIMINARY
-prelude to

PREMATURE CELEBRATION
-dancing on volcanoes

PREMATURE EJACULATION
-arriving too soon

"His specific worry, based on one unfortunate experience, was of overexcitement, of what he had heard someone describe as 'arriving too soon.' The matter was rarely out of his thoughts, but though his fear of failure was great, his eagerness—for rapture, for resolution—was far greater." Ian McEwan, *Chesil Beach*

PREMEDITATED MURDER
-malice aforethought [legal]

PREPARE
-ready yourself
-have the forethought to
-lay the groundwork for
-are being readied for
-rev up for
-pave the way for
-set the stage for
-ready for
-gird for
-provision for

Get ready.

Ready yourself.

PRESENT (ARE PRESENT)
-are assembled
-are in the flesh
-are prevalent
-are well represented

PRESENT IT
-put it

"…he put the whole thing to her as a kind of favor, an obligation he should gratefully incur." Henry James, *The Turn of the Screw*

PRESENT TO YOU
-bestow
-confer
-serve up

-bring forth
-tender
-offer up
-bring before you
-make available
-render

PRESENTATION
-rendition
-version

PRESENTED
-staged
-laid before
-put forth

PRESENTED IN POOR TASTE
-perpetrated on

PRESENTING A CAUTIOUS DEMEANOR
-sounding a note of caution

PRESENTS A PROBLEM
-poses a problem

PRESERVE
-enshrine

PRESS (THE NEWS PRESS)
-the fourth estate

PRESSURE
-bring pressure to bear
-bring to bear
-press

> We should put pressure on every member of the committee.
>
> Pressure should be brought to bear on every member of the committee.

PRESSURED INTO
-mack-trucked

"Nicole always felt mack-trucked into that one. There was a saying they used up in the nuthouse for when you got pushed into a marriage by parties larger than yourself. Mack-trucked. It was obvious to Nicole that her parents wanted her off their hands." Norman Mailer, *The Executioner's Song*

PRESTIGE
-cachet {French, *ka-SHAY*}

PRETEND
-feign
-affect

PRETEND TO BE SICK
-malinger

PRETENDING TO
-affecting
-under the pretense of
-feigning
-under the guise of
-with a façade of

PRETENDS TO
-feigns

"There are still the flowers to buy. Clarissa feigns exasperation (though she loves doing errands like this), leaves Sally cleaning the bathroom, and runs out, promising to be back in half an hour." Michael Cunningham, *The Hours*

PRETENTIOUS
-affected
-stagy
-fustian {*FUS-chen*}

PRETENTIOUS WRITER OR SPEAKER
-popinjay

PRETTY
-fairly
-somewhat

PRETTY GOOD AT
-I am something of a

PRETTY MUCH
-effectively

-for all intents and purposes
-more or less
-to a certain extent
-by and large

PREVENT
-foil
-forestall
-preclude
-avert
-hinder
-thwart
-ward off
-obviate

"He may be a good guy and all, but that does not obviate the fact that he's of little use to me."

PREVENT ME FROM
-compromise my ability to

> I will not allow you to prevent me from operating effectively.
>
> I will not allow you to compromise my ability to operate effectively.

PREVENT THE DETERIORATION OF
-save from decay

PREVENTS ME FROM
-precludes me from
-forbids me from

PREY
-quarry

PRIDE
-hubris [pejorative]

PRIESTLY
-hieratic {high-uh-RAT-ik}

PRIM AND PROPER
-staid
-reserved

PRIMITIVE FORM OF
-rudiments of

PRIOR CONDITION
-prerequisite

PRIOR EVENT
-forgoing event

PRIOR TO
-beforehand
-prelude to a

PRIORITIZE [CORPORATE CLICHÉ]
-set priorities

PRISONER
-captive

PRIVACY
-solitude

"I enjoyed such moments—but only in brief. If the talk began to wander, or cross the border into familiarity, I would soon find reason to excuse myself. I had grown too comfortable in my solitude, the safest place I knew." Barack Obama, *Dreams from My Father*

PRIVATE
-interior

"In her enigmatic remoteness Jenny was a little disquieting. Even now some interior joke seemed to be amusing her, for she was smiling to herself, and her brown eyes were like very bright round marbles." Aldous Huxley, *Chrome Yellow*

-unpeopled

"It was imperative, he knew, that he go back to sleep. He could not lie awake during these hours. He wanted to sleep, enter a lovely blackness, a dark, but not too dark, resting place, unhaunted, unpeopled, with no flickering presences." Colm Tóibín, *The Master*

PRIVATE MEETING PLACE
-conclave

PRIVATE PARTS
-nether regions

PRIVATE TIME
-stolen hours

PRIVATELY
-sub-rosa

PROACTIVE [INCORRECT USAGE]
-active

PROBABLE SUCCESSOR
-heir apparent

PROBABLY
-inclined to
-predisposed to
-presumably
-arguably
-increasingly likely that
-believed to be
-safe to say that
-most likely

> We might just do that.
> It's increasingly likely that we will.

PROBABLY SHOULD HAVE
-I might have been better advised to

PROBE INTO
-plumb

PROBLEM
-condition
-difficulty
-complexity
-sticking point
-quandary

PROBLEMATIC
-a problem

PROCEDURES
-formalities
-protocols

PRODUCE
-render
-offer up
-yield

PRODUCTIVE
-prolific
-prodigious
-gainful

PRODUCTS
-wares

PROGRAM
-regimen
-initiative

PROGRESS
-forward movement
-progression
-furtherance

PROGRESS (MAKE PROGRESS)
-make headway
-make inroads

PROHIBIT
-proscribe [academic]

PROJECT
-enterprise
-undertaking
-endeavor

PROMISE
-assurance
-covenant

PROMISE (I PROMISE)
-I assure you

PROMISING
-auspicious

PROMOTE
-cultivate
-foster
-advocate
-champion
-underwrite

-fuel
-sponsor
-propagate

PROMOTER OF AN OPERA COMPANY
-impresario {Italian, *im-pre-SAR-ee-oe*}

PROMOTION
-elevation of

PRONOUNCE
-enunciate

PROOF OF
-testament to
-evidence of
-testimony of
-attest to
-stand as proof of
-telling examples of

PROPAGANDA
-guerilla theater
-agitprop {*AJ-it-prop*}

PROPAGANDIZING PAMPHLET
-a tract on

PROPER
-de rigueur {French, *der ree-GUHR*}

PROPORTIONAL
-pro rata [academic]

PROPOSAL
-a measure
-an initiative

PROTECT
-run interference
-safeguard
-harbor

PROTECTION FROM IT
-proof against it

"There were ants scurrying everywhere, of the same kind we had in Bahia, and another pest too, living in the dunes: a tiny insect that hid between your toes *and ate its way into the flesh. Even Friday's hard skin was not proof against it: there were bleeding cracks in his feet, though he paid them no heed."* J.M. Coetzee, *Foe*

PROTECTOR
-protectant

PROTEST
-raise a hue and cry
-clamor
-register their protest

PROTOTYPE
-archetype

PROVE
-demonstrate
-suggest that
-attest
-bear witness to
-establish

"Django was a ponytailed visionary—if that's not a tautology—who, following an epiphany in Vietnam, founded the New Earth Army in order to establish whether love and peace can win wars." Anthony Lane, *The New Yorker*, Nov. 9, 2009

PROVE INNOCENT
-absolve
-exonerate
-exculpate

> I was proven completely innocent.
>
> I was absolved of any wrongdoing.

PROVE YOURSELF
-show yourself worthy

PROVES NOTHING
-produces no conclusive evidence

PROVEN
-evidenced by
-attested by
-born out by

PROVERB
-as the ___ proverb has it

PROVIDE WITH EQUIPMENT
-outfit

PROVIDE YOU WITH
-provide for the
-afford
-offer up
-give

"...And the dead tree gives no shelter, the cricket no relief..." T. S. Eliot, *The Waste Land*

PROVOKE
-wave the bloody shirt

PUBLIC
-in the public eye
-in a public forum

PUBLIC OUTCRY
-hue and cry

PUBLIC PLACES
-places essentially public

PUBLIC SHAME
-ignominy {IG-nuh-min-ee}

PUBLICIZE
-bring to much greater public notice

PUBLICLY
-on the surface
-outwardly

PUCKER
-purse

PULL
-draw
-wrest

PULLED IN
-drawn in

PULLED IT DOWNWARDS
-drew it downwards

PUNISH
-sanction
-take to the woodshed
-administer a drubbing
-mete out the ultimate punishment
-reward

"If they begged without a written permission, they were rewarded by the pillory, the whip, branding, slavery, or the gallows." Edith Sitwell, *Fanfare for Elizabeth*

PUNISHING ACTIONS
-punitive actions

PUPPETEER [METAPHORICALLY SPEAKING]
-a Svengali

PURE
-unadulterated
-intacta {Latin, in-TACK-tuh}

PURENESS
-fidelity

PURIFICATIONS
-ablutions

PURPOSE IS TO
-serves as a
-functions as a

PURSUIT OF THIS GOAL
-pursuit of this end

PUSH
-propel

PUSHED BACK BY THE CROWD
-was borne back by the crowd

PUSHED DOWN ON
-bore down upon her

PUSHED INTO A LEADING ROLE
-pressed into a leading role

PUSHING THE ENVELOPE
-operating at the margins

> You're pushing the envelope.
>
> You are operating at the margins.

PUSHY
-sharp elbowed
-bumptious

PUT A CURSE ON
-laid a curse on

PUT AN EMPHASIS ON
-laid a special emphasis on

PUT ASIDE
-lay aside

"Lay aside your personal feelings and view this as a professional matter."

PUT AT EASE
-disarm

PUT AT RISK
-imperil
-compromise

PUT DOWN
-quell
-quash

PUT FORTH
-assert
-present the case
-suggest
-adduce
-advance
-propound
-venture
-proffer

PUT IN PLACE
-install
-instate
-institute
-station
-impose
-implement
-apply

PUT ON
-don

PUT ON A BACK BURNER
-hold in abeyance [formal]

PUT ON A PEDESTAL
-sacralize
-enshrine

PUT ON A PLAY
-stage a production

PUT ON HOLD
-hold in abeyance [formal]

PUT OUT (DISSEMINATE)
-circulate
-trot out
-bandy about

PUT OUT THE FIRE
-tamp it down (of a controversy)
-douse
-extinguish

"The sultan signaled for the sole lamp to be extinguished. Darkness took over and the specters of the trees giving out a fragrant aroma were cast into semi-obscurity." Naguib Mahfouz, *Arabian Nights and Days*

PUT TO USE
-are brought to bear

PUT TOGETHER
-compiled
-cobbled together
-confected

PUT UP WITH
-withstand
-tolerate
-countenance

-endure
-abide
-a bitter pill to swallow
-bear with

"He had to accept the fate of every new-comer to a small town where there are plenty of tongues that gossip and few minds that think. He had to bear with this in spite of being a bishop and because he was a bishop." Victor Hugo, *Les Miserables*

PUT YOUR TWO CENTS IN
-weigh in with

I'd like you to put your two cents in on this.

I'd like you to weigh in on this.

PUTTING THE CART BEFORE THE HORSE
-hysteron proteron {Late Latin, *HIS-ter-on PRAH-ter-on*}

PUTTING UP WITH
-accommodating

PUZZLING
-enigmatic
-perplexing
-inexplicable
-ambiguous

Qq

QUALIFIED
-well credentialed

QUALITY
-attribute

QUENCH
-slake your thirst
-drink your thirst away

QUESTION
-take to task
-impugn
-call into question

QUESTION ASKED OF HIM
-question put to him

QUESTION CAME UP
-the question arose

QUESTION IS
-the question before us all
-the question then becomes
-it's a question of

QUESTIONABLE
-dubious
-suspect

QUESTIONING ONE'S MOTIVES OR CHARACTER
-arguing ad hominem {Latin, *add HAW-mih-num*}

QUESTIONING STARE
-interrogative stare

QUESTIONS
-inquiries

"Dr. Spears is known for his sensitivity to women's complaints; he has a way of squeezing his eyes shut when he phrases his delicate inquiries, of speaking almost poetically of nature's cycles and balances, of the tide of fertility or the consolation of fruit salts." Carol Shields, *The Stone Diaries*

QUICK LOOK
-give it a once-over
-a cursory reading

QUICKLY
-with deliberate speed
-with all deliberate speed
-in relatively short order
-hurriedly
-in an instant
-without delay
-post haste

-soon

"I enjoyed such moments—but only in brief. If the talk began to wander, or cross the border into familiarity, I would soon find reason to excuse myself. I had grown too comfortable in my solitude, the safest place I knew." Barack Obama, *Dreams from My Father*

QUICKLY ASSURED HER THAT
-was quick to assure her that

QUICKLY BECOMING
-fast becoming

QUICKLY SAW
-were quick to see

QUIET
-restrained
-stoic
-taciturn
-reserved
-hushed

QUIETLY
-with little fanfare

QUIRK
-foible
-eccentricity

QUIT
-forswear

QUOTE
-cite

Rr

RABBLE-ROUSER
-iconoclast

"Christopher Hitchens is an iconoclast of the first order."

RACIST
-xenophobe {ZEE-nuh-fobe}

RACKET (DISTURBANCE)
-commotion
-stir
-kerfuffle

RADICAL
-incendiary
-provocative
-rabid

RADICAL LEFTIST
-Jacobin {JACK-uh-bin}
-communist

RADICAL RIGHTIST
-reactionary
-intransigent
-fascist

RAIN
-the rains

RAISE DOUBTS OR OBJECTIONS
-demur

RAISE PETTY OBJECTIONS
-cavil about

RAISE QUESTIONS ABOUT
-cast doubt upon

"Several of the outfits, Ignatius noticed, were new enough and expensive enough to be properly considered offenses against taste and dignity. Possession of anything new or expensive only reflected a person's lack of theology and geometry; it could even cast doubts upon one's soul." John Kennedy Toole, *A Confederacy of Dunces*

RAISE THE SUBJECT
-broach the subject

RAISED (BORN AND RAISED)
-bred

"As for my mother, she taught me to have regard for religion, to be generous and open-handed, and not only to forbear from doing

anybody an ill turn, but not so much as to endure the thought of it. By her likewise I was bred to a plain, inexpensive way of living, very different from the common luxury of the rich." Marcus Aurelius, *Meditations*

RAISED ON
-reared on

RAMBLING
-discursive
-desultory
-digressing

RAN INTO
-encountered
-chanced upon
-came upon
-happened on

"Beyond the Indian hamlet, upon a forlorn strand, I happened on a trail of recent footprints." David Mitchell, *Cloud Atlas*

RAN THE ORGANIZATION
-oversaw

RAN UP TO
-rushed headlong up to

RANDOM
-arbitrary
-indiscriminate
-haphazard

RANGE
-scope
-gamut
-purview
-extent
-spectrum

RANK
-standing
-station
-hierarchy
-echelon
-stature
-distinctions of rank
-pecking order

-precedence

RANKED UP THERE WITH
-ranked alongside

RANKS
-the serried ranks

RARE
-rarefied
-of a rare sort

RARE EVENT
-the rarest of events

RARE EXCEPTION
-an outlier

RARE THING
-rara avis {Latin, *RARE-uh AVE-is*}
-rarity
-endangered species

RARELY
-seldom, if ever

RASH
-imprudent

RASHLY
-precipitately
-impetuously

RAT OUT
-implicate

RATIFIED
-made real

"Farmers and scholars; statesmen and patriots who had traveled across an ocean to escape tyranny and persecution finally made real their declaration of independence at a Philadelphia convention that lasted through the spring of 1787." Barack Obama, "A More Perfect Union"

RATIONAL ARGUMENT
-dialectic [academic]

RAVE OVER
-rhapsodize

RAW BEEF DISH
-steak tartare {French, *tar-TAR*}

RAW FISH DISH
-ceviche {*seh-VEE-chay*}

REACT
-respond in kind

REACTED TO WITH
-was met with
-was received with

REACTION TO EXCESSES OF A REVOLUTION
-a thermidorean reaction

READ
-consult
-peruse

READ OUT LOUD
-read aloud

READ VORACIOUSLY
-consume vast helpings of
-devour

READINESS
-preparedness

READING MY BOOK
-the reading of my book

"Whether Nature did well or ill in breaking the mould in which she formed me, is a question which can only be resolved after the reading of my book." Jean-Jacques Rousseau, *The Confessions*

READS
-proclaims

READY TO
-poised to

REAL
-bona fide
-genuine
-substantive
-tangible
-appreciable

-manifest
-palpable

REAL LIFE
-true and living

"Somewhere out there is a true and living prophet of destruction and I don't want to confront him." Cormac McCarthy, *No Country for Old Men*

REALISM
-vérité {French, *vair-ih-TAY*}

REALITY
-events on the ground

REALIZE
-perceive

"Magnificence, like the size of a fortune, is always comparative, as even Magnificent Lorenzo may now perceive, if he has happened to haunt New York in 1916; and the Ambersons were magnificent in their day and place." Booth Tarkington, *The Magnificent Ambersons*

REALIZED
-was borne in on her
-found himself
-came to that realization

"It was only toward the middle of the twentieth century that the inhabitants of many European countries came, in general unpleasantly, to the realization that their fate could be influenced directly by the intricate and abstruse books of philosophy." Czeslaw Milosz, *The Captive Mind*

REALLY (VERY)
-to a large extent
-above all
-clearly
-genuinely
-decidedly
-in no uncertain manner
-indeed
-assuredly
-so much

"My Dear Michèle, I would so much like this house to stay empty. I would hope the owners don't come back for a long time." J.M.G. Le Clézio, *The Interrogation*

REALLY (ACTUALLY)
-in actual fact
-in truth
-it is in point of fact
-in any real sense

"But even though the number of those who really think seriously before they begin to write is small, extremely few of them think about the subject itself: the remainder think only about the books that have been written on the subject, and what has been said by others. In order to think at all, such writers need the more direct and powerful stimulus of having other people's thoughts before them. These become their immediate theme; and the result is that they are always under their influence, and so never, in any real sense of the word, are original. But the former are roused to thought by the subject itself, to which their thinking is thus immediately directed. This is the only class that produces writers of abiding fame." Arthur Schopenhauer, *The Art of Literature*

REALLY LIKED
-was taken with

> She really liked his sense of style.
>
> She was taken with his sense of style.

REAPPEAR
-resurface

REASON
-motive
-grounds for
-rationale

REASON BEING IS [INCORRECT USAGE]
-the reason is
-the reason being that

REASON FOR
-cause for

"Apprehension seems to exist among the people of the Southern States that by the accession of a Republican administration their property and their peace and personal security are to be endangered. There has never been any reasonable cause for such apprehension." Abraham Lincoln, *Inaugural Address*, March 4, 1861

-this is partly accounted for by
-for the purpose of
-is the impetus for
-is being fed by
-is an outgrowth of
-is attributed to
-is behind
-catalyst for
-rooted in a desire to
-for the sake of
-in the interest of
-in consequence of
-the reason stemmed from
-what is the occasion for
-cause of

"Although I cannot yet congratulate you on the reestablishment of peace in Europe and the restoration of security to the persons and properties of our citizens from injustice and violence at sea, we have, nevertheless, abundant cause of gratitude to the source of benevolence and influence for interior tranquility and personal security..." John Adams, *State of the Union Address*, 1797

REASON FOR BEING
-raison d'être {French, *ray-zohn DET-ruh*}

REASON IS BECAUSE [INCORRECT USAGE]
-the reason is that

REASONABLE
-the voice of reason
-actions founded in reason

REASONABLE CONCLUSION
-the product of reason

REBEL
-rogue
-young Turk
-recusant {REK-you-zent}
-inserrecto {Spanish, in-sur-RECK-toe}

REBELLION
-insurrection

REBELLIOUS
-recalcitrant
-fractious
-wayward

RECAPTURE THE OLD MAGIC
-return to form

> You have finally recaptured the old magic.
>
> You have returned to form.

RECEIVE SOON
-will be forthcoming

RECEIVED
-I'm in receipt of

RECENT CONVERT
-proselyte

RECENTLY
-of late
-in recent times

RECEPTIVE TO
-well disposed to the idea of

RECHARGED
-replenished

RECKLESS
-cavalier

-impetuous
-heedless
-hasty
-harum-scarum
-haphazard
-fitful
-profligate

RECOGNIZE
-acknowledge

RECONCILIATION
-an olive branch
-a gesture
-rapprochement {French, rah-prawsh-mahn}

RECONSTRUCT
-reconstitute

RECORD
-chronicle

RECOVER
-convalesce

RED FACE
-florid face

RED FLAG
-call into question

> This throws up a red flag.
>
> This calls into question your credibility.

REDESIGN
-reconfigure

REDUCE
-curtail
-draw down
-pare

REDUCE IN IMPORTANCE
-downplay
-dismiss
-marginalize

-consign
-relegate

REDUNDANCY
-tautology [academic]

REFER
-allude to
-invoke
-cite
-point to

REFEREE
-mediator
-arbiter

REFERENCE TO
-allusion to

REFILL
-replenish

REFUSE TO ALLOW
-disallow

REFUSED
-refused to hear of it

"The woman who had suggested a case of nerves was of the opinion that an ambulance should be summoned to transport the poor man to the hospital, but the blind man refused to hear of it, quite unnecessarily, all he wanted was that someone might accompany him to the entrance of the building where he lived." José Saramago, *Blindness*

-declined
-have been reluctant to
-balked at
-failed to

"If the more sensitive among those she served or addressed failed to look at Rose, it was because her manner seemed to accuse the conscience, or it could have been, more simply, that they were embarrassed by her hair lip." Patrick White, *Voss*

REGAIN THE FAVOR OF
-propitiate

REGARDING
-as to
-apropos of {French, *a-pra-POE*}
-as regards the

REGARDLESS OF
-irrespective of

REGARDLESS OF WHAT HAPPENS
-come what may

REGION
-sphere
-domain
-realm
-dominion
-expanse

REGRET (I REGRET)
-have misgivings
-rue the day
-lament the loss of
-bemoan

REGRETFUL (IS REGRETFUL)
-source of regret

REGRETS
-misgivings
-compunctions

REGROUP
-reestablish

"They need to reestablish themselves offensively."

REGULAR
-typical of normal events

REGULARLY
-oftentimes
-customarily
-not infrequently

REHEARSAL
-dry run

REINFORCE
-bolster
-shore up

REITERATED
-reaffirmed

REJECT
-repudiate
-shrug off the idea
-rebuff
-dismiss
-spurn
-disavow
-forswear

REJECTED (WAS REJECTED)
-was poorly received

RELATED (IT IS RELATED)
-it is its cousin

"Affection may not be love, but it is at least its cousin." J.M. Coetzee, *Disgrace*

RELATED TO THE
-surrounding the

"You need to acquaint yourself with all the facts surrounding the merger."
-is in close relationship with

"My sister Margot was born in 1926 in Frankfort-on-Main, I followed on June 12th, 1929, and, as we are Jewish, we emigrated to Holland in 1933, where my father was appointed Managing Director of Travies N.V. This firm is in close relationship with the firm of Kolen and Co. in the same building, of which my father is a partner." Anne Frank, *Anne Frank: The Diary of a Young Girl*

RELATIONSHIP BETWEEN
-correlation

RELATIVE
-comparative

"Magnificence, like the size of a fortune, is always comparative, as even Magnificent Lorenzo may now perceive, if he has happened to haunt New York in 1916; and the Ambersons were magnificent in their day and place." Booth Tarkington, *The Magnificent Ambersons*

RELATIVELY SHORT PERIOD
-comparatively short period

RELAX
-set your mind at rest

RELEASE
-unbridle
-unfetter
-unleash

RELEGATE
-consign

RELENTLESS
-implacable
-will stop at nothing
-inexorable

RELENTLESSLY
-inexorably

"Year by year, slowly but inexorably, his spirit had withered. Dry of heat and dry-eyed. During his nineteen years imprisonment he had not shed a tear." Victor Hugo, *Les Miserables*

RELEVANT
-material
-germane to
-pertinent
-applicable

> That doesn't have anything to do with the conversation.
>
> That's not material to the conversation.

RELIABLE
-bankable

RELIABLE SOURCE
-good authority

"I have it on good authority."

RELIEF
-a salve

RELIEF OF TENSION (A GOOD CRY)
-a catharsis

RELIEVE
-allay
-alleviate
-give you peace

RELIGIOUS
-ecclesiastical
-exegetical [academic]

RELIGIOUS INTUITION
-gnosis {*NO-sis*}

RELUCTANT
-disinclined to
-loath to
-averse to
-reticent
-hard pressed to
-far be it from me to
-have reservations

I'm not sure about that.

I have my reservations.

RELY ON
-place your expectations on

REMAINDER
-remnant
-residual

REMAINING (IN EXISTENCE)
-extant [academic]

"There are only two extant copies, and we own them both."

REMAINING PIECES
-remnants of
-vestiges of

REMAKE
-reconstitute

REMEDY (A REMEDY)
-a panacea

REMEMBER NOW
-mind you
-let us not forget
-it bears repeating
-it is worth remembering
-it must be remembered that
-bear in mind

REMEMBER (CAN REMEMBER)
-recollect
-recall
-register in his mind the
-draw upon memory
-no memory can reach

"And these words are the truth, for they are written on the Palace of the World Council, and the World Council is the body of all truth. Thus has it been ever since the Great Rebirth, and farther back than that no memory can reach." Ayn Rand, *Anthem*

REMEMBER ME
-bring me back to mind

REMEMBER THAT YOU ARE MORTAL
-memento mori {Latin, *meh-MEN-toe MOR-ee*}

REMEMBERED AS (IS REMEMBERED AS)
-it stands in memory as

REMEMBERING
-remembrance of

"There is no remembrance of former things; neither shall there be any remembrance of things that are to come with

those that shall come after." King James Bible (Ecclesiastes)

REMINDS
-calls to mind
-provides a vivid reminder of
-pulls us back to a time when
-is reminiscent of
-is suggestive of
-is redolent of
-it recalls

> It reminds me of the saying, "Be careful what you wish for, you just might get it."
>
> It calls to mind the adage, "Be careful what you wish for, lest your wish be granted."

REMORSEFUL
-contrite

REMOVE
-dispatch
-excise
-obviate
-expunge
-dispose of

RENEWED INTEREST IN
-rebirth of interest in

RENOUNCE
-repudiate
-apostatize
-abjure

REPAIR
-restore
-carry out repairs on

REPEAT
-reiterate

REPEATED
-echoed
-recurring

-recursive
-successive

REPEATEDLY
-time and again

REPEATING THE SAME WORDS
-redundance of phrase

REPEATS ITSELF
-recurs often

REPETITION
-iteration
-recurrence

REPLACE
-displace
-supersede
-restore
-replenish
-supplant

REPLACED BY
-gave way to

REPLACEMENT
-surrogate

REPLY
-respond in like manner
-reciprocate
-retort

REPLY CLEVERLY TO AN INSULT
-he reposted

REPORT (A REPORT)
-a dispatch
-a position paper

REPRESENT
-personify
-reflect
-are the personification of
-are found
-exemplify
-are the embodiment of
-embody

"Man is explicable by nothing less than all his history. Without hurry, without rest, the human spirit goes forth from the beginning to embody every faculty, every thought, every emotion, which belongs to it, in appropriate events. But the thought is always prior to the fact; all the facts of history pre-exist in the mind as laws." Ralph Waldo Emerson, "Essay on History"

REPRESENTATION
-rendering
-portrayal

REPRESENTATIVE
-voice for
-proxy
-envoy
-emissary
-spokesperson

REPRESENTATIVE OF
-emblematic of
-illustrative of
-indicative of
-suggestive of

REPRIMAND
-chastise
-chide
-rebuke
-upbraid
-admonish
-reproach
-censure

REPUTATION
-standing
-renown
-repute
-known far and wide as

REPUTED TO BE
-putative

REQUEST (TO REQUEST)
-plea
-implore
-summon
-petition
-at the behest of

REQUIRED (ARE REQUIRED)
-compulsory
-vital
-essential
-the lifeblood of
-obligatory
-obliged to
-requisite
-indispensable

REQUIRED THING
-sine qua non {Latin, *sinn-uh kwah NON*}

REQUIREMENT
-requisite
-prerequisite
-exigency {*egg-ZIJ-en-see*} [academic]

RESEMBLE
-bear a resemblance to
-favor

"She favors her mother's side of the family."

RESIGN THE CROWN
-abdicate

RESIST
-restrain oneself
-overcome the impulse

RESOURCES
-ways and means
-wherewithal

RESPECT
-a mark of respect
-in deference to
-reverence
-high regard
-have regard for

"As for my mother, she taught me to have regard for religion, to be generous and open-handed, and not only to forbear from doing anybody an ill turn, but not so much as to endure the thought of it. By

her likewise I was bred to a plain, inexpensive way of living, very different from the common luxury of the rich." Marcus Aurelius, *Meditations*

> He is respected.
>
> He is held in high regard.

RESPECTED
-storied
-revered
-exalted
-illustrious
-venerable
-hold a high place in the public esteem
-in very good standing

RESPECTFUL
-deferential

RESPONDED
-I made response to him with a [poetic]

RESPONDING
-in reply to

RESPONSIBILITY
-that task will fall largely to
-the burden should rest with
-he is to be held accountable for
-the onus is on
-in her charge

RESPONSIBLE FOR
-played a part in
-lay behind
-were the authors of

"The terror and hurt in my story happened because when I was young I thought others were the authors of my fortune and misfortune; I did not know that a person could hold up a wall made of imaginary bricks and mortar against the horrors and cruel, dark tricks of time that assail us, and be the author therefore

of themselves." Sebastian Barry, *The Secret Scripture*

REST
-decompress

REST OF
-remainder of

RESTLESSNESS
-inquietude [academic]

RESTRAIN FROM
-forbear from
-abstain from

RESTRAINED
-forbearing

RESTRAINT
-forbearance

RESTRICT
-encumber
-circumscribe
-constrain
-place tight restrictions on

RESTRICTED
-bound
-constrained

RESTRICTION
-encumbrance
-constraint
-trammel

"Our chairs, being his patents [inventions], embraced and caressed us rather than submitted to be sat upon, and there was that luxurious after-dinner atmosphere when thought runs gracefully free of the trammels of precision." H. G. Wells, *The Time Machine*

RESULT (THIS IS THE RESULT OF)
-this is substantially owing to
-what's come of
-the fallout from
-a consequence of
-an outgrowth of

-borne of
-the product of

RESULT IN
-make for a
-provoke a
-translate into

RESULT OF
-outgrowth of
-product of

RESULTING
-consequential
-subsequent
-resultant

RESULTS
-test findings

RETALIATIONS
-reprisals

RETIRED
-emeritus [academic]

RETIREMENT
-the soft obscurities of retirement
 [Samuel Johnson]

RETURNED THE HONOR
-paid like honor to

REVEAL
-disclose
-unfold
-bring to light
-lay bare
-betray

"Princess Teodora is very dependent on me. I carry her secret in my heart. I have never breathed a word of it, and if they stretched me on the rack in the torture chamber with all its horrors, even then I should never betray anything." Pär Lagerkvist, *The Dwarf*

REVEALING
-telltale
-revelatory

"Standing among the 10,000 rare books in the stacks of the Linda Hall Library in Kansas City, Bruce Bradley, the director of the history of science special collections, pulls out a copy of 'The Starry Messenger,' the revelatory book in which Galileo detailed his astronomical observations made with his own 'spyglass'—the instrument that would later be known as the telescope." Geraldine Fabrikant, *New York Times*, Nov. 1, 2009

-illuminating
-instructive

"Those privileged to be present at a family festival of the Forsytes have seen that charming and instructive sight—an upper middle-class family in full plumage." John Galsworthy, *Forsyte Saga*

REVENGE
-get even, with interest
-reprisals

> You know there will be revenge.
> You know there will be reprisals.

REVERSING ENVIRONMENTAL DAMAGE
-remediation

REVIEWS
-literary comment

REVIVAL
-renaissance
-resurrection

REVIVING
-resurgent

REWARDS
-requisitions
-dividends

"Now, from his base on Haiti, Columbus sent expedition after expedition into the interior. They found no gold fields, but had

to fill up the ships returning to Spain with some kind of dividend. In the year 1495, they went on a great slave raid, rounded up fifteen hundred Arawak men, women and children, put them in pens guarded by Spaniards and dogs, then picked the five hundred best specimens to load onto ships." Howard Zinn, *A People's History of the United States*

-spoils
-consideration
-laurels
-trophies

REWARDS WERE GIVEN TO
-rewards were bestowed on

REWORD
-paraphrase

RHYTHM
-cadence

RICH
-well heeled
-affluent
-luxuriant
-opulent
-from a moneyed background

RIDICULOUS
-absurd
-laughable

RIDICULOUS REPRESENTATION
-a travesty

RIFT
-a falling out
-a bit of a row
-a slight estrangement
-a touch of coldness

RIGHT (A RIGHT)
-sacrament

"As a last resort, he is willing to accept the final defeat, which is death, rather than be deprived of the personal sacrament that he would call, for example, freedom. Better

to die on one's feet than to live on one's knees." Albert Camus, *The Rebel*

RIGHT (THE RIGHT TO)
-prerogative {*pri-RAW-guh-tive*}
-license

"You do not have that license."

-just claim

> That's my doughnut.
>
> I have just claim on that doughnut, I hope you know.

RIGHT MOMENT
-suitable moment

RIGHT NOW
-post haste [playful]

RIGHT OFF THE BAT
-straightaway

RIGHT ONE
-the proper one

RIGHT STUFF
-does he have the makings of a

RIGHT TO TAKE
-eminent domain

RIGHT TO TRIAL
-habeas corpus {Latin, *HAY-be-us COR-pus*}

RIGHT WHEN I WAS
-and at the very moment I was

RIGHTFUL
-inherent

RIGHT-WING CONSERVATIVE (FAR RIGHT)
-paleoconservative

RILE
-roil
-pique
-vex

RIP THEM FROM
-wrest them from

RIPPLING WATER SOUND
-purling

"A river, amber-tinted in the shadow of its banks, purled at the army's feet; and at night, when the stream had become of a sorrowful blackness, one could see across it the red, eyelike gleam of hostile camp-fires set in the low brows of distant hills." Stephen Crane, *The Red Badge of Courage*

RISING
-ascending

"Beyond opens a door into the kitchen, where there is a glimpse to be had of a range with much steam ascending from it, and many women, old and young, rushing hither and thither." Upton Sinclair, *The Jungle*

RISING AGAIN
-resurgent

RISING STAR
-considered to be on the short list for

RISK (AT RISK)
-in peril
-at hazard

RISK (TAKE A RISK)
-gambit

ROAD ALONG A CLIFF
-a cornice

ROAD KILL
-carrion

ROAMING
-marauding

ROLL
-trundle

ROLLING
-undulating

ROOKIE
-newcomer
-neophyte

ROOM (A SPECIAL ROOM)
-repository
-chamber
-sanctum

ROUGHLY
-some ten million
-on the order of
-there or thereabouts
-by and large

ROUNDABOUT
-circuitous

ROUTINE
-it was his habit to
-according to his custom

"It was Sunday, and, according to his custom on that day, McTeague took his dinner at two in the afternoon at the car conductor's coffee-joint on Polk Street." Frank Norris, *McTeague*

ROUTINELY
-as a matter of course

RSVP
-respondez s'il vous plait {French, re-spahn-day sill-voo-play, lit. respond, if you please}

RUDE
-impertinent
-insolent
-brash
-ill-mannered
-unceremonious
-undiplomatic
-brusque
-abrupt in manner
-curt
-disorderly
-short
-crisp

"The legal notice could best be described as crisp."

RUDELY BOLD
-impudent

RUIN
-it will be the death of him
-come to a very bad end
-hasten the demise of

RUINED
-marred
-tainted
-tarnished

RULE
-precept
-warrant
-convention
-precedent
-dictate
-formality
-directive
-mandate

RULE OUT
-foreclose

RULED BY
-governed by

RULER
-potentate

RULES
-tenents
-constraints
-accepted conventions
-safeguards
-formalities
-proprieties
-rules of engagement
-legal niceties
-sanctions
-dictates
-prescriptions

RULING CLASS
-powers that be

-lords of creation
-power elite

RUMOR
-canard

RUMOR HAS IT
-I have it on good authority that

RUMORED TO BE
-purported to be

RUN
-conduct
-operate
-preside
-oversee

RUN AWAY
-flee

RUN FOR MAYOR
-pursue a mayoral bid

RUN INTO
-encounter
-chance upon
-come upon
-fall upon
-fall among
-alight upon [poetic]

We ran into each other.

We had a chance encounter.

RUN INTO PROBLEMS
-encounter difficulties

I have run into problems.

I have encountered difficulties.

RUN OFF
-steal away

RUN UP AGAINST
-face

RUN-DOWN
-woebegone
-derelict

RUNNING OUT OF POWER
-starved for power

RUSTIC
-bucolic
-provincial

RUSTLE
-a little noiseless noise among the
  leaves [Keats]

RUTHLESS
-she's a carnivore

RHYTHM
-cadence

S s

SACRED
-hallowed
-sacrosanct
-arc of the _____ covenant

SACRED PLACE
-sanctum

SACRIFICING
-forfeiting
-foregoing

SAD
-poignant
-despondent
-plaintive
-doleful
-heartrending

SAD POEM
-elegy {EL-i-gee}

SAD SOUNDING
-plaintive

SADDEN
-cast a pall over
-weigh heavy upon

SADIST
-a Torquemada
-a Marquis de Sade

SADNESS
-anguish
-calvary [poetic]
-melancholy

*"For the traveler we see leaning on his
neighbor is an honest and well-meaning
man and full of melancholy, like those
Chekhov characters so laden with virtues that they never know success in life."*
Orhan Pamuk, *Snow*

SAFE
-out of harm's way
-secure
-inviolate [academic]

SAFE PLACE
-sanctuary
-place of refuge
-haven
-out of harm's way
-refuge
-held for safekeeping
-retreat

> She's in a safe place.
> She's out of harm's way.

SAFE PLACES TO PUT YOUR FEET
-safe lodgments for your feet

SAID
-expressed
-indicated
-remarked
-made clear that
-said with a touch of
-issued a statement
-said with a quiver of
-implored

-broke into the conversation
-gave full expression to
-an irreverent voice put in
-put it to her
-articulated
-dropped her voice mournfully
-she went on
-she went off into a
-as murmurs seeped through the pews
-declared
-drawled out the word
-couched in terms of
-put it to him squarely
-addressed some remark to him

SAID NOTHING
-gave no reply

"'Agua,' I said, trying Portuguese, and made a sign of drinking. He gave no reply, but regarded me as he would a seal or a porpoise thrown up by the waves, that would shortly expire and then be cut up for food." J.M. Coetzee, *Foe*

SAILING
-seafaring
-plying the northern waters

SALTY
-brackish
-saline

SALVAGE IT
-right it

SAME
-something of the same
-much the same
-commensurate with
-corresponding in degree
-of the same_____

SAME AGE
-of similar date

SAME AS
-tantamount to
-synonymous with
-akin to

SAME KIND (ALL OF THE SAME KIND)
-homogenous

"Videos of tea party events show the protesters to be a rather homogenous crowd."

SAME OLD PEOPLE
-usual suspects

SAME TIME
-meanwhile
-in the meantime
-at that same instant

SAMPLE OF
-sampling

SANE
-firmly tethered

SANITIZE ART
-bowdlerize

SARCASTIC
-caustic
-mordant
-wry
-acrid
-sardonic
-ironical

SAT
-presided at the head of the table

SAT ACROSS FROM
-sat opposite

SAT DOWN
-seated herself
-settled himself in the chair
-placed themselves about the room
-dropped on to a chair

SATISFIED
-happily sated
-then my heart will be set at rest
 [poetic]

SATISFY
-accommodate

-suffice
-sate
-satiate
-quench
-content yourself with
-slake

SATISFY A DISTASTEFUL NEED
-pander to

SATURATE
-imbue
-pervade

SAVE (RESCUE)
-salvage
-resuscitate

SAVE (SET ASIDE)
-reserve
-husband your resources
-salt away

SAVING
-redemption

"He's beyond redemption."

SAW
-came upon
-caught sight of
-our eyes had noted
-the man who met my eyes
-came within sight of

SAY
-convey
-say your piece
-articulate
-speak of it
-give voice to
-give it utterance

SAY GOOD-BYE
-part company

SAY HI
-exchange pleasantries

SAY IT IS (THAT'S WHAT THEY SAY IT IS)
-have it

That's what they say it is.

That's how they have it.

SAY IT THIS WAY
-put it to him as

SAY NO
-forbid it

SAY THAT AGAIN
-come again

SAY THAT WE SHOULD
-argue that

"Some analysts argue that a go-slow approach would be best."

SAY YOU'RE SORRY
-express remorse
-express regret

SAYING
-maxim
-adage
-aphorism
-saw
-proverb
-dictum
-refrain

SAYINGS
-dicta [academic]

SAYS
-presents a case for

SAYS HER NAME
-speaks her name

SCANDAL
-grist for the gossip pages

SCANDALOUS REPORT
-exposé {ex-poe-SAY}

SCARCE
-is at a premium
-elusive
-a rarity

SCARCITY
-dearth of

"I can assure you that there is no dearth of intellectual firepower among the experts assembled."

-few and far between
-paucity of

SCARE
-send chills through
-arouse the concerns of
-set off concern
-unnerve
-put the fear of God into

SCARED
-it had shaken me
-petrified
-gave me a bit of a fright
-gave me a severe start

SCARY
-objects of fear
-a scare

It was so scary.

It was a real scare.

SCATHING
-trenchant
-vitriolic
-acerbic
-caustic
-salty
-mordant

SCATTER
-intersperse
-disseminate
-promulgate [academic]

SCATTERED
-strewn about
-strewn with

SCENE (TO CAUSE A SCENE)
-spectacle

SCHEDULE
-itinerary

SCHEDULED
-mapped out
-appointed

"On the morning of the day that the young couple were to arrive, Princess Mary entered the antechamber as usual at the time appointed for the morning greeting, crossing herself with trepidation and repeating a silent prayer. Every morning she came in like that, and every morning prayed that the daily interview might pass off well." Leo Tolstoy, *War and Peace*

SCHEME
-contrive to
-maneuver to
-machinate

SCHEMES
-machinations
-contrivances
-maneuvers

SCHEMING
-designing
-Machiavellian

SCHOOL
-discipline
-school of thought
-field of

SCHOOL OF FISH
-shoal

SCIENCE
-scientific inquiry

SCIENTIFIC LANGUAGE
-interlingua

SCOLD
-chide
-berate
-chastise
-rebuke
-objurgate [academic]
-censure
-excoriate
-reprimand
-reprehend
-reprove [academic]
-take someone to task
-upbraid
-chasten
-he was tearing off some ripe stuff

SCOLDING (A SCOLDING)
-a reproach
-a blistering
-a matter of reproach
-a tongue lashing

SCRAPING
-abrading

SCRAPS OF FOOD
-orts

SCRATCHES
-damages

SCREAMING
-in full cry
-trumpeting

SCREECHY
-strident
-shrill

SCREW IT UP
-make a mess of it

SCUM
-beneath contempt

SEALED
-hermetic

SEARCH
-forage

-prospect
-scour
-scent out the truth
-troll for

SEARCHING FOR
-in search of
-in search for

"It was 1979, and the sun was every-where. Tripoli lay brilliant and still beneath it. Every person, animal and ant went in desperate search for shade, those occasional gray patches of mercy carved into the white of everything." Hisham Matar, *In the Country of Men*

SECLUDED
-cloistered
-far from the madding crowd

SECLUDED GARDEN
-a pleasance

SECOND RATE
-bush league
-provincial
-beneath discussion
-déclassé {French, *day-clah-SAY*}

SECOND THOUGHTS
-misgivings
-disenchantment

SECONDARY
-ancillary
-tangential
-peripheral

SECRET
-sensitive
-discreet
-covert
-behind a web of
-posing as
-behind a thin cover of
-underground
-veiled
-under the guise of
-clandestine

-in the strictest confidence
-for your eyes only
-surreptitious
-privileged information

> This is to stay secret.
>
> This is to be kept in the strictest confidence.

SECRET ARRANGEMENT TO MEET
-assignation

SECRET CODE
-cipher

SECRET GROUP
-cabal

SECRET PLACE
-lair
-inner sanctum

SECRET RITUALS
-arcane rituals

SECRETIVE
-furtive

SECRETLY
-surreptitiously
-in pectore {Latin, *in peck-TOR-ay*}

SEDUCTRESS
-femme fatale {French, *fem fe-TAL*}
-siren

SEE
-behold
-discern
-take a gander at
-trace
-make out
-come upon
-catch sight of
-foresee

SEE A DIFFERENCE
-draw a distinction

"There are really four dimensions, three of which we call the three planes of Space, and the fourth, Time. There is, however, a tendency to draw an unreal distinction between the former three dimensions and the latter, because it happens that our consciousness moves intermittently in one direction along the latter from the beginning to the end of our lives." H. G. Wells, *The Time Machine*

SEE HIM
-give him an audience

"It was the president's decision to give him an audience."

SEE YOU LATER
-au revoir {French, *or e-VWAR*}

SEEM
-strike one as
-show oneself to be
-cast oneself as
-appear to be
-tend toward the

SEEM TO BE SAYING
-seem to imply

SEEMED TO HAVE
-appeared to have

"After pointing heavenward for half a century, the steeple appeared to have swerved suddenly from its purpose, and to invite now the attention of the wayfarer to the bar beneath." E. A. G. Glasgow, *The Miller of Old Church*

SEEMING
-ostensible
-semblant

SEEMS
-often appears
-strikes me as
-has every appearance of
-has all the earmarks of
-assumes the guise of

-impresses me as being

"And yet when I take a look at my inner identity it impresses me as being precisely the same as it was thirty or forty years ago. My present station, power, the amount of worldly happiness at my command, and the rest of it, seem to be devoid of significance." Abraham Cahan, *The Rise of David Levinski*

SEEN
-discerned
-encountered
-faced

"This is one of the worst disasters this country has ever faced."

SEEN AS
-viewed as

SELECTING THE FIRST BOOK HE CAME UPON
-taking up the first book he came upon

SELF-CONFIDENCE
-aplomb

SELF-CONTROL
-forbearance
-restraint
-temperance
-abstinence

SELF-DENYING
-ascetic
-temperate
-austere
-abstemious

SELF-DEPRECATING
-diffident

SELF-DOUBTING
-channeling Hamlet

SELF-EVIDENT
-axiomatic [academic]

SELF-EVIDENT TRUTH
-an axiom

SELF-INVOLVED
-solipsistic [academic]

SELF-PROCLAIMED EXPERT
-maven

SELF-PUNISHMENT
-penance

SELF-RIGHTEOUS
-unctuous
-smug
-sanctimonious

SELF-SATISFIED
-smug
-no modest violet

SELFISH
-not overlooking himself
-self-absorbed

SELFLESSNESS
-altruism

SELL
-retail
-tout

SELLING YOUR SOUL
-engaged in a Faustian bargain

SEMI-DRY (WINE)
-demi-sec {French, *dem-ee-SEK*}

SEND
-unleash
-dispatch
-forward
-send along

SEND AWAY
-dismiss

SEND MY
-convey my

SENSATIONAL
-lurid

SENSATIONAL REPORTING
-yellow journalism

SENSE
-sensibility

SENSITIVE TO
-more attuned to

SENT
-sent off

SENTIMENTAL
-maudlin
-mawkish
-saccharine

SENTIMENTAL ART
-schmaltz

SEPARATE BETWEEN
-differentiate
-draw a distinction between

> You shouldn't separate the two.
> You shouldn't draw a distinction between the two.

SEPARATE ENTITIES
-discrete entities

SEPARATE GROUPS
-disparate groups
-separate entities

SEPARATED ITSELF WITH
-parted company with

SEPARATING
-distinguishing

"He was aware that the qualities distinguishing her from the herd of her sex were chiefly external, as though a fine glaze of beauty and fastidiousness had been applied

to vulgar clay." Edith Wharton, *The House of Mirth*

SEPARATING (PHYSICAL SEPARATION)
-disengaging ____ from____

SEPARATION
-a divorce between

SERIES (A SERIES OF)
-a spate of
-a rash of
-a battery of
-a cavalcade of
-a litany of
-a parade of
-a skein of [pejorative]

"The public disclosure of his views has heightened existing tensions between senior military officers and General Eikenberry, who left the military in April to become Mr. Obama's emissary. Several military officials complained bitterly that his latest cables were part of a skein of pessimistic and defeatist memos the ambassador has sent since taking over in Kabul." Mark Landler and Jeff Zeleny, *New York Times*, Nov. 12, 2009

-a procession of
-a sequence of
-a flurry of
-a drumbeat of
-a barrage of
-cascade of
-a progression of
-a line of
-a succession of

"Poetry is a succession of questions which the poet constantly poses." Vicente Aleixandre

SERIOUS
-sobering
-grievous
-grave

SERIOUS AND COMICAL
-seriocomic

SERIOUS ENOUGH TO
-sufficient to warrant

SERIOUSLY
-all joking aside
-I tell you it's true
-in earnest

SERIOUSNESS
-gravity
-enormity
-gravitas
-earnestness
-sobriety

> I understand the seriousness of the situation.
>
> I understand the gravity of the situation.

SERMON
-homily

SERVED WITH ICE CREAM
-à la mode {French, *ah lah* MODE, lit. in the style}

SET ASIDE
-assign
-apportion
-earmark
-appropriate

SET FIRE TO
-set ablaze

SET IN
-ensconced in

SET RIGHT
-remedy
-redress

"The public has a right to a clear understanding of BP's commitment to redress all of the damage that has occurred or that will occur in the future as a result of the oil spill. Therefore, in the event that our understanding is inaccurate, we request immediate public clarification of BP's true intentions." Ken Salazar and Janet Napolitano, May 14, 2010 Letter to British Petroleum

SET UP
-establish

SETTING
-theater
-within the confines of
-backdrop

SETTLED IN
-ensconced
-entrenched

SEVERAL
-a number of
-any number of
-no less than
-a wide array of
-a spate of
-a rash of
-a host of
-a goodly number of
-a fair amount of

> That comes with several new sets of problems.
>
> That carries with it a host of corresponding problems.

SEVERE
-harsh
-acute
-austere
-with severity

> That kind of severe punishment will only make things worse.
>
> That kind of severity will only make things worse.

"As she moved beside him, in her long, light step, Seldon was conscious of taking a luxurious pleasure in her nearness: in the modeling of her little ear, the crisp upward wave of her hair—was it ever so lightly brightened by art?" Edith Wharton, *The House of Mirth*

SEX
-gender

SEX DRIVE
-libido

SEX MANUAL
-Kama Sutra {Sanskrit, *kah-mah SUE-tra*}

SEXUAL
-carnal

SEXUAL DESIRE
-eros {*AIR-aws*}
-libido

SEXUALLY EXCESSIVE
-lascivious
-lecherous
-licentious
-prurient

SHADOWY
-dusky

SHADY
-unprincipled
-roguish

SHALLOW
-superficial

SHAMEFUL
-inglorious
-ignominious {*ig-no-MIN-ee-us*}

SHAPE
-contour
-geometry
-modeling

SHAPED
-contoured

SHAPED BY
-wrought by

SHARP
-acute

SHARPEN
-hone

SHARPNESS
-acuity

SHE DIDN'T MIND THE DISAPPOINTMENT
-she was philosophical

SHE HAD THREE SONS
-she bore three sons

SHE IS
-I have found her to be
-I find her quite
-hers is a _____ nature
-the _____ of her person is
-she may suffer from spells of
-her ___ manner never abandoned her
-she is given to
-she has shown herself to be
-she is the product of
-she has a taste for
-she is learned in
-she could easily be classified as
-she is of the sort who's

SHEDDING
-deciduous [academic]

SHEETS
-bed linen
-linens

SHELTERED
-cloistered

SHINE
-luster

"The Utopians wonder how any man should be so much taken with the glaring doubtful luster of a jewel or stone, that can look up to a star, or to the sun himself." Sir Thomas More, *Utopia*

SHINY
-lustrous

SHINY BLACK
-obsidian black

SHIP SHAPE
-in Bristol fashion [humorous]

SHIP WRECKAGE
-flotsam and jetsam {*FLAWT-sum*}

SHIPMENT OF
-consignment of

SHIVER OF EXCITEMENT
-a frisson {French, *fri-SONE*}

SHOCKED
-blindsided
-badly shaken
-mortified

SHOCKING
-arresting
-sobering

SHOCKINGLY BAD
-egregious

> Anything this bad has got to be dealt with.
>
> Anything this egregious has got to be dealt with.

SHODDY
-slipshod

SHORT
-of small stature
-short in stature

SHORT (BRIEF)
-fleeting
-momentary

SHORT AND CLEVER
-aphoristic
-gnomic {*NO-mick*}

"And once again he lets loose in this carefully cluttered dreamscape an assortment of human creatures who both ponder their existences in gnomic declarations and run around crashing into walls like Keystone Kops." Ben Brantley, *New York Times*, Nov. 5, 2009

SHORT-LIVED
-ephemeral
-transient
-evanescent

SHORT STAY
-cameo appearance

SHORT STORY
-anecdote
-vignette {*vin-YET*}
-chestnut

SHORTAGE OF
-deficit of
-want of
-dearth of

SHORTEN
-abridge
-truncate
-abbreviate
-contract

SHORTLY AFTER
-thereupon

SHORTNESS
-brevity

SHOULD
-might well consider
-it would behoove you to
-be well advised
-are advised to
-would be wise to
-ought to

"I have to thank my great-grandfather that I did not go to a public school, but had good masters at home, and learned to know that one ought to spend liberally on such things." Marcus Aurelius, *Meditations*

-shall
-what news am I to take to
-it would be as well to
-would do well to

SHOULD BE
-is to be

"Public approval is to be avoided above all. It is absolutely necessary to forbid the public entry if one wants to avoid confusion. I further emphasize that it is vital to keep the public exasperated at the door by a system of defiance and provocation." Andre Breton

SHOULD BE GOOD ENOUGH
-should suffice

SHOULD DO WHAT THEY SAY
-should defer to the

SHOULD HAVE
-ought to have

SHOULD HE
-is he to

SHOULD NOT
-ought not to

"He taught me also to put my own hand to business upon occasion, to endure hardship and fatigues, and to throw the necessities of nature into a little compass; that I ought not to meddle in other people's business, nor be easy in giving credit to informers." Marcus Aurelius, *Meditations*

SHOULD NOT BE
-is not to be

"A serious writer is not to be confounded with a solemn writer. A serious writer may be a hawk or a buzzard or even a popinjay, but a solemn writer is always a bloody owl." Ernest Hemingway

SHOULD NOT FORGET
-it is worth remembering

SHOULD NOT HAVE
-ought not to have

SHOUT
-yammer

SHOW
-depict
-portray
-demonstrate
-tell us
-represent
-present
-reflect
-indicate
-display
-suggest
-bear the words
-reveal
-brandish
-parade
-illustrate
-exhibit
-project
-evidence
-showcase
-offer the sight of

"The feet did indeed look swollen. He was prepared to offer the sight of those bulging boots to his mother as evidence of her thoughtlessness." John Kennedy Toole, *A Confederacy of Dunces*

SHOW CONFUSION
-flounder

SHOW HOW
-school her

SHOW NO EMOTION
-betray no emotion

SHOW OF
-veneer of

"Pine floorboards creak above my head as my mother steps before my father's bed, checking his breathing mask. The old floor is thin and while I can't make out her words I recognize the tone, it's veneer of cheerfulness layed on anxiety." Geraldine Brooks, *Foreign Correspondence*

SHOW-OFF (A SHOW-OFF)
-showboat
-one with a penchant for
 self-aggrandizement

SHOW OFF (LIKES TO SHOW OFF)
-flaunt it
-lord it over us

SHOW RESPECT
-pay court to the king

SHOW SIGNS OF
-exhibit signs of

SHOW UP
-put in an appearance
-give the pleasure of one's company
-appear on the scene
-present oneself
-bob up [British]
-emerge
-surface

SHOWDOWN
-high noon

SHOWED NO EMOTION
-betrayed no emotion

SHOWED NO SURPRISE
-showed not the slightest surprise

SHOWER OF
-hail of
-salvo of
-barrage of

SHOWINESS
-éclat {French, *ay-KLAH*}

SHOWN
-featured
-depicted

SHOWY
-ostentatious
-pretentious
-meretricious posturing
-affected
-contrived

> That's too showy.
>
> That's too ostentatious.

SHREWD LAWYER
-a Philadelphia lawyer

SHUNNING
-balking at
-eschewing [academic]

SHY
-unassuming
-retiring
-demure
-diffident

SICK
-in ill health
-indisposed
-taken ill
-his health was in a precarious state

SICK (THE SICK)
-the ailing

SICK LOOKING
-cadaverous

SICKENING EXCESS
-cloying

SICKNESS
-malady
-affliction
-disorder

"*Depression is a disorder of mood, so mysteriously painful and elusive in the way it becomes known to the self—to the mediating intellect—as to verge close to being beyond description.*" William Styron, *Darkness Visible*

SIDE BY SIDE
-cheek by jowl
-placed in juxtaposition [academic]

SIDE VIEW
-seen in profile

SIGN (A NOTICE)
-placard

SIGN (A SIGNAL)
-harbinger
-foreshadowing
-in what may be a telling sign of
-precursor

SIGN OF
-mark of

"*This was still the era—it would end later in that famous decade—when to be young was a social encumbrance, a mark of irrelevance, a faintly embarrassing condition for which marriage was the beginning of a cure.*" Ian McEwan, *Chesil Beach*

SIGN OF A CRITICAL DECISION MADE
-in a puff of white smoke

SIGN OF THE CROSS (MAKE THE)
-she crossed herself as she knelt

SIGN OF THINGS TO COME
-a portent
-an auger

SIGNER OF A CONTRACT
-signatory

SIGNIFICANT
-appreciable
-substantive
-a factor of no little importance

SILENCE
-lucid stillness [T. S. Elliot]
-quietude

SILENT
-mute
-taciturn
-is heard no more [Shakespeare]
-grows quiet

SILENTLY
-without sound

"*The walls are cracked and water runs upon them in thin threads without sound, black and glistening as blood.*" Ayn Rand, *Anthem*

SILLINESS
-this folly

SIMILAR
-reminiscent of
-like-minded
-of like mind
-analogous
-akin to
-bear the hallmarks of
-close in style to
-have close affinities to
-have much in common with
-show great similarity
-closely allied to
-of similar form
-bear a resemblance to
-might be mistaken for

SIMILAR TO WITH ONE EXCEPTION
-not unlike ____, only with ____

SIMILARITIES
-parallels
-resemblances of things

SIMILARLY
-likewise
-in kind
-in specie [academic]
-in a similar vein

SIMPLE
-provincial
-modest
-spartan
-straightforward and unadorned
-elemental

"The landscape is elemental, austere, with a kind of monumental elegance. The formal lines of the fields and hills not only speak of the severity of life in the prehistoric past, but would also match some well-tended parkland belonging to an earl." Henry Shukman, *New York Times*, Nov. 1, 2009

SIMPLICITY
-economy
-irreducible simplicity

SIMPLIFIED FORM
-reductive
-schematic

SIN (A SIN)
-a transgression
-a moral failing

SINCE (IT'S ONLY BEEN ___ WEEKS SINCE YOU)
-removed from a

"We are only two weeks removed from the midterm elections, and you are already campaigning for 2012."

SINCE THEN
-from that day forth

SINCERE
-heartfelt

-artless
-unaffected
-unpretending

"Unpretending mediocrity is good, and genius is glorious; but a weak flavor of genius in an essentially common person is detestable." Oliver Holmes, *The Autocrat of the Breakfast-Table*

SINGLE
-singular
-solitary

"The wine was from France, though no particular region was mentioned on the label, which was embellished with a solitary darting swallow." Ian McEwan, *Chesil Beach*

SITE
-venue

SITTING ON
-it was upon

SITUATED
-resided

SITUATION
-circumstance
-condition of affairs
-state of affairs

SIZE
-scale
-order of magnitude

SKEPTICS
-naysayers

SKETCHY
-anecdotal at best

SKILL
-prowess
-expertise

SKILLED
-practiced
-accomplished

-adroit
-formidable
-adept

> She is good a skilled deceiver
>
> She is practiced in the art of deception. [The Rolling Stones]

SKILLFUL
-deft
-adroit
-artful

SKILLFULLY PUT TOGETHER
-well wrought

SKIM OVER
-hardly touch on

SKIN (COFFEE SKIN)
-sarcoma

"She swiveled in her seat, snatched up the mug and recoiled as her lips met the cold sarcoma that had formed on the coffee's surface." Tim Winton, *Dirt Music*

SKINNY
-emaciated
-skeletal
-of slight figure

SKIRT CHASER
-casual in his affections

SLAM DUNK
-a foregone conclusion

SLAVE
-captive
-helot
-serf

SLAVERY
-servitude

SLEEP
-slumber [poetic]

SLEEP WITH
-bed down with

SLIGHT
-faint
-remote

SLIGHT CHANCE
-outside chance

SLIGHTLY
-somewhat
-faintly

"This was still the era—it would end later in that famous decade—when to be young was a social encumbrance, a mark of irrelevance, a faintly embarrassing condition for which marriage was the beginning of a cure." Ian McEwan, *Chesil Beach*

SLIGHTLY OPEN
-ajar

SLIP OF THE TONGUE
-Freudian slip

SLOB
-unkempt

SLOPE
-gradient

SLOW
-halting
-hesitant
-faltering

SLOW AND STEADY
-three yards and a cloud of dust

SLUR
-a generalized term of abuse
-colorful language

SMALL
-small scale
-diminutive
-Lilliputian

SMALL AMOUNT OF MONEY
-modest sum

SMALL NUMBER OF PEOPLE ASSIGNED
-thin force of

SMALL OFFENSE
-a peccadillo

SMALL TALK
-preliminaries
-an exchange of pleasantries

SMALL TWEAKS
-marginal tweaks
-tweaking around the edges

SMART
-well advised

> It would be smart to keep your distance.
>
> You would be well advised to keep your distance.

SMART-MOUTHED
-impudent
-impertinent

SMARTS
-quick wit
-sharp wit
-cerebral
-noetic {no-ET-ik}
-gifted
-of sound intellect

SMELL
-aroma
-bouquet
-nose

"The shop was doing a tasting of the Domaine des 2 Ânes, a biodynamic red from the south of France, and its funky nose and earthy, quirky flavors justified the $16 price tag." Matt Gross, *New York Times*, Oct. 28, 2009

SMELLED GOOD
-gave a good smell

"Under the live oaks, shady and dusty, the maidenhair flourished and gave a good smell, and under the musty banks of the water courses whole clumps of five-fingered ferns and goldy-backs hung down." John Steinbeck, *East of Eden*

SMELLED LIKE
-there was a strong smell of
-he smelt strongly of
-from _____ came the aroma of
-she smelled of
-she carried with her the odors of

"She used no cosmetics. She had learned only a few English words. It even seemed to Herman that she carried with her the odors of Lipsk; in bed she smelled of camomile. From the kitchen now came the aroma of beets cooking, of new potatoes, of dill, and something else summery and earthy that he couldn't name but that evoked a memory of Lipsk." Isaac Bashevis Singer, *Enemies, A Love Story*

SMOKE
-columns of smoke

SMOOTH
-fluid

SMOOTHLY
-seamlessly

SNAIL
-escargot {French, es-kar-GO}

SNEAK AWAY
-steal away

SNEAK ATTACK
-a fragging

SNEAKY
-under false pretenses

-surreptitious
-clandestine
-furtive
-sub rosa

> That's not why she's here.
>
> She is here under false pretenses.

SO
-consequently
-as such
-hence
-thus
-hereby
-hereupon
-it follows, therefore

SO ____ IT'S ____
-____ to the point of ____
-so ____ as to be ____
-so ____as to verge on____

SO ARE HIS OTHER
-so are other of his

"He has never been much of a teacher; in this transformed and, to his mind, emasculated institution of learning he is more out of place than ever. But then, so are other of his colleagues from the old days, burdened with upbringings inappropriate to the tasks they are set to perform; clerks in a post-religious age." J.M. Coetzee, *Disgrace*

SO-CALLED
-supposed
-professed

SO DOES
-as does

SO FAR
-heretofore
-as yet
-thus far
-to date

SO HARD
-with such force

"It rained with such force."

SO IS
-as is

SO LONG AS
-provided

SO MUCH THAT
-to such a degree that
-to such an extent that

SO-SO
-generating little enthusiasm

SO THAT
-so as to
-so as not to
-in order that I may
-that I might

"For if I summoned you abruptly and made you travel to the out-of-the-way place where I live, it was solely that I might see you, that you might hear me." André Gide, *The Immoralist*

SO TO SPEAK
-if you will
-in a manner of speaking
-in some sense
-as it were
-metaphorically speaking

SO WHAT
-what of it

SO YOUNG
-at so tender an age

SOAKING UP
-absorption
-assimilation

"'Scientific people,' proceeded the Time Traveler, after the pause required for the proper assimilation of this, 'know very well that time is only a kind of space.'" H. G. Wells, *The Time Machine*

SOCIABLE
-gregarious

SOCIAL CONVENTIONS
-decorum

SOCIAL GRACE
-savoir faire {French, *sav-war fare*}

SOCIAL HARMONY
-sweetness and light

SOCIAL MISTAKE
-faux pas {French, *foe PAH*}
-impropriety

SOGGY
-sodden

SOLD FOR ___
-it brought ___

SOLID GROUND
-terra firma

"'That's St. Jude,' Thomas says. 'You know what he's the saint of?' Cedric, unaware of Catholic dogma, shrugs, though he's happy to feel the conversation land on the terra firma of religion. 'Causes beyond hope,' Thomas says. 'Hope for the hopeless.'" Ron Suskind, *A Hope in the Unseen*

SOLVE
-remedy
-overcome

SOME THINK THAT
-it has been suggested that

SOMEHOW
-by some means

SOMEONE
-a figure of

SOMEONE LIKE ME
-the likes of me

SOMETHING FOR SOMETHING
-quid pro quo {Latin, *quid proh kwoh*}
-transactional

"*The voters in his district are more loyal, and a little less transactional.*"

SOMETHING GOING ON
-something astir

SOMETHING HE HAD NEVER DONE BEFORE
-a thing he had never done before

SOMETHING I REALLY HATE
-this is anathema to me

SOMETHING STICKING OUT
-protuberance

SOMETHING TO BE AFRAID OF
-an object of fear
-a bugaboo

SOMETIMES
-on occasion
-at times

SOMETIMES THEY
-they sometimes

SOMEWHAT
-to some extent
-to some degree
-in a measure
-rather
-in some sense

SOMEWHERE ELSE
-elsewhere

SONG (CLASSICAL)
-a piece of music

Beethoven's "Ode to Joy" is a beautiful song.

Beethoven's "Ode to Joy" is a beautiful piece of music.

SOON
-at hand
-in due course

-in the days to come
-by and by

"He reached out and with the back of his hand touched my arm. He is trying my flesh, I thought. But by and by my breathing slowed and I grew calmer. He smelled of fish, and of sheepswool on a hot day." J. M. Coetzee, *Foe*

-in the weeks to come
-in short order
-destined soon to
-in time
-momentarily
-in a short time

"The divorce was arranged and Robert Cohn went out to the coast. In California he fell among literary people and, as he still had a little of the fifty thousand left, in a short time he was backing a review of the Arts." Ernest Hemingway, *The Sun Also Rises*

SOON ENOUGH
-in due time
-in due course

SOONER OR LATER, THE TRUTH WILL COME OUT
-the truth will out [Shakespeare]

SOPHISTICATED
-well traveled

SORROWFUL
-elegiac {el-uh-JIE-uk}

SORRY
-contrite
-remorseful
-penitent
-repentant

SORT OF
-of sorts
-shall we say
-rather
-in a manner of speaking
-quasi

SOUL
-being
-psyche

SOUL MATE
-kindred spirit

SOUND
-rumble forth
-reverberate

SOUND MORE ENGLISH
-anglicize

He made his name sound more English.

He anglicized his name from Mikhail to Michael.

SOUND OF (MUSIC)
-to the strains of ____
-to the passages of a sonata

SOUNDS (IT SOUNDS)
-to the ear

SOUR
-acerbic

SOURCE OF
-mother lode of
-wellspring of

SOUTHERN LIFE
-Faulknerian
-Tara-like grandeur

SPACE
-cosmos
-the outermost reaches of
-the expanse of

SPACIOUS
-airy
-capacious [academic]

SPANISH FIELD OR PLAIN
-vega {Spanish, VAY-ga}

SPARE TIME
-vacant hours

"The Author has himself acquainted the Publick, that the following Treatise was the fruit of his vacant hours, and the relief he sometimes had recourse to, when tired with his other studies." Sir Isaac Newton, *The Chronology of Ancient Kingdoms Amended*

-off hours

SPARK
-rouse our thought
-rouse our interest

SPEAK
-say a word to

SPEAK ABOUT
-speak of the need for

SPEAK AUTHORITATIVELY
-discourse on a subject [academic]

SPEAK FOR THE ____
-present the ____'s view
-give voice to the concerns of the

SPEAK IN A BORING MANNER
-drone

SPEAK TO
-have a few words with

SPEAKING ABILITY
-oracy [academic]

SPEAKING IN PUBLIC
-holding forth

"In later years, holding forth to an interviewer or to an audience of aging fans at a comic book convention, Sam Clay liked to declare, apropos of his and Joe Kavalier's greatest creation, that back when he was a boy, sealed and hog-tied inside the airtight vessel known as Brooklyn, New York, he had been haunted by dreams of Harry Houdini." Michael Chabon, *The Amazing Adventures of Kavalier & Clay*

SPEAKING TO HIM
-directing his remarks to him
-addressing him

SPECIAL
-select

SPECIAL DAY
-a red-letter day

SPECIAL PLACE
-an enclave of

SPECIALIZED VOCABULARY (LINGO)
-argot {AR-go}

SPECIALTY
-my bailiwick
-my forte {FOR-tay}

SPECIFIC
-well defined
-peculiar

SPECIFIC WAY
-given manner

SPECIFICALLY
-on closer inspection
-namely that
-most notably
-pointedly
-that is to say

SPECTATORS
-onlookers

SPECULATE
-surmise

SPECULATION
-conjecture
-largely a matter for speculation
-open speculation

SPEECHLESS
-words fail me
-I'm at a loss for words
-the words escape me
-allow me to collect my thoughts

> I'm having a brain freeze.
>
> Allow me to collect my thoughts.

SPEED
-with deliberate speed
-haste
-celerity [academic]
-breakneck speed

> We need to get the hell out of here.
>
> We need to move with all deliberate speed.

SPEEDING UP
-quickening his march

SPELL
-incantation

SPELLED OUT
-enunciated

"Although he devotes hours of each day to his new discipline, he finds its first premise, as enunciated in the Communications 101 handbook, preposterous: 'Human society has created language in order that we may communicate our thoughts, feelings and intentions to each other.' His own opinion, which he does not air, is that the origins of speech lie in song, and the origins of song in the need to fill out with sound the overlarge and rather empty human soul."
J. M. Coetzee, *Disgrace*

SPEND
-expend

SPEND A NIGHT ON VACATION
-resort for the night

SPEND SOME TIME
-devote some time

-invest some time

SPEND TIME DOING
-busy oneself in
-give themselves to the study of

SPEND TIME IN THE SUMMER AT
-we summer in

SPEND TIME IN THE WINTER AT
-we winter in
-hibernate

SPEND YOUR WAY OUT OF IT
-employing Keynesian tactics

SPENDS HIS TIME
-devotes

SPENT THE WHOLE AFTERNOON IN
-passed a whole afternoon in

SPENT TIME DOING
-she gave her time to

SPIRIT
-verve

SPIRITED
-exuberant

SPIRIT OF THE LAW
-intendment [academic]

SPIRIT OR MOOD OF A CULTURE OR TIME
-zeitgeist
-geist
-genius loci [academic]
-local god
-ethos
-spirit that pervades it

SPIRITS EXIST IN ANIMALS (THE BELIEF THAT)
-animism

SPIRITUAL
-transcendent
-larger than life

-ethereal
-otherworldly
-numinous

SPIRITUAL POWER OF A PLACE
-numen

"This archeological site possesses an indescribable numen."

SPIT (TO SPIT)
-to expectorate [academic]

SPITE (IN SPITE OF)
-despite

SPLASH
-douse

SPLIT (A SPLIT)
-a schism

SPLIT (TO SPLIT)
-diverge

SPOIL
-blight
-defile
-vitiate

SPOILED RICH KIDS
-the jeunesse dorée {French, *zhen-us daw-RAY*}

SPOKE ABOUT
-spoke of the need to

SPONSOR
-benefactor
-patron

SPONSORSHIP
-under the auspices of
-under the aegis of

SPONTANEOUS
-impromptu

SPRAINED HERSELF
-she received a sprain

SPREAD
-widened
-was exported to
-diffused
-proliferated

SPREAD OUT
-fan out

SPREADING
-rampant
-in circulation

SPREADING GOSSIP
-retailing the latest gossip

SPREADING OUT OVER
-straying over

"And the cottages of these coal-miners, in blocks and pairs here and there, together with odd farms and homes of the stockingers, straying over the parish, formed the village of Bestwood." D. H. Lawrence, *Sons and Lovers*

SPRINKLE
-just a hint of

SPUNKY
-plucky

SPYING
-the great game
-espionage

SQUANDERING OF RESOURCES
-dissipation [academic]

STABILITY
-continuity

STABLE
-well adjusted

STAFFED
-peopled

"He funded charitable enterprises, used interest-free loans to put influential citizens in his debt, provided the less affluent with sustenance, and peopled his payroll

with the best political operatives money could buy." Hendrik Hetzberg, *The New Yorker*

STAGE (A STAGE IN A PROCESS)
-a gradation

STAGNANT
-moribund

STAND (CAN'T STAND)
-bear
-endure

STAND GUARD
-mount guard

STAND IN FRONT OF
-stand before

STAND TOGETHER
-close ranks
-stay on message

STANDARD
-caliber
-criterion
-touchstone
-ideal

STANDING
-your station in life

STANDING CLOSE TOGETHER IN ROWS
-serried ranks of soldiers

STANDING OUT
-conspicuous

STARE
-scowl
-glower

START
-initiate
-establish
-arise
-commence
-inaugurate
-set about

-take up
-embark upon
-enter upon
-launch into
-begin the task of
-fire the opening salvo
-if we could get to
-begin its course

START TALKING
-get into conversation

"As soon as a boy asks if he may bicycle home with me and we get into conversation, nine out of ten times I can be sure that he will fall head over heels in love immediately and simply won't allow me out of his sight. After a while it cools down of course, especially as I take little notice of ardent looks and pedal blithely on." Anne Frank, *Anne Frank: The Diary of a Young Girl*

START USING
-adopt

STARTED
-took to

"In his last year at Princeton he read too much and took to wearing spectacles." Ernest Hemingway, *The Sun Also Rises*

STARTED ASSOCIATING WITH
-fell among

"The divorce was arranged and Robert Cohn went out to the coast. In California he fell among literary people and, as he still had a little of the fifty thousand left, in a short time he was backing a review of the Arts." Ernest Hemingway, *The Sun Also Rises*

STARTED UP AGAIN
-resumed

STARTS OUT
-goes forth

"Man is explicable by nothing less than all his history. Without hurry, without rest, the *human spirit goes forth from the beginning to embody every faculty, every thought, every emotion, which belongs to it, in appropriate events. But the thought is always prior to the fact; all the facts of history pre-exist in the mind as laws."* Ralph Waldo Emerson, "Essay on History"

STASH
-cache

STATE
-assert
-affirm
-intone
-proclaim
-annunciate
-mention

STATE DEPARTMENT (WASHINGTON DC)
-Foggy Bottom

STATEMENT
-communiqué
-assertion

STATUES
-statuary

Look at all the statues.

~~Look at the statuary.~~

STATUS
-position on the food chain
-pecking order
-hierarchy

STAY
-remain
-hold true
-linger

STAY CALM
-keep your composure

STAY TOO LONG
-tarry

STAY WITH ME
-be with me

STEADFAST BELIEFS
-beliefs held, come what may

STEADY
-unswerving

STEADY YOUR
-still your

STEAL
-make off with
-pilfer
-siphon
-misappropriate
-purloin
-spirit away
-filch

STEEP
-precipitous

"For the greater part of its course the river Drina flows through narrow gorges between steep mountains or through deep ravines with precipitous banks." Ivo Andric, *The Bridge on the Drina*

STEP BY STEP
-chronologically
-incrementally

STEPPING STONE
-way station
-precursor

STEPS TO TAKE
-measures

STEREOTYPICAL
-proverbial

STEREOTYPICAL OPERA (LIKE WHEN THE FAT LADY SINGS)
-Wagnerian {vahg-NEAR-ee-un}

"It's funny how a Viking helmet can give anything a Wagnerian feel."

STICK OUT
-protrude

STIFFNESS
-formality
-reticence

STILL
-be that as it may
-nonetheless
-nevertheless
-that's all well and good, but
-that being said
-just the same
-yet

"There must be acceptance and the knowledge that sorrow fully accepted brings its own gifts. For there is an alchemy in sorrow. It can be transmuted into wisdom, which, if it does not bring joy, can yet bring happiness." Pearl S. Buck, *The Child Who Never Grew*

STILL ARE
-they remain

STILL CONTINUE TO [INCORRECT USAGE]
-they continue to

STILL IN EXISTENCE
-extant [academic]

STILL THERE
-still in place

STILTED AND CAUTIOUS
-lawyerly

STIMULATE
-whet

STINGING QUESTION
-pointed question
-barbed question

STINGRAY (COOKED)
-skate

STINGY
-parsimonious

STIPULATION
-with the caveat that
-with the proviso that

STIR TO ACTION
-galvanize support

STIR UP TROUBLE
-foment

STOLEN GOODS
-spoils
-loot

STONE CUTTER (PRECIOUS STONES)
-a lapidary

STOOD (IT STOOD)
-there stood a

STOOP (WILLING TO STOOP)
-she is not above it

STOP
-put a stop to
-draw to a close
-contain
-put an end to
-check
-refrain from further
-desist [academic]
-forbear from
-declare an end to
-bring an end to
-choke off the flow of
-negate the effects of
-restrain
-halt
-relent
-thwart
-dispense with
-quiet
-cease from

"We shall not cease from exploration/ And the end of all our exploring/ Will be to arrive

where we started/ And know the place for the first time." T. S. Eliot, *Four Quartets*

-arrest

"In those days cheap apartments were almost impossible to find in Manhattan, so I had to move to Brooklyn. This was in 1947, and one of the pleasant features of that summer which I so vividly remember was the weather, which was sunny and mild, flower-fragrant, almost as if the days had been arrested in a seemingly perpetual springtime." William Styron, *Sophie's Choice*

> It's too early to say that the recession is over.
>
> It's too early to declare an end to the recession.

STOP IT
-come now

STOP TALKING
-break off their conversation

STOP WASTING TIME ON
-close the book on

STOP YOUR
-quiet your

STOPPED
-quitted

STOPPED BEING
-ceased to be

"The planet Mars, I scarcely need remind the reader, revolves about the sun at a mean distance of 140,000,000 miles, and the light and heat it receives from the sun is barely half of that received by this world. It must be, if the nebular hypothesis has any truth, older than our world; and long before this earth ceased to be molten, life upon its surface must have begun its course." H. G. Wells, *The War of the Worlds*

STORAGE PLACE
-depository

STORE OF
-wealth of
-repository of

STORMY
-tempestuous

STORIES
-histories
-incidents

STORY
-narrative
-account
-saga
-parable
-reminiscence
-history

STORY ABOUT (THERE IS A STORY ABOUT)
-the story is told of a
-the plot centers on

STORY-TELLER
-a griot {GREE-oh}

STORY-TELLING
-the telling of stories

"Three years he had spent between fear and hope, between death and expectation; three years spent in the telling of stories; and, thanks to those stories, Shahrzad's lifespan had been extended." Naguib Mahfouz, *Arabian Nights and Days*

STRAIGHT TALKER
-forthright
-forthcoming

STRAIGHTFORWARD
-without nuance

> Be straightforward with me.
>
> Give it to me without nuance.

STRANGE
-peculiar
-idiosyncratic
-curious
-eccentric
-he has his peculiarities
-strange in his manner
-enigmatic
-alien

STRANGE THINGS
-curiosities
-little curios

STRANGENESS OF
-the surreality of

STRANGERS
-alien visitors

STRATEGIES
-initiatives
-schemes
-stratagems [academic]

STRAYING
-errant

STRENGTHEN
-bolster
-temper
-shore up

STRETCHED THEIR NECKS
-craned their necks

STRICT
-stringent
-austere

STRICT MORAL BEHAVIOR
-puritanical

STRIFE FILLED
-contentious
-combative

STRIKE
-smite

STRIPPED OF ITS
-divested of its

STRONG
-unwavering
-robust
-penetrating
-muscular

STRONG FLAVOR
-sapid

STRONG SMELL
-penetrating

STRONGEST
-predominant

STRUCK DOWN
-felled

"Felled, dazed, silent, he has fallen; knocked full length on the cobbles of the yard. His head turns sideways; his eyes are turned toward the gate, as if someone might arrive to help him out. One blow, properly placed, could kill him now." Hilary Mantel, *Wolf Hall*

STRUCTURE
-fabric
-framework

STRUGGLING
-grappling with
-beleaguered
-floundering
-beset

STUBBORN
-steadfast
-intransigent
-immovable
-obdurate [academic]
-intractable
-adamant
-obstinate
-uncompromising

STUCK
-mired
-entrenched

STUDENT
-protégé

STUDENT OF
-devotee of

STUDIED THEM
-applied himself to them

"He had covered the plotting table immediately with piles of papers from his briefcase; and he applied himself to them except when General Beal, turning his head, addressed some remark to him." James Gould Cozzens, *Guard of Honor*

STUDY (TO STUDY)
-read

"Simon would have regarded with impotent fury the disturbance between the North and the South, as it left his descendants stripped of everything but their land, yet the tradition of living on the land remained unbroken until well into the twentieth century, when my father, Atticus Finch, went to Montgomery to read law, and his younger brother went to Boston to study medicine." Nelle Harper Lee, *To Kill a Mockingbird*

STUDYING
-making a study of

"All the time he had lived there, the nephew had secretly been making a study of him. The nephew, who had taken him in under the name of Charity, had at the same time been creeping into his soul by the back door, asking him questions that meant more than one thing, planting traps around the house and watching him fall into them, and finally coming up with a written study of him for a schoolteacher magazine." Flannery O'Connor, *The Violent Bear It Away*

STUPID
-inane

-bovine
-none-too-bright
-benighted
-daft
-of questionable intellect
-obtuse

STUPID THING (TO DO)
-ill-advised
-ill-conceived
-lacks the intellectual sophistication of

> That would be stupid.
> That would be ill-advised.

STUPIDITY
-absence of thought

STYLE
-tradition
-approach
-convention
-influence
-treatment
-genre
-sensibility
-character
-color
-mold
-the idiom of
-a vocabulary of gesture
-the character of their art

STYLE OF SPEECH
-locution [academic]

SUBDUE
-quell
-temper
-chasten your urge to

SUBDUED (IN TONE)
-sober

"In the vestibule and on the stairway, directing them or watching them pass, were men who looked like functionaries or

bailiffs, *dressed in sober grey suits, mostly young, efficient-looking, discreet, the type that one meets everywhere in such places; ministries, the residences of heads of state, or headquarters of important organizations."* Claude Simon, *The Invitation*

SUBJECT
-focus
-subject matter
-topic
-line of inquiry

"Our subject being Poetry, I propose to speak not only of the art in general but also of its species and their respective capacities; of the structure of plot required for a good poem; of the number and nature of the constituent parts of a poem; and likewise of any other matters in the same line of inquiry. Let us follow the natural order and begin with the primary facts." Aristotle, *The Poetics*

SUBMISSIVE
-obliging
-complaisant
-compliant
-amenable
-deferential
-retiring

SUBMIT
-tender

SUBORDINATE ISSUES
-ancillary issues

SUBSTITUTE
-surrogate

SUBTLE
-nuanced

SUBURBS
-environs

SUCCEED IN
-manage to

SUCCEEDED
-have met with success a number of times

SUCCESS
-good fortune

SUCCESSFUL
-enjoying some commercial success

SUCCESSFUL BUSINESSPERSON
-a rainmaker

SUCCESSFULLY
-to great effect

SUCK
-draw

SUCK UP TO
-kowtow {Chinese, *cow-tou*}

SUDDENLY
-all at once

"We were strolling one night down a long dirty street, in the vicinity of the Palais Royal. Being both, apparently, occupied by thought, neither of us had spoken a syllable for fifteen minutes at least. All at once Dupin broke forth with these words..." Edgar Allan Poe, "The Murders in the Rue Morgue"

SUE HAPPY
-litigious

> Be careful, she's sue happy.
>
> Be careful, she has a litigious history.

SUFFER
-endure
-withstand
-tolerate
-bear

SUFFERING
-affliction

-plight
-scourge

SUFFICE TO SAY [INCORRECT USAGE]
-suffice it to say

SUGARCOAT IT
-to put it kindly
-to be generous
-to put it charitably

SUGGEST
-give the opinion that
-posit
-postulate
-proffer
-submit

SUGGESTS
-carries certain connotations
-the implication being
-is suggestive of

SUIT YOURSELF
-as you like

SUMMARY
-an abstract
-a distillation of

SUMMER HOUSE
-retreat
-arbor

SUN
-daystar [poetic]

SUPERIORITY
-preeminence

SUPERIORS
-higher-ups

SUPERVISE
-preside over
-oversee

SUPERVISION
-oversight

SUPPLIERS OF
-purveyors of

SUPPLIES
-provisions

SUPPORT
-bear the weight of

SUPPORTER
-adherent of
-constituent
-advocate
-proponent
-champion of
-defender of the faith
-partisan
-expositor [academic]

SUPPOSED
-putative
-reputed

SUPPOSED TO
-are in theory

SUPPOSED TO BE
-are said to be

"How is it that Americans, so solicitous of the animals they keep as pets, are so indifferent to the ones they cook for dinner? The answer cannot lie in the beasts themselves. Pigs, after all, are quite companionable, and dogs are said to be delicious." Elizabeth Kolbert, *The New Yorker*, Nov. 9, 2009

SUPREMACY
-primacy

SUPREME
-transcendent
-sovereign

SURE ENOUGH
-indeed

"'Ready to sleep,' she says; and indeed, en route, she falls asleep briefly, her head slumped against the window." J.M. Coetzee, *The Lives of Animals*

SURE OF
-resolved

"He was glad for one thing: the rope was off his neck. That had given them an unfair advantage; but now that it was off, he would show them. They would never get another rope around his neck. Upon that he was resolved." Jack London, *The Call of the Wild*

-have no doubt
-we may be sure that
-assured

"The existence of which we are most assured and which we know best is unquestionably our own, for of every other object we have notions which may be considered external and superficial, whereas, of ourselves, our perception is internal and profound." Henri Bergson, *Creative Evolution*

SURELY
-he will be sure to
-by all means
-no doubt

"No one even knows I have a story. Next year, next week, tomorrow, I will no doubt be gone, and it will be a small size coffin they will need for me, and a narrow hole. There will never be a stone at my head, and no matter." Sebastian Barry, *The Secret Scripture*

SURRENDER TO IT
-cede to it

"Nothing is more certain than the indispensable necessity of government, and it is equally undeniable, that whenever and however it is instituted, the people must cede to it some of their natural rights in order to vest it with requisite powers." John Jay, *"The Federalist Papers, No. 2"*

SURENESS
-certitude

SURGING
-onrushing

SURPASSED
-eclipsed

SURPRISE
-defy expectations

> You continue to surprise me.
> You continue to defy expectations.

SURPRISE ATTACK
-preemptive strike

SURPRISED
-blindsided
-bemused
-taken aback
-astounded
-thrown for a loss
-caught unawares

SURPRISINGLY
-to my surprise

SURRENDER POWER
-abnegate

SURROUND
-enfold
-encircle

SURROUNDED
-hemmed in

SURVEY
-take soundings
-canvass

SURVIVAL
-subsistence

SURVIVE
-emerge unscathed
-escape the ravages of
-persevere
-eke out

SURVIVE ON
-subsist on

SURVIVED FOR A LONG TIME
-have long survived the

SURVIVING INFLUENCES
-vestiges of

SURVIVOR
-holdover from

SUSCEPTIBLE
-predisposed to

SUSPICION
-initial suspicion fell on
-a cloud of suspicion

SUSPICIOUS OF
-wary of

SWALLOW UP
-engulf

SWAMPED
-engulfed

SWAMPLAND
-glade
-swale

SWEAR WORDS
-expletives
-colorful language
-language in full technicolor
-profane expressions

"His conversation was garnished at convenient intervals with various profane expressions, which not even the desire to be graphic in our account shall induce us to transcribe." Harriet Beecher Stowe, *Uncle Tom's Cabin*

SWEARING
-using colorful language
-shouting course abuse

SWEETS
-confections

SWELL
-swimmingly [humorous or sarcastic]

SWISS BANKERS
-the gnomes of Zurich

SWOLLEN
-distended
-tumid

SYMBOL
-icon
-totem
-token
-hallmark
-standard

SYMBOLIC OF
-emblematic of

SYMPATHIZE WITH
-commiserate with

SYMPATHIZER
-fellow traveler

SYMPATHY
-consolation

SYMPTOM
-manifestation of

SYSTEMATIZE
-codify

T t

TACKY
-garish
-lurid
-meretricious

TACTFUL
-discreet

TAG ALONG
-caddy for

TAKE
-appropriate
-procure
-commandeer
-wrest from
-help oneself to
-preempt

TAKE A FEW MINUTES
-it will only be a matter of minutes

TAKE A LOOK AT
-let me direct your attention to

TAKE A POSITION
-stake out a divisive position

TAKE ACTION
-go on the offensive
-act upon

TAKE ADVANTAGE OF
-avail herself of
-exploit
-seize upon
-leverage

> Feel free to take advantage of everything I have to offer.
>
> Feel free to avail yourself of everything I have to offer.

TAKE ANOTHER LOOK AT
-revisit
-reappraise

TAKE APART
-dismantle
-disassemble

TAKE AWAY PROPERTY
-expropriate

TAKE AWAY THE WORTH OF
-detract from

TAKE AWAY YOUR
-rid you of your

TAKE BACK
-withdraw
-retract
-recant
-countermand

TAKE BACK WHAT WAS SAID
-backpedal
-you may want to roll that one back

TAKE CARE OF
-attend to
-address
-look after
-see after
-bring to the floor

TAKE COMFORT IN
-take solace in

TAKE CONTROL OF
-reign in your

TAKE DOWN
-unseat

TAKE FROM
-glean
-extract
-draw on

TAKE IT
-seize upon it

TAKE LEGAL ACTION
-consider other options
-adjudicate the matter

TAKE OFF
-take wing

TAKE OFF YOUR
-remove your
-off with your

TAKE ON
-adopt the cause of
-assume

"He will assume all fund-raising duties."

TAKE ON A PROBLEM
-address

TAKE OVER
-supervene
-commandeer
-arrogate to themselves

TAKE POSSESSION OF
-expropriate

TAKE QUESTIONS
-field questions

> I need you to take questions.
>
> I need you to field questions.

TAKE THE LEAD
-come to the fore

TAKE THE PLACE OF
-supersede

TAKE UP
-adopt

TAKE YOU TO
-he will conduct you to [formal]

TAKEN FROM
-derived from
-culled from
-excerpted from
-gleaned from

TAKEN OFF
-taken wing

TAKEN THE POSITION
-adopted the stance

TAKEOFF ON
-parody
-send-up
-pastiche {pas-TEESH} (of a play or book)

TAKES FROM
-draws on

TAKES RISKS
-she runs what risks she chooses

TAKES SETBACKS IN STRIDE
-is philosophical

TAKES UP ALL OF HER TIME
-consumes her life

TAKING A SECOND LOOK
-paying renewed attention to
-revisiting

TAKING EVERYTHING INTO ACCOUNT
-all things considered

TAKING FROM ME
-depriving me of

TAKING HER GOOD TIME
-dallying
-dawdling
-lollygagging

TAKING INTO ACCOUNT
-in view of the fact that
-given the
-in light of

TAKING ON A NEW JOB
-translating his abilities to

TAKING OUT
-wresting

TALENT
-a real faculty for

TALENTED
-gifted

TALK
-converse
-confer

TALK ABOUT
-speak of
-point to
-cite
-note
-feature

-highlight
-address
-mention
-allude to
-remark upon
-talk of
-engage the issue of
-hit upon the
-make excellent comment upon
-give some account of

"Although it has no direct bearing on the tale we have to tell, we must nevertheless give some account of the rumours and gossip concerning him which were in circulation when he came to occupy the Diocese."
Victor Hugo, *Les Miserables*

> She did talk about it.
>
> She made mention of it.

TALK ABOUT IT
-speak of it

TALK FOOLISHLY
-prate on about
-prattle

TALK OUT OF
-dissuade

TALK WITH
-converse with

TALKED ABOUT
-has spoken of
-spoke of it
-made mention of it

TALKED ME OUT OF
-convinced me otherwise

TALKATIVE
-communicative
-garrulous

TALKING
-passing remarks back and forth
-conversing

TALKING ABOUT
-speaking of _____
-the _____ in question

"The author in question is believed to have lived a life of obscurity."

TALKING HEADS
-the commentariate

TALKING POINTS (EMPTY WORDS)
-shibboleths {Hebrew, *SHI-bu-leths*}

TAME (IS TAME)
-docile

TAME (TO TAME)
-domesticate

TANGLED UP
-enmeshed in

TAPER OFF
-wane
-ebb

TARGET
-take aim at
-cater to
-court the rich

TASK
-ordeal

TASTE FOR
-penchant for
-predilection for
-partiality to

TASTED (IT TASTED)
-it tasted of
-I drank the taste of

"I poured myself a glass of water and drank the mealy taste of my tongue." Herta Müller, *The Appointment*

> It tasted just like licorice.
>
> It tasted of licorice.

TASTELESS JUNK
-kitsch {German, *kich*}

TASTES BAD
-is unfit for human consumption
-is unpalatable
-is displeasing

TAUGHT (WAS TAUGHT)
-brought up in the ___ tradition

TAX ON IMPORTS
-tariff
-excise

TEACH
-instill
-develop in her those qualities which
-school
-awaken you to all the

TEACHER
-guru
-mentor

TEACHING
-instilling
-helping others to
-imparting

TEACHING PROPS
-realia {ree-AL-ee-uh}

TEACHINGS
-doctrine

TEAM MORALE
-esprit de corps {French, *es-PREE de KOR*}

TEAR (A TEAR)
-rent

"Diseases were forever flitting in and out of the provinces and old age carried away some of the more admirable citizens. That is why it was so surprising that the Peruvians should have been especially touched by the rent in the bridge of San Luis Rey." Thornton Wilder, *The Bridge of San Luis Rey*

TEAR APART
-rive
-rend [poetic]

"It was said that to descend into the world beneath the world was to learn the secrets of heaven and hell, to go mad, to speak in tongues, to rend the veil, to become immortal, to witness the destruction of the universe and the birth of a new order of being..." Steven Millhauser, *Martin Dressler: The Tale of an American Dreamer*

TEAR DOWN
-raze

TEASE
-tantalize

TECHNICAL
-arcane
-cryptic
-Talmudic

TECHNIQUES (USING ALL TECHNIQUES)
-using all manner of means

TELL
-relate
-convey in the most forceful terms
-impart a secret
-share it with you
-recount

TELL (I COULD TELL)
-I could judge

TELL SOMEONE A SECRET
-take someone into one's confidence
-confide in

TELL THE POLICE
-the police should be informed

TELL THE TRUTH
-lay bare your soul [poetic]

TELL THEM ABOUT
-tell them of

TELL US SOMETHING ABOUT
-throw some light on

"When on board H.M.S. Beagle, as naturalist, I was much struck with certain facts in the distribution of the inhabitants of South America, and in the geological relations of the present to the past inhabitants of that continent. These facts seemed to me to throw some light on the origin of species— that mystery of mysteries, as it has been called by one of our greatest philosophers." Charles Darwin, *On the Origin of Species*

TELL YOU THAT IT WAS
-did he put it to you as

TELLING STORIES
-yarning about his supposed encounter
-regaling
-recounting

TELLS US THAT
-points to
-demonstrates
-indicates
-suggests
-seems to suggest
-if ___ is any indication, then…
-speaks of

"The marks on his rib cage speak of the violence he endured before death."

TEMPORARY
-ephemeral
-fleeting
-transitory
-for a time
-in the interim
-makeshift
-impermanent
-momentary
-provisional
-transient

"No one would have believed in the last years of the nineteenth century that this world was being watched keenly and closely by intelligences greater than man's and yet as mortal

as his own; that as men busied themselves about their various concerns they were scrutinized and studied, perhaps almost as narrowly as a man with a microscope might scrutinize the transient creatures that swarm and multiply in a drop of water." H. G. Wells, *The War of the Worlds*

TEMPERATURES BETWEEN [INCORRECT USAGE]
-temperatures from -20 to + 80 Celsius

TEMPT
-entice

TEMPTATIONS
-enticements
-seductions

TEMPTED (TO BE TEMPTED)
-surrender to impulse
-fall to temptation

TEND TO
-are inclined to
-are predisposed to
-are prone to
-are given to

TEND TO (HELP)
-address
-treat
-minister to

TENDENCY
-inclination
-penchant
-propensity
-predisposition
-proclivity
-bent
-adherence to

TERRIBLE
-dire

TERRITORY
-dominion
-sphere of influence
-domain

-realm
-province
-principality

TEST (A TRIAL BY FIRE)
-a crucible

TEST LAB
-proving ground

TESTIFY TO
-bear witness to

"I would like to write down what happened in my grandmother's house the summer I was eight or nine, but I am not sure if it really did happen. I need to bear witness to an uncertain event. I feel it roaring inside me—this thing that may not have taken place." Anne Enright, *The Gathering*

TEXTBOOK (BASIC)
-primer

THANK
-to laud and congratulate

THANK GOODNESS THAT
-it was a comfort that

THANK YOU
-much obliged
-many thanks

THANKFUL
-much obliged

THAT
-with which
-as is
-on which
-to which
-such is the
-according to which

THAT ARE FOUND ON
-that populate

THAT DOESN'T MEAN
-it does not follow that

THAT HAS NOTHING TO DO WITH WHAT WE'RE TALKING ABOUT
-that is a non sequitur {Latin, *non SEK-wih-tor*}

THAT I NOTICED
-that caught my eye

THAT IS A GIVEN
-that is a foregone conclusion

THAT IS BOTH ____ AND ____
-that is at once ____ and ____

"In 'La Danse' you watch closely as dancers and choreographers break complex movements down into their constituent gestures, a process that is at once tedious and entirely engrossing." A. O. Scott, *New York Times*, Nov. 4, 2009

THAT IS ENOUGH
-that will do

THAT IS FINE WITH ME
-so much the better

THAT IS NOT WHAT WILL HAPPEN
-anyone expecting ____ is likely to be disappointed

THAT IS OFFENSIVE
-I take exception to

THAT IS RIDICULOUS
-come now
-what do you hope to accomplish

THAT IS SOMETHING ELSE
-that's another matter

THAT IS WHAT IS SO SCARY ABOUT IT
-that's the horror of it

THAT IS WHAT THEY CALLED HIM
-that is how they called him

THAT IS WHY SHE
-simply for that she
-it is for this reason that she

THAT KIND OF _____ IS
-_____ of that kind is

THAT MOST THINGS HAVE
-peculiar to most things

THAT WAY
-thus

"Then, since we could not stay thus forever, I sat up and again began to make motions of drinking. I had rowed all morning. I had not drunk since the night before, I no longer cared if he killed me afterwards so long as I had water." J.M. Coetzee, *Foe*

THAT WAY SHE COULD
-in this way she could

THAT WE CAN SEE
-that are discernible

_____ THAT WE'RE TALKING ABOUT WERE
-the _____s in question were

THAT WOULDN'T DO ANY GOOD
-no purpose would be served

THAT'S ALL I ASK
-I ask no more

THAT'S ENOUGH
-that will do

THAT'S FOR SURE
-I can tell you that

"Humboldt was just what everyone had been waiting for. Out in the Midwest I had certainly been waiting eagerly, I can tell you that. An avant-guard writer, the first of a new generation, he was handsome, fair, large, serious, witty, he was learned. The guy had it all." Saul Bellow, *Humboldt's Gift*

THAT'S WHAT HAPPENS WHEN YOU
-such is the result of

THE BEST SO FAR
-as yet unequalled

_____ THE EMBATTLED
-_____ Agonistes

THE EXACT OPPOSITE
-the very opposite
-on the contrary

THE FACT THAT A
-that a

THE FOLLOWING:
-as follows:

THE HIGHEST QUALITY _____
-a _____ of the highest quality

THE KIND OF
-what manner of

THE KIND OF _____ YOU SEE
-a _____ of the kind you see

"With slow strokes, my long hair floated about me, like a flower of the sea, like an anemone, like a jellyfish of the kind you see in the waters of Brazil. I swam towards the strange island, for a while swimming as I had rowed, against the current, then all at once free of its grip, carried by the waves into the bay and on to the beach." J.M. Coetzee, *Foe*

THE LAST ONE TO LEAVE
-last of all

"She had left the church last of all, and, desiring to arrive first at the hall, had issued orders to the coachman to drive faster." Upton Sinclair, *The Jungle*

THE ONE RESPONSIBLE FOR
-the owner

"The owner of the voice was nowhere to be found."

-the maker

"Through rotting kelp, sea cocoa-nuts and bamboo, the tracks led me to their maker..." David Mitchell, *Cloud Atlas*

THE ONES WHO
-those who

THE OPPOSITE IS TRUE
-quite the contrary

THE OPPOSITE OF
-the very opposite of

"Theatergoers who use plays as mood-setting preludes to romantic evenings had better look elsewhere. 'Quartett,' which opened Wednesday night and runs through Nov. 14, may well be the sexually frankest play in New York this side of a backroom peephole. But with a cast led by the formidable French actress Isabelle Humpert in a magnificently mannered performance, it is the very opposite of an aphrodisiac." Ben Brantley, *New York Times*, Nov. 6, 2009

THE POWER OF
-the agency of

"And like a big teacup at the county fair, they would sit and spin in their little round boat, and want for rain and want for land, until they had only to want for the agency of God."

THE REST OF THE
-the remainder of the

THE SAME AS
-tantamount to

> That is the same thing as treason.
>
> That is tantamount to treason.

THE SAME KIND OF
-something of the

"I gave her something of the shock that I had received." Henry James, *The Turn of the Screw*

THE SAME PERSON
-they are one and the same

THE TYPE OF
-what manner of

THE WAY IT IS
-as it stands

THE WAY THAT
-the manner in which

"They were hungry for breakfast which they ate at the café, ordering brioche and café au lait and eggs, and the type of preserve that they chose and the manner in which the eggs were to be cooked was an excitement." Ernest Hemingway, *Garden of Eden*

THE WAY THEY ARE USED
-in their application

THE WAY THINGS ARE
-the way of things

"It seems ridiculous to suppose the dead miss anything. If you're a grown man when you read this—it is my intention for this letter that you read it then—I'll have been gone a long time. I'll know most of what there is to know about being dead, but I'll probably keep it to myself. That seems to be the way of things." Marilynne Robinson, *Gilead*

THEATRICS
-histrionics
-melodrama

THEME
-motif {moe-TEEF}
-leitmotiv {German, LITE-moe-teef}

THEMSELVES
-in and of themselves
-unto themselves
-of their own accord

THEN
-at this
-after which
-whereupon
-thereafter

-subsequently
-at that instant
-whereafter we
-at the time
-in turn
-at this I
-and with that she
-it was then he noticed

"We were sitting in the blind that Wanderobo hunters had built of twigs and branches at the edge of the salt-lick when we heard the truck coming. At first it was far away and no one could tell what the noise was. Then it was stopped and we hoped it had been nothing or perhaps only the wind." Ernest Hemingway, *The Green Hills of Africa*

THEORETICAL
-conjectural
-academic
-notional
-ideological

THEORY
-school of thought
-theory now being pursued by
-theorem

THERE (ARE THERE)
-are on hand

THERE ARE ___ OF THEM
-they number ___

> There are seventeen of them.
>
> They number seventeen in all.

THERE ARE FOUR OF US CHILDREN
-we are four children

"We are four children; there is my sister Diana and the three men—Chaddy, Lawrence, and myself. Like most families in which the children are out of their twenties, we have been separated by business,

marriage, and war." John Cheever, *The Stories of John Cheever*

THERE ARE ONLY
-there are but

THERE FOR EVERYONE TO SEE
-there on fairly generous display

THERE IS
-we find
-there lies

THERE IS A DIFFERENCE BETWEEN
-one must distinguish between

THERE IS NO ___
-the ___ is nonexistent

THERE IS NO REASON TO THINK THAT
-there is no reason to suppose that

THERE IS NOTHING AS
-there is nothing so

THERE IS STILL
-there remains

THERE MAY BE
-there are believed to be

THERE WAS A TIME WHEN
-time was,

THERE WILL STILL BE
-there will remain

THERE YOU HAVE IT
-Q.E.D. (playfully appended to the conclusion of a statement of logic)

"If you can't explain it in five seconds, then you haven't thought about it long enough. Q.E.D."

THEREFORE
-thus
-accordingly
-consequently
-hence

-ergo [academic]

-as such

THESE

-such

"That such artifacts escaped the ravages of time is remarkable."

THESE ARE ____

-how____ are these

THESE ARE EXCELLENT QUESTIONS

-excellent questions all

THESE NO LONGER HAVE

-these have no longer

"These have no longer any hope of death." Dante, *Inferno, Canto III*

THEY ARE NEVER

-never are they

THEY ARE USED TO

-to which they have become accustomed

THEY DON'T ALL AGREE ON

-there is little agreement on

> They can't agree on anything.
> There is little agreement.

THEY HAVE A BAD REPUTATION FOR BEING

-they have acquired a bad reputation for being

THEY LIKED IT

-it was well received

THEY SAT ON THE MANTLE

-their place was upon the mantle

THEY SAY

-it is said that

-it was said of him

THEY USED TO SAY THAT HE WOULD

-it was said of him that he would

THEY WILL NEVER KNOW

-they'll be none the wiser

THICK-SKINNED

-impervious

THIN OUT

-diffuse

-disperse

THING (A THING)

-an entity

-a construct

-a factor

-a consideration

-an aspect

-a matter

-an element

-an animal

-an affair

"The houses of this street were poor grey affairs, two-story houses of grey brick, with grey shutters, all dusted over with grey dust which had been thrown up from bomb craters and shell holes." John Hersey, *A Bell for Adano*

THING TO DO

-course of action

THING YOU HATE OR FEAR

-a bête noire {French, *betn-WAHR*}

THINGS HAPPEN THE WAY THEY DO BECAUSE

-things happen as they do because

"The customers of cafes are people who believe that things happen as they do because they happen and that it is never worthwhile to put anything right. At Doña Rosa's they all smoke and most of them meditate, each alone with himself, on those small, kindly, intimate things which make their lives full or empty." Camilo Jose Cela, *The Hive*

THINGS LIKE
-from the likes of

THINGS TO ENJOY
-there was a pleasure to be had from

THINGS TO THINK ABOUT
-considerations

> These are the things to think about.
>
> These are the considerations.

THINGS YOU JUST KNOW WITH-OUT HAVING TO LEARN
-a priori assumptions {Latin, *ay pree-OR-ee*}

THINK (I THINK)
-I suspect
-I imagine
-I hold the opinion
-I am of the belief
-I think that in actual fact
-I have a mind to
-I consider
-I reckon

THINK ABOUT IT
-take into consideration
-consult and consider
-entertain the idea
-deliberate
-ruminate
-ponder over
-take stock of
-meditate upon
-take account of circumstances
-give the matter your best consideration
-reflect upon
-play with the idea of

THINK DEEPLY
-ruminate on

THINK I AM
-most people look on me as rather

THINK IT IS OUR DUTY
-we think it our duty

THINK OF
-regard
-consider
-deem
-look upon as
-reckon as
-envisage
-conceive of

THINK OUT LOUD
-muse

THINK THE SAME WAY
-think in similar terms
-of like mind

THINK TO ONESELF
-ruminate

THINK WHAT YOU WANT
-think what you will
-think what you please

THINKING ABOUT
-contemplating
-being occupied with thought

"We were strolling one night down a long dirty street, in the vicinity of the Palais Royal. Being both, apparently, occupied by thought, neither of us had spoken a syllable for fifteen minutes at least. All at once Dupin broke forth with these words..." Edgar Allan Poe, "The Murders in the Rue Morgue"

THINKING IN NEW WAYS
-thinking along new lines

THINKING SHE WAS
-thinking herself

THINKS OF HIMSELF AS_____
-gives himself airs of a _____
-thinks himself a ____

THIRD CLASS (A THIRD CLASS)
-a tertiary

THIRSTY
-parched

THIS
-such

THIS ALONE MUST HAVE MADE
-this in itself must have made

THIS AND THAT
-this thing and the other

"She racked her brains, and tried this thing and the other, but could not find anything successful. The failure made deep lines come into her face." D. H. Lawrence, "The Rocking-Horse Winner"

THIS IS A
-ours is a
-mine is a

THIS IS A MAN WHOSE THOUGHTS
-we see a man whose thoughts

THIS IS HOW
-in this way we

THIS IS WHAT HAPPENS WHEN
-this is what comes of

THIS IS WHERE
-once home to

THIS IS WHY
-it is for this reason that

THIS KIND OF _____
-_____s of this sort were

THIS WAY
-in this way

THOROUGH
-exhaustive
-intensive
-painstaking
-rigorous
-exacting

THOROUGH, YET CONCISE
-compendious [academic]

THOROUGHNESS
-a breadth of treatment

THOSE
-such

"I enjoyed such moments—but only in brief. If the talk began to wander, or cross the border into familiarity, I would soon find reason to excuse myself. I had grown too comfortable in my solitude, the safest place I knew." Barack Obama, *Dreams from My Father*

THOSE RESPONSIBLE FOR
-those who orchestrated
-the architects of

THOSE WHO
-they who

THOUGHT (HE THOUGHT)
-felt
-contemplated
-the idea occurred to him
-thought it only proper that
-had thought fit to
-supposed

"This is a tale of a meeting between two lonesome, skinny, fairly old white men on a planet which was dying fast. One of them was a science fiction writer named Kilgore Trout. He was a nobody at the time, and he supposed his life was over. He was mistaken." Kurt Vonnegut, *Breakfast of Champions*

THOUGHT (A THOUGHT)
-sentiment
-conception
-the whole tenor of his thoughts
-it figured in his mind as
-her train of thought

THOUGHT ABOUT IT
-deliberated
-entertained the idea that

-turned it over
-after a few moments reflection

THOUGHT AT ALL ABOUT
-gave a thought to

"*No one gave a thought to the older worlds of space as sources of human danger, or thought of them only to dismiss the idea of life upon them as impossible or improbable.*" H. G. Wells, *The War of the Worlds*

THOUGHT BY MANY
-widely presumed

> She is thought by many to be the heir apparent.
>
> She is widely presumed to be the heir apparent.

THOUGHT HE WAS
-believed him to be
-found him to be
-thought himself

> I thought that he was honest.
>
> I believed him to be honest.

THOUGHT IT APPROPRIATE TO
-thought fit to

THOUGHT OF AS A
-thought a

THOUGHT OF HERSELF AS A
-she thought herself a
-she fancied herself a

THOUGHT OF YOU
-my thoughts returned to you

THOUGHT OUT
-a good deal of thought has been given to
-a considered _____

"*Month after month he sets, collects, reads, and annotates their assignments, correcting lapses in punctuation, spelling and usages, interrogating weak arguments, appending to each paper a brief, considered critique.*" J.M. Coetzee, *Disgrace*

THOUGHT SO
-I've felt so myself

THOUGHT THAT HE WAS
-looked upon him as

THOUGHTLESS
-improvident

THREATEN
-hold out the possibility that
-bluster

THREATENING
-forbidding

THREE-PERSON RULE
-triumvirate

THREESOME
-troika
-trio

THREE-WAY MASTERFUL MANEUVER
-Tinker to Evers to Chance

THREW AT
-he thrust upon him the

THRIFTY
-frugal

THRILL
-frisson {free-SOHn}

THRIVED
-abounded

THRIVING
-burgeoning
-flourishing

THROUGH
-throughout
-by way of

THROUGH THICK AND THIN
-come what may

THROUGHOUT
-in the course of

THROUGHOUT THE DAY
-as the day wore into

THROW AROUND
-bandy them about

THROW AWAY
-dispose of
-jettison
-cast away
-discard

THROW UNDER THE BUS
-throw to the wolves

THROW UP
-purge

THROW YOUR WEIGHT AROUND
-ride roughshod over

THROWN OUT OF OFFICE
-ousted

TIME (AT THIS TIME)
-at this moment

TIME (OMINOUS)
-at the witching hour

TIME OFF
-a hiatus {high-AY-tus}

TIME PASSES
-as time rolls away

TIME RELATED
-temporal

TIME TO GO TO SLEEP
-it's time you were asleep

TIME TO MYSELF
-stolen hours

TIME WHEN
-years that saw

TIME WILL TELL
-in time we'll know

TIMES (MULTIPLIED)
-____ -fold

TINY
-miniscule
-Lilliputian

TINY BIT
-hint
-scintilla
-trace

TIP OF MY TONGUE
-the words escape me

TIP OF THE ICEBERG
-only begin to tell the story

TIPTOED
-walked on tiptoe

TIPTOEING AROUND
-treading wearily around

TIRED
-spent
-anemic
-listless

TIRED-LOOKING
-haggard
-zombish

TIRED OF (GET TIRED OF)
-weary of
-you never tire of it

> You never get tired of it.
> You never tire of it.

TIREDNESS
-languor
-lassitude
-lethargy
-ennui {on-WEE}

TITLE (THE NAME YOU GO BY)
-appellation

TO
-to that of

"Its tailbone is similar in shape to that of other dinosaurs."

-in which to

"We have only five days in which to file a claim."

-to one of
-to those of

TO BE
-to serve as

TO BE ABLE TO
-the means by which

TO BE GOTTEN
-to be had

"Beyond opens a door into the kitchen, where there is a glimpse to be had of a range with much steam ascending from it, and many women, old and young, rushing hither and thither." Upton Sinclair, *The Jungle*

TO BE HONEST
-to speak truly

"The young man reveres men of genius, because, to speak truly, they are more himself than he is." Ralph Waldo Emerson, "The Poet"

TO DO THAT
-to do so

TO EVER
-ever to

TO IMPRESS
-for effect

TO MAKE IT WORSE
-to make matters worse

TO MORE EASILY
-for greater convenience

TO NEVER
-never to be

TO QUOTE
-to borrow from
-to approximate _____'s remark

"It was only that, having written down the first few fine paragraphs, I could not produce any others—or, to approximate Gertrude Stein's remark about a lesser writer of The Lost Generation—I had the syrup but it wouldn't pour." William Styron, *Sophie's Choice*

TO THE END
-to the last

TO THE LETTER
-religiously

TO THE POINT
-terse
-succinct

____ TO THE RESCUE
-____ ex machina {Latin, *ex MAHK-ih-nuh*}

TO THEM
-in their eyes

TODAY
-in the present day
-of our day
-this day

"Play the man, Master Ridley; we shall this day light such a candle, by God's grace, in England, as I trust shall never be put out." Hugh Latimer, Bishop of Worchester, speaking to Nicholas Ridley, as they were being burned alive

TOGETHER
-in concert
-coupled with
-in conjunction with

TOKEN OF REMEMBRANCE
-a requiem

TOLD HER
-acquainted her with
-informed her
-mentioned to her

TOLERATE
-suffer

TONE DOWN
-temper

TONS OF
-legions of
-ample
-loads of
-oodles of [playful]
-masses of
-a predominance of

> There were tons of prospective buyers at the convention.
>
> There were legions of prospective buyers at the convention.

TOO BAD
-a matter of regret
-a pity
-more's the pity

TOO COMPLICATED
-overwrought with

TOO DISGUSTED
-too much disgusted

TOO EARLY
-premature

TOO HIGH IN PRICE
-prohibitive

> The cost is way too high.
>
> The cost is prohibitive.

TOO IMPORTANT TO BE INTERFERED WITH
-sacrosanct

TOO LATE
-useless

"Do not write to my sister yet. When all is a 'fait accompli' then we will tell her, because then it will be useless for her to do other than to accept." D. H. Lawrence, *Selected Letters*

TOO MANY
-untold numbers of

TOO MUCH
-in excess
-excessive
-an embarrassment of

TOO MUCH TO TAKE
-insufferable
-intolerable
-just so much I can take

TOO OFTEN (TO THE POINT OF DISGUST)
-ad nauseam {Latin, *add* NAUS-ee-um}

TOO SWEET
-saccharine
-an embarrassment of sugar

TOOK A LONG TIME TO
-was long in

"Every moving thing lifted the dust into the air; a walking man lifted a thin layer as high as his waist, and a wagon lifted the dust as high as the fence tops, and an automobile boiled a cloud behind it. The dust was long in settling back again." John Steinbeck, *The Grapes of Wrath*

TOOK IT AS
-received it as

"He used to tell a curious story about Southampton, and as a child I received it as the gospel truth. It may have been true for all that." Sebastian Barry, *The Secret Scripture*

TOOK OFF AND HID
-absconded

TOOK OFF FOR
-set off

TOOK ON INCREASING IMPORTANCE
-assumed increasing importance

TOOK THE ROAD THAT LED
-she went by the road that led

TOOK THEIR TIME IN
-were slow to

"It happened at the end of winter, in a year when the poppies were strangely slow to shed their petals; for mile after mile, from Benares onwards, the Ganga seemed to be flowing between twin glaciers, both its banks being blanketed by thick drifts of white-petalled flowers." Amitav Ghosh, *Sea of Poppies*

TOOL
-vehicle
-implement
-a new vocabulary of expression

TOPPED
-crowned

TORE
-rent

"But the idiot's cry was the saddest of all. It rent the sky. It was a long-drawn-out inhuman wail." Miguel Angel Asturias, *The President*

TOTAL IDIOT
-perfect idiot

TOTAL NUMBER
-all told
-to the tune of

> I'd say the total number is about 200,000.
> All told, I'd say about 200,000.

TOUCHED A NERVE
-touched a tender spot

TOUCHED OUR HEARTS
-softened our hearts

TOUCHING
-heart-rending
-poignant

TOUCHY
-petulant

TOUCHY SITUATION
-ticklish situation

TOUGH
-hard-boiled

TOWARDS THE REAR OF THE SHIP
-go aft

TRACE
-chronicle

TRACE OF
-hint of
-slight indication of
-vestige of

TRACES
-vestiges
-remnants

TRADEMARK
-hallmark

TRADITION
-folklore

TRADITIONALIST
-classicist
-purist
-textualist

TRAINED
-trained in the tradition of
-groomed
-well schooled in
-practiced in
-seasoned

TRAINED FOR TWO YEARS UNDER _____
-was for two years under _____

TRAINING
-grounding

TRAITOR
-apostate

TRAITOROUS GROUP
-a fifth column

TRAITS
-graces

TRANSFORM
-metamorphose
-transfigure
-transmute

"There must be acceptance and the knowledge that sorrow fully accepted brings its own gifts. For there is an alchemy in sorrow. It can be transmuted into wisdom, which, if it does not bring joy, can yet bring happiness." Pearl S. Buck, *The Child Who Never Grew*

TRANSFORM GROTESQUELY
-transmogrify
-mutate

TRANSFORMATIVE DESTRUCTION
-a terrible beauty

TRANSITION FROM
-segue {SEG-way}

TRANSLATE
-render
-paraphrase

TRANSLATION
-rendering
-rendition

TRANSMITTER OF DISEASE
-vector of disease

TRANSPARENT
-translucent
-limpid

TRAPPED
-ensnared

TRASH
-schlock

TRAVEL
-traverse

TRAVELED
-found its way to

TRAVELER
-wayfarer

"After pointing heavenward for half a century, the steeple appeared to have swerved suddenly from its purpose, and to invite now the attention of the wayfarer to the bar beneath." E. A. G. Glasgow, *The Miller of Old Church*

TRAVELING
-itinerant
-nomadic
-globetrotting

TRAVELING BEHIND THEM
-in the wake of

TRAVELS
-migrations

TRAVELS A LOT
-is well traveled

TREACHERY
-duplicity
-perfidy [academic]

TREASURE
-spoils
-booty
-bounty
-a trove of

TREASURED BELONGINGS
-lares and penates
{Latin, *LAY-reez and pi-NAY-teez*}

TREAT BADLY
-maltreat

TREND
-convention
-mode
-vogue

TRESPASSING
-errant

TRIBUTE TO
-pay homage to {*HOM-ij*}

TRICK (A TRICK)
-a ruse
-a canard {*ken-ARD*}
-a mare's nest
-a ploy

I'm on to your little trick.

I'm on to your ruse.

TRICK (TO TRICK)
-dupe
-hoodwink

TRIED OUT ON
-hawked

"His witty sayings were hawked about by other writers for years."

TRIED SO HARD
-took such pains

We've tried really hard to remove all offensive material.

We've taken great pains to remove all offensive material.

TRIED TO
-sought to
-went to unusual lengths to
-took pains to

TRIED TO HELP
-went to great lengths to help

TRIED TO SAY
-endeavored to convey

TRIP
-excursion
-jaunt
-outing

TRIVIA
-niceties

TROOPS IN CLOSE FORMATION
-a phalanx

TROUBLE
-imposition
-difficulty
-adversity

TROUBLED
-disconcerted
-distressed
-flustered
-it caused some heartburn among
-beleaguered
-beset with difficulties

TROUBLEMAKER
-provocateur

TROUBLING
-disconcerting
-disquieting
-a source of concern

TRUCE
-détente {French, *day-TAHNT*}

TRUE
-it is so
-that is the case
-true enough

TRUE (REAL)
-a natural born _____

TRUE AFTER ALL
-true for all that

"He used to tell a curious story about Southampton, and as a child I received it as the gospel truth. It may have been true for all that." Sebastian Barry, *The Secret Scripture*

TRULY
-verily

TRUST
-in someone's confidence
-I enjoy her full confidence

TRUSTWORTHY
-credible

TRUTHS
-imperishable truths
-verities

"From the Christian standpoint, we are charged with denying the reality and seriousness of human undertakings, since, if we reject God's commandments and the eternal verities, there no longer remains anything but pure caprice, with everyone permitted to do as he pleases, and incapable, from his own point of view, of condemning the points of view and acts of others." Jean-Paul Sartre, *Existentialism and Human Emotion*

TRUTHFULNESS
-veracity
-probity [academic]
-rectitude [academic]

TRY
-try as we might

TRY HARD ENOUGH
-sufficient pains taken in finding

TRY IT
-try your hand at

TRY SOMETHING NEW
-endorse a new approach

> We've decided to try something new.
>
> We've decided to endorse a new approach.

TRY TO
-labor to
-seek to
-endeavor to
-make every effort to
-struggle to
-try your luck as
-attempt to do so
-go about
-dare to
-I do what I can to
-in a bid to
-have a go at
-venture to
-in a push for
-strive to
-contrive to

"He knew that if she did not wish to be seen that she would contrive to elude him; and it amused him to think of putting her skill to the test." Edith Wharton, *The House of Mirth*

TRY TO DECIDE
-wrestle with the question of

TRYING TO RECOVER FROM
-reeling from

TURF
-orbit
-circles

TURN AWAY
-avert your eyes

TURN INTO
-transform
-resolve itself into a
-evaporate into

TURN LEMONS INTO LEMONADE
-make a virtue of

TURN OUT TO BE
-prove to be

TURN UPSIDE DOWN
-turn turtle

TURNED AROUND
-faced around

TURNED ON THE LIGHTS
-put the lights on

"We stood up and made our way out of the blind and out through the trees, walking on the sandy loam, feeling our way between trees and under branches, back to the road. A mile along the road was the car. As we came along side, Kamau, the driver, put the lights on." Ernest Hemingway, Green Hills of Africa

TURNED OUT TO BE
-proved to be

> It may turn out to be harmless after all.
>
> It may prove to be harmless after all.

TURNING POINT
-watershed event

TWIST
-writhe

TWISTED
-entwined
-intertwined

TWITTER USER-NAME
-nom de tweet

TYPE
-variant of
-species of
-of what order
-orientation
-genre {ZHAWN-ruh}
-of the sort which
-the likes of which

TYPICAL OF
-representative of

TYPICALLY
-commonly

U u

UGLY
-unflattering
-homely

ULTIMATE ACHIEVEMENT
-ne plus ultra {Latin, *nee plus UL-truh*}

"The Reagan Revolution is widely considered to be the ne plus ultra of the conservative movement."

UN_____ (UNINTERESTING)
-of no _____ (of no interest)

UNABLE TO
-incapable of
-at a loss how to

UNABLE TO COMMUNICATE
-incommunicado {Spanish,
 in-cah-MUNE-ih-CAH-toe}

UNAFFECTED BY
-impervious to

UNAPOLOGETIC
-make no apologies for

UNASHAMEDLY
-unabashedly

UNATTAINABLE DREAM
-châteaux en Espagne {French, shah-TOE
ah-nes-PAHN-ye, lit. castles in Spain}
-tilting at windmills

UNAUTHENTIC
-apocryphal

UNAVOIDABLE
-inexorable

UNAWARE
-incognizant

UNBEARABLE
-insufferable

UNBELIEVABLE
-I find that hard to accept
-implausible
-frankly it stretches credulity
-incredulous
-scarcely to be imagined
-it flies in the face of credulity
-beyond belief

UNBIASED
-disinterested
-impartial

UNBREAKABLE
-inviolable

UNCARED FOR
-in disrepair

UNCARING
-indifferent

-apathetic
-blithe
-with indifference

UNCARING ATTITUDE
-insouciance {in-SOO-see-unce}
-nonchalance

UNCERTAIN
-precarious
-ambivalent
-at a loss
-infirm of purpose
-casting doubt on the future course of
-dubious
-dicey
-far from clear

UNCERTAINTY
-ambiguity
-irresolution

*"She stood apart from the crowd, letting
it drift by her to the platform or the street,
and wearing an air of irresolution which
might, as he surmised, be the mask of a
very definite purpose."* Edith Wharton,
The House of Mirth

UNCHANGEABLE
-inalterable

UNCHANGED
-changeless in its _____

UNCHANGING
-immutable
-perpetual

UNCIVILIZED
-barbarous

UNCLEAR
-not immediately clear
-incoherent
-incomprehensible
-ambiguous
-obscure

*"I am amazed at how little has changed in
the more than fifty years that have gone by*

since I was last here. Amazed, and disappointed, I would go so far as to say appalled, for reasons that are obscure to me, since why should I desire change, I who have come back to live amidst the rubble of the past?" John Banville, *The Sea*

UNCOMFORTABLE
-ill at ease

UNCOMPLAINING
-stoic
-philosophical

UNCONCERNED
-cavalier
-unengaged
-nonchalant

UNCONFIDENT
-diffident

UNCONQUERABLE
-impregnable

UNCONTROLLABLE
-irrepressible

UNCONTROLLED
-unbridled

UNCONVENTIONAL
-willing to zig while others zag
-bohemian
-unorthodox

UNCOOPERATIVE
-disobliging
-less than forthcoming

UNCRITICAL
-undiscerning

UNCRITICAL FOLLOWERS
-the amen corner

UNDECORATED
-spartan
-unembellished
-austere
-modest

UNDER
-beneath

UNDER ATTACK
-put upon
-beleaguered
-embattled
-besieged
-set upon

UNDER DISCUSSION
-at issue

UNDER NO CIRCUMSTANCES
-on no account

UNDER THE UMBRELLA OF
-under the rubric of

UNDERCOVER AGENT
-provocateur

UNDERSTAND (I UNDERSTAND THAT)
-I take it that
-I recognize
-I can gather
-I can't fathom
-I comprehend
-I can't make out why
-the _____ does not escape him

"The irony does not escape him: that the one who comes to teach learns the keenest of lessons, while those who come to learn learn nothing. It is a feature of his profession on which he does not remark to Soraya." J. M. Coetzee, *Disgrace*

-I grasp the situation
-I am given to understand
-I have come to understand
-it is not lost on me
-I arrive at understanding
-I have it that

"It is simply this. That Space, as our mathematicians have it, is spoken of as having three dimensions, which one may call length, breadth, and thickness, and is always definable by reference to three planes,

each at right angles to the others." H. G. Wells, *The Time Machine*

> As far as I know, the flow of oil has stopped.
>
> I am given to understand that the flow of oil has stopped.

UNDERSTAND YOUR PROBLEM
-I am sympathetic to your problem

UNDERSTOOD BY ONLY A FEW
-arcane
-esoteric

UNDERTAKING
-an initiative

UNDERWAY
-under full sail

UNDERWAY FOR FIVE MINUTES
-five minutes underway

"Before the feast has been five minutes underway, Tamoszius Kuszleika has risen in his excitement; a minute or two more and you see that he is beginning to edge over toward the tables." Upton Sinclair, *The Jungle*

UNDESIRABLE GROUP
-bad company

UNDEVELOPED
-latent

UNDOUBTEDLY
-decidedly

UNDRESS
-disrobe

UNEASINESS
-disquiet

UNEASY FEELING
-pang

-qualm
-misgiving

UNEMOTIONAL
-stoic
-stolid
-philosophical

UNEQUAL SIZE
-disparate size

UNEXPLORED TERRITORY
-terra incognita {Latin, *TEAR-uh in-COG-ni-tuh*}

UNFAIR
-unwarranted
-invidious
-discriminatory

UNFAVORABLE
-adverse

UNFEELING
-callous
-indifferent
-changed to me

UNFINISHED
-a work in progress

UNFOLD (AS DEVELOPMENTS UNFOLD)
-unfurl

UNFORGETTABLE
-indelible

UNFORTUNATELY
-sadly

UNFRIENDLY
-less accommodating
-remote
-aloof
-ill-disposed
-offish
-distant
-very cool toward

UNGRATEFUL PERSON
-ingrate

UNGRATEFULNESS
-ingratitude

UNHAPPY
-disgruntled
-disconsolate
-discontented
-displeased

UNHARMED
-unscathed

UNHEALTHY
-baneful
-noxious

UNHURT
-unscathed

UNIMPORTANT
-inconsequential
-immaterial
-negligible
-trifling
-of no consequence

UNIMPORTANT DETAILS
-minutiae

UNIMPORTANT PERSON
-nonentity

UNIMPRESSED
-underwhelmed
-jaded

UNIMPRESSIVE
-unimposing
-tame

UNINSPIRING
-sterile

UNINTENTIONAL
-inadvertent

UNINTERESTING
-of no interest

UNINVITED GUESTS
-unbidden guests {un-BID-nn}

UNIQUE
-stands apart from
-inimitable
-sui generis {Latin, SOO-eye
 JEN-er- us}
-singular

UNITY
-cohesion

UNIVERSE
-cosmos
-world without end

UNKIND
-uncharitable

She had some unkind things to say.

She was uncharitable in her critique.

UNKNOWN
-obscure
-indeterminate
-alien to

UNLESS
-barring any

UNLIKE
-in contrast to
-apart from
-alien to

UNLIMITED
-unbounded
-knows few equals and few bounds
-boundless

"His curiosity is boundless but also disciplined, and he forgoes explanation in favor of a visual version of what anthropologists call thick description." A. O. Scott, *New York Times*, Nov. 4, 2009

UNLIMITED AUTHORITY
-carte blanche {French, *kart blahnsh*}

UNLOVED
-forsaken

UNLUCKY PERSONS
-poor souls

UNNECESSARY
-nonessential
-superfluous

UNNOTICED
-inconspicuous
-unobtrusive

UNOFFICIAL
-de facto

UNORGANIZED
-in disarray

UNORIGINAL
-derivative

UNPLANNED
-impromptu

UNPOPULAR
-generating little enthusiasm

UNPREDICTABLE
-vagrant
-wayward
-quicksilver

UNPREDICTABLE CHANGE
-caprice

UNPREPARED
-ill-prepared

UNPROVEN
-groundless

These accusations are unproven lies.
These accusations are groundless.

UNREALISTIC
-fanciful

UNREASONABLE BEHAVIOR
-perverse behavior

UNRESERVED
-demonstrative

"They have never been a demonstrative family. A hug, a few murmured words, and the business of greeting is done." J.M. Coetzee, *The Lives of Animals*

-effusive

"In bed Soraya is not effusive. Her temperament is in fact rather quiet, quiet and docile." J.M. Coetzee, *Disgrace*

UNRESTRAINED
-abandoned
-wayward
-unstinted
-unsparing
-unbridled
-irrepressible

UNRESTRAINT
-abandon

UNSATISFACTORY
-dissatisfactory

UNSATISFIED
-insatiable

UNSEEN ASSETS
-intangibles

UNSOLVABLE
-insoluble

UNSOPHISTICATED
-homespun
-provincial
-untraveled

UN-SOPHISTICATION
-naiveté

UNSOUND
-fallacious

UNSPOKEN
-tacit
-implicit
-unsounded

UNSTOPPABLE FORCE
-a juggernaut

UNSTOPPING
-inexorable
-relentless

UNSUITABLE AS
-miscast as

UNSURE
-hesitant
-reluctant
-curious

UN-TALKATIVE
-taciturn

UNTHINKING
-in the heat of the moment
-knee-jerk
-impetuous

UNTIL NOW
-heretofore [academic]

UNTIL THEY LET THEIR GUARD DOWN
-till vigilance is laid asleep [Machiavelli]

UNTOUCHED
-pristine

UNTRUE STORY
-of dubious authenticity
-apocryphal
-unfounded
-a canard
-spurious
-fallacious

UNTRUTHFUL
-less than forthcoming
-mendacious [academic]

UNUSED
-to lie fallow

UNUSUAL
-an aberration
-an anomaly
-out of keeping with
-peculiar
-unaccustomed
-unwonted
-unorthodox
-preternatural

UNUSUAL GROUP OF PEOPLE OR ANIMALS
-a menagerie

UNWELCOME PERSON
-she's persona non grata {Latin, *per-SOHN-u non GRAHT-uh*}
-an interloper

UNWISE
-ill-advised
-imprudent
-ill-conceived
-ill-considered
-ill-fated
-impolitic {*im-PAUL-ih-tic*}

UP
-upwards
-skywards
-heavenward

"After pointing heavenward for half a century, the steeple appeared to have swerved suddenly from its purpose, and to invite now the attention of the wayfarer to the bar beneath." E. A. G. Glasgow, *The Miller of Old Church*

UP AGAINST
-faced with

UP AND DOWN THE COAST
-up the coast and down

"They gathered mountains and valleys, rivers and whole horizons, the way a man might now gain title to building lots. These

tough, dried-up men moved restlessly up the coast and down." John Steinbeck, *East of Eden*

UP AND RUNNING
-in full swing

UP CLOSE
-on close examination

UP FOR GRABS
-in the balance

UP HIGH
-on high

UP IN THE AIR
-inconclusive

> The results are still up in the air.
>
> The results are inconclusive.

UP ON YOUR _____
-conversant with
-versed in
-properly schooled in mythology

UP TO DATE
-abreast
-apprised

UP TO YOU
-incumbent upon you
-at your discretion

UP UNTIL (TIL) NOW
-as yet
-thus far
-heretofore

UPFRONT
-forthcoming
-candid
-forthright
-frank
-veracious

UPLIFTED
-buoyed with

UPS AND DOWNS
-vagaries
-vicissitudes

UPSET
-troubled
-unnerved
-dismayed
-distressed
-rankled

UPSETTING
-disconcerting

UPSTART
-a parvenu {French, *PAR-ve-new*}

UPTIGHT
-prudish
-puritanical

URGE (AN URGE)
-an impulse

URGE (TO URGE)
-enjoin
-press

URGENT
-dire
-imperative
-pressing

URGING
-exhortation

USE (TO USE)
-avail oneself of
-draw on existing
-apply
-exploit
-incorporate
-adopt
-deploy
-employ
-put to good use

-draw upon
-make use of

"The sergeant with him was Leonard Borth, an M.P., who was to be in charge of matters of security in Adano: he was to help weed out the bad Italians and make use of the good ones." John Hersey, *A Bell for Adano*

USE OF (TO HAVE USE OF)
-have recourse to

USE UP
-expend
-deplete
-draw down

USED
-employed
-adopted by
-served to
-continued in use
-made full use of
-put to good use
-used to great effect

USED BY
-reserved for

USED BY EVERYONE
-it gained currency in
-it's ubiquitous

USED TO
-accustomed to
-familiar with
-conversant with
-in the practice of

> They are not used to being treated that way.
>
> They are unaccustomed to being treated that way.

USED TO BE
-had been formerly

USED TO SOMETHING UNPLEASANT
-inured

"I've become inured to your hostile attitude."

USED UP
-exhausted

USEFUL
-of use to him
-worthwhile

USELESS
-of no use
-fruitless
-of no avail
-futile
-weary, stale, flat and unprofitable [Shakespeare]

> It's useless to me.
>
> It's of no use to me.

USELESS ACT
-a fool's errand

USELESS POSSESSION
-a white elephant

USES
-makes use of
-involves the use of

USES PROPER SOURCES
-she does not write from hearsay

USING
-making use of it

USING EVERY
-she was bringing out every

USUAL
-customary
-obligatory
-wonted
-conventional
-stock

-standing topics
-accustomed way

USUALLY
-tended to
-more often than not
-customarily
-in practice
-as is the custom
-nearly always

UTILITARIAN
-institutional

"Get some plaster, he said, propped up in the bed, which looked odd and institutional among the Persian rugs and Colonial furniture and dozens of antique clocks." Paul Harding, *Tinkers*

V v

VAGUE
-ill-defined
-nebulous
-amorphous
-imprecise
-indistinct
-allow a wide latitude of interpretation
-murky
-ambiguous
-equivocal (vague by intent)

> Why are you being so vague?
>
> Why are you being so equivocal?

VALUE
-place a high emphasis on
-he reserves his highest esteem for
-hold dear
-treasure
-prize

VALUED
-prized
-highly sought after
-widely accepted
-a darling of
-an object of much attention
-much in demand

VARIABLES
-imponderables

VARIATION OF
-a variant of

VARIED
-sundry
-diverse
-manifold [academic]

VARIOUS
-assorted

VEHICLE
-conveyance

VERBAL ATTACK
-diatribe
-tongue lashing
-verbal drive-by
-polemic

VERIFY
-attest to

VERSATILE
-protean [academic]

VERSION
-adaptation
-rendition
-reimagining

VERY
-you are nothing if not
-terribly
-desperately
-all too
-most
-markedly
-highly

-particularly
-exceptionally
-well
-fiercely
-intensely
-exceedingly
-profoundly
-startlingly
-immensely
-only too
-far and away
-much
-painfully
-fearfully
-more than a bit
-acutely
-heartily
-decisively
-in the worst way
-to a great extent
-ever so
-considerably
-by far
-_____ to an extreme
-clearly
-indeed
-assuredly
-so much

"My Dear Michèle, I would so much like this house to stay empty. I would hope the owners don't come back for a long time." J.M.G. Le Clézio, *The Interrogation*

VERY AGREEABLE
-complaisant
-obliging

VERY BAD
-abject
-egregious
-execrable [academic]

VERY DIFFERENT FROM
-far removed from

VERY ENTHUSIASTIC
-rhapsodic

VERY GOOD AT
-highly accomplished

VERY GOOD FRIENDS
-immense friends

VERY EXACT
-scrupulous
-punctilious
-exacting

VERY EXCITED
-were much excited

VERY HIGH
-rarified

VERY LARGE
-imposing

VERY LITTLE
-scant

VERY MUCH
-in no small measure

VERY SMALL
-minuscule

VERY UNIQUE [INCORRECT USAGE]
-unique

VERY WELL
-if you like
-well enough

VIA
-by means of
-by way of

VIBRATO
-tremolo {*TREM-uh-low*}

VICTIM
-casualty

VIEW
-vista

VIEW
-I look upon

-I looked on the thing as
-my take on

VIEWER
-onlooker
-beholder
-spectator

VIEWS IT AS THE SAME
-does not distinguish between

VIGOR
-brio

VILLAIN
-a heavy

VINEGARY
-acetic {uh-SEE-tic}

VIOLATION
-a breach
-a transgression

VIOLENCE BETWEEN GROUPS
-sectarian violence
-convulsions
-strife

VIOLENT BEHAVIOR
-militancy

VIOLENT LANGUAGE
-martial language

"Like many talk-show hosts, he [Limbaugh] uses martial language to rouse the faithful: 'The enemy camp is the White House right now,' he says. Former Alaska governor turned media star Sarah Palin posted on her Facebook page a list of House Democrats who voted for health-care reform with crosshairs aimed at their home districts, while tweeting to her followers, 'Don't Retreat, Instead—RELOAD!'" Evan Thomas and Eve Conant, "Hate." *Newsweek,* April 19th, 2010

VIP
-above-the-line talent
-A-listers

VIRGIN
-innocent of sex
-virgo intacta {Latin, *VEER-go in-TAHK-tah*}

VIRTUALLY
-it is in effect
-for all intents and purposes

VIRTUALLY DESTROYED
-tattered
-decimated

VISIBLE
-discernible
-manifest

VISIBLY
-markedly
-manifestly

VISIT
-make our visit
-call on

VISITED
-went among
-paid a visit to
-had occasion to visit

"Among the diplomats whom he had occasion to visit was none other than the Secretary of State."

VISITING
-paying her visits

VISUAL
-pictorial

VOCAL
-outspoken
-no shrinking violet

VOICE OUT OF NOWHERE
-disembodied voice

VOLATILE SITUATION
-tinderbox

VOLUNTARILY
-of one's own accord
-presumptuously [pejorative]

VOLUNTEER
-I took it upon myself to

VOTED AGAINST
-voted in dissent

VOUCH FOR (OR CONFIRM)
-attest to
-bear witness to

> I am here to confirm the horrors of that war.
>
> I am here to bear witness to the horrors of that war.

VULGAR
-indelicate
-crass

W w

WAFFLE
-equivocate

"Stop equivocating and answer the question."

-prevaricate

WAGED WAR
-made war upon

"In the year before Christ 1125 Mephres Reigned over the upper Egypt from Syene to Heliopolis, and his Successor Misphragmuthosis made a lasting war upon the Shepherds soon after, and caused many of them to fly into Palestine, Idumæa, Syria, and Libya..." Sir Isaac Newton, *The Chronology of Ancient Kingdoms*

WAIT
-lie in wait

WAIT A MINUTE!
-Now look here!

WAIT PATIENTLY
-bide one's time

WAITED FOR
-wanted

"They awakened when the rushing wind was gone. They lay quietly and listened deep into the stillness. Then the roosters crowed, and their voices were muffled, and the people stirred restlessly in their beds and wanted the morning." John Steinbeck, *The Grapes of Wrath*

-lay in wait

"Even he saw that she was gone, and over the years he had become an expert in the appearance and disappearance of things. But he knew that she would come again, and he lay in wait for her, his cold hand spread over the sheet." Bernice Rubens, *The Elected Member*

WAITED FOR HIM
-awaited him

WAITING FOR
-awaiting

WAIVER
-a dispensation
-a derogation [academic]

WAKE UP
-rouse
-awaken

WALK
-stride
-file into
-amble
-mosey
-saunter
-hoof it

-escort
-accompany

WALK AROUND
-walk about

> He would walk around the room
> with microphone in tow.
>
> He would walk about the room
> with microphone in tow.

WALK CLUMSILY
-lumber over

WANDER
-meander

WANDERING
-itinerant

"Many of this nation's agricultural concerns rely on low-wage itinerant farmhands."

WANT
-favor
-require
-intend for
-covet
-desire
-care to
-wish to
-long for
-have designs on
-long to

WANTED TO
-had hoped to
-felt very much inclined to
-it had been the ambition of ___ to be
-burned to

"He had burned several times to enlist. Tales of great movements shook the land. They might not be distinctly Homeric, but there seemed to be much glory in them. He had read of marches, sieges, conflicts, and he had longed to see it all. His busy mind had drawn for him large pictures extravagant in color, lurid with breathless deeds." Stephen Crane, *The Red Badge of Courage*

-desired to
-longed to be
-cared to
-did so want to
-yearned to

"It was not that I no longer wanted to write, I still yearned passionately to produce the novel which had been for so long captive in my brain." William Styron, *Sophie's Choice*

WANTS ME TO
-wishes me to

WARM WEATHER
-balmy weather

WAR
-disturbance

"Simon would have regarded with impotent fury the disturbance between the North and the South, as it left his descendants stripped of everything but their land, yet the tradition of living on the land remained unbroken until well into the twentieth century, when my father, Atticus Finch, went to Montgomery to read law, and his younger brother went to Boston to study medicine." Nelle Harper Lee, *To Kill a Mockingbird*

WARN
-caution
-foretell
-presage
-foreshadow
-forewarn
-admonish
-raise the specter of
-add a cautionary note
-serve notice
-portend

WARNING
-caveat {CAV-ee-ot}

-cautionary tale
-portent
-omen of grave portent

> And to this discussion let me add an important warning.
>
> And to this discussion let me add an important caveat.

WAS
-it proved
-became subject to
-showed signs of
-struck her as
-constituted [academic]
-was a [poetic]

"The sea was a very blue."

WAS ABOUT
-touched on

"The conversation touched on many things."

WAS BECAUSE OF
-it came of
-was due in large part to

> It was because of her greatness in spirit.
>
> It came of her greatness in spirit.

WAS BORN
-had come into the world

WAS BOTH
-was at once _____ and _____

"Everything about her was at once vigorous and exquisite, at once strong and fine." Edith Wharton, *The House of Mirth*

WAS CRITICIZED
-was the object of his criticism

WAS FOR (WAS FOR TWO WEEKS)
-provided for

"Her itinerary provided for two weeks in Paris, and she had suffered through one week of it when, like an angel from heaven, an Englishman called Tippy Akenside showed up at her hotel at the very moment when she was about to dissolve in tears and book passage home." Jean Stafford, *The Collected Stories of Jean Stafford*

WAS GONE
-gone was

WAS IN EFFECT
-was the order of the day

WAS IT THAT
-did it happen that

"Amid the distractions and frivolities that occupied his life, did it happen that he was suddenly overtaken by one of those mysterious and awful revulsions which, striking to the heart, change the nature of a man who cannot be broken by outward disasters affecting his life and fortune? No one can say. All that is known is that when he returned from Italy he was a priest." Victor Hugo, *Les Miserables*

WAS KILLED
-came to a violent end

WAS LIKE
-was like that of

"And that was the long Salinas Valley. Its history was like that of the rest of the state." John Steinbeck, *East of Eden*

WAS LUCKY ENOUGH TO
-had the good luck to

"About thirty years ago, Miss Maria Ward, of Huntingdon, had the good luck to captivate Sir Thomas Bertram, of Mansfield Park, in the county of Northampton, and to be thereby raised to the rank of baronet's lady, with all the comforts and consequences of a handsome house and large income." Jane Austen, *Mansfield Park*

WAS MADE OF
-was of

WAS NOT
-was not to be _____
-was nothing of the kind

"In Jenny's opinion, her breasts were too large; she thought the ostentation of her bust made her look 'cheap and easy.' She was nothing of the kind. In fact, she had dropped out of college when she suspected that the chief purpose of her parents' sending her to Wellesley had been to have her dated by and eventually mated to some well-bred man." John Irving, *The World According to Garp*

WAS NOT A GOOD THING
-this was not so good a thing

WAS NOT AFRAID
-was in no fear
-felt little trepidation
-feared not [poetic]

WAS NOT ONE OF
-could not be counted among

WAS OUR
-formed our

"Within the fence, protected from the apes, grew a patch of wild bitter lettuce. This lettuce, with fish and birds' eggs, formed our sole diet on the island, as you shall hear." J. M. Coetzee, *Foe*

WAS OVER
-was ended

"...and the warm heavy smell of turkey and ham and celery rose from the plates and dishes and the great fire was banked high and red in the grate and the green ivy and red holly made you feel so happy and when dinner was ended the big plum pudding would be carried in, studded with peeled almonds and sprigs of holly, with bluish fire running around it and a little green flag flying from the top." James Joyce, *Portrait of an Artist as a Young Man*

WAS PROOF OF
-attested

"The initialism SPQR attested her allegiance to Rome."

WAS THAT
-being that

WAS THERE
-was on hand

WAS WAITING
-awaited them

"One behind the other they passed through the door, crossed a vestibule, climbed two flights of stairs, walked along a corridor, and emerged in the chamber where the secretary-general awaited them." Claude Simon, *The Invitation*

WASHED ASHORE
-borne ashore

"Off the island grew beds of brown seaweed which, borne ashore by the waves, gave off a noisome stench and supported swarms of large pale fleas." J.M. Coetzee, *Foe*

WASTE
-squander
-fritter away

WASTE AWAY
-atrophy

WASTE OF TIME
-a boondoggle

WASTE TIME
-lollygag
-trespass on your time

WASTEFUL PEOPLE
-profligates

WASTEFULLY EXTRAVAGANT
-profligate
-prodigal

WATCH
-survey
-study

"When the weather was good, my room-mate and I might sit out on the fire escape to smoke cigarettes and study the dusk wash-ing blue over the city…" Barack Obama, *Dreams from My Father*

WATCH OVER
-superintend
-keep vigil over

WATCHED
-looked on
-beheld them from afar
-kept his eyes compulsively fixed on her

WATCHING
-keeping a watch on

WATCHWORD
-mantra

WAVE
-a swell
-an undulation

WAVE A KNIFE
-brandish a knife

WAY
-means by which
-a manner
-a mechanism for
-process by which
-means whereby
-mode of operation
-course

"It is not because the truth is too difficult to see that we make mistakes…we make mis-takes because the easiest and most comfort-able course for us is to seek insight where it accords with our emotions—especially self-ish ones." Alexander Solzhenitsyn

WAY (DEMEANOR)
-his manner
-a way about her
-a presence
-an air

WAY OF DEALING WITH
-an approach

WAY OF DOING SOMETHING
-it was her practice to
-it was his convention to
-modus operandi {Latin, *MOE-dus o-per-AND-ee*}

> The killer's way of doing it never changes.
>
> The killer's modus operandi never changes.

WAY OF LIFE
-modus vivendi {Latin, *MOE-dus vi-VEN-dee*}

WAY OF SEEING THINGS
-perspective
-mindset
-predilection
-slant
-proclivity

WAY OF THINKING
-turn of mind

"Get the jury to empathize with the defen-dant's particular turn of mind, and we will win this trial."

-currents of thought
-particular school of interpretation
-orthodoxy
-doctrine

WAY TO GO
-weren't you good to think of it

"Weren't you good to think of going!" Ernest Hemingway, *A Moveable Feast*

WAY TOO
-much too

WAYS
-traditions
-ideals
-respects

WE ARE HERE AT
-we're coming to you from

WE ARE JUDGES
-judges that we are

____ WE CAN DO
-____ is in our power

"Kindness is in our power, even when fondness is not." Samuel Johnson

WE CANNOT
-school policy prohibits us from
-current conditions do not warrant

WE DON'T KNOW THAT YET
-that remains to be seen

WE HAD AGREED TO
-it had been agreed between us

WE HAD NOT BEEN IN THE NEIGHBORHOOD FOR LONG
-we had not been a great while in the
 neighborhood

WE HAVE BEGUN TO QUESTION
-we have come to question

"We have come to question the tenets on which that philosophy is based."

WE KNOW SO LITTLE
-so little is known

WE THINK
-it is believed that

"No matter what its name or provenance, it is believed that the arrival of the Europeans on Hispaniola unleashed the fukú on the world, and we've all been in the shit ever since." Junot Diaz, *The Brief Wondrous Life of Oscar Wao*

WE WERE ____
-____ as we were

WEAK
-tenuous
-precarious
-feckless
-inert
-sagging
-lagging
-lackluster
-a bit groggy at the knees
-given the sorry nature of
-qualities in which you are deficient

WEAKENED
-compromised
-undermined
-enervated [academic]
-enfeebled
-abated
-debilitated
-attenuated
-waned
-dwindled

WEAKNESS
-shortcoming
-failing
-defect
-foible
-drawback
-infirmity
-deficiency

WEALTH
-means

WEALTHY
-of considerable means
-moneyed
-well heeled

WEARING
-sporting
-clad in

WEAVE
-plait {plate}

WEIGHT OF
-heavy freight of

"*Every facial twitch had its own score. Every smile ate up two and a half pages of sheet music. Every little thing walked around with this heavy freight of meaning.*" Colson Whitehead, *Apex Hides the Hurt*

WELCOME!
-it's an honor and a pleasure
-delighted to make your acquaintance
-I am pleased to welcome you

WELCOMED (WAS WELCOMED)
-was initially greeted with
-was received warmly

WELFARE
-your livelihood
-your lot

WELL
-suitably

"*He was suitably attired for the occasion.*"

WELL CHOSEN FOR THE OCCASION
-felicitous

"*The awkward moment threatened to derail the talks, when out of nowhere came a felicitous remark to save the day.*"

WELL DONE
-kudos {Greek, *KOO-doze*, lit. praise}

"*Kudos to you for ruining Christmas.*" [sarcastic]

WELL EDUCATED
-well read
-erudite
-learned

WELL FURNISHED
-well appointed

WELL-INFORMED PEOPLE (CULTURALLY)
-the cognoscenti {Italian, con-ya-SHEN-tee}

"*The art exhibit attracted everyone from the cognoscenti to the just plain curious.*"

WELL INTENTIONED
-well disposed

"*He was fortunate to work for a company so well disposed to the needs and ambitions of its employees.*"

WELL KEPT
-in good repair

WELL KNOWN
-widely circulated
-of wide repute

> That rumor has been going around for months.
>
> That rumor has been widely circulated for months.

WELL LIKED
-well thought of
-held in high regard

WELL QUALIFIED
-well credentialed

> He's comes very qualified.
>
> He comes well credentialed.

WELL TIMED
-opportune

WENT
-made her way to
-pushed as far as
-went forth [poetic]
-extended far beyond
-repaired

"*We repaired to a crappy bar for a round of kamikazes and a good cry. For several hours we swam in a pool of sad stories from our childhoods."* Nancy Balbirer, "Friendly Fire"

WENT ABOUT THEIR BUSINESS
-busied themselves

"No one would have believed in the last years of the nineteenth century that this world was being watched keenly and closely by intelligences greater than man's and yet as mortal as his own; that as men busied themselves about their various concerns they were scrutinized and studied, perhaps almost as narrowly as a man with a microscope might scrutinize the transient creatures that swarm and multiply in a drop of water." H. G. Wells, *The War of the Worlds*

WENT AROUND IT
-circumvented

WENT AWAY
-dispersed

WENT UP TO
-drew near

WENT WITH
-attended
-accompanied

WENT WRONG
-have gone seriously awry

WERE
-showed themselves to be

WE'RE TALKING ABOUT
-the one in question

WHAT _____ ARE MADE OF
-of what _____ are made

"And now, my boys and girls, I must first tell you of what candles are made." Michael Faraday, *The Chemical History of a Candle*

WHAT ABOUT
-what is there to say about

-what of

"But what of those who travel alone? Why should Vinnie Miner, whose comfort has been disregarded by others by most of her adult life, disregard her own comfort?" Alison Lurie, *Foreign Affairs*

WHAT AM I SUPPOSED TO DO?
-what would you have me do?

WHAT DID HE DIE OF?
-of what did he die?

WHAT DO I HAVE TO DO WITH THAT
-what have I to do with that

WHAT DO YOU CARE?
-what is that to you?

WHAT DO YOU HAVE TO
-what have you to

"'What have you to justify your identity?' asked the man with the carbine." Ernest Hemingway, *For Whom the Bell Tolls*

WHAT DO YOU EXPECT WITH
-what can you expect with

WHAT DO YOU THINK ABOUT
-what have you to say for
-what do you make of
-to your thinking

WHAT DOES IT HAVE TO DO WITH
-what has it to do with
-of what consequence is it

WHAT DOES IT MATTER
-of what matter is it

WHAT DOES THAT HAVE TO DO WITH ANYTHING
-that is apropos of nothing

WHAT FRUSTRATES ME MOST IS
-the thing that gives me most frustration is

"We tend to disagree on other matters too, but the thing that gives me most frustration is trying to make her understand why I like country music." James Alan MacPherson, *Elbow Room*

WHAT HAPPENED TO
-what became of

"I had two elder brothers, one of whom was lieutenant-colonel to an English regiment of foot in Flanders, formerly commanded by the famous Colonel Lockhart, and was killed at the battle near Dunkirk against the Spaniards. What became of my second brother I never knew, any more than my father or mother knew what became of me." Daniel Defoe, *Robinson Crusoe*

WHAT HE DOES AS A RULE
-he is quick to
-that's his calling card
-he is given to

"He is given to ostentatious words and long winded speeches."

WHAT HE DOES FOR A LIVING
-by occupation he is
-by profession he is

"By profession he is, or has been, a scholar, and scholarship still engages, intermittently, the core of him." J.M. Coetzee, *Disgrace*

WHAT HE LIKES
-he is taken to

"He is taken to old things like rare books and vintage hunting rifles."

WHAT HE SAID
-his words

"He was dismayed at the president's words."

WHAT HE WILL THINK
-how he will view the matter

WHAT I MEAN IS
-what I mean to say is

WHAT I SAID
-my mention of

WHAT IS
-that which is

WHAT IS GOING ON (THIS IS WHAT IS GOING ON)
-this is how the matter stands

WHAT IS HIS NAME
-what is he called [poetic]

WHAT IT WAS LIKE
-how it was to

"We asked him how it was to live under Communism, and he said that it was terrible at first, because everybody had to work so hard, and because there wasn't much shelter or food or clothing." Kurt Vonnegut, *Slaughterhouse-Five*

WHAT IT'S LIKE TO
-I know what it is to

WHAT KIND OF
-what manner of

WHAT LITTLE THERE IS
-such as it is

"Only her compassion and mercy—such as it is—can save you now."

WHAT SHOULD I DO
-what's to be done
-what am I to do

WHAT SHOULD OUR
-what is to be our

WHAT SOMEONE DOES
-her _____ manner never abandons her
-he's given to
-her penchant for
-she's a practitioner of

WHAT THEY WERE DOING
-the goings on of
-the doings of

"She took little interest in the doings of the glitterati."

WHAT WE ARE ABOUT TO SEE
-what we are about to receive

"The disembodied voice, sounding like God with a hangover, lets us know in detail what we are about to receive. 'Ladies and gentlemen,' the voice rumbles by way of a preshow announcement for Richard Forman's 'Idiot Savant,' a play that is some kind of wonderful. 'In the course of this evening the following objects will appear onstage.'" Ben Brantley, New York Times, Nov. 5, 2009

WHAT WE'RE IN FOR
-what lay before us

WHAT WERE YOU THINKING
-what possessed you to

WHAT WILL HAPPEN TO
-what will become of

WHAT WILL ____ DO FOR YOU
-where will ____lead you

WHAT WOULD YOU LIKE ME TO
-what would you have me

WHAT YOU SHOULD DO
-what is expected of you

WHATEVER
-very well
-so be it

WHATEVER THE
-whatever were the

WHATEVER YOU WANT
-do what you will

> Whatever you want to call them is fine.
>
> Call them what you will.

WHAT'S YOUR NAME?
-How are you called? [poetic]

"'How are you called? I have forgotten.' It was a bad sign to him that he had forgotten. 'Anselmo,' the old man said. 'I am called Anselmo and I come from Barco de Avila...'" Ernest Hemingway, For Whom the Bell Tolls

WHEN ALL IS SAID AND DONE
-in the final analysis

WHEN HE HAD NO EXAMPLES, HE WOULD
-in default of examples he would

"In default of examples he would invent parables." Victor Hugo, Les Miserables

WHEN HE SEES
-when his eyes fall on

"Then one Saturday morning everything changes. He is in the city on business; he is walking down St. George's Street when his eyes fall on a slim figure ahead of him in the crowd." J.M. Coetzee, Disgrace

WHEN I CAME DOWN FOR THE WINTER
-on my coming down for the winter

WHEN I HEARD THAT
-on hearing that

WHEN I HEARD THE CRY
-when the cry went up

"As chaplain, I had no orders, and so placed myself where I believed I could do most good. I was in the rear, praying with the wounded, when the cry went up: Great God, they are upon us!" Geraldine Brooks, March

WHEN I WAS
-some years ago, as a

WHEN IT'S TIME TO LEAVE
-when the time has come to leave

WHEN LEAVING
-on going away

WHEN SHE AWOKE
-on waking in the morning

WHEN SHE DID THIS
-at this

WHEN THE VISIT WAS OVER
-when the visit was ended

WHEN USED
-when applied

WHEN YOU GET A CHANCE
-at your earliest convenience

WHEN YOU GET BACK FROM
-on your return from

WHENEVER HE WANTED TO
-with impunity
-at will
-as the mood struck him

WHERE
-in which
-wherein
-by which

WHERE ARE YOU GOING?
-Where are you off to?

WHERE SHE WAS
-her whereabouts

WHERE THERE ARE SIGNS OF
-where _____ are in evidence

WHERE THERE WASN'T ONE BEFORE
-where there was none before

WHERE YOU DON'T BELONG
-out of your element

WHEREVER I LOOKED
-wherever I turned my view

WHETHER HE MEANT TO OR NOT
-deliberately or otherwise

> I don't care if you meant to or not.
>
> I don't care if it was deliberate or otherwise.

WHETHER IT'S TRUE OR FALSE
-be it true or false
-whether it be true or false

"What is reported of men, whether it be true or false, may play as large a part in their lives, and above all in their destiny, as the things they do." Victor Hugo, *Les Miserables*

WHETHER THEY ARE
-be they

WHICH
-from which
-to which he had been

WHICH ARE
-as may be

"Whatever may be the result of this mission, I trust that nothing will have been omitted on my part to conduct the negotiation to a successful conclusion, on such equitable terms as may be compatible with the safety, honor and interest of the United States." John Adams, *State of the Union Address*, 1797

WHICH ARE NOT
-none of which are

WHICH IS WHAT WE DID
-all of which we did

WHICH SOME CALL_____
-which by some is called_____

"...there lies a small market town or rural port, which by some is called Greensburgh, but which is more generally and properly

known by the name of Tarry Town."
Washington Irving, *The Legend of Sleepy Hollow*

WHICH WOULD MEAN
-in which case

WHILE
-for some time
-for a spell

WHILE EVERYONE IN THE HOUSE WAS SLEEPING
-while the house slept

WHILE ON THE CONTRARY
-whereas

WHIM
-a velleity {*vuh-LEE-uh-tee*}

WHINE
-lament

WHINING SPEECH
-diatribe
-jeremiad

WHISPER
-a murmur
-in an undertone
-a veiled voice
-in an aside
-a muttering

WHITE WINE
-a white

WHO
-who among us
-for whom

WHO IS A
-who serves as

WHO WAS HIS
-in his

"The late owner of this estate was a single man, who lived to a very advanced age, and who for many years of his life, had a constant companion and housekeeper in his sister." Jane Austen, *Sense and Sensibility*

WHOEVER
-whosoever

WHOLE NINE YARDS
-the alpha and omega of

WHY?
-Where's the sense of it?
-Why so?
-Why then?
-To what purpose?

WHY ARE YOU DIFFERENT WITH ME?
-Why are you so changed to me?

WHY IS IT THAT
-how is it that

"How is it that Americans, so solicitous of the animals they keep as pets, are so indifferent to the ones they cook for dinner? The answer cannot lie in the beasts themselves. Pigs, after all, are quite companionable, and dogs are said to be delicious." Elizabeth Kolbert, *The New Yorker*, Nov. 9, 2009

WHY IS THIS
-why should this be

WHY SHOULD I CARE IF
-what do I care if

WIDE-RANGING
-eclectic

WIDESPREAD
-pervasive
-systemic
-far-reaching

WIDTH
-breadth

WILL (I WILL)
-intend
-shall
-will be compelled to

-mean to
-will not hesitate to
-am to
-will think fit to
-will resolve to
-I have a mind to

WILL (MY WILL)
-volition
-strength of will
-discretion
-inclination

WILL BE
-is likely to be
-is to be

WILL BE ENOUGH
-will suffice

WILL BE THERE
-are to be there

WILL BE THREE IN JUNE
-will turn three in June

WILL CONTINUE
-will persist

WILL HAVE
-shall have

WILL WORK (IT WILL WORK)
-it will do

WILL YOU
-will you not

WILLED BY GOD
-willed on high

WILLING
-inclined to
-disposed to

WILLINGNESS
-alacrity

WILLPOWER
-resolve
-with singular force of will

WIN
-carry the day
-gain a decisive victory
-prevail

WIN AWARDS
-garner praise

WIN OVER
-co-opt

WINDING
-sinuous {SIN-you-us}
-serpentine {SUR-pen-teen}

WINE
-vintage

WINE STEWARD
-sommelier {French, sum-all-YAY}

WINNER
-victor

"In my soul rages a battle without victor. Between faith without proof and reason without charm." Sully Prudhomme

WIPE IT OUT
-eradicate

WISE
-prudent
-judicious
-astute

WISE AND PITHY
-gnomic {NO-mik}

WISE PERSON
-a sage

WITCH DOCTOR
-conjure doctor

"Their preachers and conjure doctors have always known many things besides how to save men's lives and souls." Julia Peterkin, *Scarlet Sister Mary*

WITCHCRAFT
-diablerie {French, dee-AH-blu-ree}

WITH
-among
-attended
-in possession of

"It is a truth universally acknowledged, that a single man in possession of a good fortune, must be in want of a wife." Jane Austen, *Pride and Prejudice*

-accompanied by
-in league with
-of

"We were sitting in the blind that Wanderobo hunters had built of twigs and branches at the edge of the salt-lick when we heard the truck coming." Ernest Hemingway, *The Green Hills of Africa*

-with that of
-in the company of
-in tow
-in concert with
-by

"They were gentlemen-magicians, which is to say they had never harmed any one by magic—nor done any one the slightest good." Susanna Clarke, *Jonathan Strange and Mr. Norrell*

WITH A LITTLE _____
-tinged with _____

WITH ALL THE POMP AND CIRCUMSTANCE OF
-with all the parade of
-with all the ceremony of

WITH BAITED BREATH
-everyone waited expectant

> Everyone waited with baited breath.
>
> Everyone waited expectant.

WITH CONTEXT
-with thick description

WITH FEELING
-poignant

WITH GRAVY
-au jus {French, *oh*-ZHOOS, lit. with juice}

WITH MY EYES CLOSED
-in my dark

"I let the mop push me back to the wall and smile and try to foul her equipment up as much as possible by not letting her see my eyes—they can't tell so much about you if you got your eyes closed. In my dark I hear her rubber heels hit the tile and the stuff in her wicker bag clash with the jar of her walking as she passes me in the hall." Ken Kesey, *One Flew Over the Cuckoo's Nest*

WITH THAT GOAL IN MIND
-to that end

WITH THE HELP OF
-by means of
-under the auspices of

WITH THE WORDS
-emblazoned with the words

WITH THEM
-in their company

"...you get some who blow kisses or try to get hold of your arm, but then they are definitely knocking at the wrong door. I get off my bicycle and refuse to go further in their company, or I pretend to be insulted and tell them in no uncertain terms to clear off." Anne Frank, *Anne Frank: The Diary of a Young Girl*

WITH THIS IN MIND
-against this background
-in this light

WITH THIS LETTER
-herewith

WITH YOUR PERMISSION
-by your leave [humorous]

WITHDRAW
-disengage

WITHIN
-in the midst of
-inherent

WITHIN REACH
-near at hand

WITHIN THE COUNTRY
-on its soil

WITHOUT
-empty of

"Baba never found out about Mama's illness; she only fell ill when he was away on business. It was as if, when the world was empty of him, she and I remained as stupid reminders, empty pages that had to be filled with the memory of how they had come to be married." Hisham Matar, In the Country of Men

-in default of
-sans _____
-devoid of
-independent of
-without the least trace of
-destitute of

"Destitute of beauty but not without use, the scaly ant-eater is frequently seen; but the most common of all the beasts is an odious species of large lizard, nearly three feet long, which resembles a flabby-skinned crocodile and feeds on carrion." Winston Churchill, *The Story of The Malakand Field Force*

WITHOUT A PROBLEM
-without issue

WITHOUT ANY HELP FROM
-without the patronage of

WITHOUT BEING THERE
-in absentia {Latin, *in ab-SENT-shee-uh*}

WITHOUT EFFORT OR THOUGHT
-perfunctory

WITHOUT EVEN THINKING ABOUT IT
-out of hand
-arbitrarily
-indiscriminately
-with indifference to
-in a perfunctory manner

WITHOUT GETTING INTO QUESTIONS WHICH
-without entering into questions which

WITHOUT HURTING HIMSELF
-without disaster to himself and others

WITHOUT MAKING THEM SUSPICIOUS
-without arousing suspicion

Don't make them suspicious.

Do not arouse suspicion.

WITHOUT PENALTY
-with impunity

WITHOUT RESENTMENT
-ungrudging

WITHOUT SIN
-in a state of grace

WITHOUT SOUNDING
-without casting yourself as

WITHOUT THE
-unadorned by the

WITHOUT THE LEAST BIT OF
-without the least trace of

WITS
-in matters of the mind [Homer]

WITTY REMARK
-retort
-sally
-jeu d'esprit {French, *zhu de SPREE*}
-repartee {French, *reh-par-TAY*}

WITTY SAYING
-witticism
-aphorism

"If you are your own worst enemy; don't do yourself any favors."

WIZ KID
-wunderkind {German, *voon-der-kind,* kind as in wind}

WOKE UP TO
-awoke to

WOMAN-HATING
-misogynistic

WOMEN'S FASHIONS
-couture {French, *koo-TOUR*}

WON AWARDS
-garnered praise

WON THE
-netted the

WONDERED
-mused

WONDERING
-I was curious

WON'T TAKE NO FOR AN ANSWER
-she's pretty emphatic

WORD FOR WORD
-ipsissima verba {Latin, *ip-SIS-imuh VER-buh*} [academic]

WORD MOST APPROPRIATE (THE PERFECT WORD)
-mot juste {French, *moe ZHOOST*}

WORDED AS
-couched in the rhetoric of

WORDY
-garrulous {*GAIR-uh-lus*}
-windy
-loquacious
-turgid
-prolix [academic]

WORK FOR
-am accountable to
-work under the patronage of
-in the service of

"He does not impress me as he does the others, but I like to be in the service of a master who is so impressive. I will not deny that he is a great man; but nobody is great to his dwarf. I follow him constantly, like a shadow." Pär Lagerkvist, *The Dwarf*

WORK HARD
-work tirelessly
-he will make his name by his industry

WORK OF ART
-a confection

"It was a confection of light and shadow like no other."

WORK OUT
-hammer out

WORK TO
-undertake
-endeavor to
-labor to
-toil

WORK TOGETHER
-collaborate

WORKED FOR
-took employment under

WORKED FOR ME
-was in my employ

WORKERS
-the rank and file

WORKING
-laboring

WORKING ON IT
-working to address it

WORKING WITH
-in concert with

WORKMANLIKE
-yeoman

"The book is a yeoman work of historical fiction, with fact grinding against historical fact. It is also a monotonous piece of storytelling, one that has little pliancy or narrative push. Its 681 pages of text are at times as grueling as a forced march across the Mongolian steppe." Dwight Garner, *New York Times*, Nov. 3, 2009

WORKS
-lends itself to

WORKS AGAINST
-undermines the credibility of

WORKS AT
-earns his living at

"About his own job he says little, not wanting to bore her. He earns his living at the Cape Technical University, formerly Cape Town University College." J.M. Coetzee, *Disgrace*

WORLD
-realm
-landscape of

WORLDLY
-secular
-temporal
-terrestrial

WORM YOUR WAY IN
-insinuate yourself into
-ingratiate yourself

WORN OUT
-haggard

WORRIED
-raised concern among
-expressed concern
-was especially concerned that
-had a foreboding that

WORRY
-angst
-apprehension
-disquiet

WORSE THAN
-are more to be feared than

WORSHIP
-deify
-idealize
-lionize

WORST
-scaliest

WORST THING FOR
-the bane of

WORTH
-merits
-well worth

WORTHY
-there is nothing beneath you in it

WOULD BE GOOD FOR YOU
-would do you good
-you could stand to benefit

WOULD HAVE BEEN
-was to be

WOULD HAVE MY
-took my

"My name, in those days, was Susan Trinder. People called me Sue. I know the

year I was born in, but for many years I did not know the date, and took my birthday at Christmas." Sarah Waters, *Fingersmith*

WOULD NOT
-he declined to

> He would not answer any more questions.
>
> He declined to answer any further questions.

WOULD RATHER NOT
-I had rather not

WOULD YOU LIKE SOME
-shall I bring

WOUNDING
-bloodying

WRAPPED IN
-swathed in

WRITE
-commit something to paper
-produce

"It was only that, having written down the first few fine paragraphs, I could not produce any others—or, to approximate Gertrude Stein's remark about a lesser writer of The Lost Generation—I had the syrup but it wouldn't pour." William Styron, *Sophie's Choice*

-take it down
-draft
-set down

"The final reason for setting down this story is that I want my child's life to be of use in her generation. She is one who has never grown mentally beyond her early childhood, therefore she is forever a child, although in years she is old enough now to have been married and to have children of her own—my grandchildren who will

never be." Pearl S. Buck, *The Child Who Never Grew*

WRITE AT THE TOP OF THE PAGE
-superscribe

WRITE LETTERS
-dash off letters

WRITING
-the author's hand

"But Douglas, without heeding me, had begun to read with a fine clearness that was like a rendering to the ear of the beauty of his author's hand." Henry James, *The Turn of the Screw*

WRITINGS
-inscriptions
-narrative
-prose

WRITTEN
-put to paper
-commited to paper
-emblazoned on
-composed

WRITTEN IN
-enshrined in

WRONG (IMMORAL)
-unconscionable

WRONG (INCORRECT)
-that's faulty reasoning
-it flies in the face of reality
-it is founded on a misconception

"You must follow me carefully. I shall have to controvert one or two ideas that are almost universally accepted. The geometry, for instance, they taught you in school is founded on a misconception." H. G. Wells, *The Time Machine*

WRONG (MISGUIDED)
-under the illusion that
-he's got a wrong notion about
-is aberrant

WRONG (SOMETHING'S WRONG)
-is askew
-is awry

WRONG NAME FOR SOMETHING
-misnomer

WRONG OPINION
-misconception

WRONG WORD (A WORD USED MISTAKENLY)
-malapropism {MAL-ih-proh-pih-sum}

WRONGDOING
-malfeasance

WRONGED (THE WRONGED)
-the aggrieved
-they that you've acted wrongly by

WRONGHEADED
-ill-advised
-ill-conceived

WROTE
-took it down

WROTE GOOD THINGS ABOUT
-made favorable mention of
-wrote highly of

I said good things about her in my report.

I made favorable mention of her in my report.

Xx Yy Zz

YEAR IN AND YEAR OUT
-unfailingly

YEAR OF TRAVELING
-my wanderjahr {German, VOHN-der-yar}

YEARS
-generations

YEARS AGO
-in former days

"...there lies a small market town or rural port, which by some is called Greensburgh, but which is more generally and properly known by the name of Tarry Town. This name was given, we are told, in former days, by the good housewives of the adjacent country, from the inveterate propensity of their husbands to linger about the village tavern on market days." Washington Irving, *The Legend of Sleepy Hollow*

YEARS OLD
-a man of seventy five
-_____ years of age

"The stranger's eyes were green, his hair burnt to a straw colour. I judged he was sixty years of age." J.M. Coetzee, *Foe*

YEARS SINCE
-many years removed from
-since many years I have

YELL AT
-chastise
-scathe
-voice disdain

YELLED OUT
-bellowed

YELLOW
-primrose
-saffron
-flaxen

YELLOWISH COMPLEXION
-sallow
-jaundice

YES
-precisely
-so it seems
-to be sure
-no doubt

-it would seem so
-most assuredly
-without reservations
-such is the case

YES IT IS
-so it is
-it is so

YESTERDAY
-it's only a day since

YET
-yet to be
-at last
-as yet

"Sayward awoke this day with the feeling that something had happened to her. What it was, she didn't know as yet, or if it was for better or for worse, but inside of her a change had taken place." Conrad Richter, *The Town*

YOU ARE ALL STUPID FOR
-how stupid you all are for

YOU ARE HANGING OUT WITH
-you've taken up with

YOU CAN GET IT
-it can be had

YOU CAN'T HAVE ANY
-you are not to have any

YOU CAN'T WIN THEM ALL
-even Homer nods

YOU COULD SAY THAT
-it would be true to say
-it may be imagined

YOU DID THIS
-this is your doing

YOU DON'T CARE
-it's of no consequence to you

YOU DON'T KNOW ANYTHING ABOUT
-you know nothing of

YOU DON'T SEEM TO GET
-the point, which seems to elude you

YOU HAVE PLANNED NOTHING
-nothing have you planned

YOU HAVE TO ADMIT
-you must admit

YOU HAVE THE ABILITY TO
-you have the capacity for

YOU INSULT ME
-you pay me a great insult [humorous]

YOU SHOULD
-I would advise you to

YOU SHOULD KNOW
-mind you
-it is only fair to say that
-I must tell you
-it's worth noting, if only to
 demonstrate

YOU SHOULD NOT BE SURPRISED IF
-it should come as no surprise that

YOU SHOULD NOT THINK, HOWEVER, THAT
-it must not be thought, however, that

YOU WERE WRONG
-you acted wrongly

YOU WON'T HAVE TO WORRY ABOUT ANYTHING
-it will be no trouble to you

YOU WOULD LOVE THIS IF YOU WERE STILL ALIVE
-_____, shouldst thou be living at
 this hour

YOU WOULD THINK
-one would think

YOU'LL BE SORRY IF YOU DON'T
-it'll be the worse for you if you don't

YOUNGER
-_____ years his junior

YOUR
-one's
-a woman's
-a man's

"It was a rasping nervous wind, and the dust particles cut into a man's skin and burned his eyes." John Steinbeck, *East of Eden*

YOUR FAULT
-a predicament of your own making

YOUR OWN LITTLE WORLD
-in a world of your invention
-a world of your own making

YOUR RESPONSIBILITY TO
-it's incumbent upon you to

YOU'RE TALKING ABOUT
-the one in question

YOU'RE WELCOME
-think nothing of it

YOUTH
-my salad days
-at a tender age

ZERO IN ON
-train your sights on

200 Well-Spoken Alternatives to Common Words and Phrases

1. **it seems**
   -it strikes me as

2. **talking about**
   -talking of

3. **walking around**
   -walking about

4. **absolutely**
   -without question

5. **a lot**
   -a great deal

6. **a little**
   -to some extent

7. **blame**
   -find fault

8. **I like**
   -I favor

9. **admittedly**
   -albeit

10. **advice**
    -counsel

11. **on**
    -upon

12. **anyhow**
    -be that as it may

13. **fake**
    -faux

14. **it reminds me of**
    -it recalls

15. **an amount of**
    -a measure of

16. **She lied.**
    -She was less than forthcoming.

17. **I don't see a difference between**
    -I draw no distinction between

18. **uncertain**
    -precarious

19. we are affected by
-we are subjected to

20. I'm afraid that
-I fear that

21. right after
-in the wake of

22. they have an effect on
-they inform

23. now that I think about it
-in retrospect

24. it goes with
-it's in keeping with

25. they are still
-they remain

26. all kinds of
-all manner of

27. in nobody's debt
-beholden to no one

28. are good for
-lend themselves to

29. it comes from
-it stems from

30. it doesn't matter
-it's of little consequence

31. are proof of
-they attest to the

32. look like
-bear a resemblance to

33. just as good as
-comparable to

34. asked to do
-called upon to do

35. asking for trouble
-courting disaster

36. at risk
-at hazard

37. I don't claim to
-I make no pretenses

38. They don't like her.
-They hold her in very low regard.

39. makes him mad
-displeases him

40. filled with
-laden with

41. soon to arrive
-forthcoming

42. I'm aware of
-I'm mindful of

43. bad
-perverse

44. It ended dramatically.
-It ended in dramatic fashion.

45. bare
-spartan

46. **I'm offended by**
    -I take exception to

47. **get a grip on yourself**
    -steel yourself

48. **because of**
    -in light of

49. **I'm not likely to**
    -I'm less inclined to

50. **become a victim**
    -fall victim to

51. **the previously mentioned**
    -the aforementioned

52. **heard it through the grapevine**
    -have it on good authority

53. **without my knowledge**
    -unbeknownst to me

54. **kind of mean way to put it**
    -rather uncharitable

55. **a black sheep**
    -a pariah

56. **bossy**
    -imperious

57. **run into**
    -chance upon

58. **you came here willingly**
    -you came of your own accord

59. **keep it away**
    -keep it at bay

60. **believable**
    -plausible

61. **believe**
    -embrace

62. **keep from us**
    -deprive us of

63. **It's on the tip of my tongue.**
    -The word escapes me.

64. **I can't find them.**
    -They are nowhere to be found.

65. **I can't see her.**
    -I've lost sight of her.

66. **can't stand it**
    -can't bear it

67. **we really care about**
    -we give great importance to

68. **I'll let her know you called.**
    -I'll leave word.

69. **what's more,**
    -moreover,

70. **on purpose**
    -by design

71. **not used to**
    -unaccustomed to

72. **on the condition that**
    -with the proviso that

73. **She came across very well.**
    -She acquitted herself well.

74. are confirmed by
-are borne out by

75. not required to
-not obliged to

76. the current
-the prevailing

77. the opposite view
-the countervailing view

78. don't look at it
-avert your eyes

79. wrong-headed
-ill-conceived

80. started crying
-fell to tears

81. swear words
-colorful language

82. an excuse
-a pretext

83. I decided not to do that
-I thought better of it

84. put your two cents in
-weigh in

85. how much
-the extent to which

86. I'm not here to defend
-I'm no apologist for

87. I've wanted that for a while.
-I've had designs on that for a while.

88. He never told us that.
-He made no mention of that.

89. I don't know
-I cannot say

90. I don't like doing this
-I take no pleasure in it

91. I do not understand
-the point escapes me

92. do without
-forego

93. broken down
-in disrepair

94. is down to earth
-has few pretentions

95. has ill-feelings for
-harbors ill-feelings for

96. the ignorant
-the benighted

97. Who knows?
-It remains to be seen.

98. involve yourself in
-indulge in

99. envy
-begrudge

100. **even so**
-be that as it may

101. **exaggerate**
-embellish

102. **except for**
-apart from

103. **a huge amount of time**
-an inordinate amount of time

104. **expose**
-lay bare

105. **get to know**
-acquaint yourself with

106. **fancy**
-extravagant

107. **feel it the worst**
-bear the brunt of

108. **force myself to**
-bring myself to

109. **for no reason**
-without cause

110. **for practical purposes**
-for all intents and purposes

111. **former friend**
-erstwhile friend

112. **forget about it**
-think no more of it

113. **we found**
-we came upon

114. **freak out**
-come unglued

115. **free from**
-independent of

116. **get ready**
-ready yourself

117. **give it up for good**
-foreswear it

118. **go there**
-frequent

119. **goes beyond**
-transcends

120. **get back up**
-right yourself

121. **got closer**
-drew near

122. **tons of**
-legions of

123. **it hurts to**
-it pains me to

124. **has a habit of**
-is given to

125. **has gained acceptance**
-has gained currency

126. **hardly any**
-none to speak of

127. **we said hello**
-we exchanged pleasantries

128. How do you mean?
-In what respect?

129. I might even
-I have a mind to

130. I admit that
-I make no secret of my

131. I don't like it.
-It is not to my liking.

132. I don't like to complain
-I'm not one to complain

133. I know what it's like to
-I know what it is to

134. The truth is
-truth be told

135. I would never
-far be it from me to

136. if I wanted to
-if I were so inclined

137. if you say so
-as you please

138. That's iffy.
-That's open to question.

139. in case you
-lest you

140. in a timely fashion
-with deliberate speed

141. in many ways
-in many respects

142. in on the conversation
-privy to the conversation

143. plain and average looking
-nondescript

144. we were told that
-we were given to understand that

145. is both _____ and _____
-is at once _____ and _____

146. is no longer
-has ceased to be

147. It is no use.
-It is to no avail.

148. The jury's still out on that one.
-It remains a matter of dispute.

149. keep in mind
-bear in mind

150. a lame argument
-an unconvincing argument

151. lately
-of late

152. a lead-up to
-a prelude to

153. make a fool of yourself
-expose yourself to ridicule

154. prevent
-preclude

155. **It makes me want more.**
    -It leaves me wanting more.

156. **maybe a little**
    -to some extent, yes

157. **me neither**
    -neither do I

158. **mournful**
    -plaintive

159. **the nerve**
    -the temerity

160. **a trick**
    -a ruse

161. **take advantage of**
    -avail yourself of

162. **Just because you** _____
    -That you _____

163. **nosy**
    -inquisitive

164. **unnecessary**
    -unwarranted

165. **not to mention**
    -to say nothing of

166. **will turn out to be**
    -will prove to be

167. **off the cuff**
    -impromptu

168. **on his orders**
    -at his behest

169. **there is only one**
    -there is but one

170. **outrageous**
    -beyond the pale

171. **out of the blue**
    -quite by chance

172. **get around the regulations**
    -circumvent the regulations

173. **par for the course**
    -pretty standard fare

174. **sound phony**
    -sound affected

175. **say something positive about her**
    -say something complimentary about her

176. **pressure was put on**
    -pressure was brought to bear

177. **He never gets tired of it.**
    -He never tires of it.

178. **problems**
    -difficulties

179. **put at risk**
    -imperil

180. **put on**
    -don

181. **tends to**
    -is predisposed to

182. ask questions
  -make inquiries

183. raise the subject
  -broach the subject

184. rat out
  -implicate

185. regardless of
  -irrespective of

186. a slam dunk
  -a foregone conclusion

187. sometimes
  -on occasion

188. reword
  -paraphrase

189. the right to
  -license to

190. run into problems
  -encounter difficulties

191. in a safe place
  -out of harm's way

192. she said nothing
  -she gave no reply

193. it was scary
  -it was a real scare

194. screwed it up
  -made a mess of things

195. shy
  -retiring

196. bragged about it
  -lorded it over us

197. showy
  -ostentatious

198. good at
  -practiced in the art of

199. get busy
  -busy yourself

200. sneak away
  -steal away

About the Author

....

Tom Heehler is a degree student at the Harvard University Extension School and creator of Fluent in Five Languages, the free online language course where students learn to speak four languages simultaneously—French, Italian, Spanish, and Romanian. You can find this novel approach to language acquisition at FreeLanguageCourses.blogspot.com.